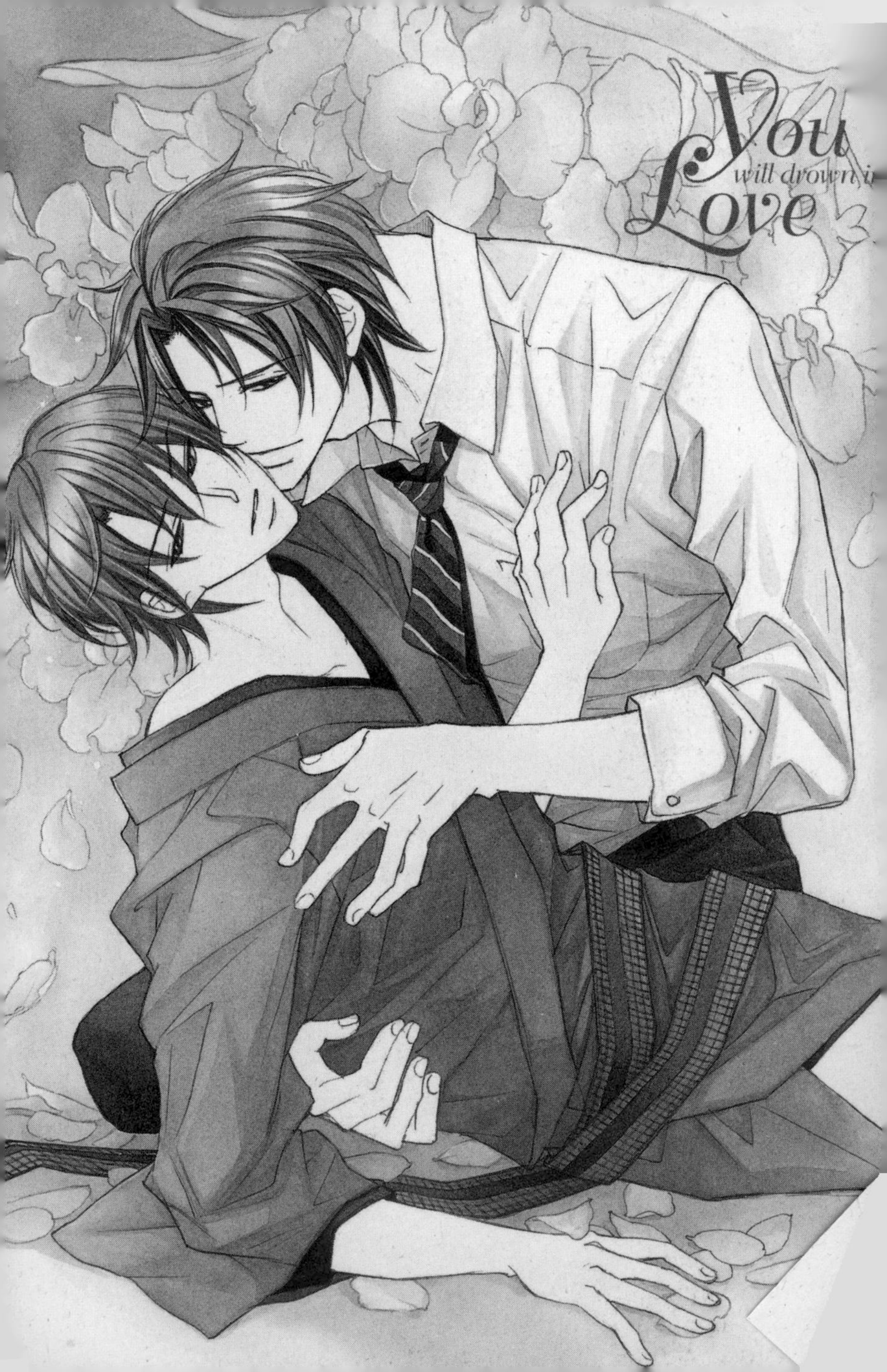
You
will drown
Love

CONTENTS

You Will Drown in Love Act. 6   005

You Will Drown in Love Act. 7   037

You Will Drown in Love Act. 8   069

You Will Drown in Love Act. 9   101

You Will Drown in Love Act. 10   129

You Will Drown in Love epilogue   163

Postscript   174

Presented by Hinako Takanaga

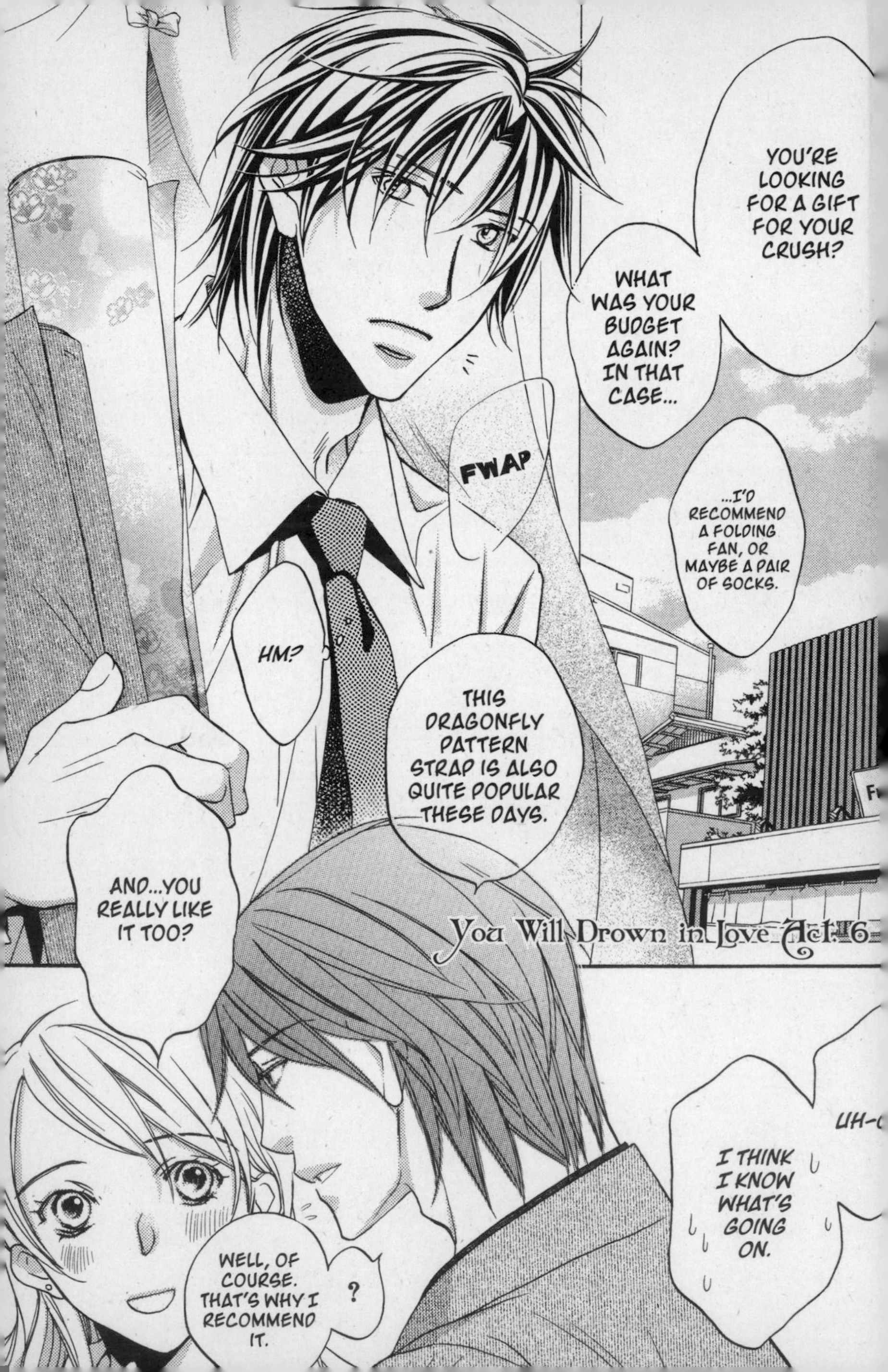
YOU'RE LOOKING FOR A GIFT FOR YOUR CRUSH?
WHAT WAS YOUR BUDGET AGAIN? IN THAT CASE...
FWAP
...I'D RECOMMEND A FOLDING FAN, OR MAYBE A PAIR OF SOCKS.
THIS DRAGONFLY PATTERN STRAP IS ALSO QUITE POPULAR THESE DAYS.
HM?
AND...YOU REALLY LIKE IT TOO?
You Will Drown in Love Act. 6
UH-
I THINK I KNOW WHAT'S GOING ON.
?
WELL, OF COURSE. THAT'S WHY I RECOMMEND IT.

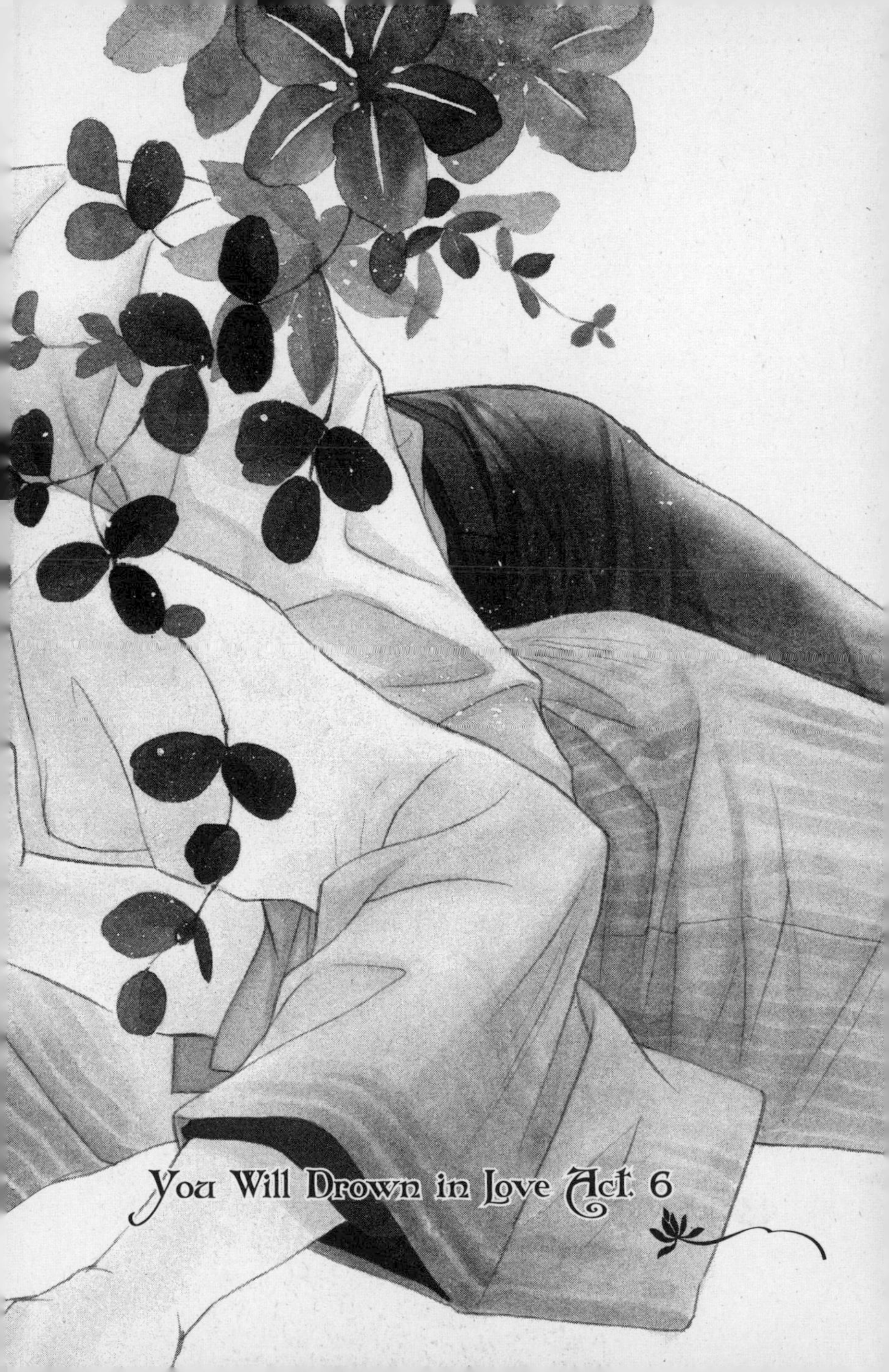
You Will Drown in Love Act. 6

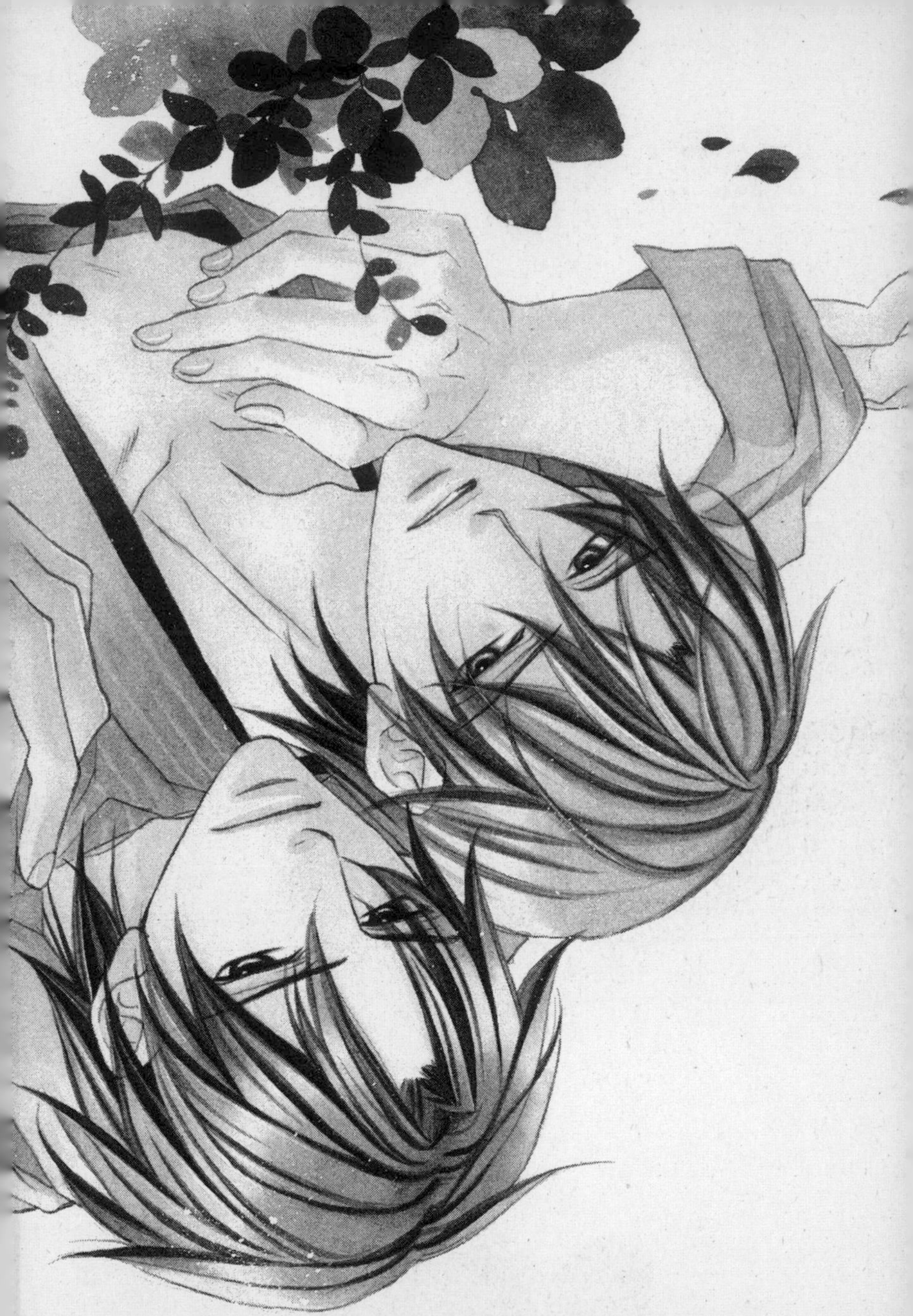

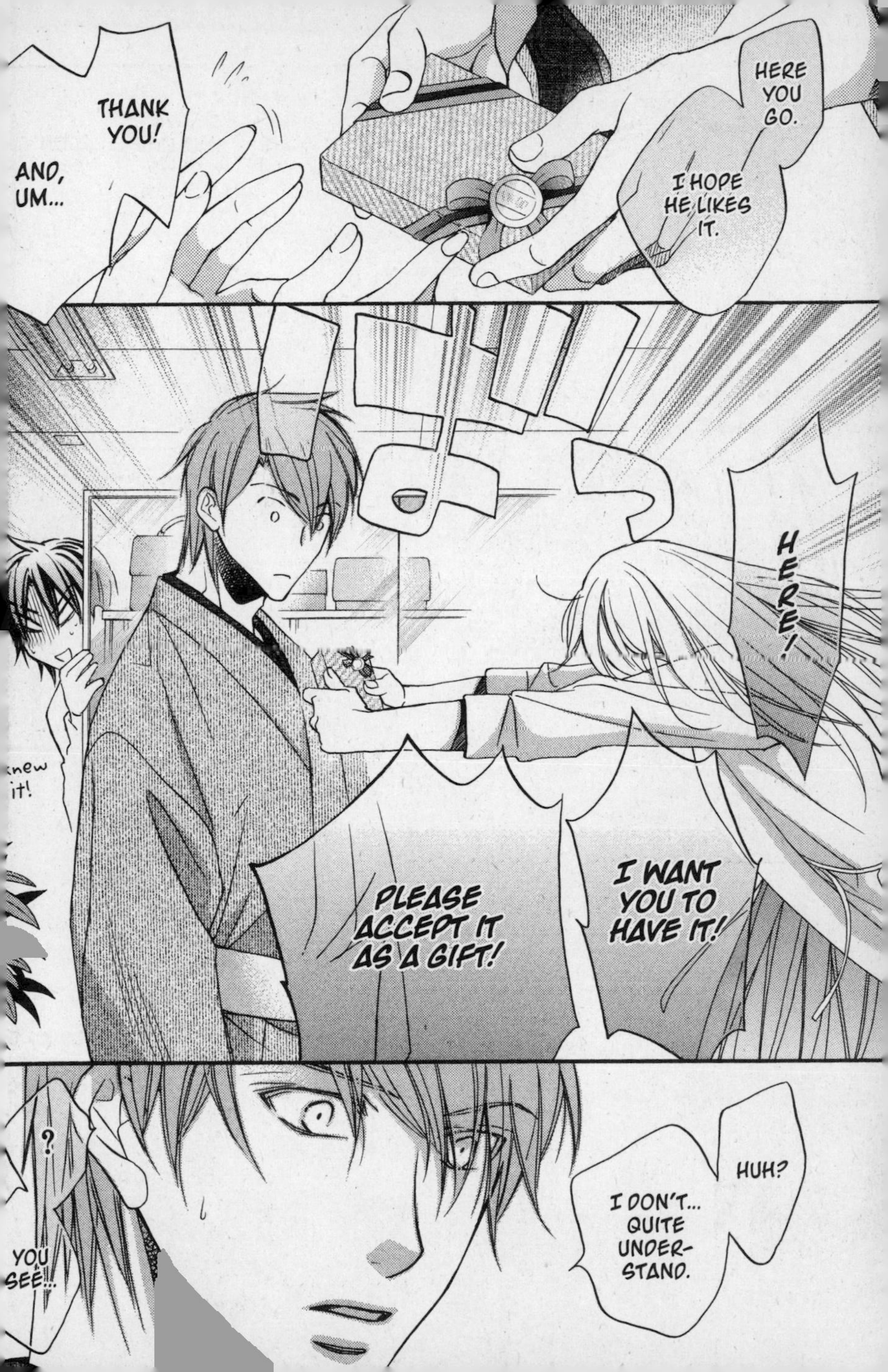
HERE YOU GO.
I HOPE HE LIKES IT.
THANK YOU!
AND, UM...
HERE!
I WANT YOU TO HAVE IT!
PLEASE ACCEPT IT AS A GIFT!
knew it!
HUH?
I DON'T... QUITE UNDER-STAND.
?
YOU SEE...

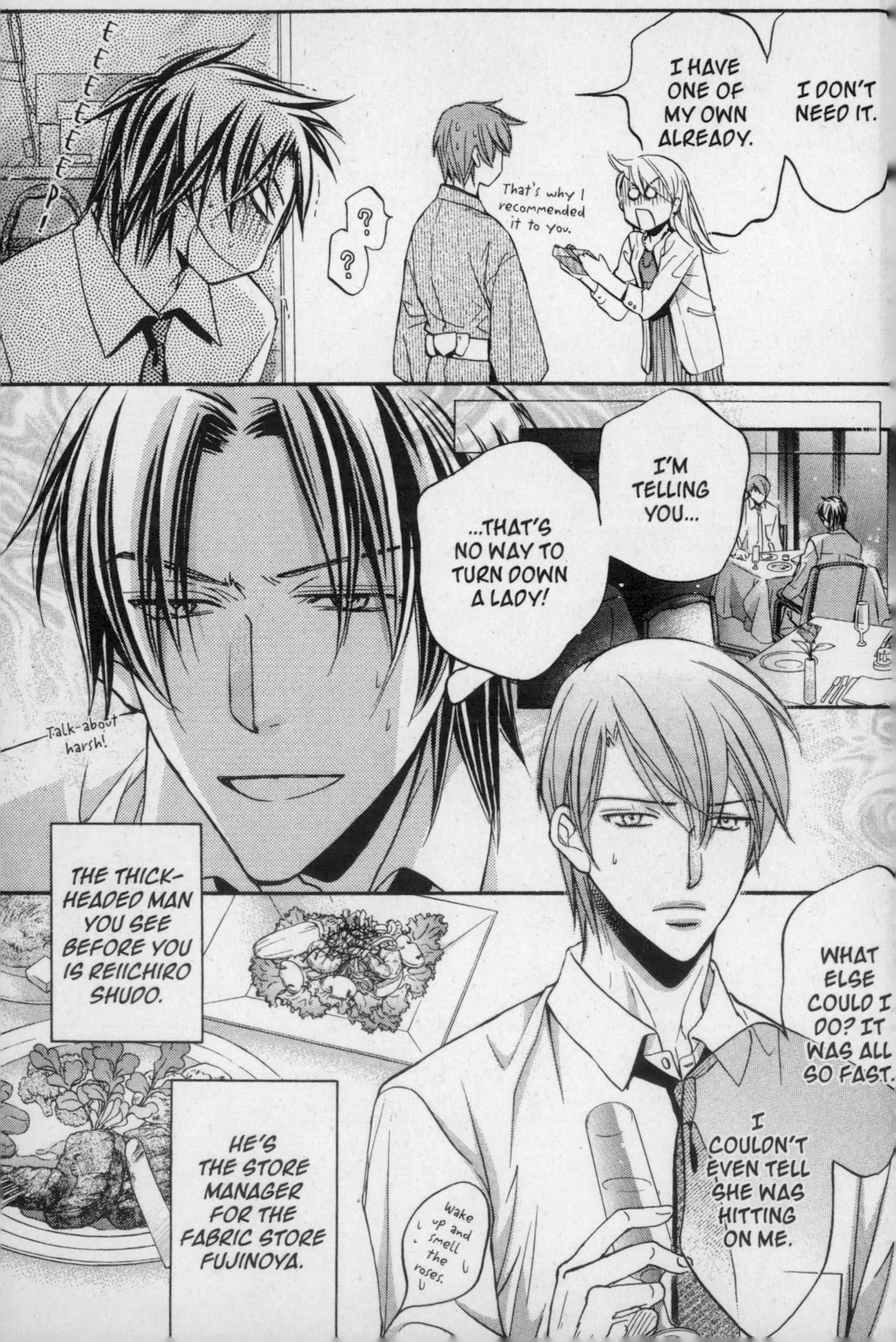
I DON'T NEED IT.
I HAVE ONE OF MY OWN ALREADY.
That's why I recommended it to you.
? ?
EEEEEEEEP!
I'M TELLING YOU...
...THAT'S NO WAY TO TURN DOWN A LADY!
Talk about harsh!
WHAT ELSE COULD I DO? IT WAS ALL SO FAST.
I COULDN'T EVEN TELL SHE WAS HITTING ON ME.
Wake up and smell the roses.
THE THICK-HEADED MAN YOU SEE BEFORE YOU IS REIICHIRO SHUDO.
HE'S THE STORE MANAGER FOR THE FABRIC STORE FUJINOYA.

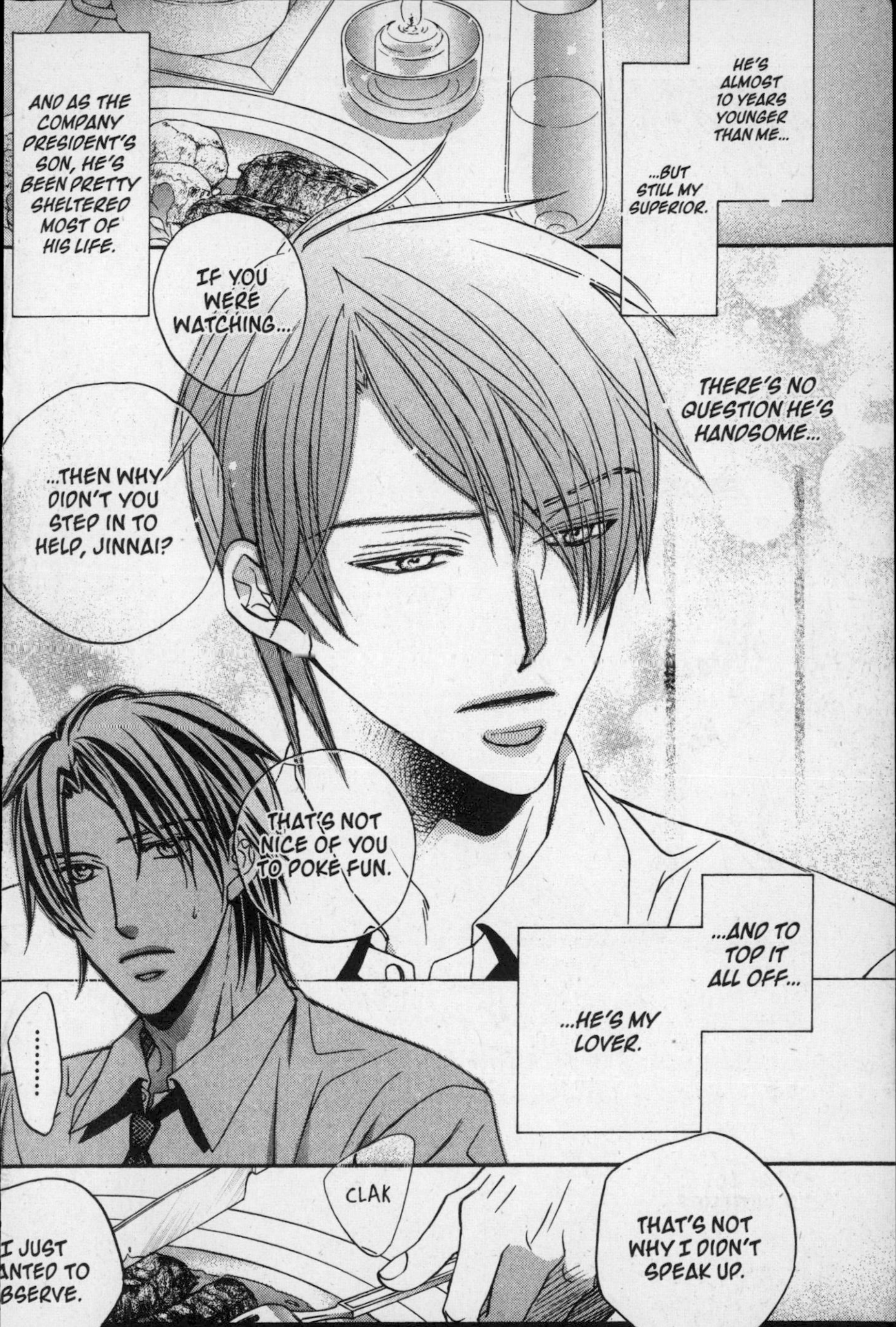
HE'S ALMOST 10 YEARS YOUNGER THAN ME...
...BUT STILL MY SUPERIOR.
AND AS THE COMPANY PRESIDENT'S SON, HE'S BEEN PRETTY SHELTERED MOST OF HIS LIFE.
IF YOU WERE WATCHING...
THERE'S NO QUESTION HE'S HANDSOME...
...THEN WHY DIDN'T YOU STEP IN TO HELP, JINNAI?
THAT'S NOT NICE OF YOU TO POKE FUN.
...AND TO TOP IT ALL OFF...
...HE'S MY LOVER.
......
THAT'S NOT WHY I DIDN'T SPEAK UP.
CLAK
I JUST ANTED TO BSERVE.

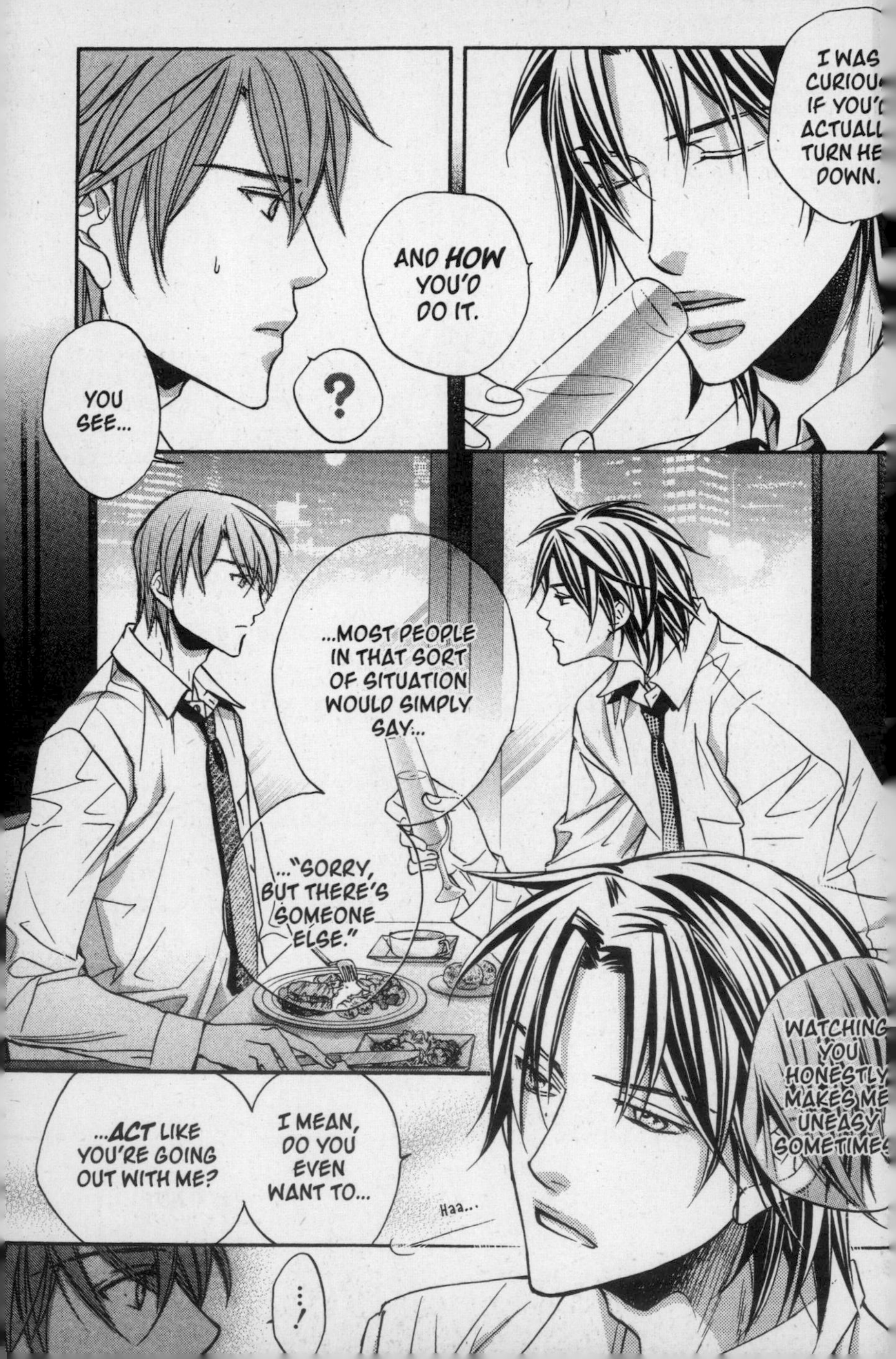
I WAS CURIOUS IF YOU'D ACTUALLY TURN HER DOWN.
AND HOW YOU'D DO IT.
?
YOU SEE...
...MOST PEOPLE IN THAT SORT OF SITUATION WOULD SIMPLY SAY...
..."SORRY, BUT THERE'S SOMEONE ELSE."
WATCHING YOU HONESTLY MAKES ME UNEASY SOMETIMES.
Haa...
I MEAN, DO YOU EVEN WANT TO...
...ACT LIKE YOU'RE GOING OUT WITH ME?
...!

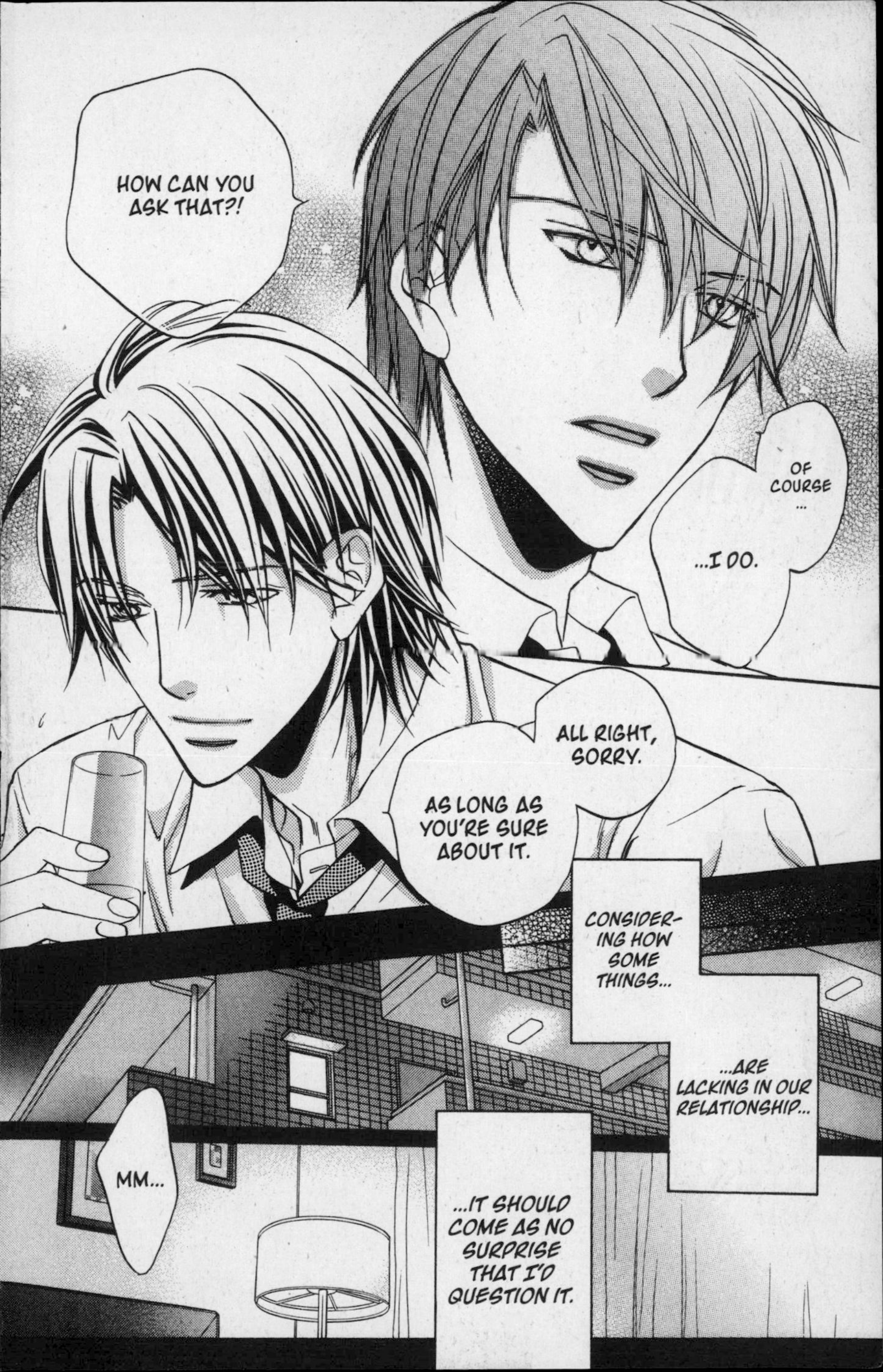
HOW CAN YOU ASK THAT?!
OF COURSE ...
...I DO.
ALL RIGHT, SORRY.
AS LONG AS YOU'RE SURE ABOUT IT.
CONSIDER-ING HOW SOME THINGS...
...ARE LACKING IN OUR RELATIONSHIP...
...IT SHOULD COME AS NO SURPRISE THAT I'D QUESTION IT.
MM...

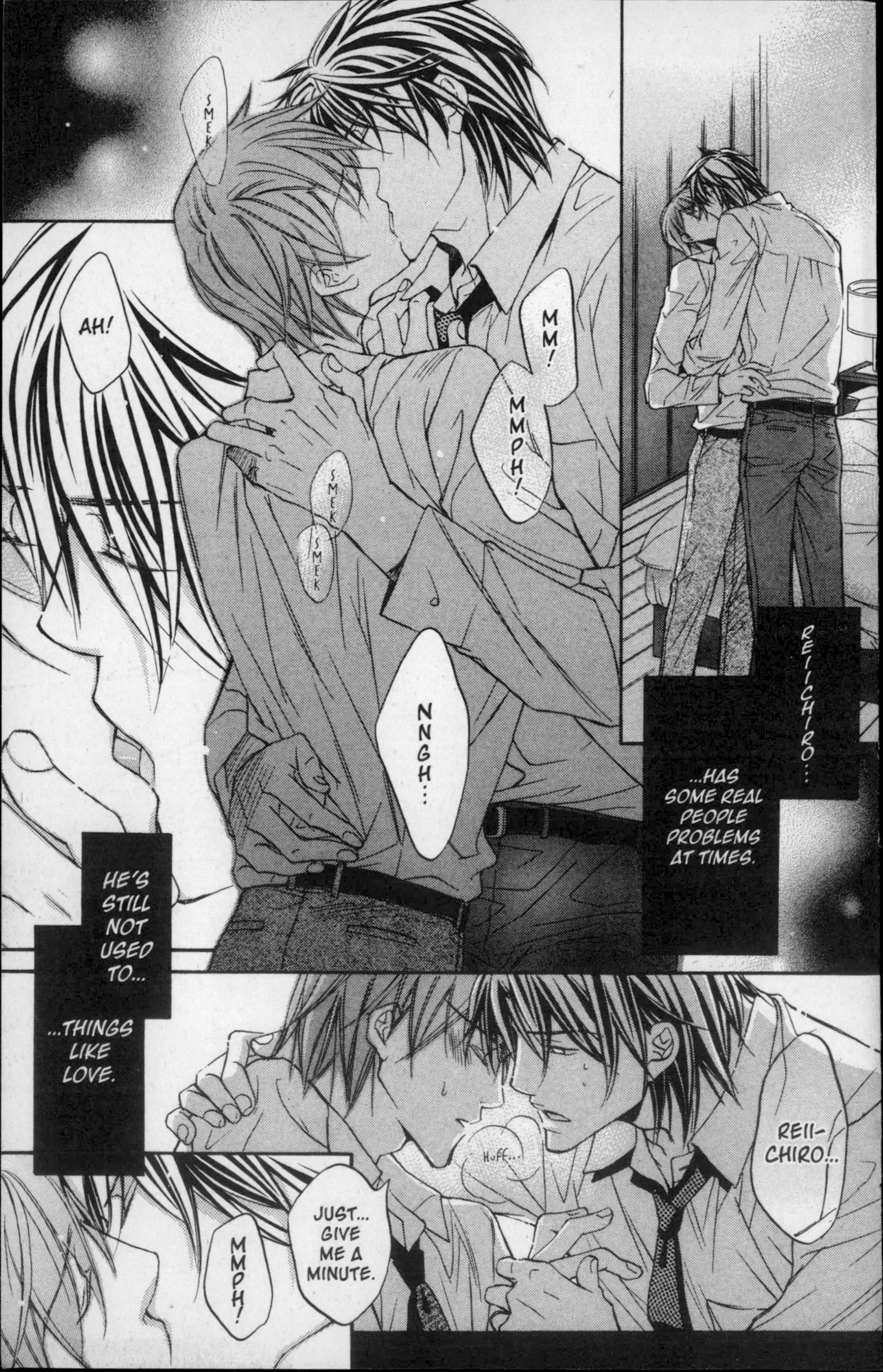
REIICHIRO...
...HAS SOME REAL PEOPLE PROBLEMS AT TIMES.
SMEK
MM!
MMPH!
SMEK
SMEK
AH!
NNGH...
HE'S STILL NOT USED TO...
REII-CHIRO...
HUFF...
JUST... GIVE ME A MINUTE.
MMPH!
...THINGS LIKE LOVE.

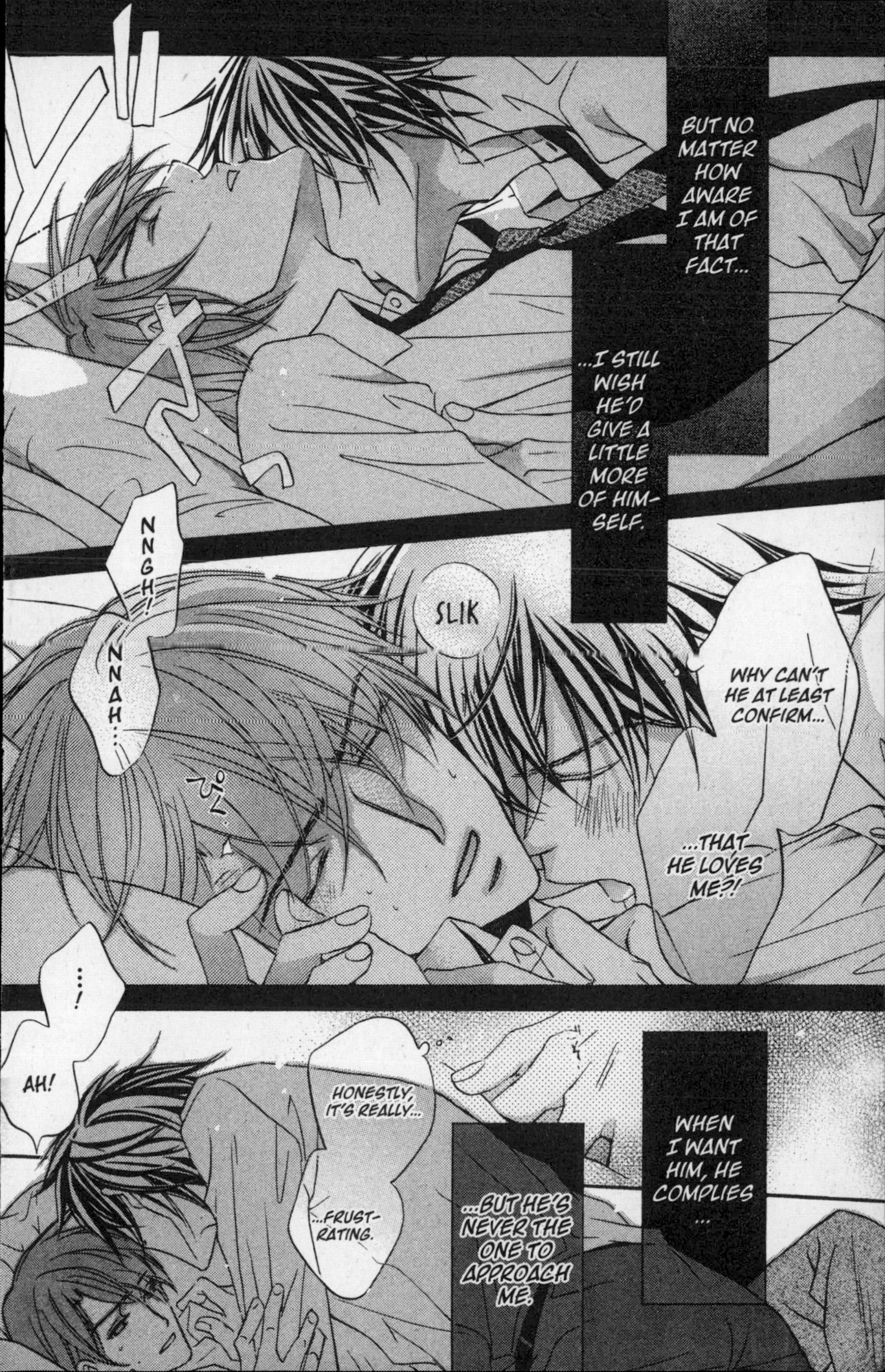
BUT NO MATTER HOW AWARE I AM OF THAT FACT...
...I STILL WISH HE'D GIVE A LITTLE MORE OF HIM-SELF.
SLIK
WHY CAN'T HE AT LEAST CONFIRM...
...THAT HE LOVES ME?!
NNGH!
NNAH...
WHEN I WANT HIM, HE COMPLIES...
...BUT HE'S NEVER THE ONE TO APPROACH ME.
HONESTLY, IT'S REALLY...
...FRUST-RATING.
...!
AH!

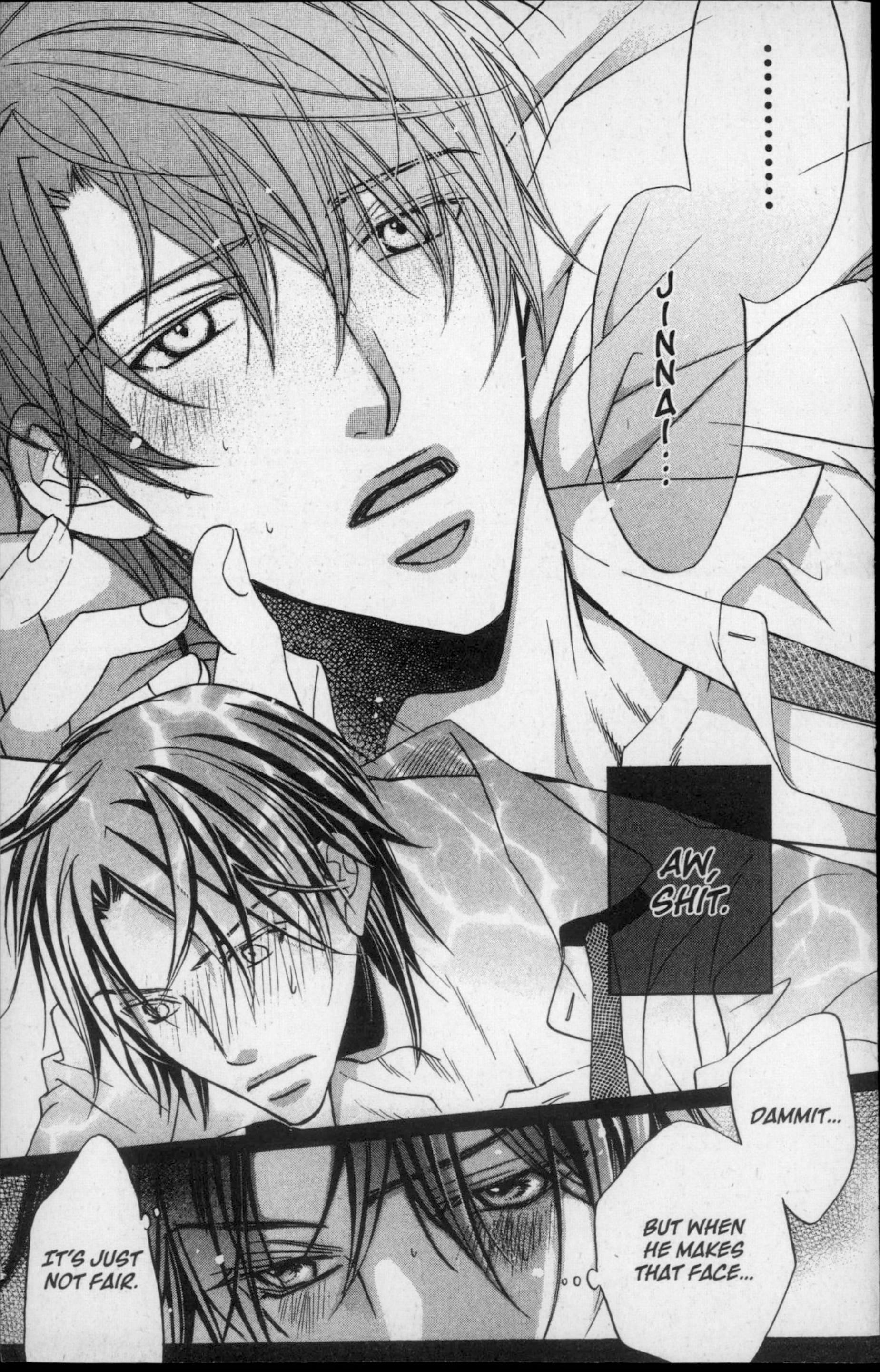
....
JINNAI...
AW, SHIT.
DAMMIT...
BUT WHEN HE MAKES THAT FACE...
IT'S JUST NOT FAIR.

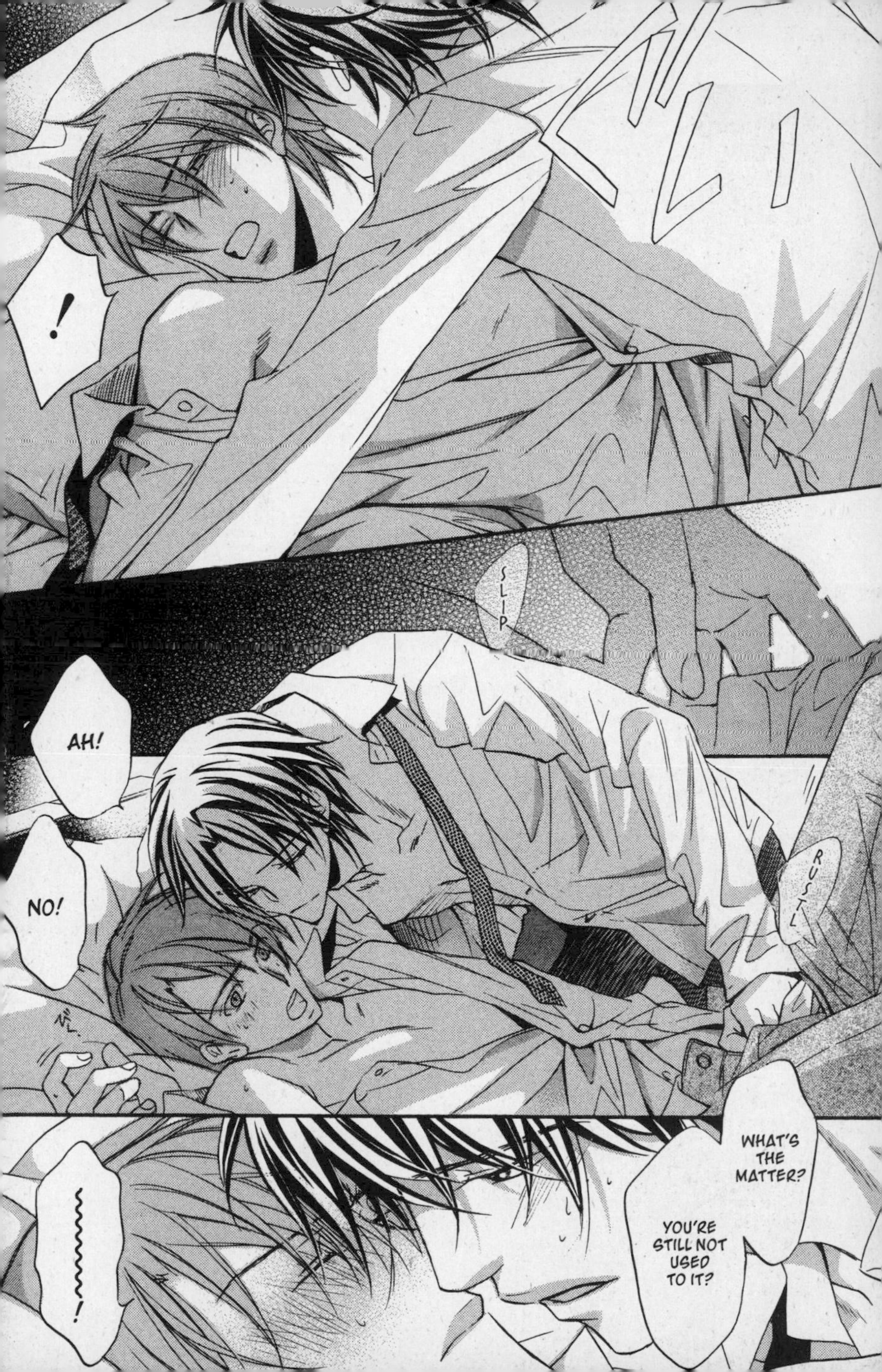
!
SLIP
AH!
RUSTL
NO!
WHAT'S THE MATTER?
YOU'RE STILL NOT USED TO IT?
~~~~~!
~~~~~

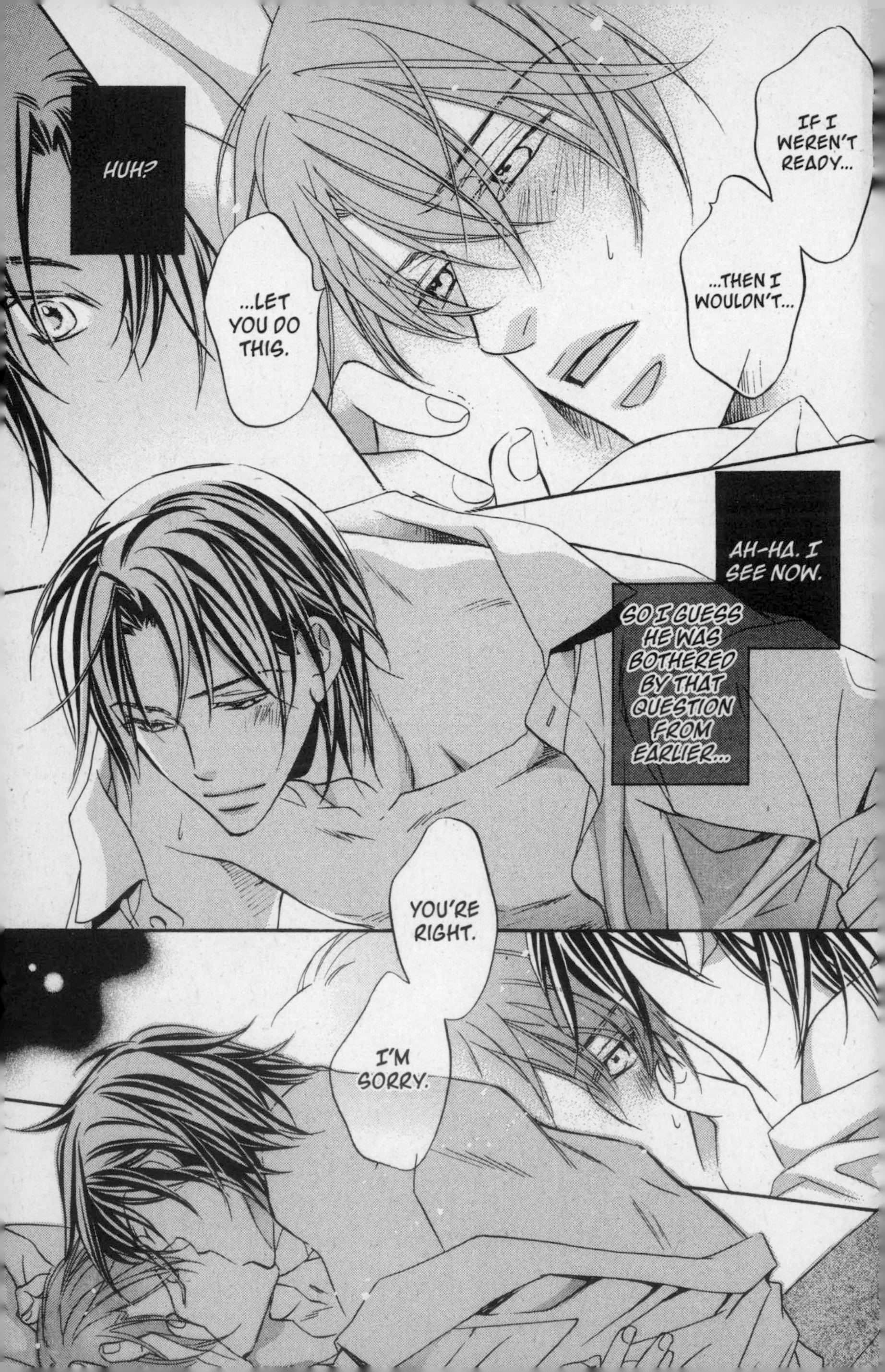
IF I WEREN'T READY...
...THEN I WOULDN'T...
...LET YOU DO THIS.
HUH?
AH-HA. I SEE NOW.
SO I GUESS HE WAS BOTHERED BY THAT QUESTION FROM EARLIER...
YOU'RE RIGHT.
I'M SORRY.

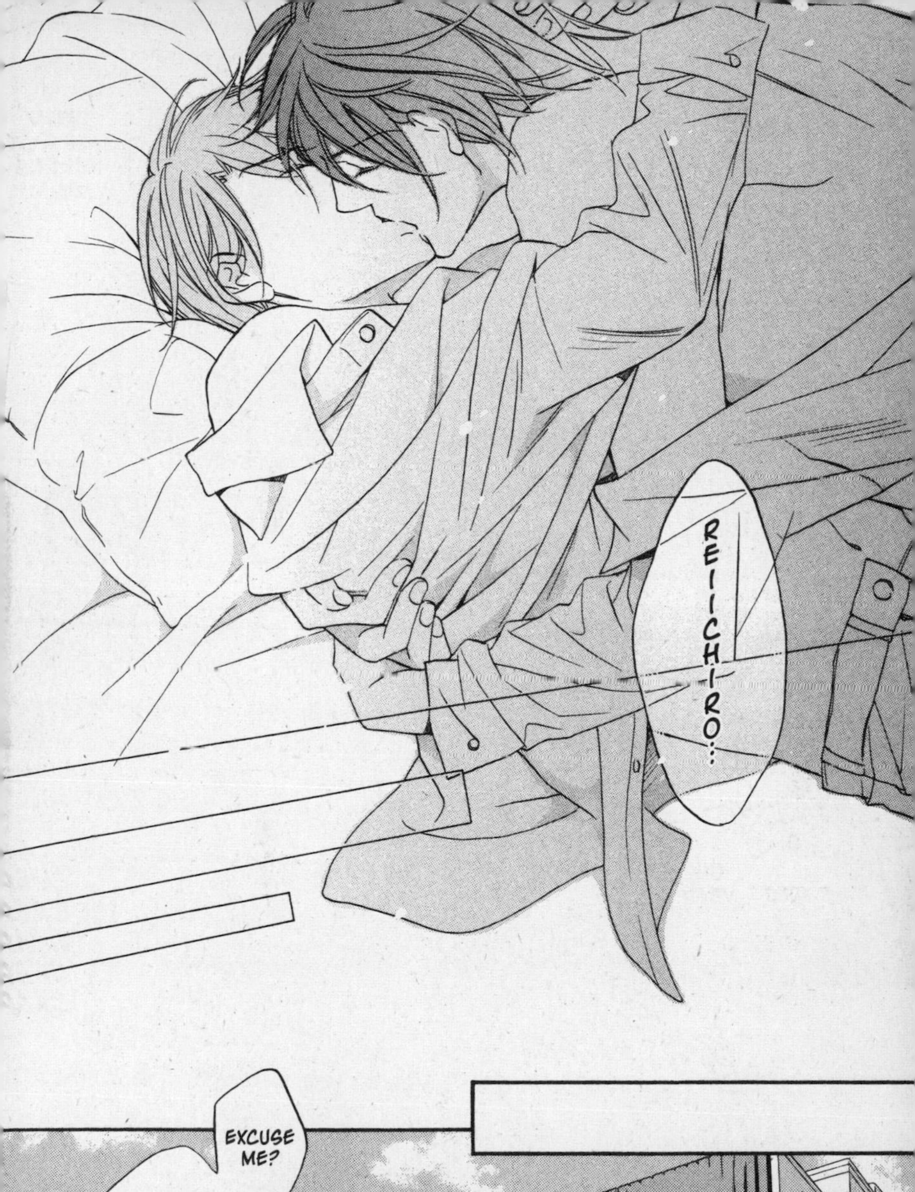
REIICHIRO...

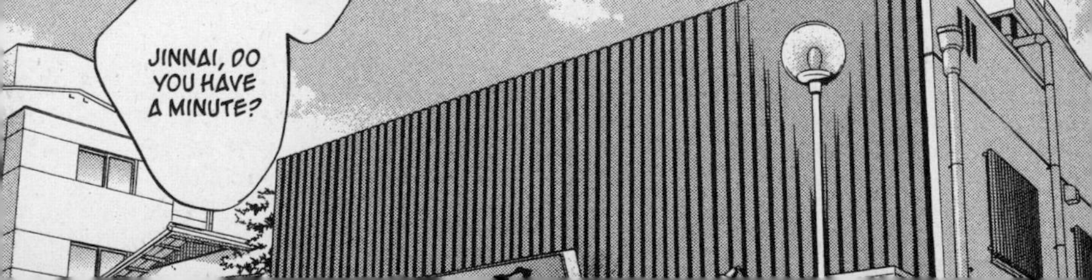
EXCUSE ME?
JINNAI, DO YOU HAVE A MINUTE?

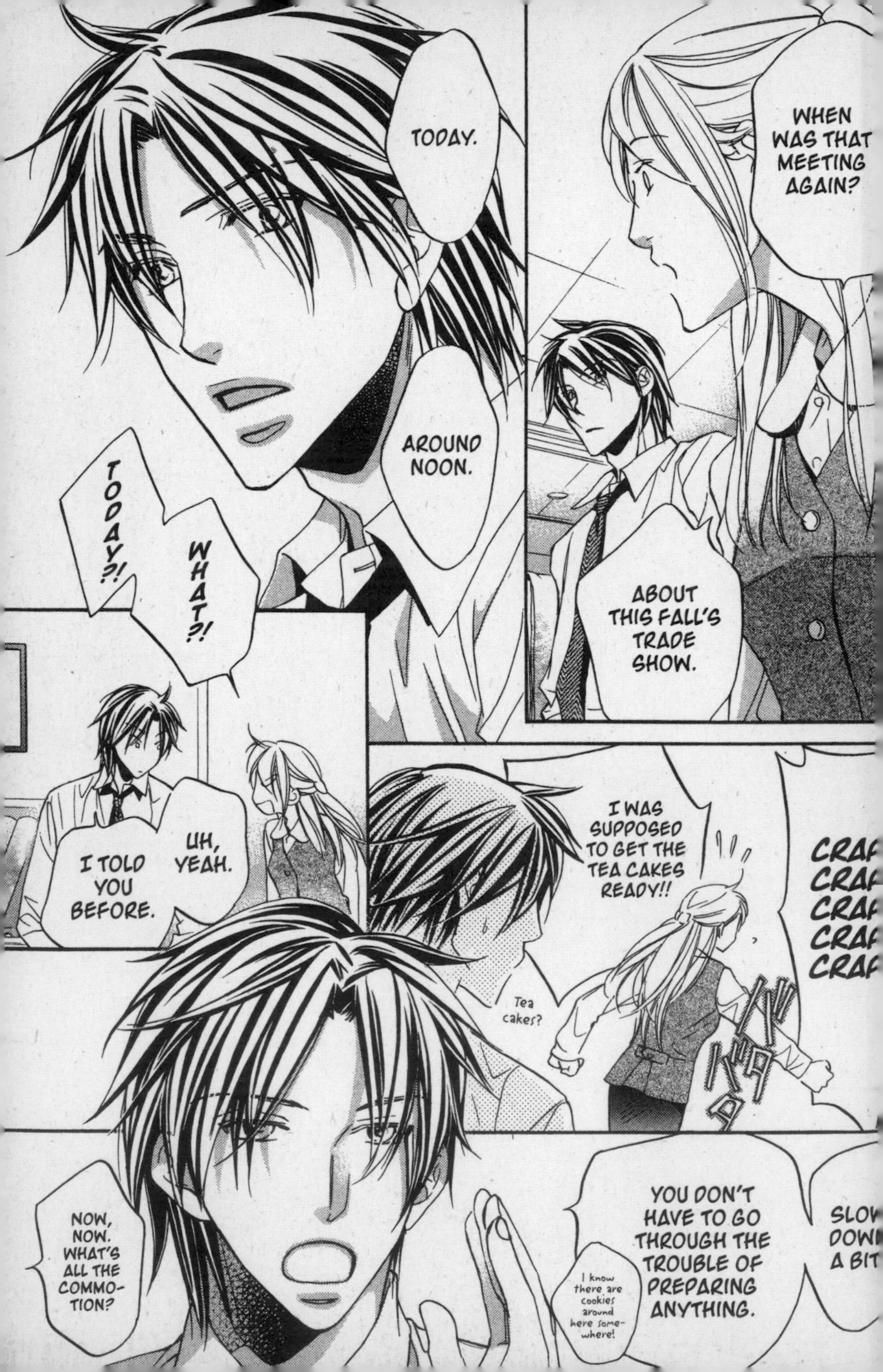
WHEN WAS THAT MEETING AGAIN?
ABOUT THIS FALL'S TRADE SHOW.
TODAY.
AROUND NOON.
WHAT?!
TODAY?!
CRAP CRAP CRAP CRAP CRAP
I WAS SUPPOSED TO GET THE TEA CAKES READY!!
Tea cakes?
UH, YEAH.
I TOLD YOU BEFORE.
SLOW DOWN A BIT
YOU DON'T HAVE TO GO THROUGH THE TROUBLE OF PREPARING ANYTHING.
I know there are cookies around here somewhere!
NOW, NOW. WHAT'S ALL THE COMMOTION?

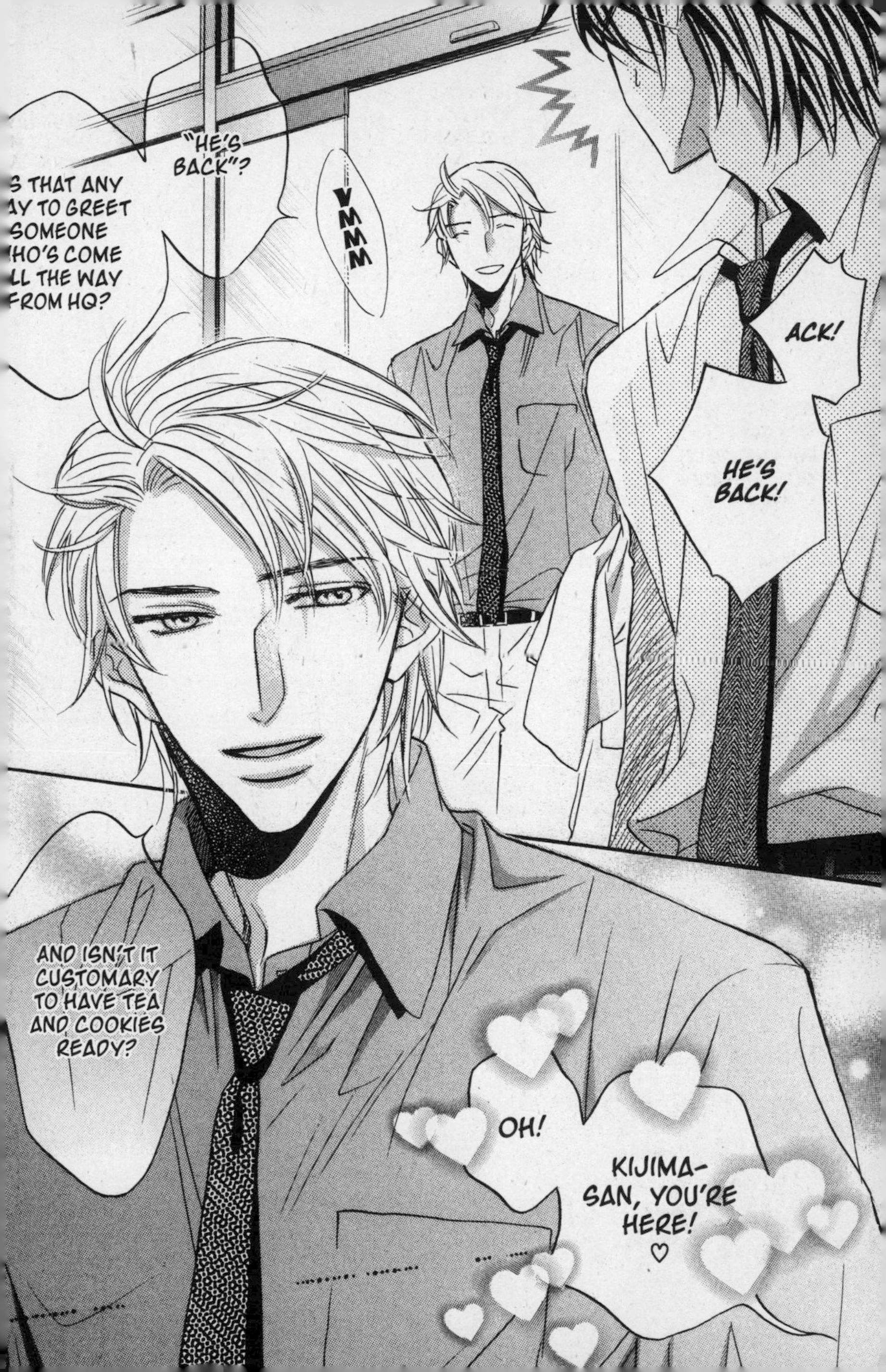
ACK!
HE'S BACK!
VMMM
"HE'S BACK"?
S THAT ANY AY TO GREET SOMEONE HO'S COME LL THE WAY FROM HQ?
OH!
KIJIMA-SAN, YOU'RE HERE! ♡
AND ISN'T IT CUSTOMARY TO HAVE TEA AND COOKIES READY?

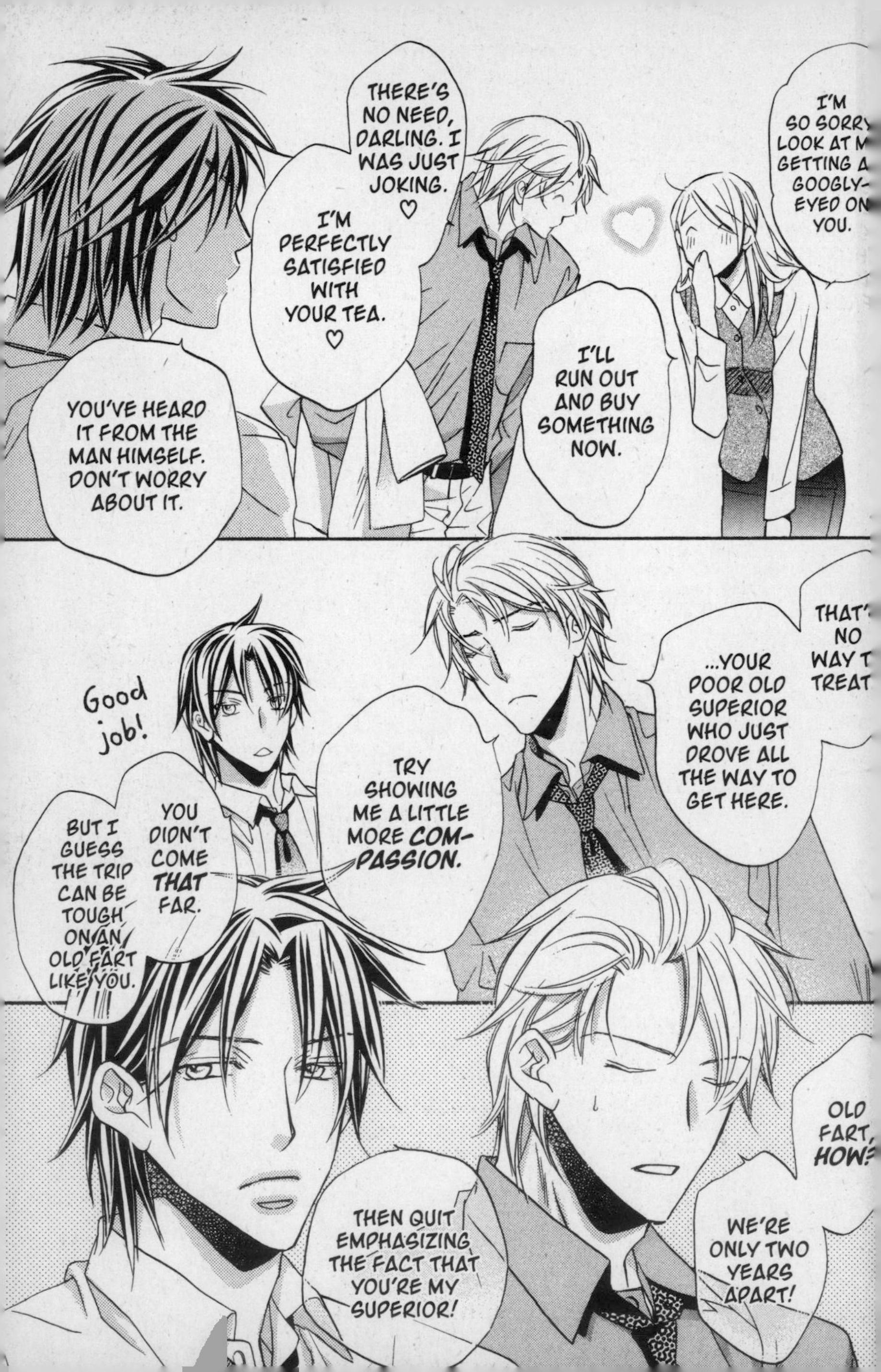
I'M SO SORR LOOK AT M GETTING A GOOGLY-EYED ON YOU.
I'LL RUN OUT AND BUY SOMETHING NOW.
THERE'S NO NEED, DARLING. I WAS JUST JOKING. ♡
I'M PERFECTLY SATISFIED WITH YOUR TEA. ♡
YOU'VE HEARD IT FROM THE MAN HIMSELF. DON'T WORRY ABOUT IT.
THAT NO WAY T TREAT
...YOUR POOR OLD SUPERIOR WHO JUST DROVE ALL THE WAY TO GET HERE.
TRY SHOWING ME A LITTLE MORE COM-PASSION.
Good job!
YOU DIDN'T COME THAT FAR.
BUT I GUESS THE TRIP CAN BE TOUGH ON AN OLD FART LIKE YOU.
OLD FART, HOW
WE'RE ONLY TWO YEARS APART!
THEN QUIT EMPHASIZING THE FACT THAT YOU'RE MY SUPERIOR!

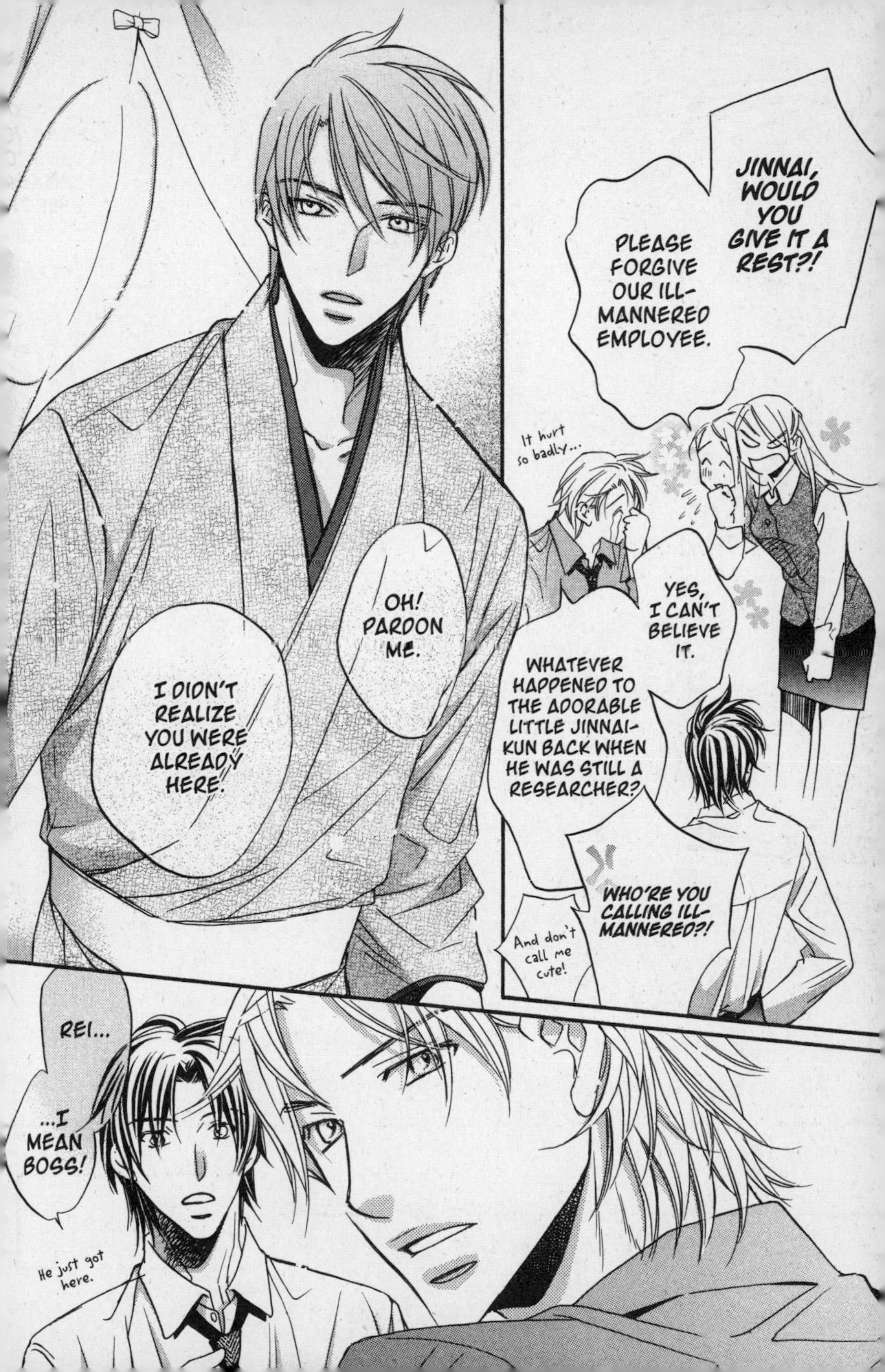
JINNAI, WOULD YOU GIVE IT A REST?!
PLEASE FORGIVE OUR ILL-MANNERED EMPLOYEE.
It hurt so badly...
YES, I CAN'T BELIEVE IT.
WHATEVER HAPPENED TO THE ADORABLE LITTLE JINNAI-KUN BACK WHEN HE WAS STILL A RESEARCHER?
WHO'RE YOU CALLING ILL-MANNERED?!
And don't call me cute!
OH! PARDON ME.
I DIDN'T REALIZE YOU WERE ALREADY HERE.
REI...
...I MEAN BOSS!
He just got here.

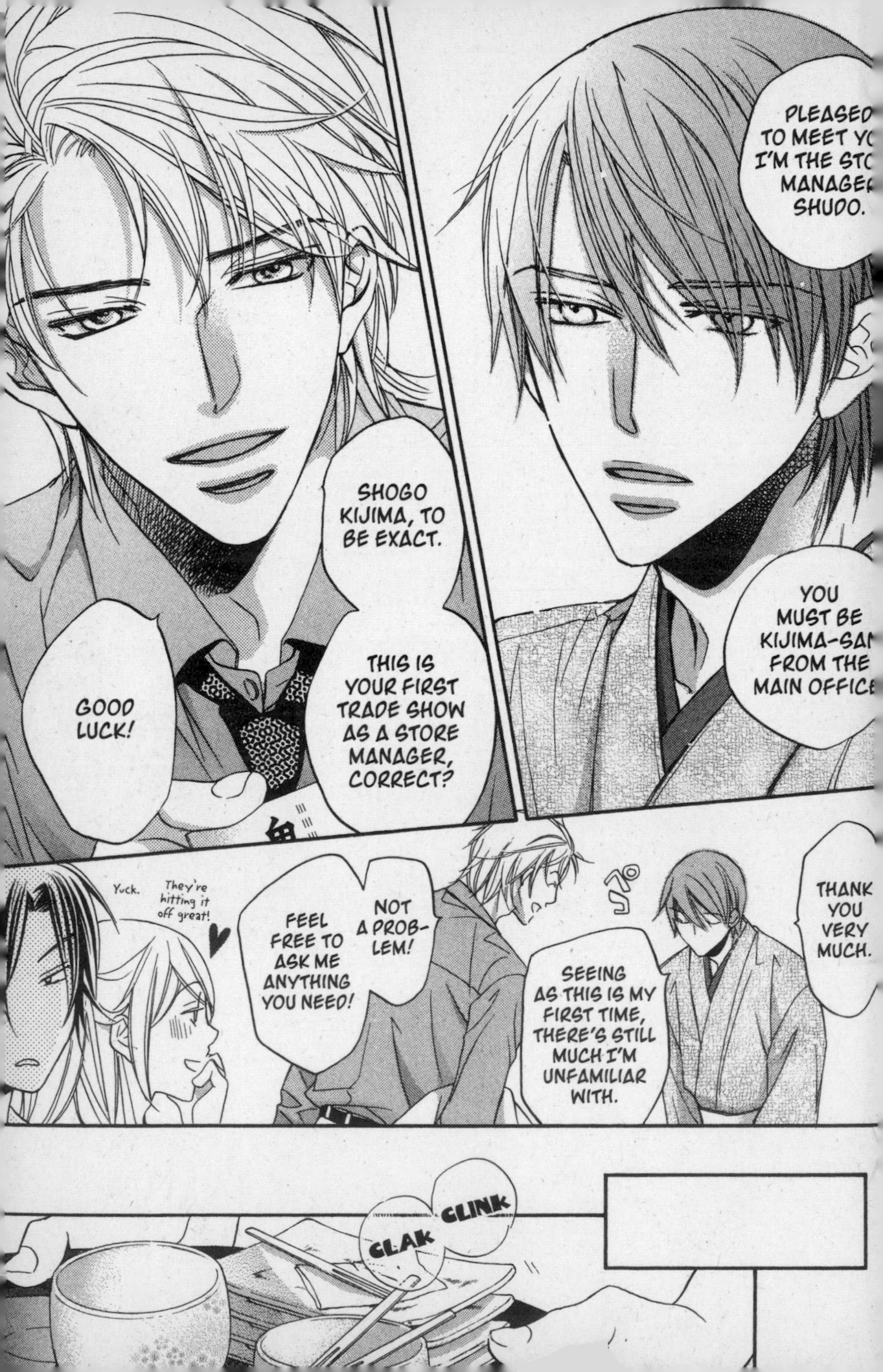
PLEASED TO MEET YO I'M THE STO MANAGER SHUDO.
YOU MUST BE KIJIMA-SA FROM THE MAIN OFFIC
SHOGO KIJIMA, TO BE EXACT.
THIS IS YOUR FIRST TRADE SHOW AS A STORE MANAGER, CORRECT?
GOOD LUCK!
THANK YOU VERY MUCH.
SEEING AS THIS IS MY FIRST TIME, THERE'S STILL MUCH I'M UNFAMILIAR WITH.
NOT A PROB-LEM!
FEEL FREE TO ASK ME ANYTHING YOU NEED!
They're hitting it off great!
Yuck.
CLINK
CLAK

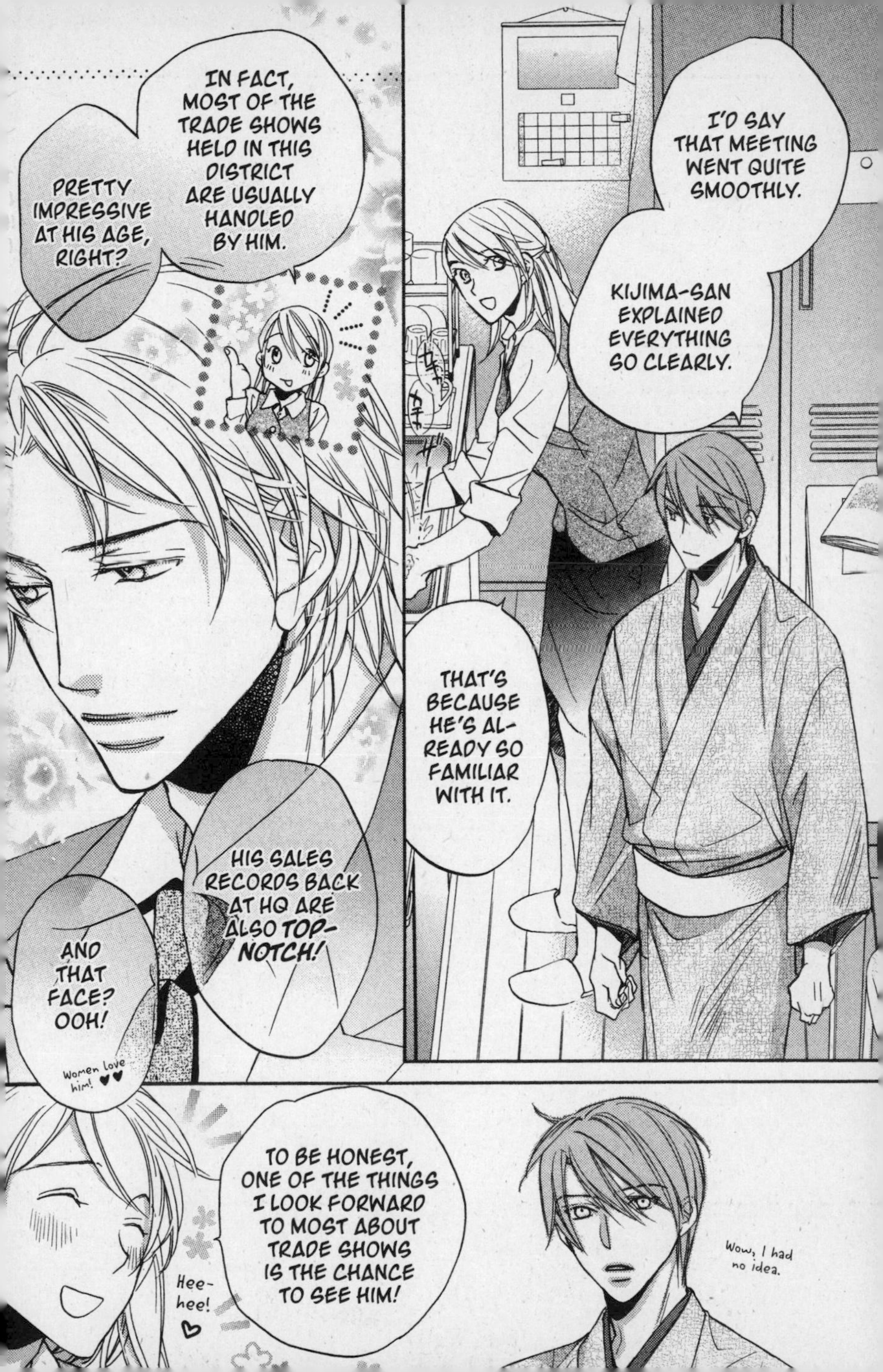
I'D SAY THAT MEETING WENT QUITE SMOOTHLY.
KIJIMA-SAN EXPLAINED EVERYTHING SO CLEARLY.
THAT'S BECAUSE HE'S AL-READY SO FAMILIAR WITH IT.
IN FACT, MOST OF THE TRADE SHOWS HELD IN THIS DISTRICT ARE USUALLY HANDLED BY HIM.
PRETTY IMPRESSIVE AT HIS AGE, RIGHT?
HIS SALES RECORDS BACK AT HQ ARE ALSO TOP-NOTCH!
AND THAT FACE? OOH!
Women love him! ♥♥
TO BE HONEST, ONE OF THE THINGS I LOOK FORWARD TO MOST ABOUT TRADE SHOWS IS THE CHANCE TO SEE HIM!
Hee-hee! ♥
Wow, I had no idea.

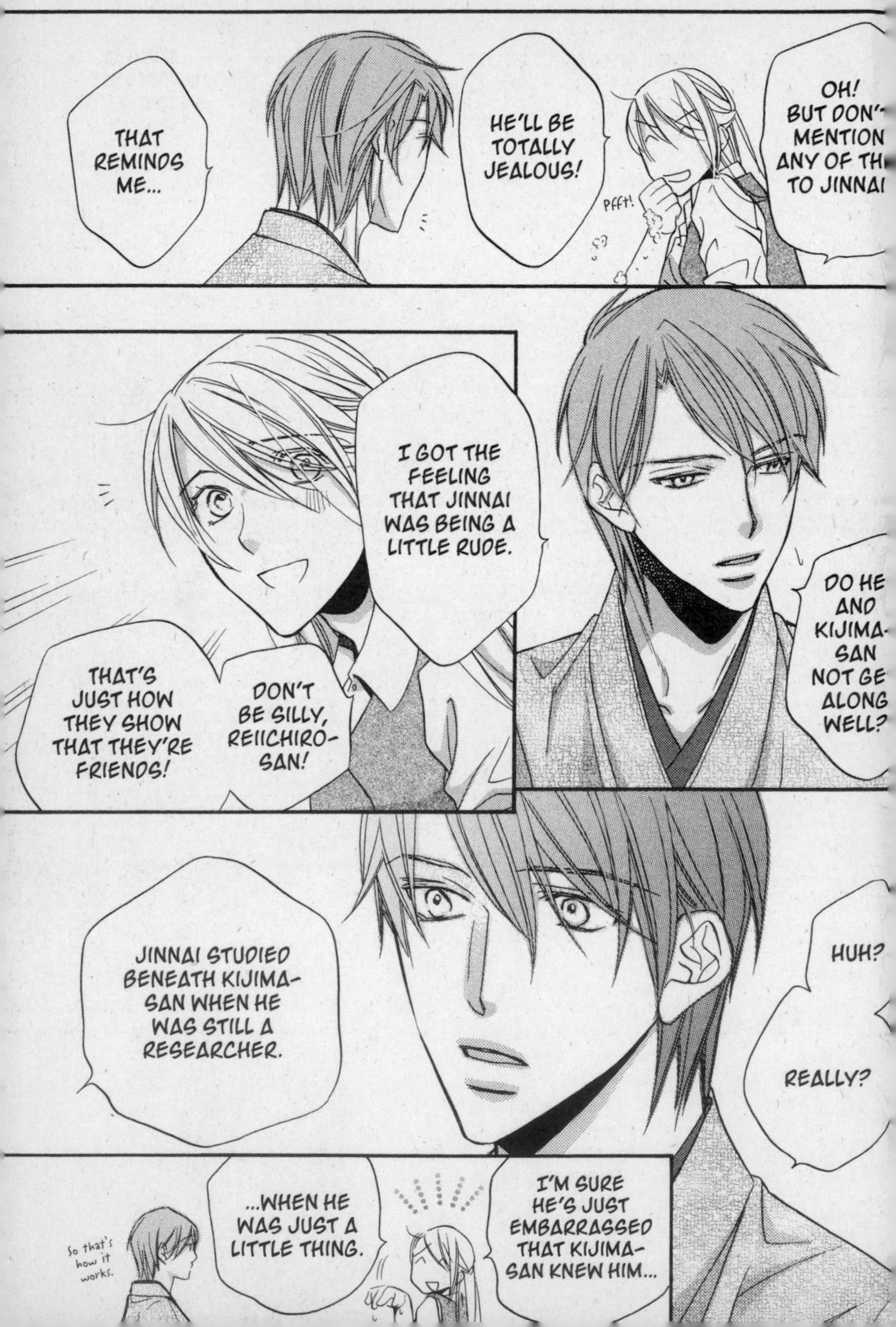
OH! BUT DON'- MENTION ANY OF TH TO JINNAI
PFFT!
HE'LL BE TOTALLY JEALOUS!
THAT REMINDS ME...
DO HE AND KIJIMA-SAN NOT GE ALONG WELL?
I GOT THE FEELING THAT JINNAI WAS BEING A LITTLE RUDE.
DON'T BE SILLY, REIICHIRO-SAN!
THAT'S JUST HOW THEY SHOW THAT THEY'RE FRIENDS!
HUH?
REALLY?
JINNAI STUDIED BENEATH KIJIMA-SAN WHEN HE WAS STILL A RESEARCHER.
I'M SURE HE'S JUST EMBARRASSED THAT KIJIMA-SAN KNEW HIM...
...WHEN HE WAS JUST A LITTLE THING.
So that's how it works.

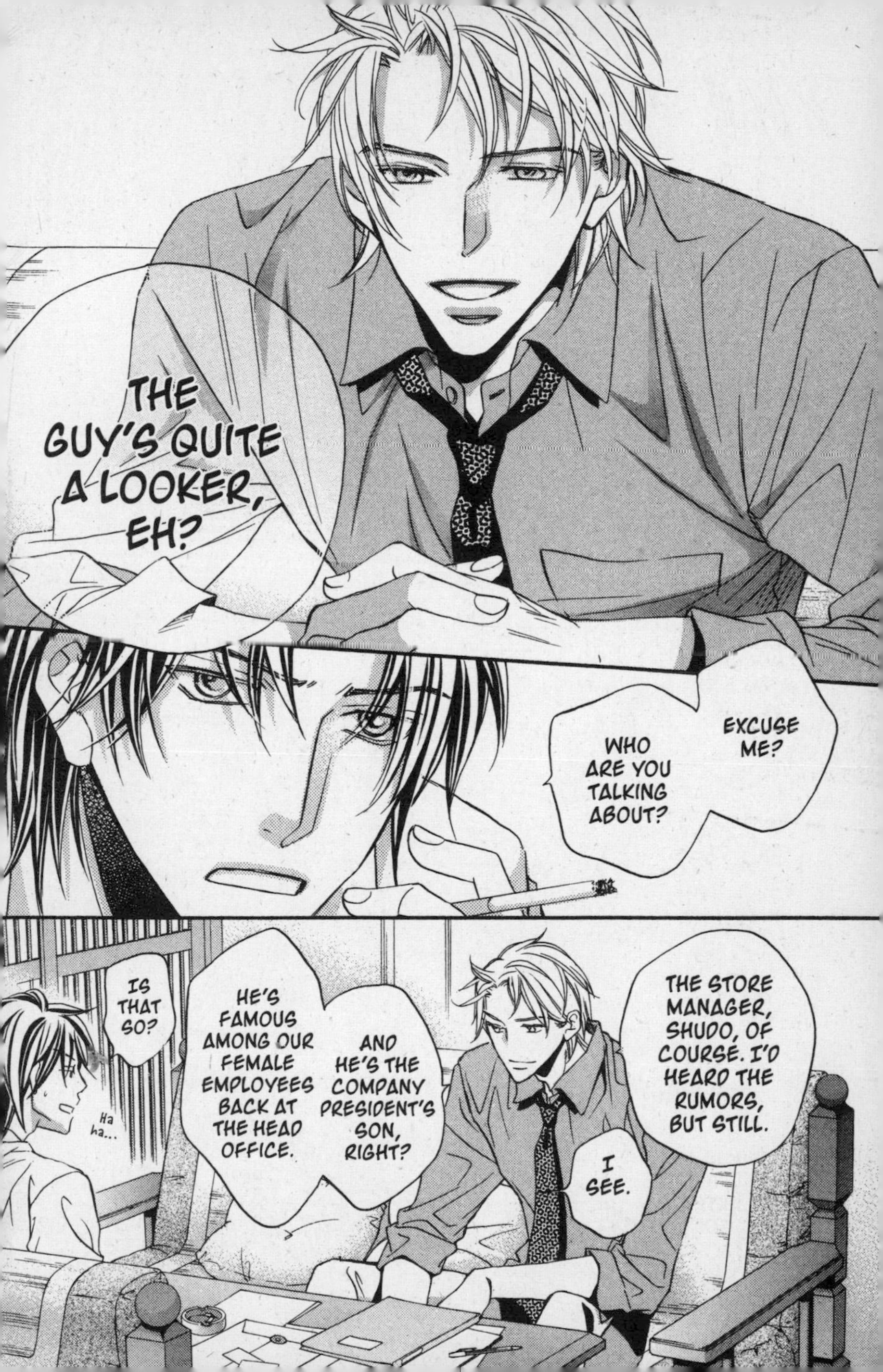
THE GUY'S QUITE A LOOKER, EH?
EXCUSE ME?
WHO ARE YOU TALKING ABOUT?
THE STORE MANAGER, SHUDO, OF COURSE. I'D HEARD THE RUMORS, BUT STILL.
I SEE.
AND HE'S THE COMPANY PRESIDENT'S SON, RIGHT?
HE'S FAMOUS AMONG OUR FEMALE EMPLOYEES BACK AT THE HEAD OFFICE.
IS THAT SO?
Ha ha...

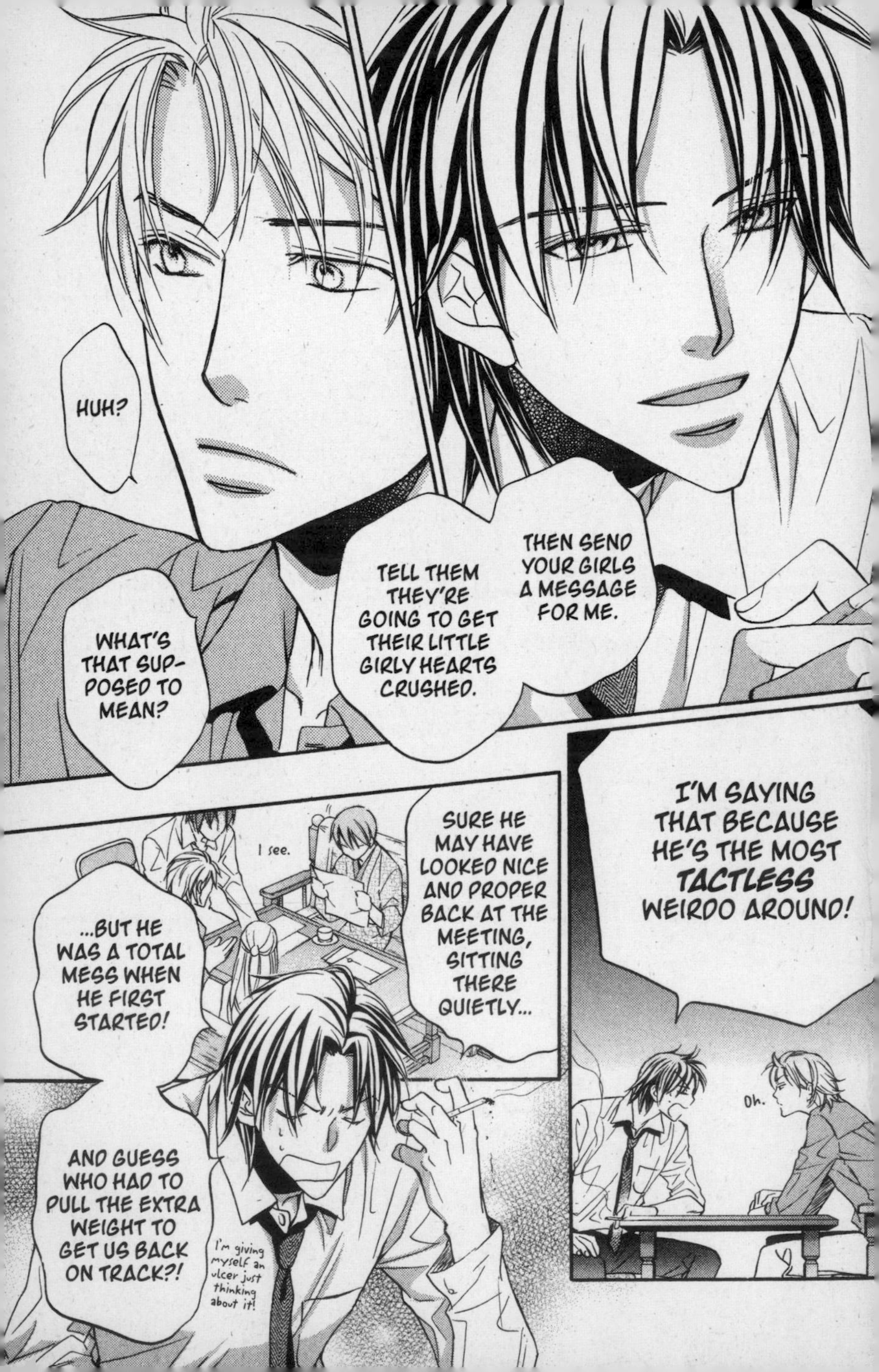
THEN SEND YOUR GIRLS A MESSAGE FOR ME.
TELL THEM THEY'RE GOING TO GET THEIR LITTLE GIRLY HEARTS CRUSHED.
HUH?
WHAT'S THAT SUP-POSED TO MEAN?
I'M SAYING THAT BECAUSE HE'S THE MOST *TACTLESS* WEIRDO AROUND!
Oh.
SURE HE MAY HAVE LOOKED NICE AND PROPER BACK AT THE MEETING, SITTING THERE QUIETLY...
I see.
...BUT HE WAS A TOTAL MESS WHEN HE FIRST STARTED!
AND GUESS WHO HAD TO PULL THE EXTRA WEIGHT TO GET US BACK ON TRACK?!
I'm giving myself an ulcer just thinking about it!

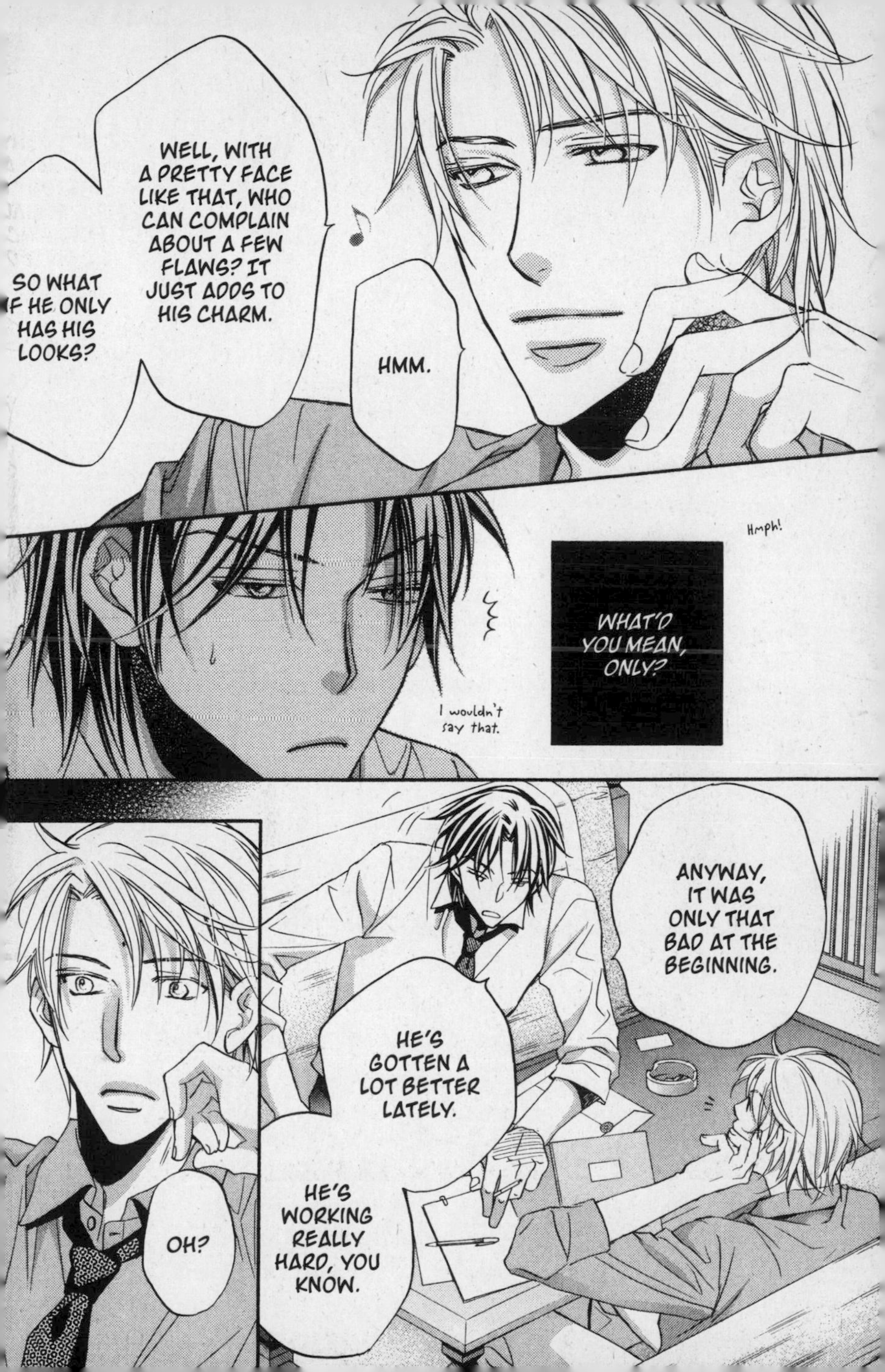
HMM.
WELL, WITH A PRETTY FACE LIKE THAT, WHO CAN COMPLAIN ABOUT A FEW FLAWS? IT JUST ADDS TO HIS CHARM.
SO WHAT IF HE ONLY HAS HIS LOOKS?
Hmph!
WHAT'D YOU MEAN, ONLY?
I wouldn't say that.
ANYWAY, IT WAS ONLY THAT BAD AT THE BEGINNING.
HE'S GOTTEN A LOT BETTER LATELY.
HE'S WORKING REALLY HARD, YOU KNOW.
OH?

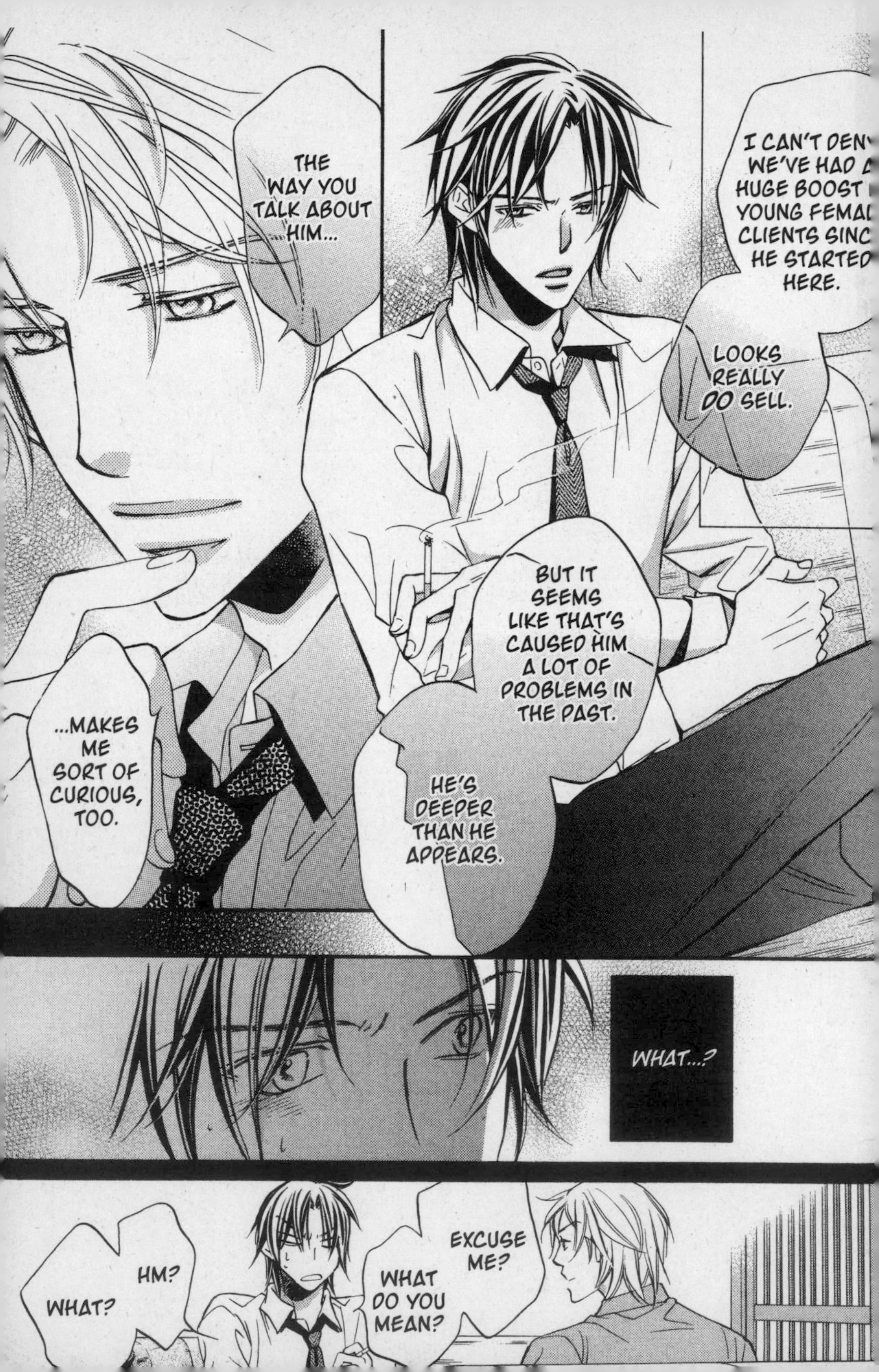
I CAN'T DENY WE'VE HAD A HUGE BOOST IN YOUNG FEMALE CLIENTS SINCE HE STARTED HERE.
LOOKS REALLY DO SELL.
BUT IT SEEMS LIKE THAT'S CAUSED HIM A LOT OF PROBLEMS IN THE PAST.
HE'S DEEPER THAN HE APPEARS.
THE WAY YOU TALK ABOUT HIM...
...MAKES ME SORT OF CURIOUS, TOO.
WHAT...?
EXCUSE ME?
WHAT DO YOU MEAN?
HM?
WHAT?

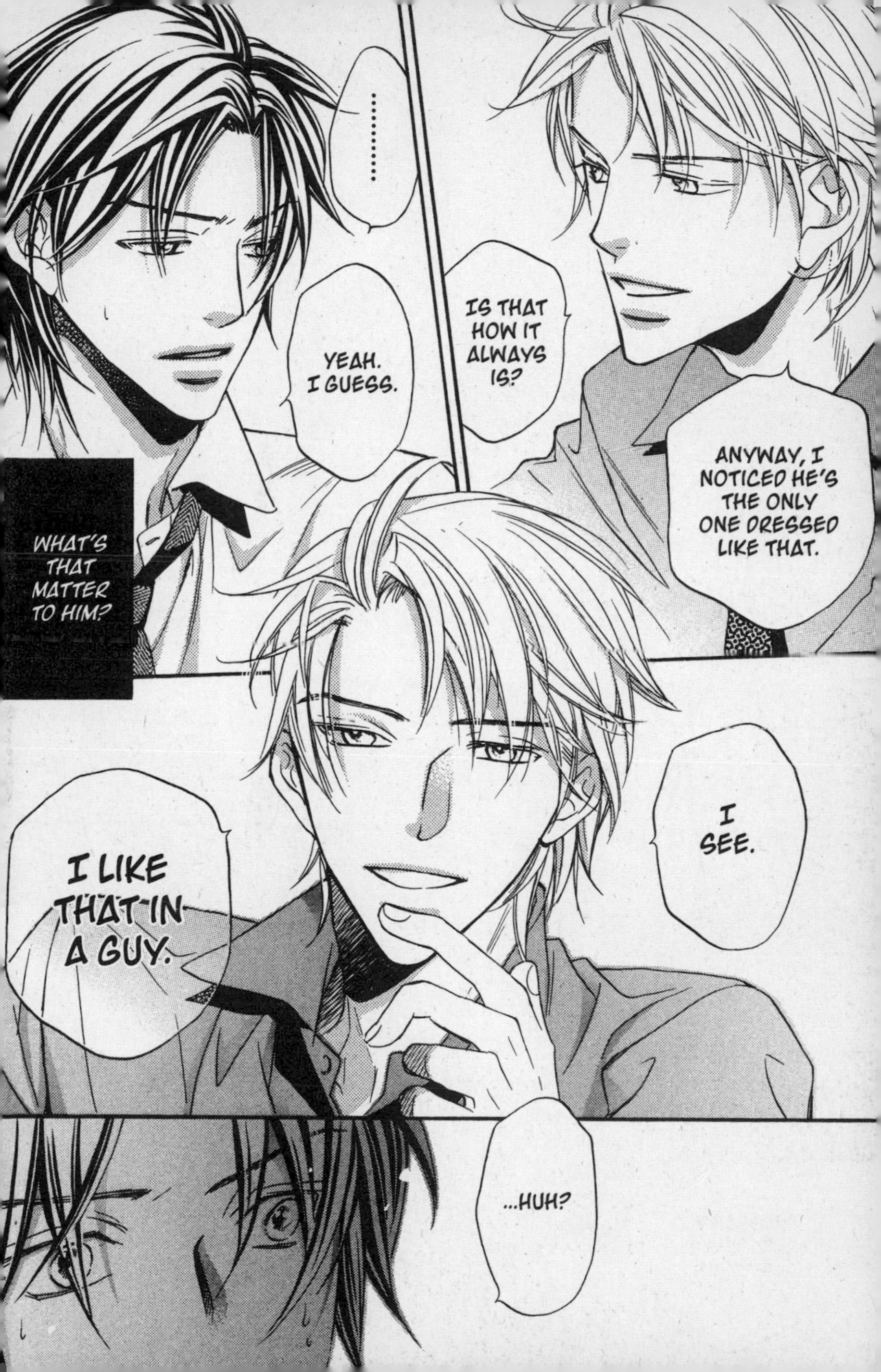
ANYWAY, I NOTICED HE'S THE ONLY ONE DRESSED LIKE THAT.
IS THAT HOW IT ALWAYS IS?
......
YEAH. I GUESS.
WHAT'S THAT MATTER TO HIM?
I SEE.
I LIKE THAT IN A GUY.
...HUH?

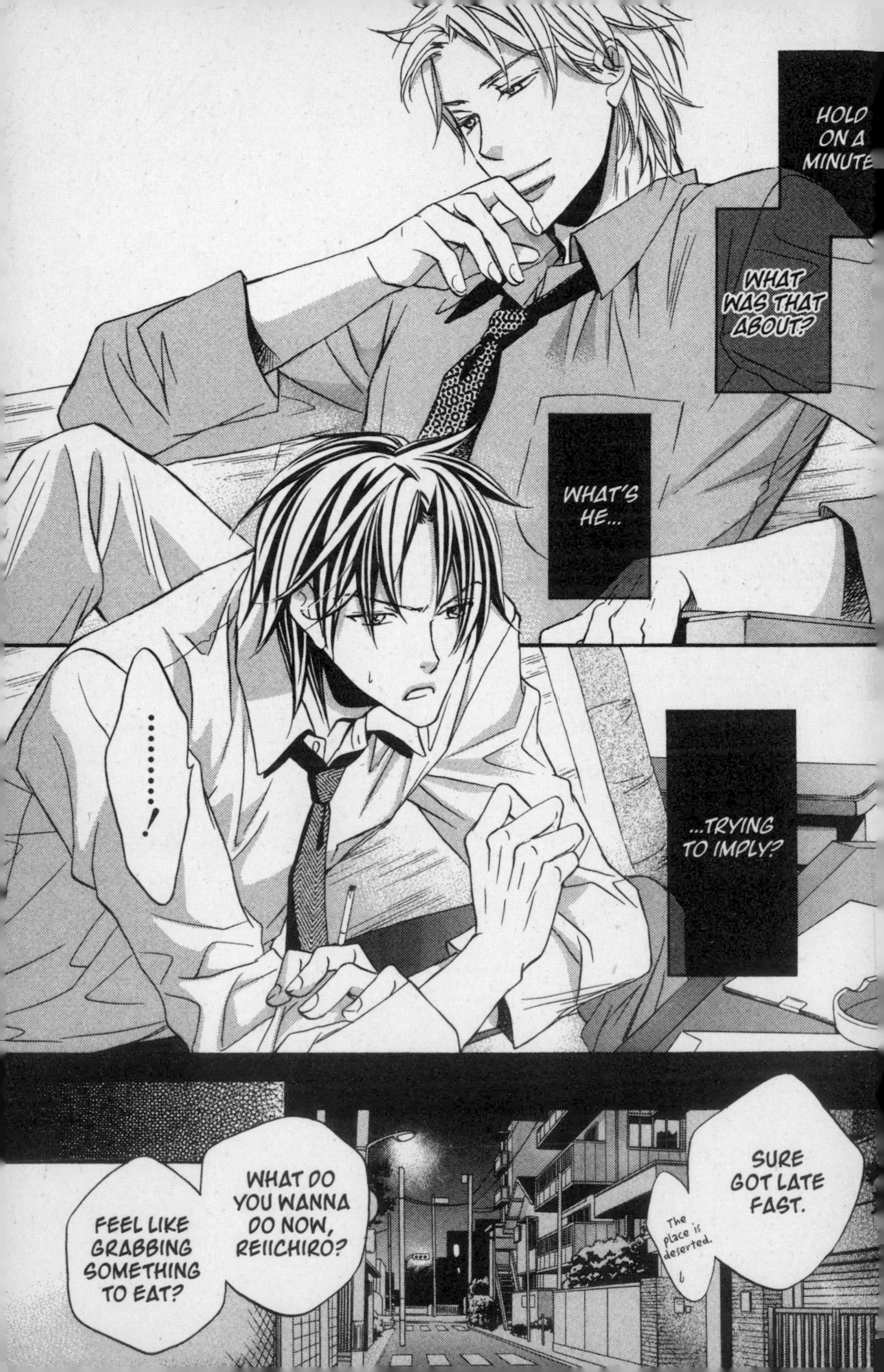
HOLD ON A MINUTE
WHAT WAS THAT ABOUT?
WHAT'S HE...
...TRYING TO IMPLY?
......!
SURE GOT LATE FAST.
The place is deserted.
WHAT DO YOU WANNA DO NOW, REIICHIRO?
FEEL LIKE GRABBING SOMETHING TO EAT?

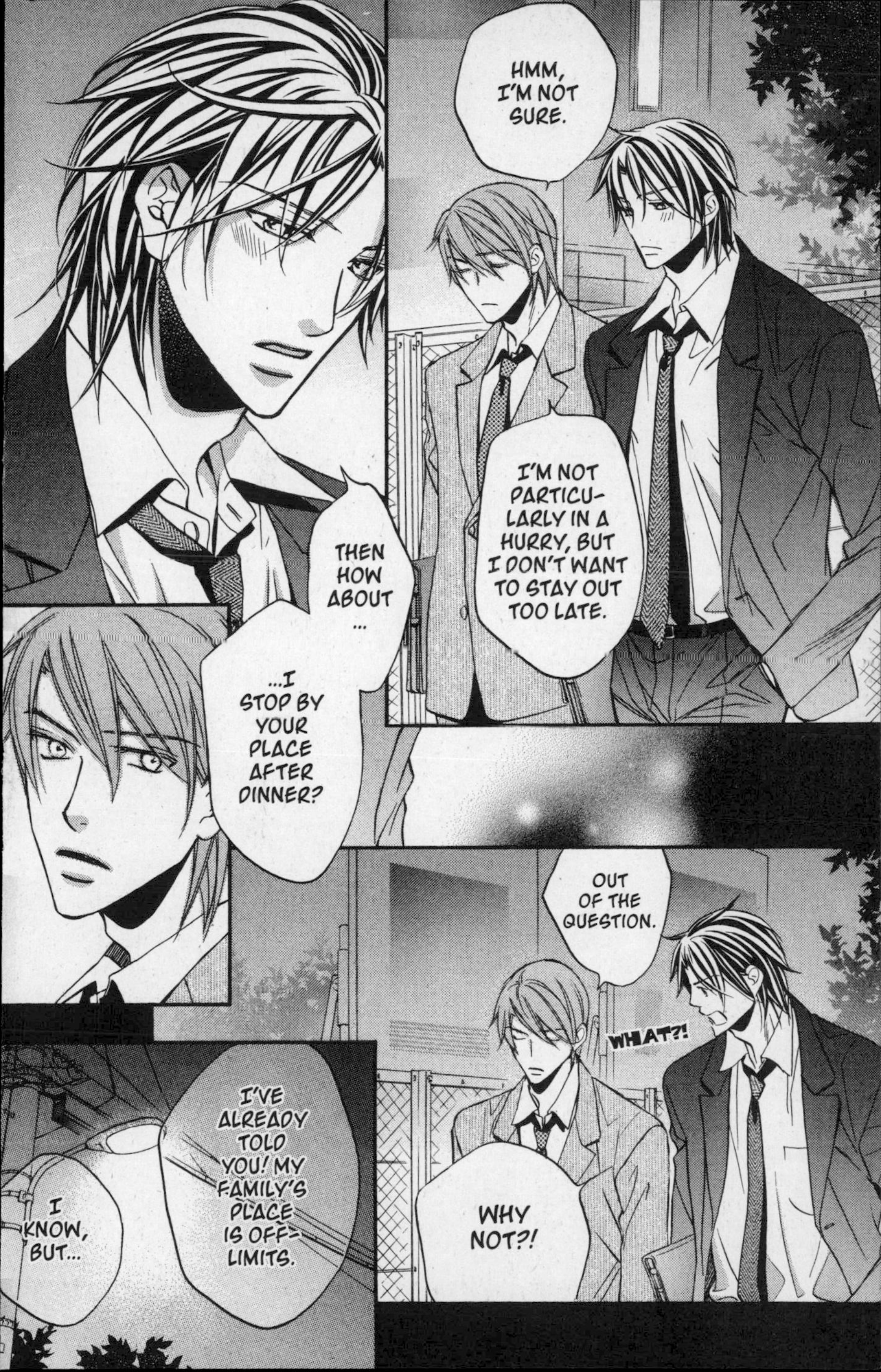
HMM, I'M NOT SURE.
I'M NOT PARTICU-LARLY IN A HURRY, BUT I DON'T WANT TO STAY OUT TOO LATE.
THEN HOW ABOUT ...
...I STOP BY YOUR PLACE AFTER DINNER?
OUT OF THE QUESTION.
WHAT?!
WHY NOT?!
I'VE ALREADY TOLD YOU! MY FAMILY'S PLACE IS OFF-LIMITS.
I KNOW, BUT...

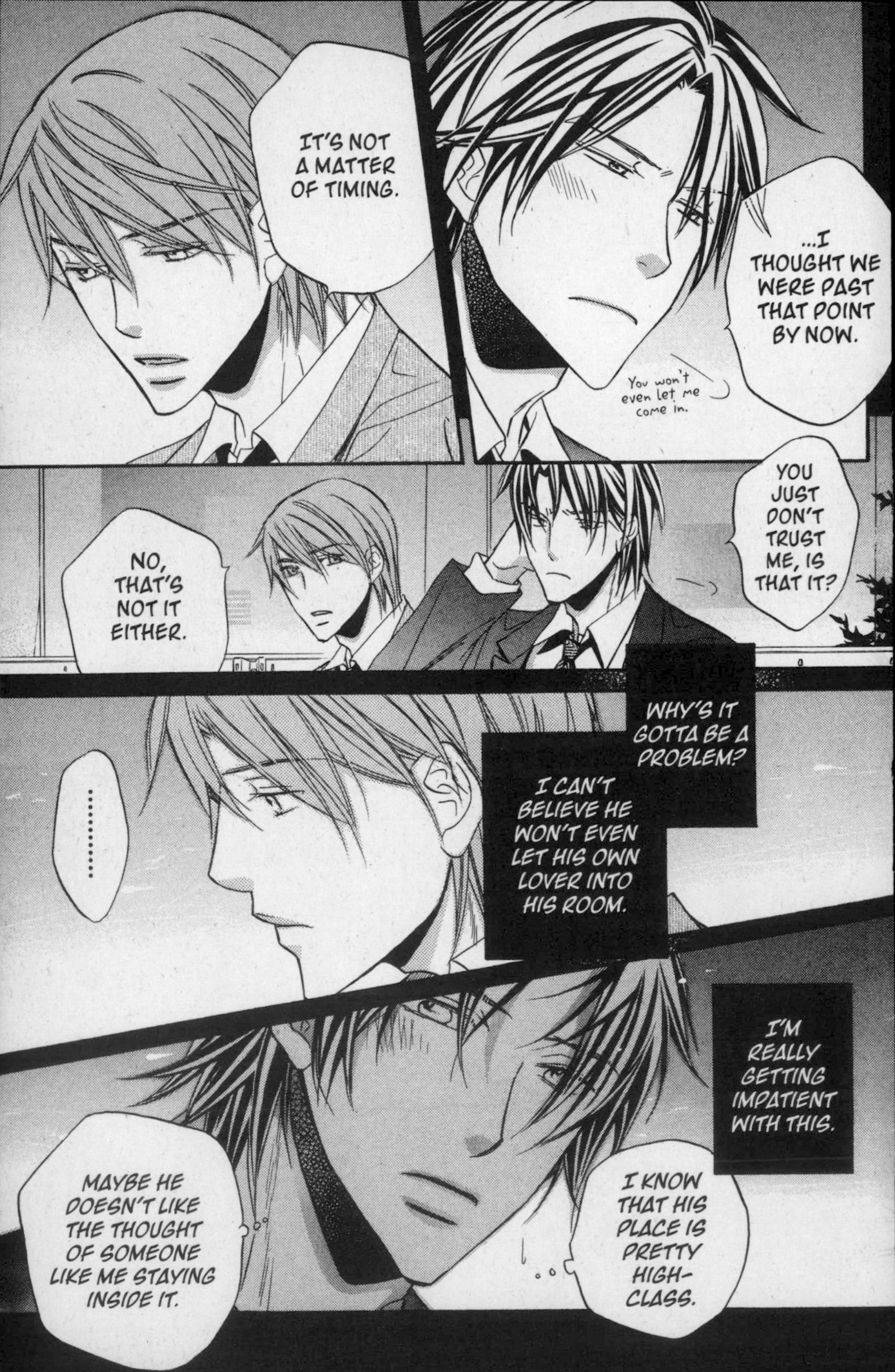
...I THOUGHT WE WERE PAST THAT POINT BY NOW.
You won't even let me come in.
IT'S NOT A MATTER OF TIMING.
YOU JUST DON'T TRUST ME, IS THAT IT?
NO, THAT'S NOT IT EITHER.
WHY'S IT GOTTA BE A PROBLEM?
I CAN'T BELIEVE HE WON'T EVEN LET HIS OWN LOVER INTO HIS ROOM.
......
I'M REALLY GETTING IMPATIENT WITH THIS.
I KNOW THAT HIS PLACE IS PRETTY HIGH-CLASS.
MAYBE HE DOESN'T LIKE THE THOUGHT OF SOMEONE LIKE ME STAYING INSIDE IT.

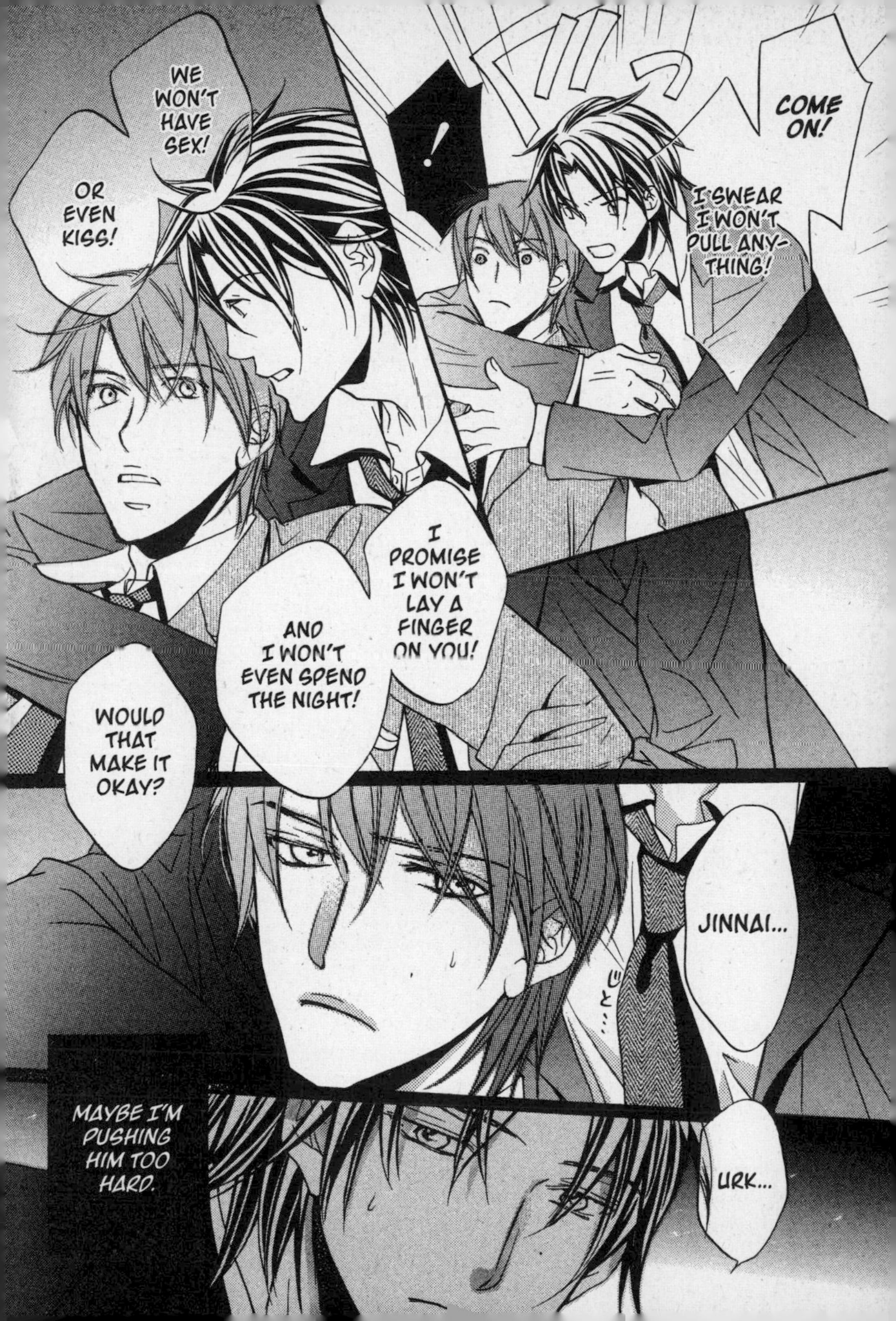
COME ON!
I SWEAR I WON'T PULL ANY-THING!
!
WE WON'T HAVE SEX!
OR EVEN KISS!
I PROMISE I WON'T LAY A FINGER ON YOU!
AND I WON'T EVEN SPEND THE NIGHT!
WOULD THAT MAKE IT OKAY?
JINNAI...
MAYBE I'M PUSHING HIM TOO HARD.
URK...

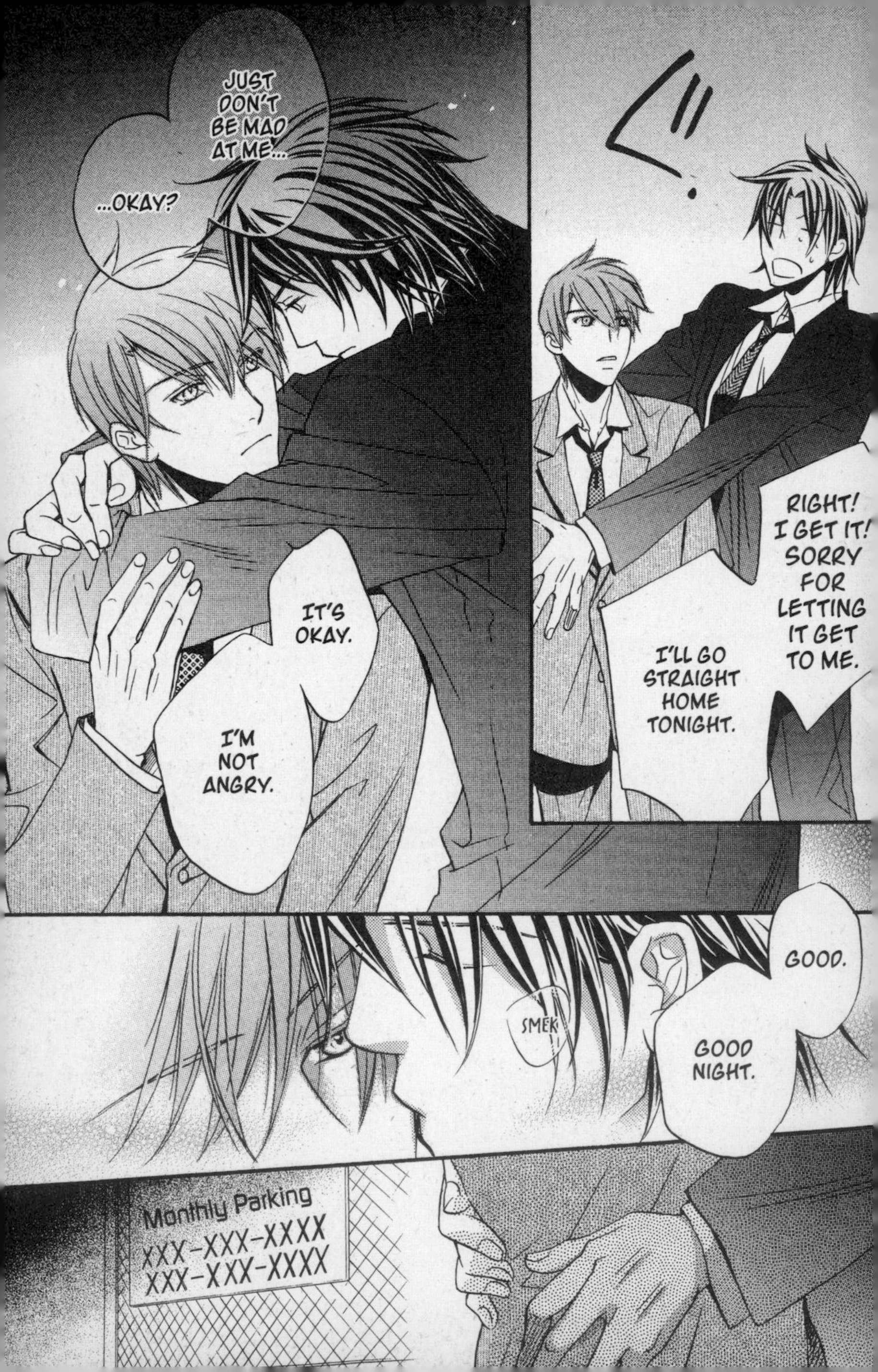
!!
RIGHT! I GET IT! SORRY FOR LETTING IT GET TO ME.
I'LL GO STRAIGHT HOME TONIGHT.
JUST DON'T BE MAD AT ME...
...OKAY?
IT'S OKAY.
I'M NOT ANGRY.
GOOD.
GOOD NIGHT.
SMEK
Monthly Parking
XXX-XXX-XXXX
XXX-XXX-XXXX

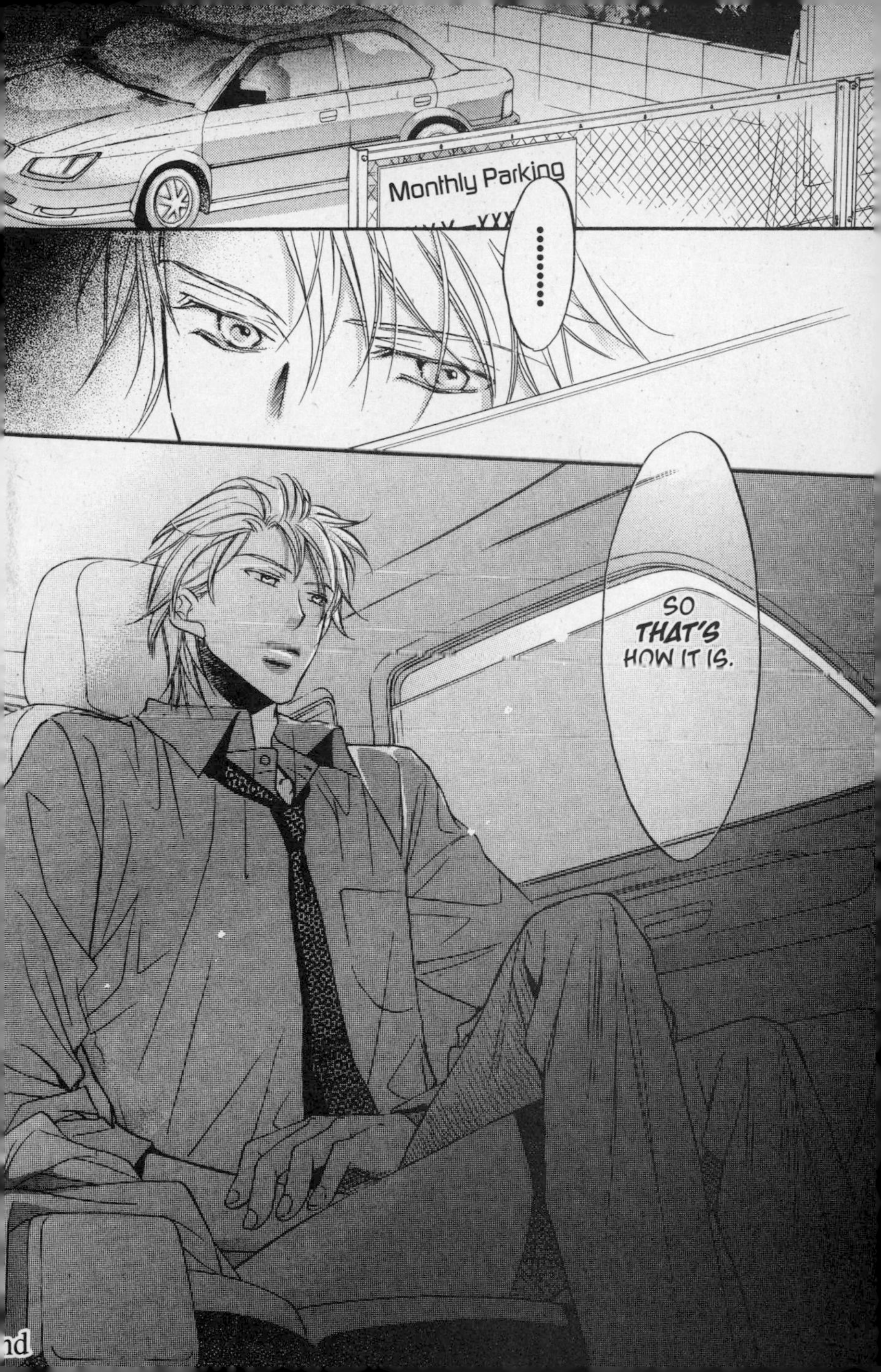
Monthly Parking
....
SO THAT'S HOW IT IS.

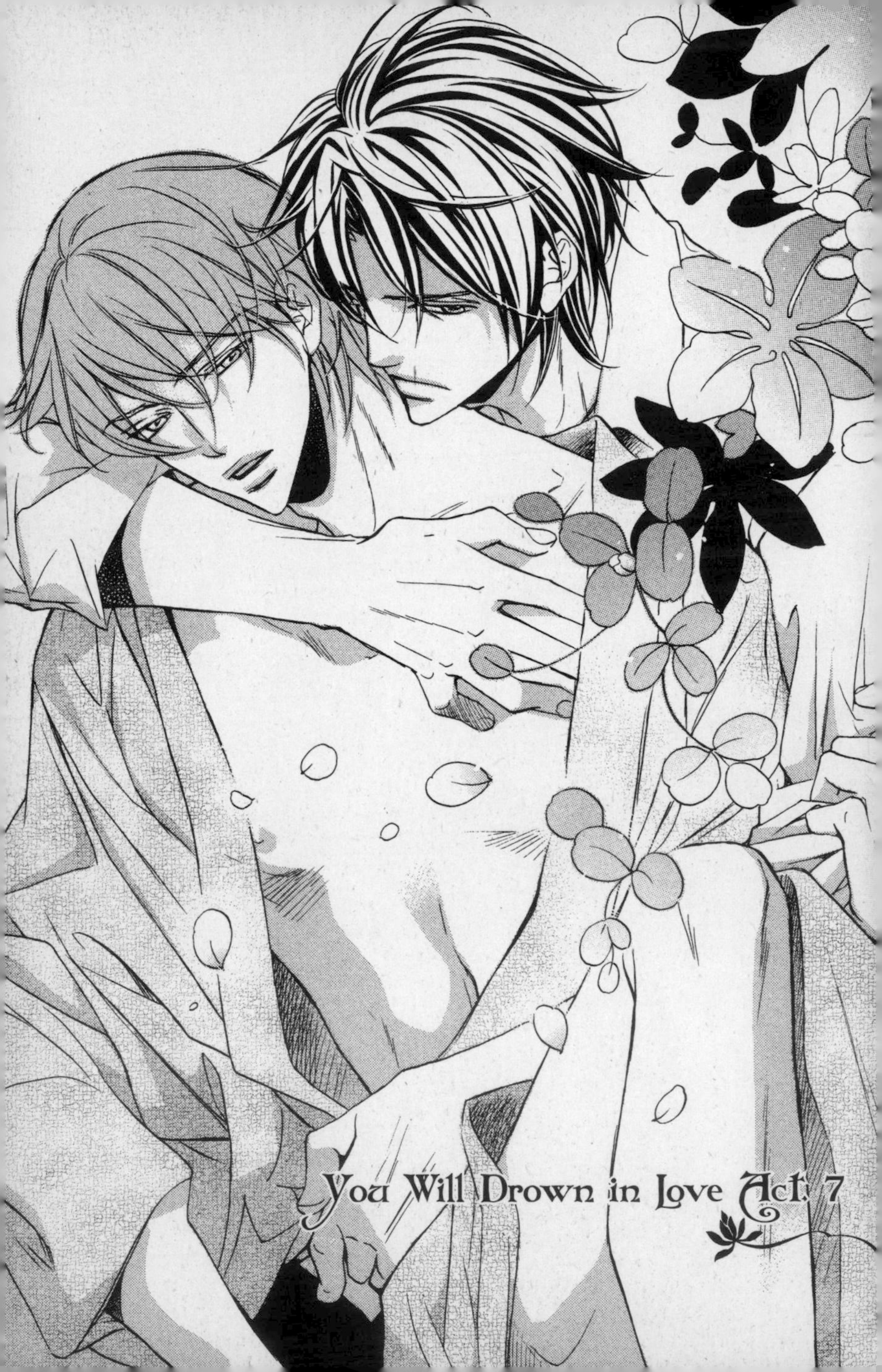
You Will Drown in Love Act: 7

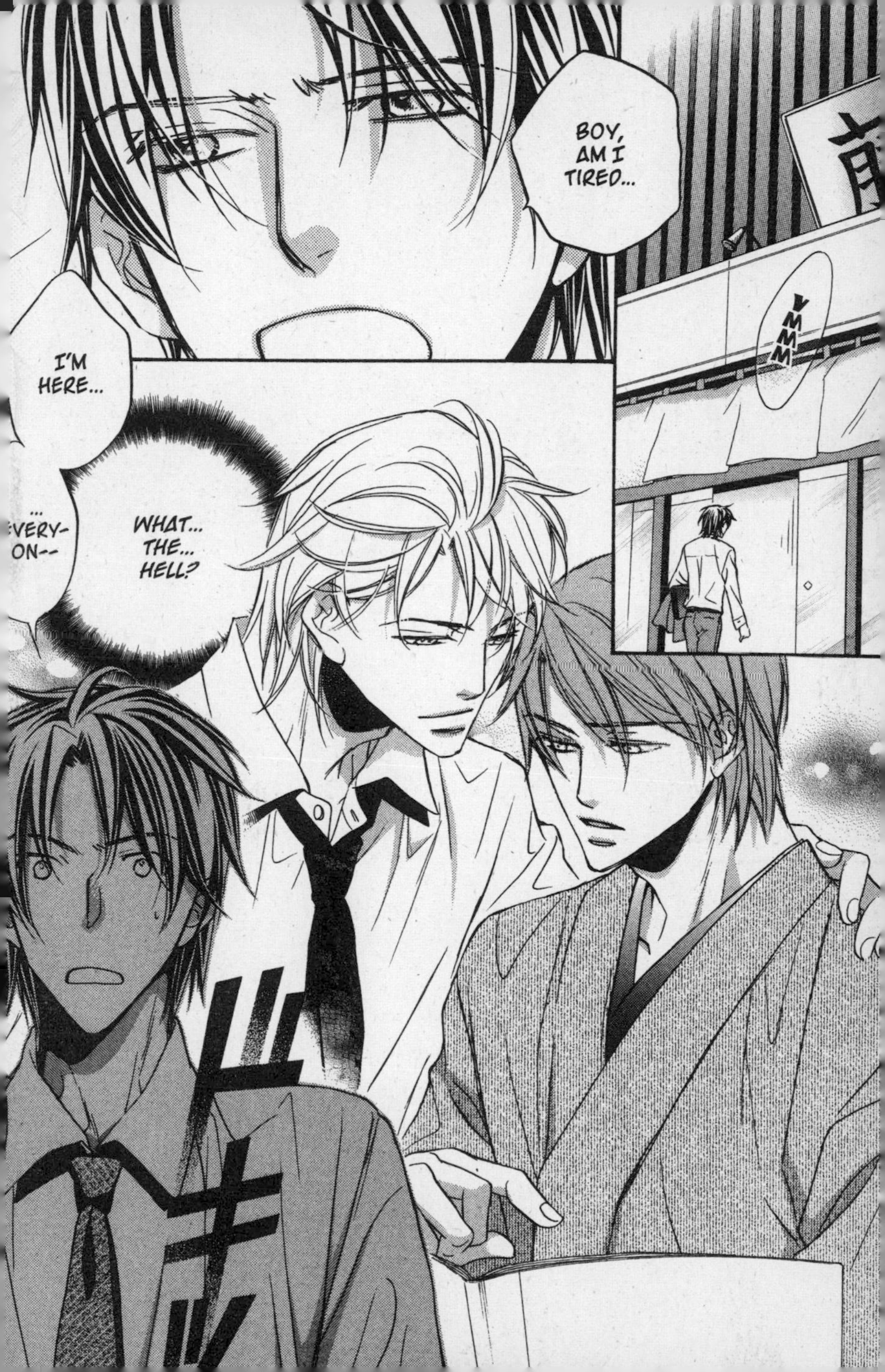
VMMM
BOY, AM I TIRED...
I'M HERE...
...EVERY-ON--
WHAT... THE... HELL?

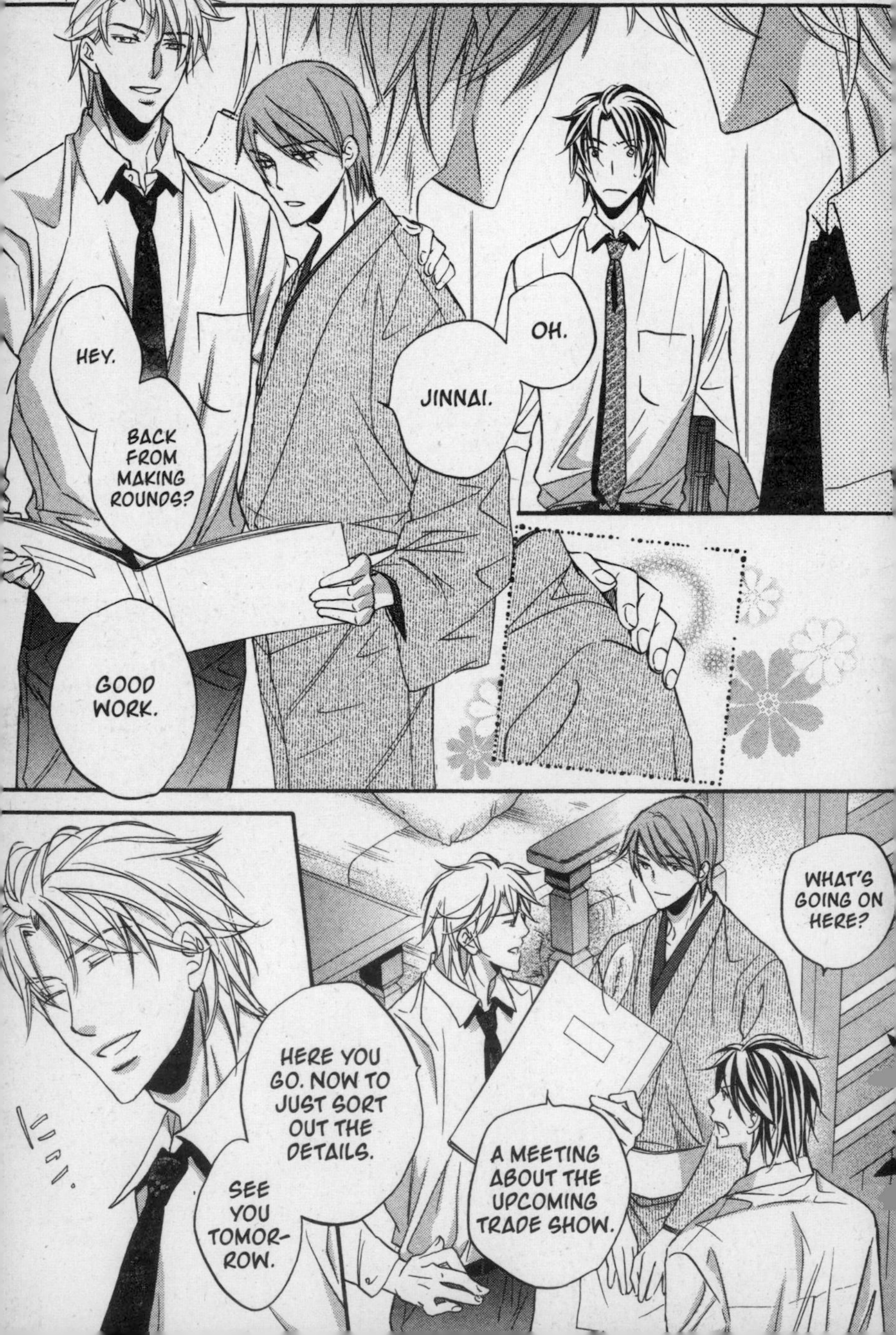
OH.
JINNAI.
HEY.
BACK FROM MAKING ROUNDS?
GOOD WORK.
WHAT'S GOING ON HERE?
A MEETING ABOUT THE UPCOMING TRADE SHOW.
HERE YOU GO. NOW TO JUST SORT OUT THE DETAILS.
SEE YOU TOMOR-ROW.

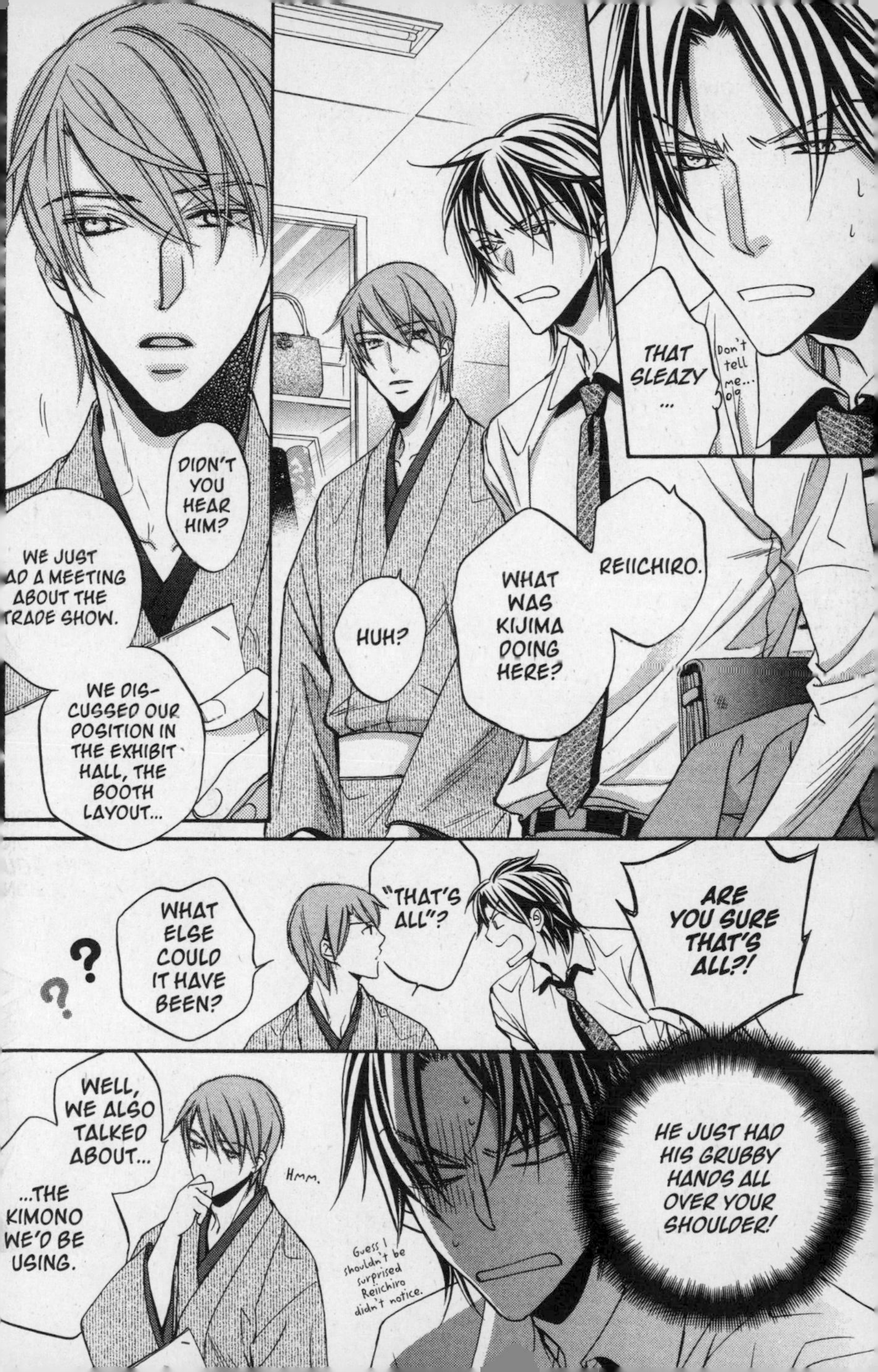
THAT SLEAZY ...
Don't tell me... 9
REIICHIRO.
WHAT WAS KIJIMA DOING HERE?
HUH?
DIDN'T YOU HEAR HIM?
WE JUST AD A MEETING ABOUT THE TRADE SHOW.
WE DIS-CUSSED OUR POSITION IN THE EXHIBIT HALL, THE BOOTH LAYOUT...
ARE YOU SURE THAT'S ALL?!
"THAT'S ALL"?
WHAT ELSE COULD IT HAVE BEEN?
? ?
HE JUST HAD HIS GRUBBY HANDS ALL OVER YOUR SHOULDER!
Guess I shouldn't be surprised Reiichiro didn't notice.
Hmm.
WELL, WE ALSO TALKED ABOUT...
...THE KIMONO WE'D BE USING.

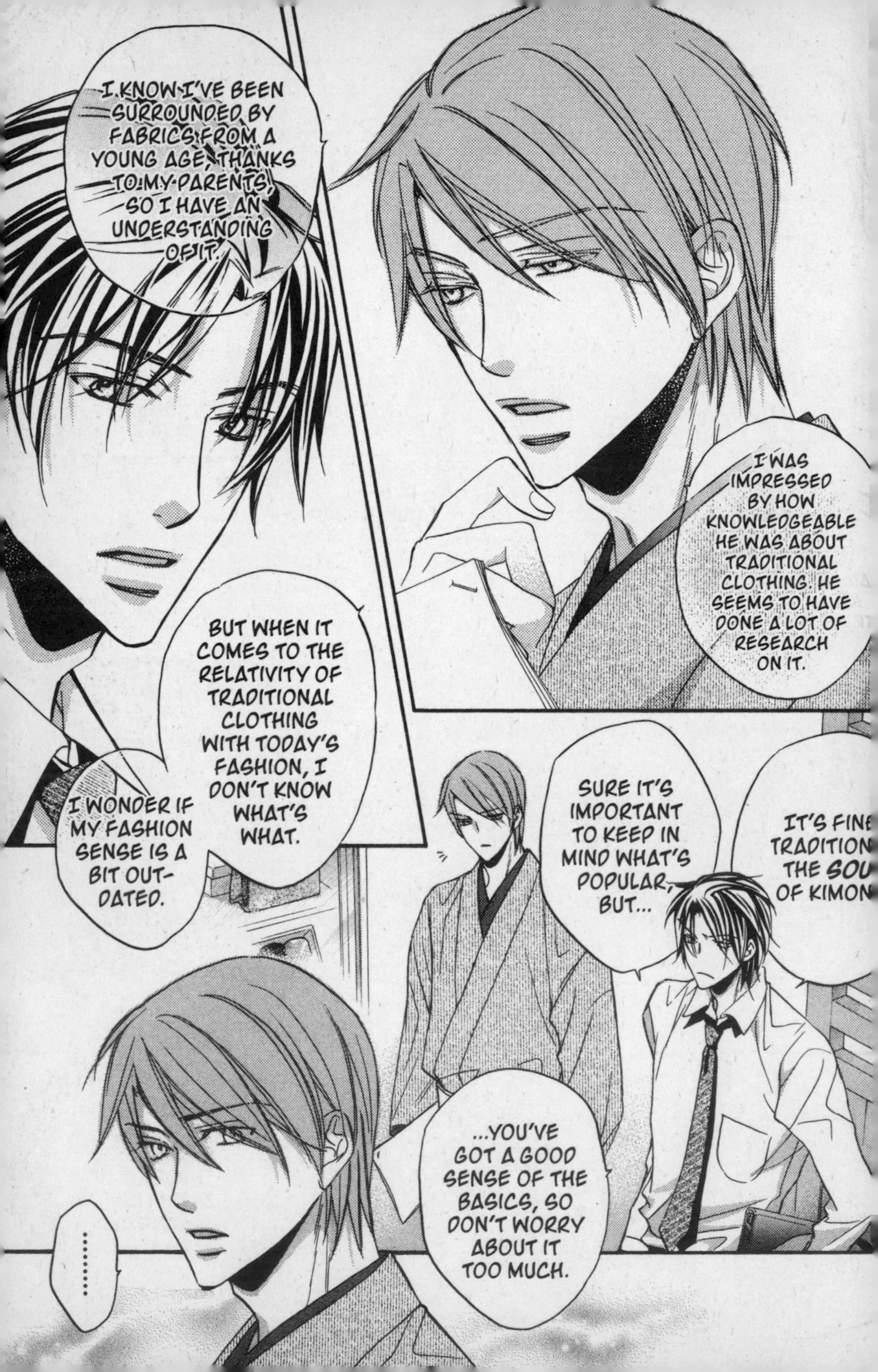
I WAS IMPRESSED BY HOW KNOWLEDGEABLE HE WAS ABOUT TRADITIONAL CLOTHING. HE SEEMS TO HAVE DONE A LOT OF RESEARCH ON IT.
I KNOW I'VE BEEN SURROUNDED BY FABRICS FROM A YOUNG AGE, THANKS TO MY PARENTS, SO I HAVE AN UNDERSTANDING OF IT.
BUT WHEN IT COMES TO THE RELATIVITY OF TRADITIONAL CLOTHING WITH TODAY'S FASHION, I DON'T KNOW WHAT'S WHAT.
I WONDER IF MY FASHION SENSE IS A BIT OUT-DATED.
IT'S FINE TRADITION THE SOU OF KIMON
SURE IT'S IMPORTANT TO KEEP IN MIND WHAT'S POPULAR, BUT...
...YOU'VE GOT A GOOD SENSE OF THE BASICS, SO DON'T WORRY ABOUT IT TOO MUCH.
......

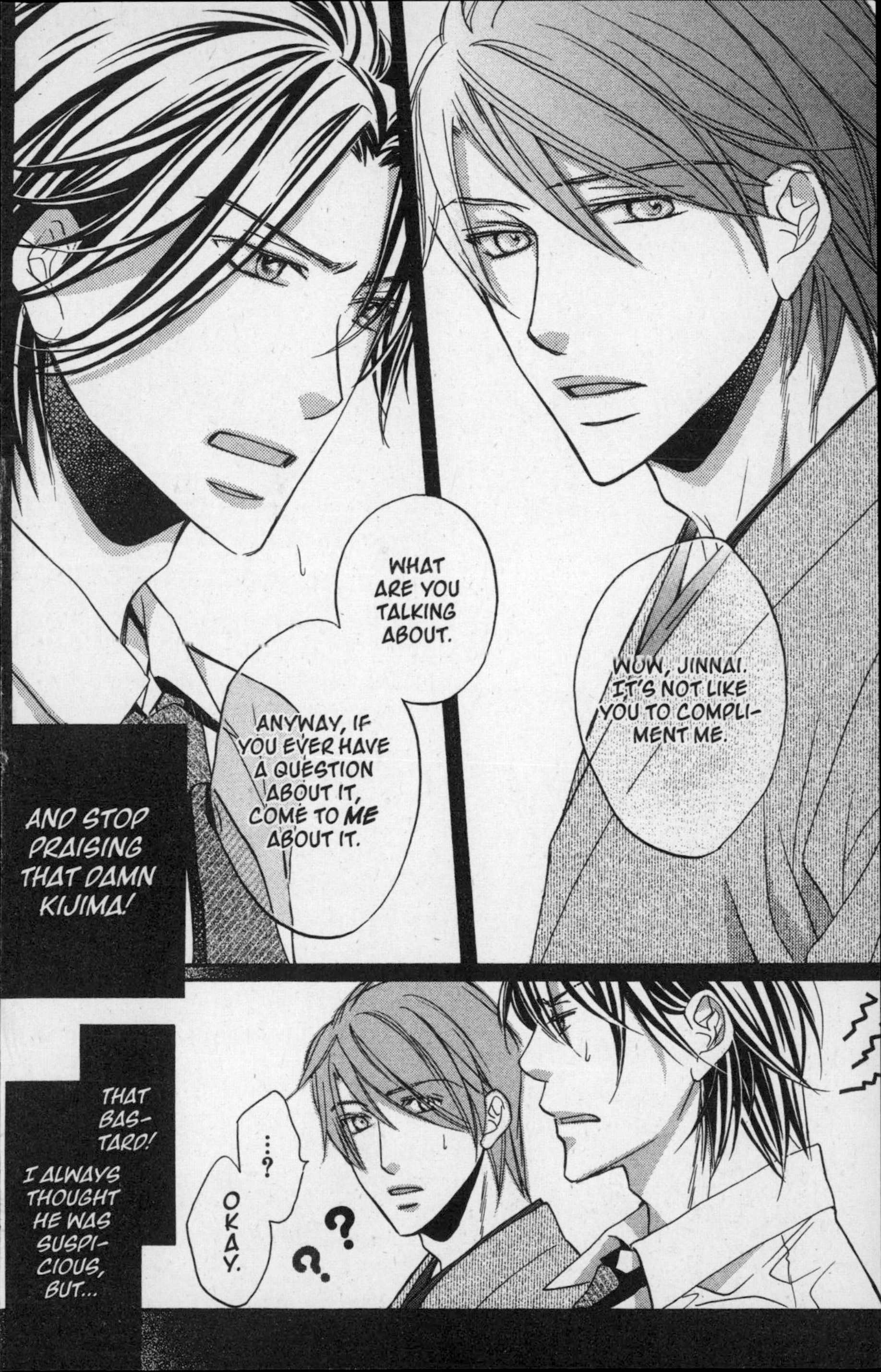
WOW, JINNAI. IT'S NOT LIKE YOU TO COMPLIMENT ME.
WHAT ARE YOU TALKING ABOUT.
ANYWAY, IF YOU EVER HAVE A QUESTION ABOUT IT, COME TO *ME* ABOUT IT.
AND STOP PRAISING THAT DAMN KIJIMA!
...?
OKAY.
? ?
THAT BASTARD!
I ALWAYS THOUGHT HE WAS SUSPICIOUS, BUT...

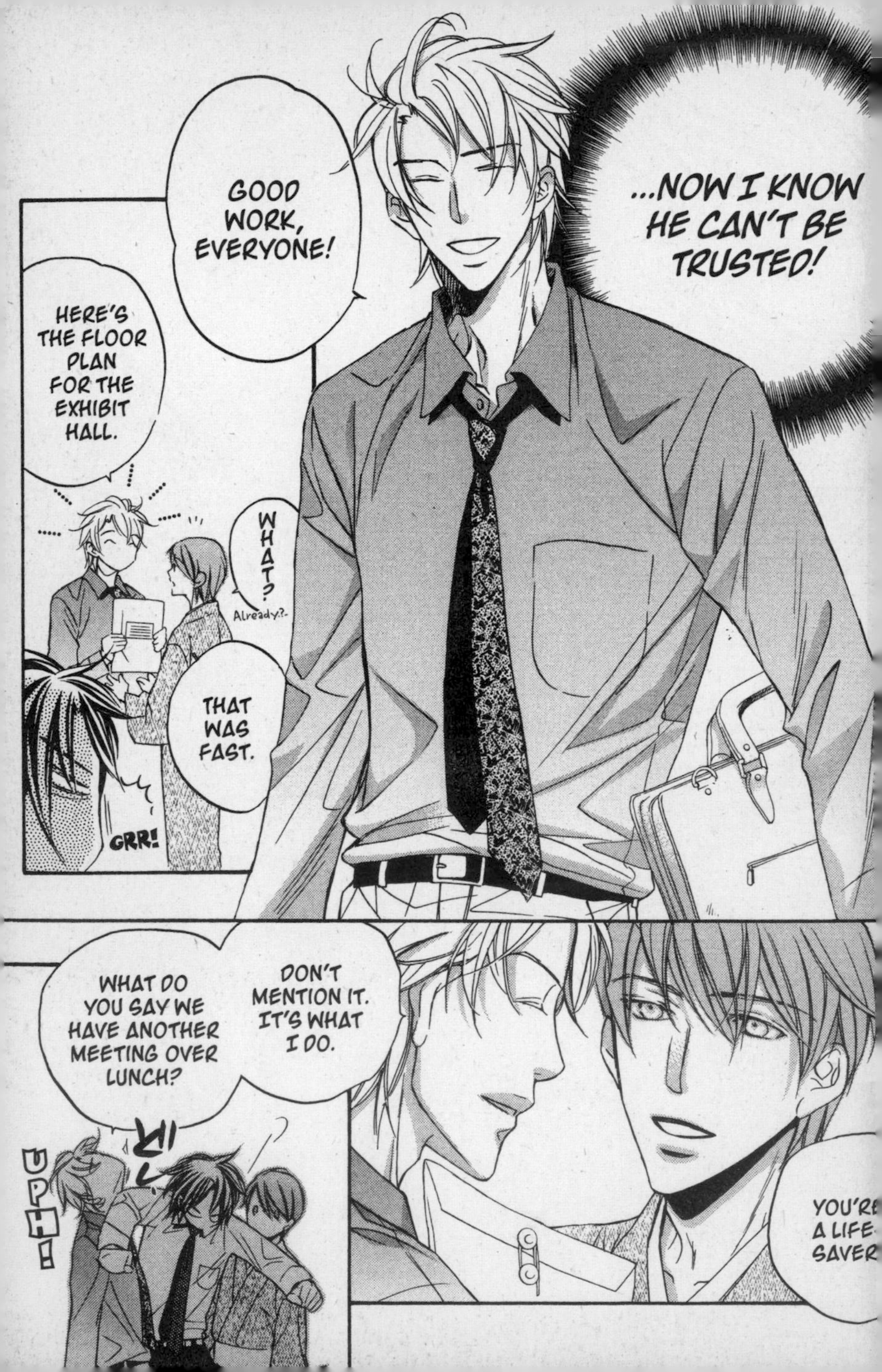
...NOW I KNOW HE CAN'T BE TRUSTED!
GOOD WORK, EVERYONE!
HERE'S THE FLOOR PLAN FOR THE EXHIBIT HALL.
WHAT?
Already?-
THAT WAS FAST.
GRR!
YOU'RE A LIFE-SAVER
DON'T MENTION IT. IT'S WHAT I DO.
WHAT DO YOU SAY WE HAVE ANOTHER MEETING OVER LUNCH?
UPH!

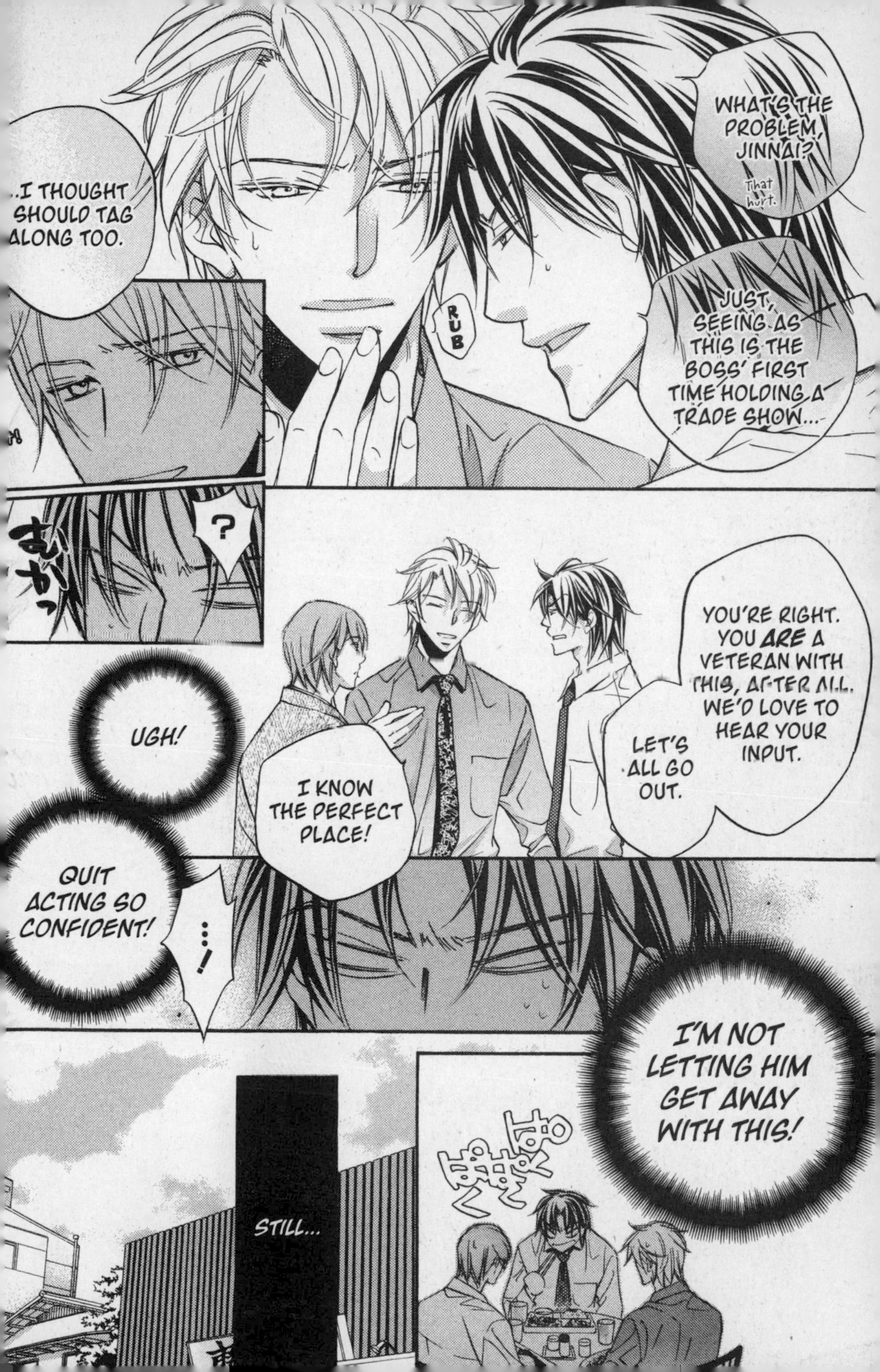
WHAT'S THE PROBLEM, JINNAI?
That hurt.
JUST, SEEING AS THIS IS THE BOSS' FIRST TIME HOLDING A TRADE SHOW...
RUB
...I THOUGHT SHOULD TAG ALONG TOO.
?
YOU'RE RIGHT. YOU ARE A VETERAN WITH THIS, AFTER ALL. WE'D LOVE TO HEAR YOUR INPUT.
LET'S ALL GO OUT.
I KNOW THE PERFECT PLACE!
UGH!
...!
QUIT ACTING SO CONFIDENT!
I'M NOT LETTING HIM GET AWAY WITH THIS!
STILL...

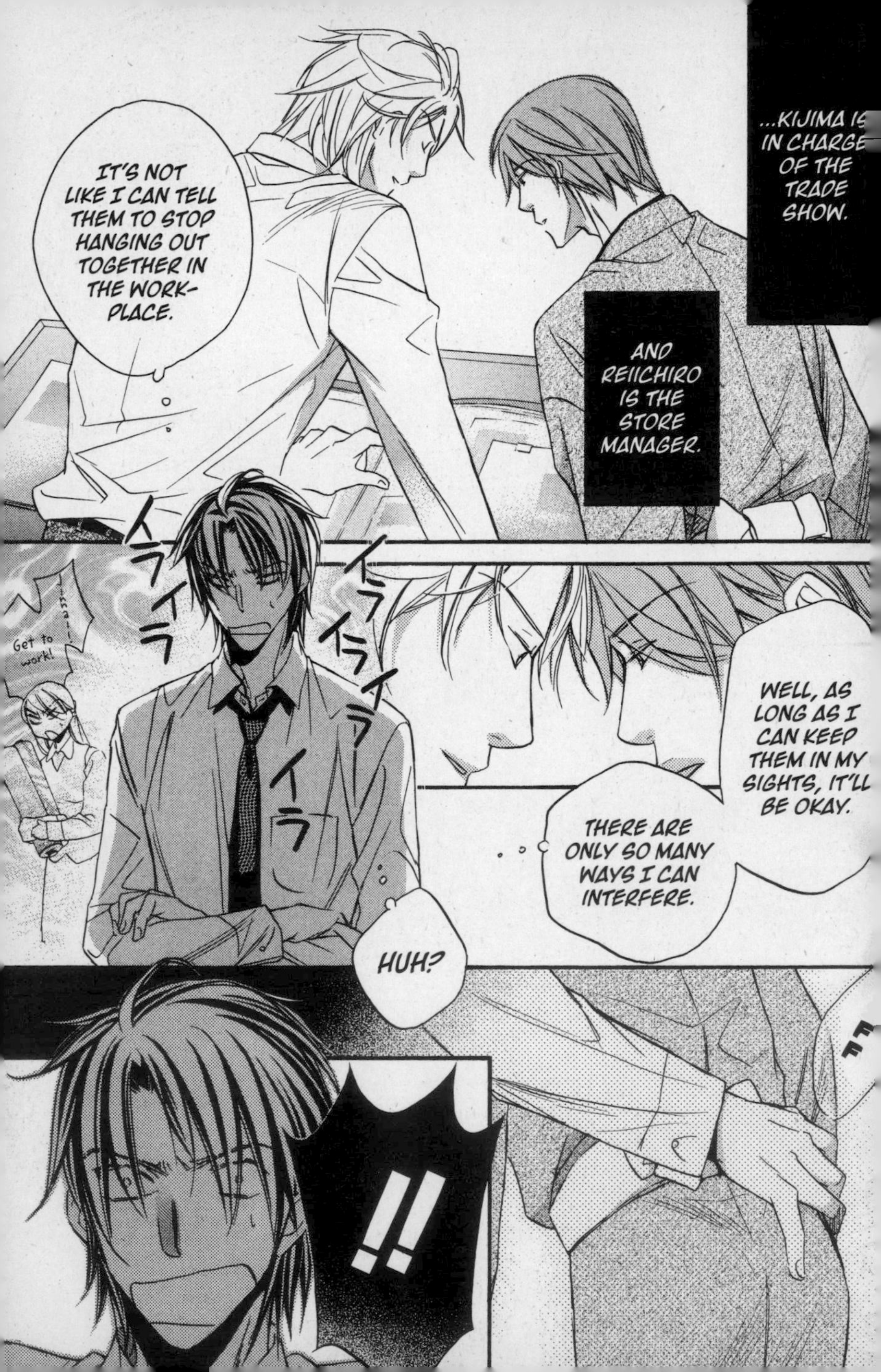
...KIJIMA IS IN CHARGE OF THE TRADE SHOW.
AND REIICHIRO IS THE STORE MANAGER.
IT'S NOT LIKE I CAN TELL THEM TO STOP HANGING OUT TOGETHER IN THE WORK-PLACE.
WELL, AS LONG AS I CAN KEEP THEM IN MY SIGHTS, IT'LL BE OKAY.
THERE ARE ONLY SO MANY WAYS I CAN INTERFERE.
イライラ
イライライラ
Get to work!
HUH?
!!

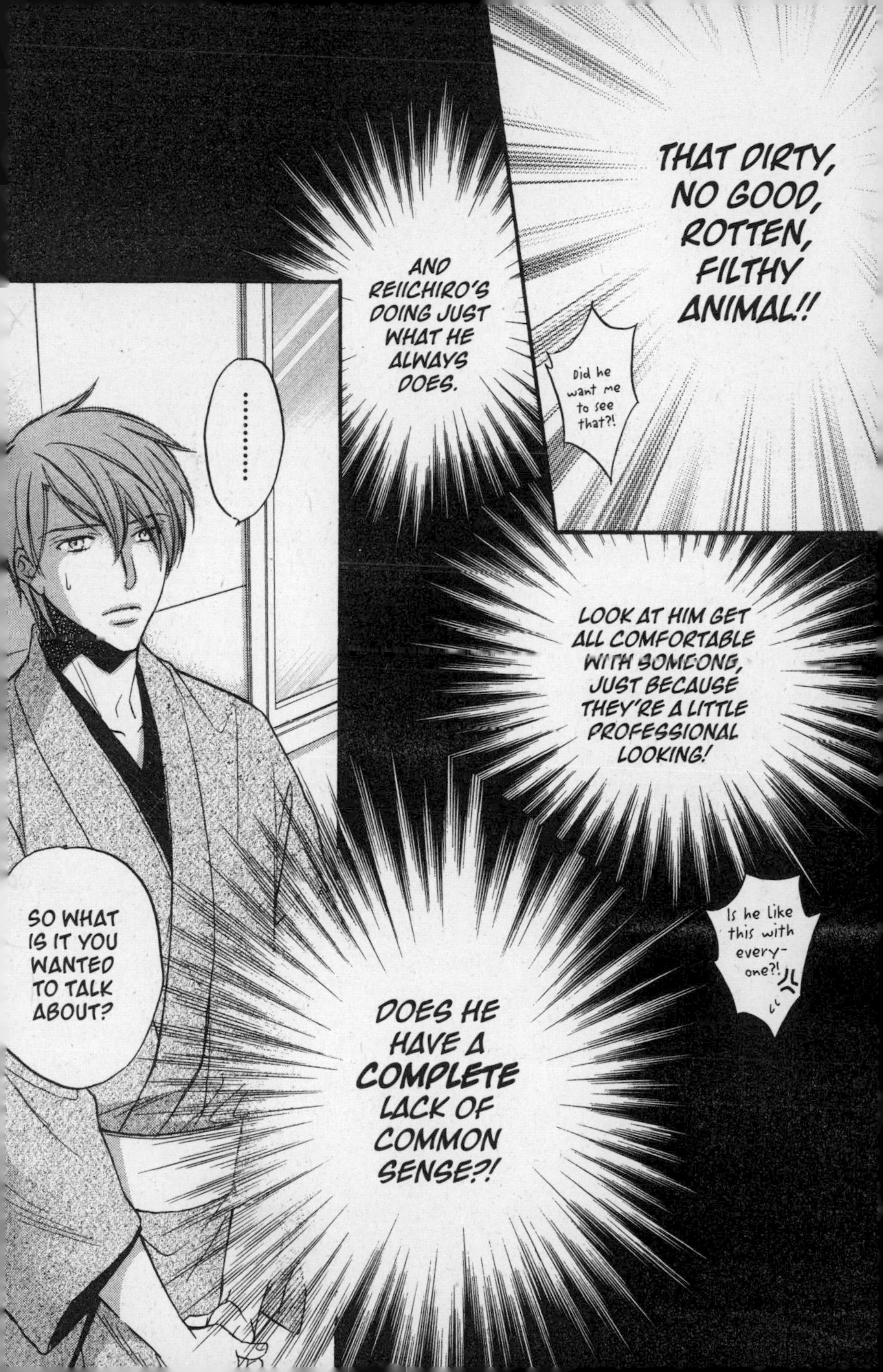
THAT DIRTY, NO GOOD, ROTTEN, FILTHY ANIMAL!!
Did he want me to see that?!
AND REIICHIRO'S DOING JUST WHAT HE ALWAYS DOES.
......
LOOK AT HIM GET ALL COMFORTABLE WITH SOMEONE, JUST BECAUSE THEY'RE A LITTLE PROFESSIONAL LOOKING!
Is he like this with every-one?!
DOES HE HAVE A COMPLETE LACK OF COMMON SENSE?!
SO WHAT IS IT YOU WANTED TO TALK ABOUT?

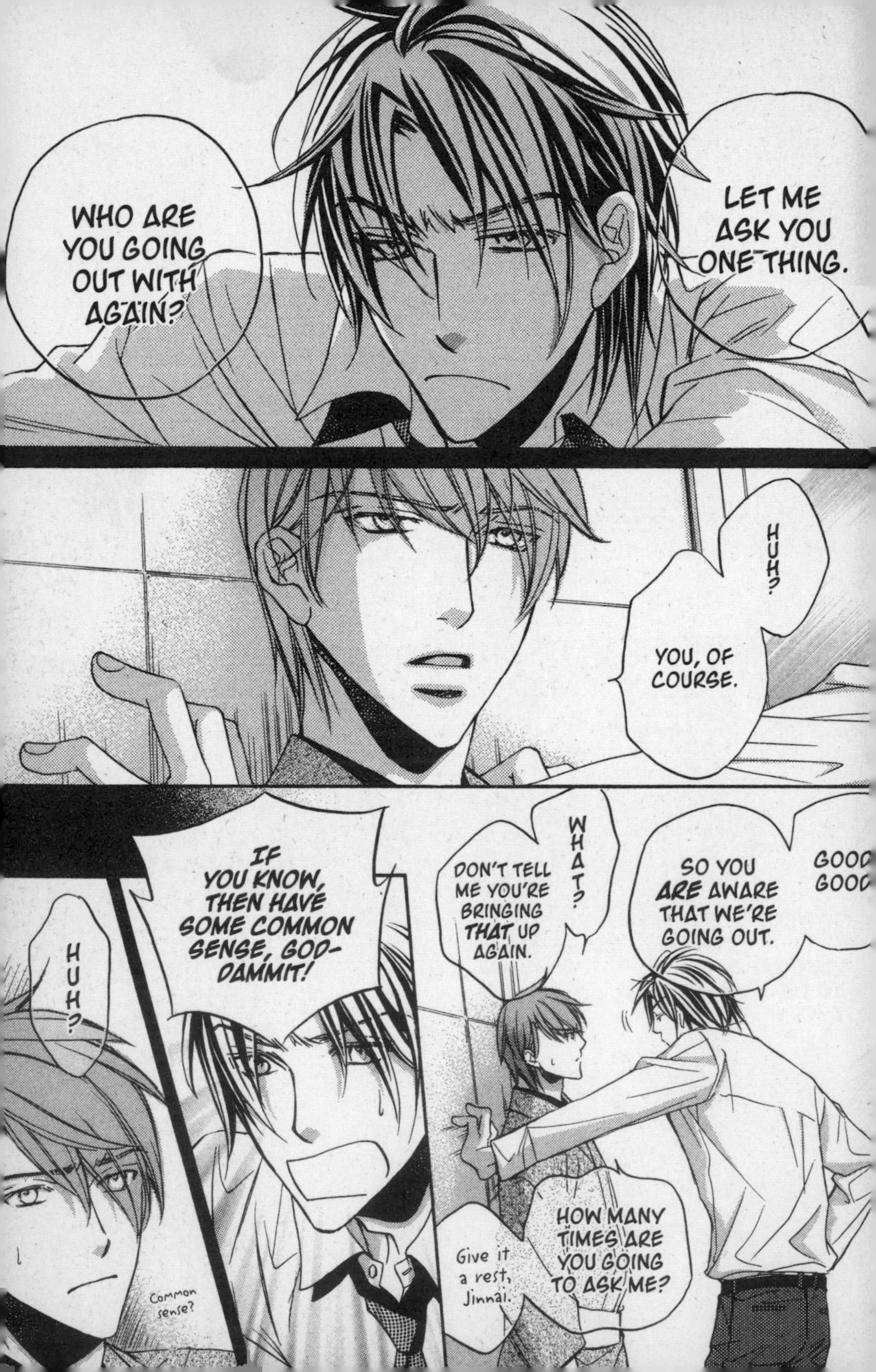
LET ME ASK YOU ONE THING.
WHO ARE YOU GOING OUT WITH AGAIN?
HUH?
YOU, OF COURSE.
GOOD GOOD
SO YOU ARE AWARE THAT WE'RE GOING OUT.
WHAT?
DON'T TELL ME YOU'RE BRINGING THAT UP AGAIN.
HOW MANY TIMES ARE YOU GOING TO ASK ME?
Give it a rest, Jinnai.
IF YOU KNOW, THEN HAVE SOME COMMON SENSE, GOD-DAMMIT!
HUH?
Common sense?

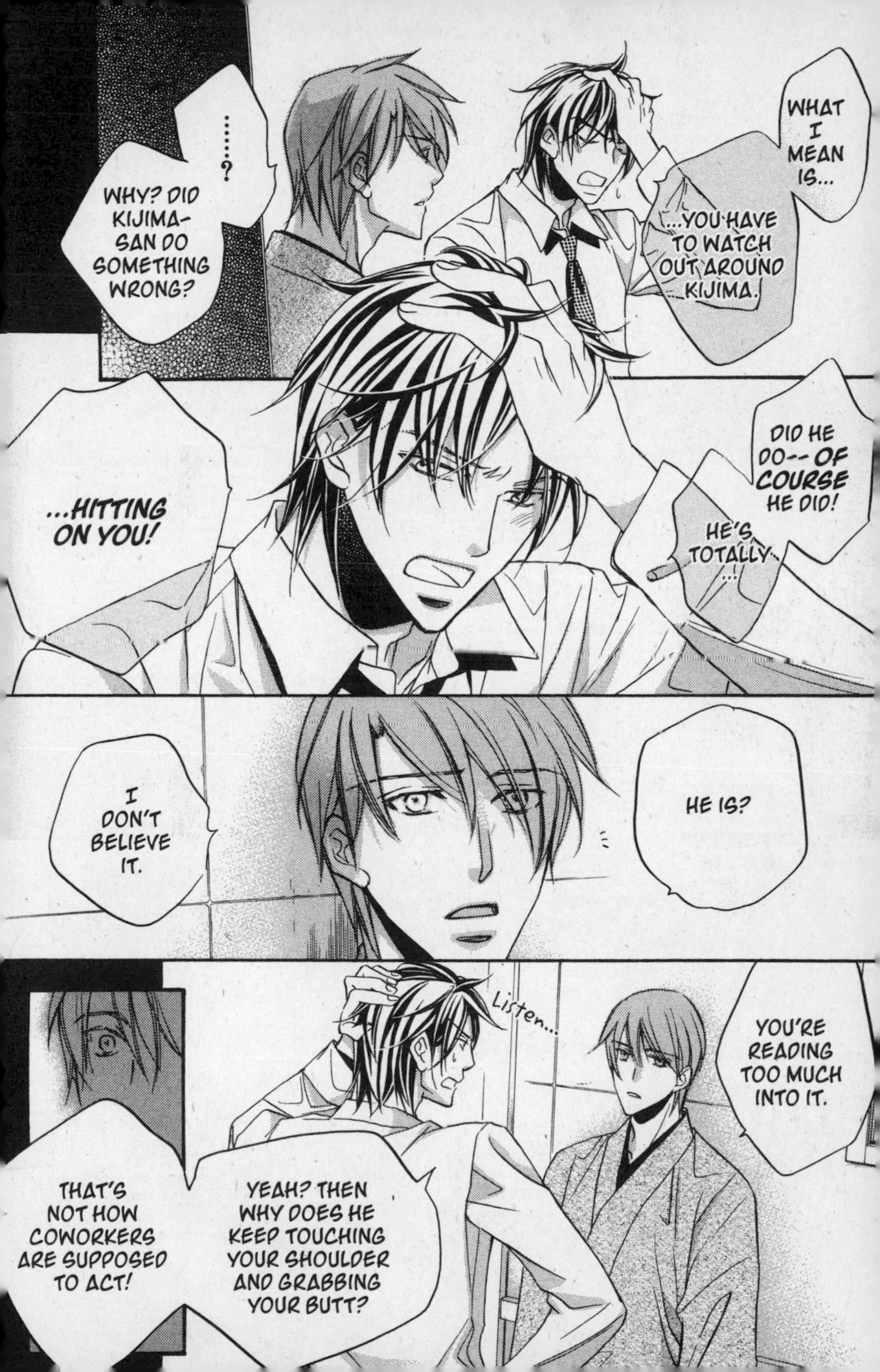
WHAT I MEAN IS...
...YOU HAVE TO WATCH OUT AROUND KIJIMA.
......?
WHY? DID KIJIMA-SAN DO SOMETHING WRONG?
DID HE DO-- OF COURSE HE DID!
HE'S TOTALLY...
...HITTING ON YOU!
HE IS?
I DON'T BELIEVE IT.
YOU'RE READING TOO MUCH INTO IT.
Listen...
YEAH? THEN WHY DOES HE KEEP TOUCHING YOUR SHOULDER AND GRABBING YOUR BUTT?
THAT'S NOT HOW COWORKERS ARE SUPPOSED TO ACT!

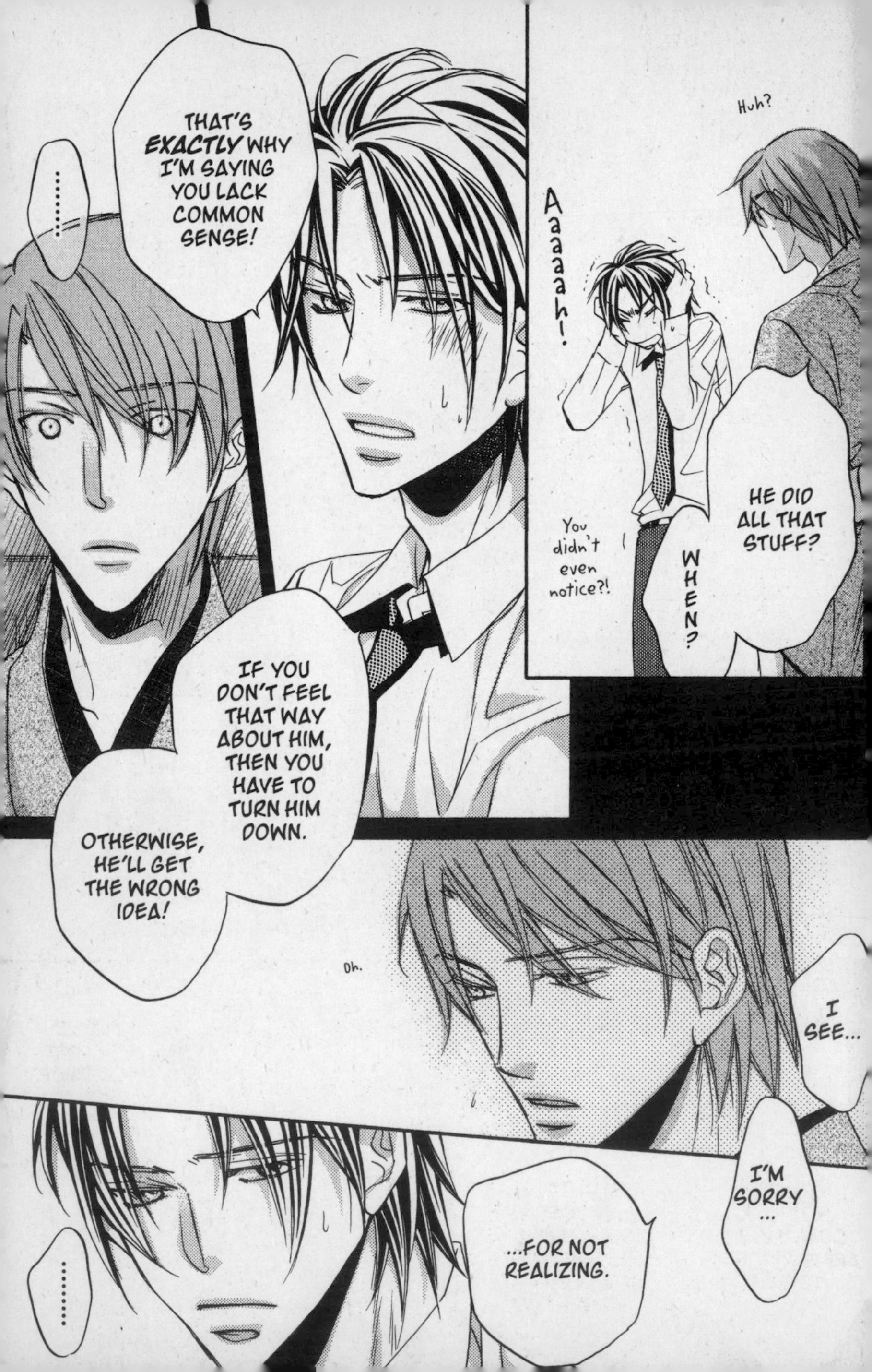
Huh?
HE DID ALL THAT STUFF?
WHEN?
You didn't even notice?!
Aaaaah!
THAT'S EXACTLY WHY I'M SAYING YOU LACK COMMON SENSE!
......
IF YOU DON'T FEEL THAT WAY ABOUT HIM, THEN YOU HAVE TO TURN HIM DOWN.
OTHERWISE, HE'LL GET THE WRONG IDEA!
Oh.
I SEE...
I'M SORRY...
...FOR NOT REALIZING.
......

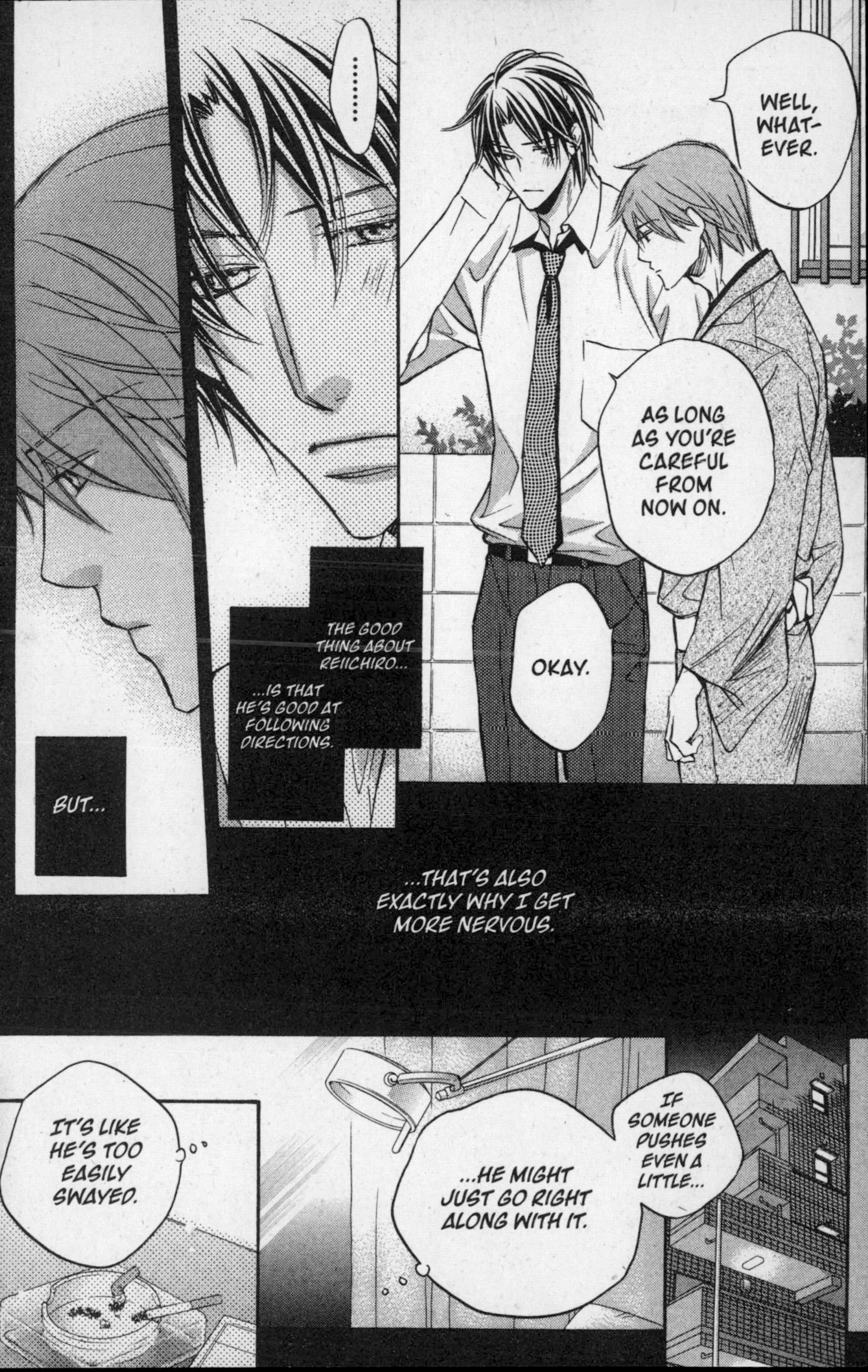
WELL, WHAT-EVER.
AS LONG AS YOU'RE CAREFUL FROM NOW ON.
OKAY.
......
THE GOOD THING ABOUT REIICHIRO...
...IS THAT HE'S GOOD AT FOLLOWING DIRECTIONS.
BUT...
...THAT'S ALSO EXACTLY WHY I GET MORE NERVOUS.
IF SOMEONE PUSHES EVEN A LITTLE...
...HE MIGHT JUST GO RIGHT ALONG WITH IT.
IT'S LIKE HE'S TOO EASILY SWAYED.

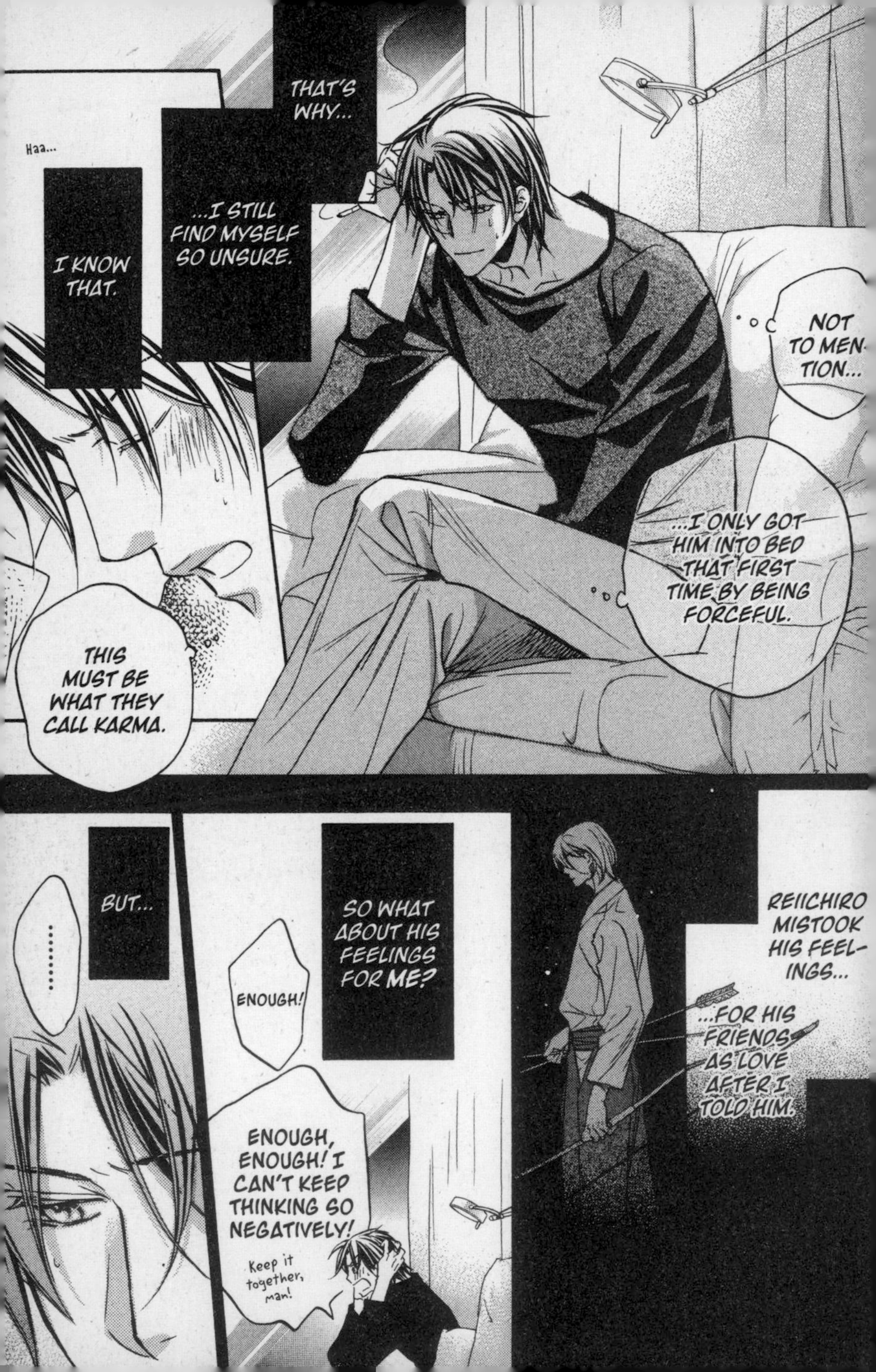
NOT TO MEN-TION...
...I ONLY GOT HIM INTO BED THAT FIRST TIME BY BEING FORCEFUL.
THAT'S WHY...
...I STILL FIND MYSELF SO UNSURE.
I KNOW THAT.
Haa...
THIS MUST BE WHAT THEY CALL KARMA.
REIICHIRO MISTOOK HIS FEEL-INGS...
...FOR HIS FRIENDS AS LOVE AFTER I TOLD HIM.
SO WHAT ABOUT HIS FEELINGS FOR ME?
ENOUGH!
ENOUGH, ENOUGH! I CAN'T KEEP THINKING SO NEGATIVELY!
Keep it together, man!
BUT...
....

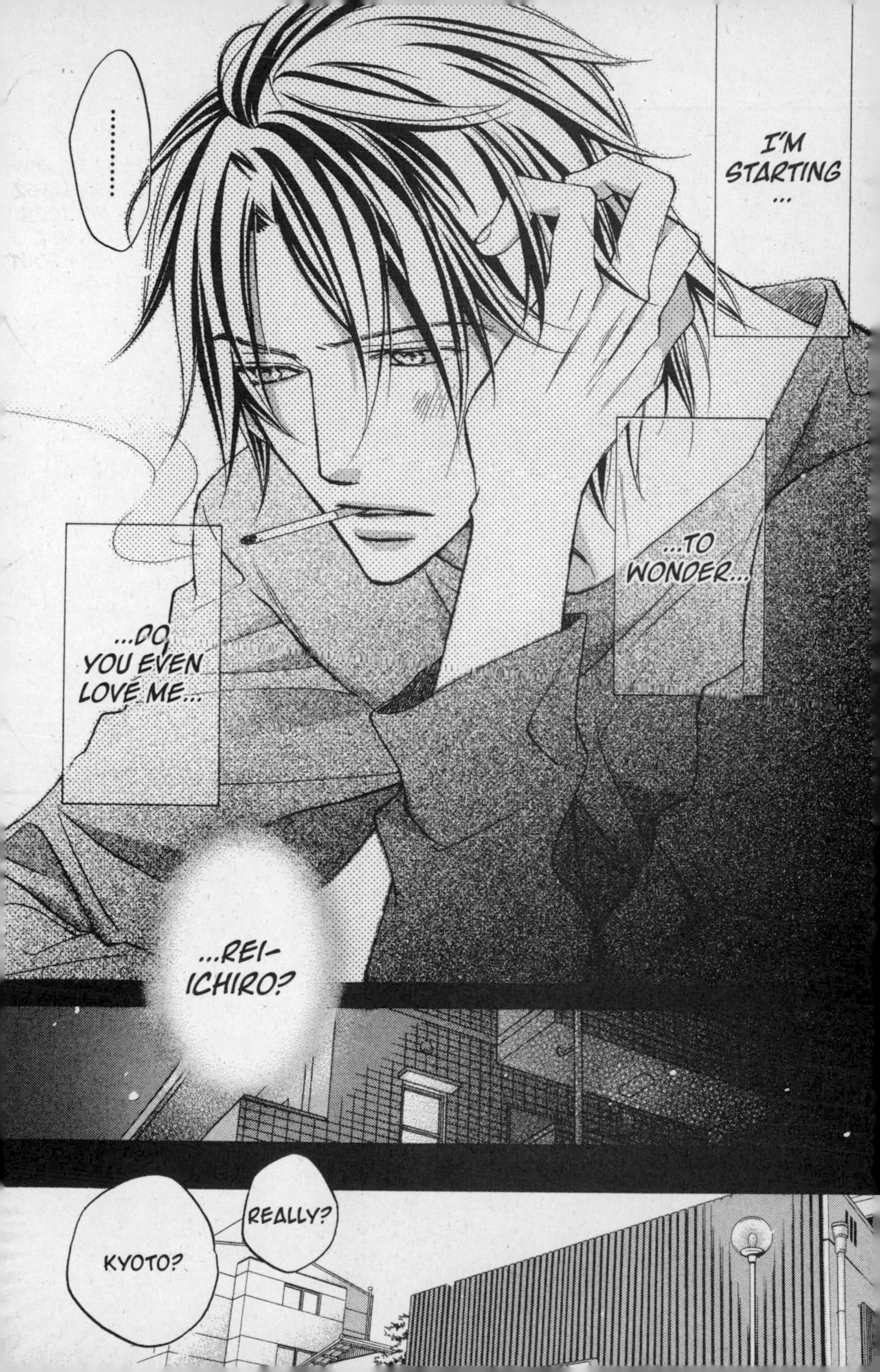
I'M STARTING ...
...TO WONDER...
...DO YOU EVEN LOVE ME...
......
...REI-ICHIRO?
REALLY?
KYOTO?

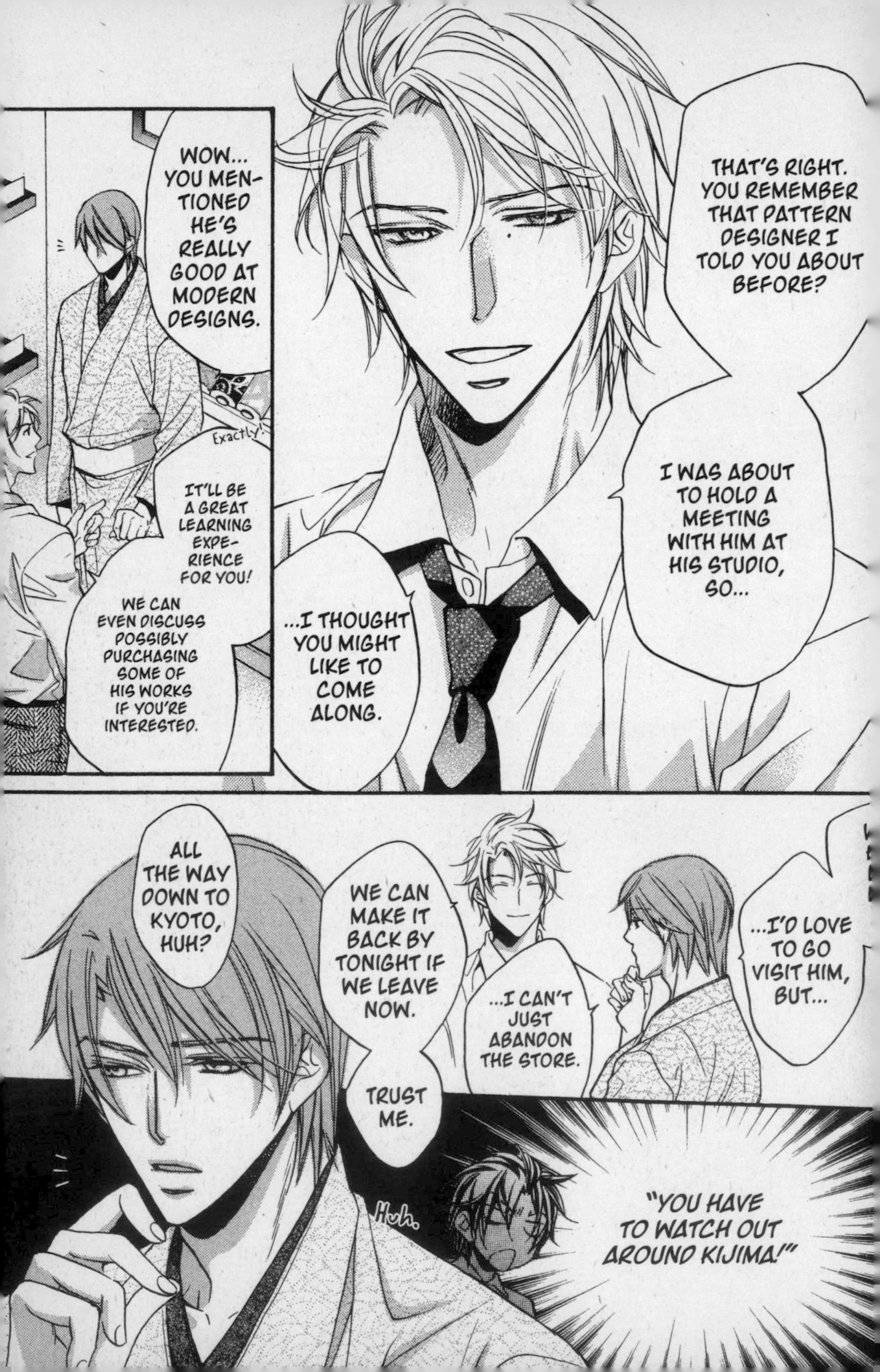
THAT'S RIGHT. YOU REMEMBER THAT PATTERN DESIGNER I TOLD YOU ABOUT BEFORE?
I WAS ABOUT TO HOLD A MEETING WITH HIM AT HIS STUDIO, SO...
...I THOUGHT YOU MIGHT LIKE TO COME ALONG.
WOW... YOU MEN-TIONED HE'S REALLY GOOD AT MODERN DESIGNS.
Exactly!
IT'LL BE A GREAT LEARNING EXPE-RIENCE FOR YOU!
WE CAN EVEN DISCUSS POSSIBLY PURCHASING SOME OF HIS WORKS IF YOU'RE INTERESTED.
...I'D LOVE TO GO VISIT HIM, BUT...
...I CAN'T JUST ABANDON THE STORE.
WE CAN MAKE IT BACK BY TONIGHT IF WE LEAVE NOW.
TRUST ME.
ALL THE WAY DOWN TO KYOTO, HUH?
"YOU HAVE TO WATCH OUT AROUND KIJIMA!"
Huh.

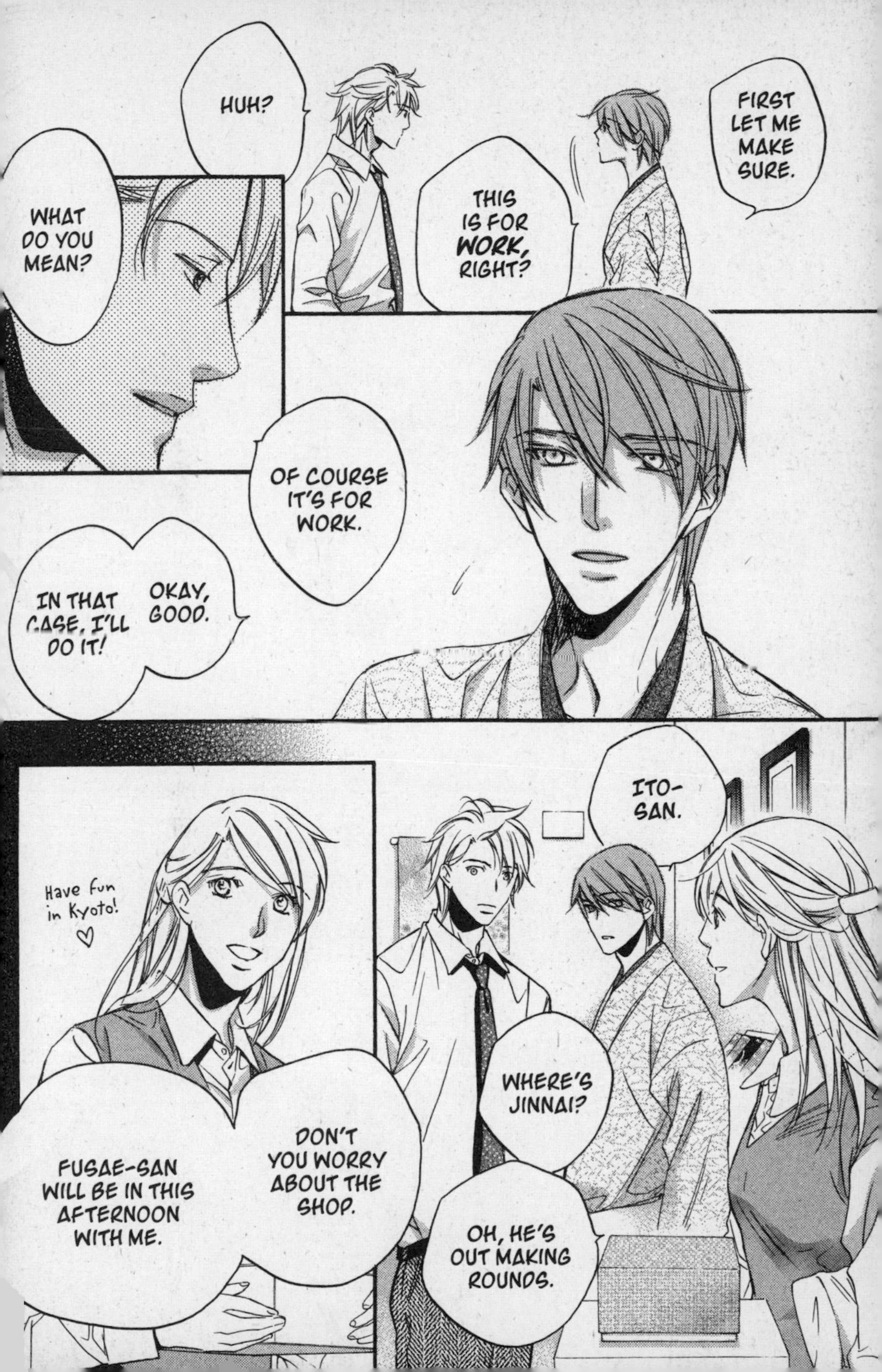
FIRST LET ME MAKE SURE.
THIS IS FOR **WORK**, RIGHT?
HUH?
WHAT DO YOU MEAN?
OF COURSE IT'S FOR WORK.
OKAY, GOOD.
IN THAT CASE, I'LL DO IT!
ITO-SAN.
WHERE'S JINNAI?
OH, HE'S OUT MAKING ROUNDS.
DON'T YOU WORRY ABOUT THE SHOP.
FUSAE-SAN WILL BE IN THIS AFTERNOON WITH ME.
Have fun in Kyoto! ♡

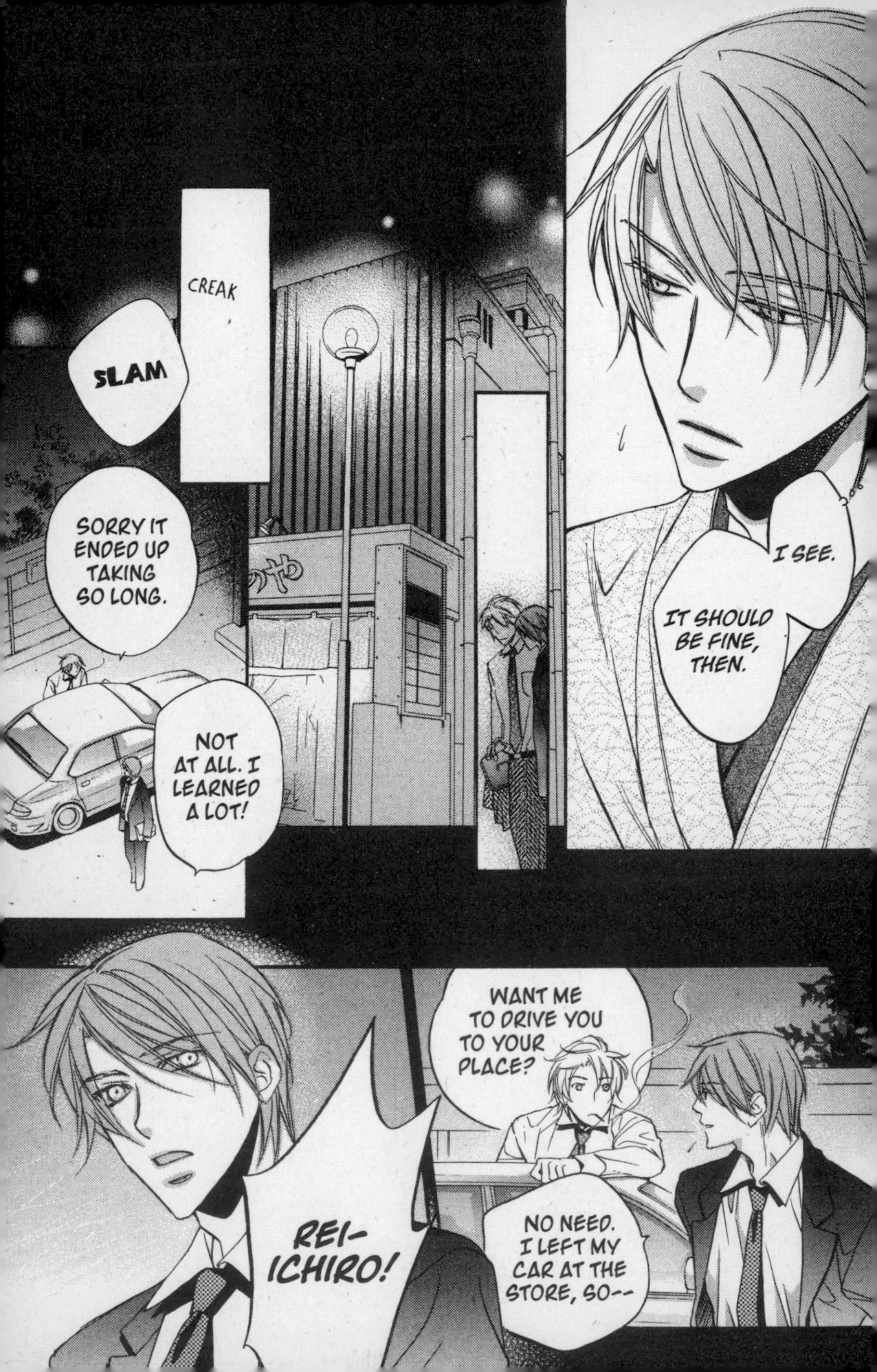
I SEE.
IT SHOULD BE FINE, THEN.
CREAK
SLAM
SORRY IT ENDED UP TAKING SO LONG.
NOT AT ALL. I LEARNED A LOT!
WANT ME TO DRIVE YOU TO YOUR PLACE?
NO NEED. I LEFT MY CAR AT THE STORE, SO--
REI-ICHIRO!

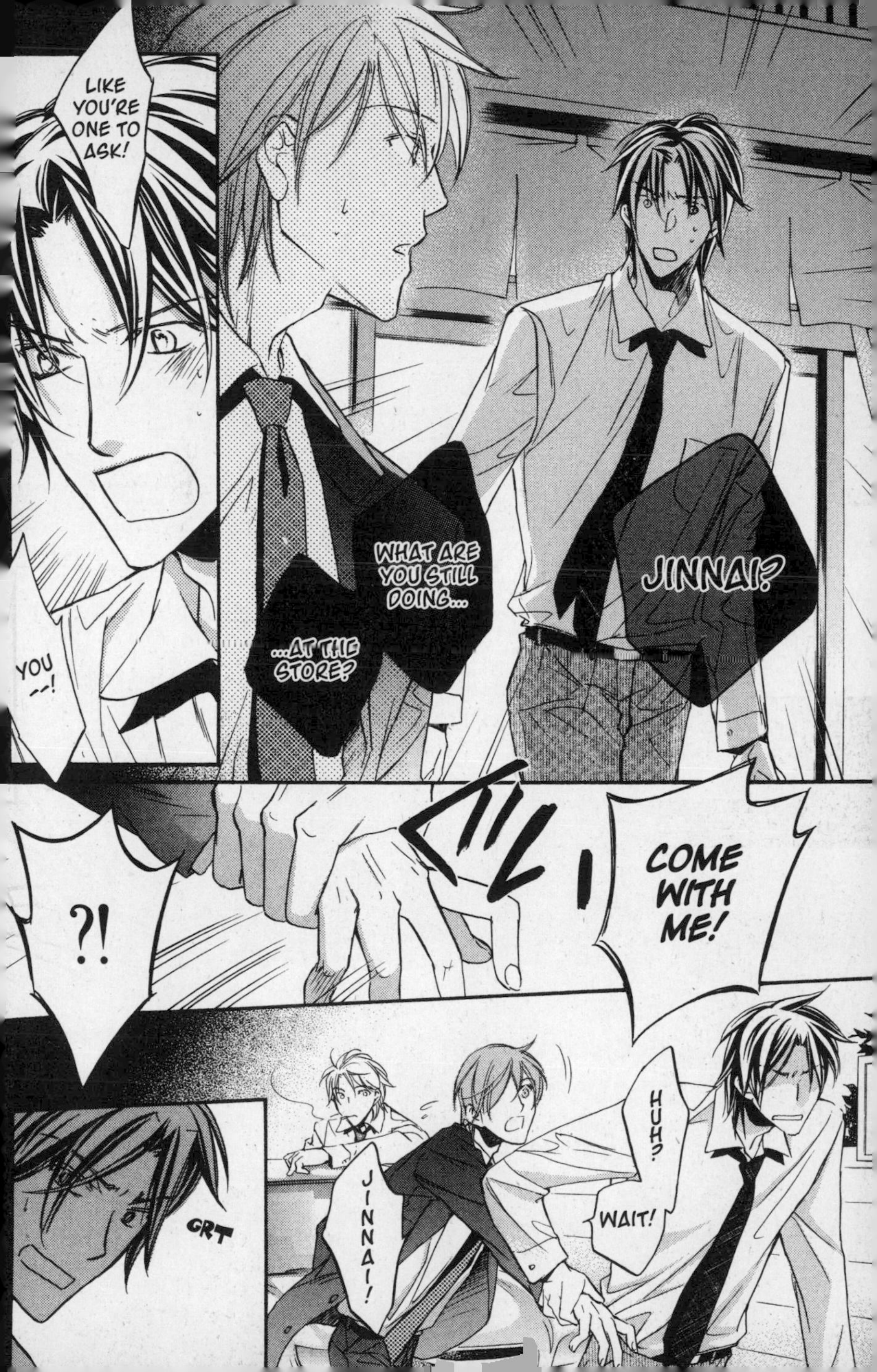
JINNAI?
WHAT ARE YOU STILL DOING...
...AT THE STORE?
LIKE YOU'RE ONE TO ASK!
YOU --!
COME WITH ME!
?!
HUH?
WAIT!
JINNAI!
GRT

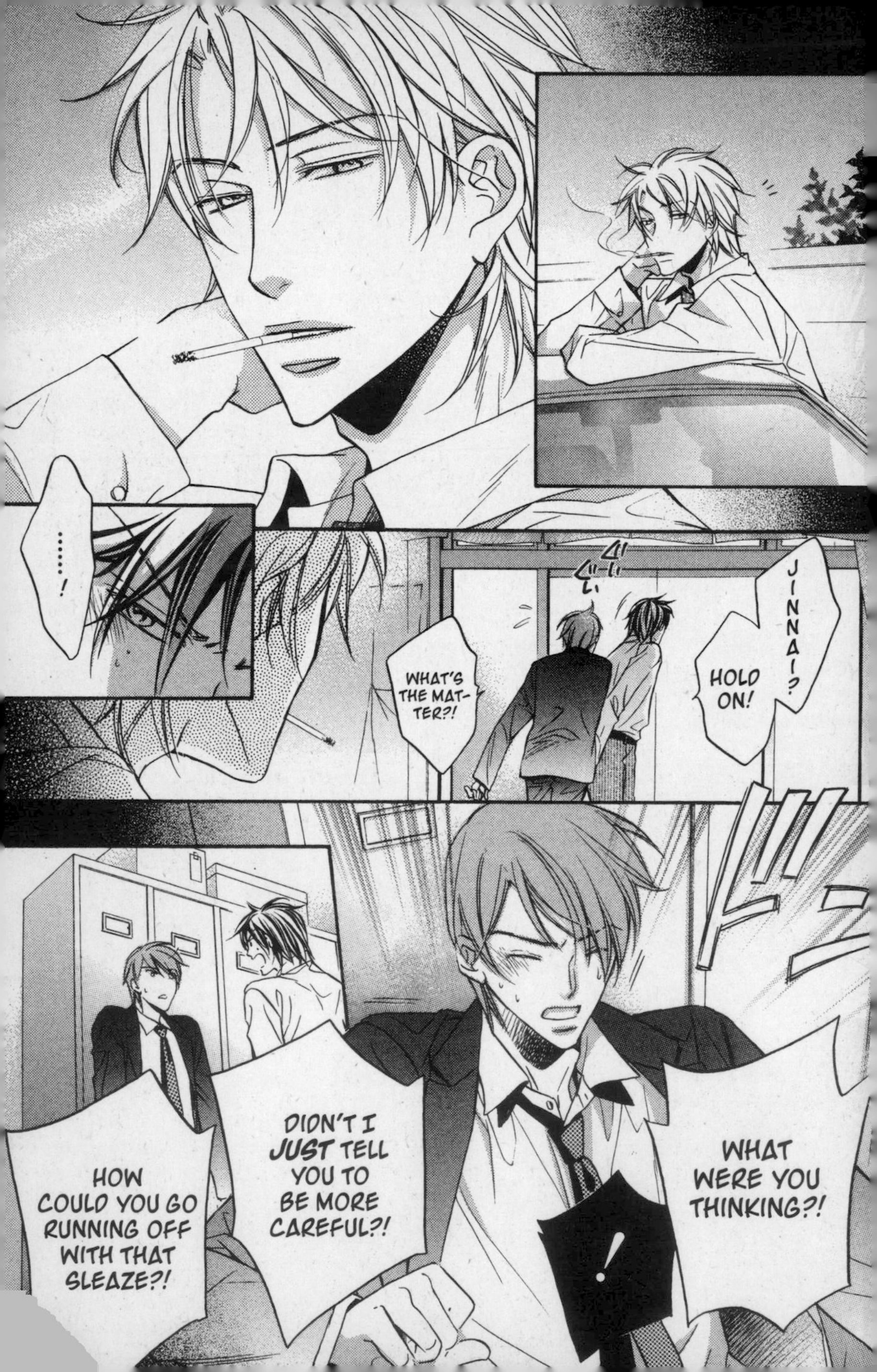
JINNAI?
HOLD ON!
WHAT'S THE MAT-TER?!
......!
WHAT WERE YOU THINKING?!
DIDN'T I JUST TELL YOU TO BE MORE CAREFUL?!
HOW COULD YOU GO RUNNING OFF WITH THAT SLEAZE?!

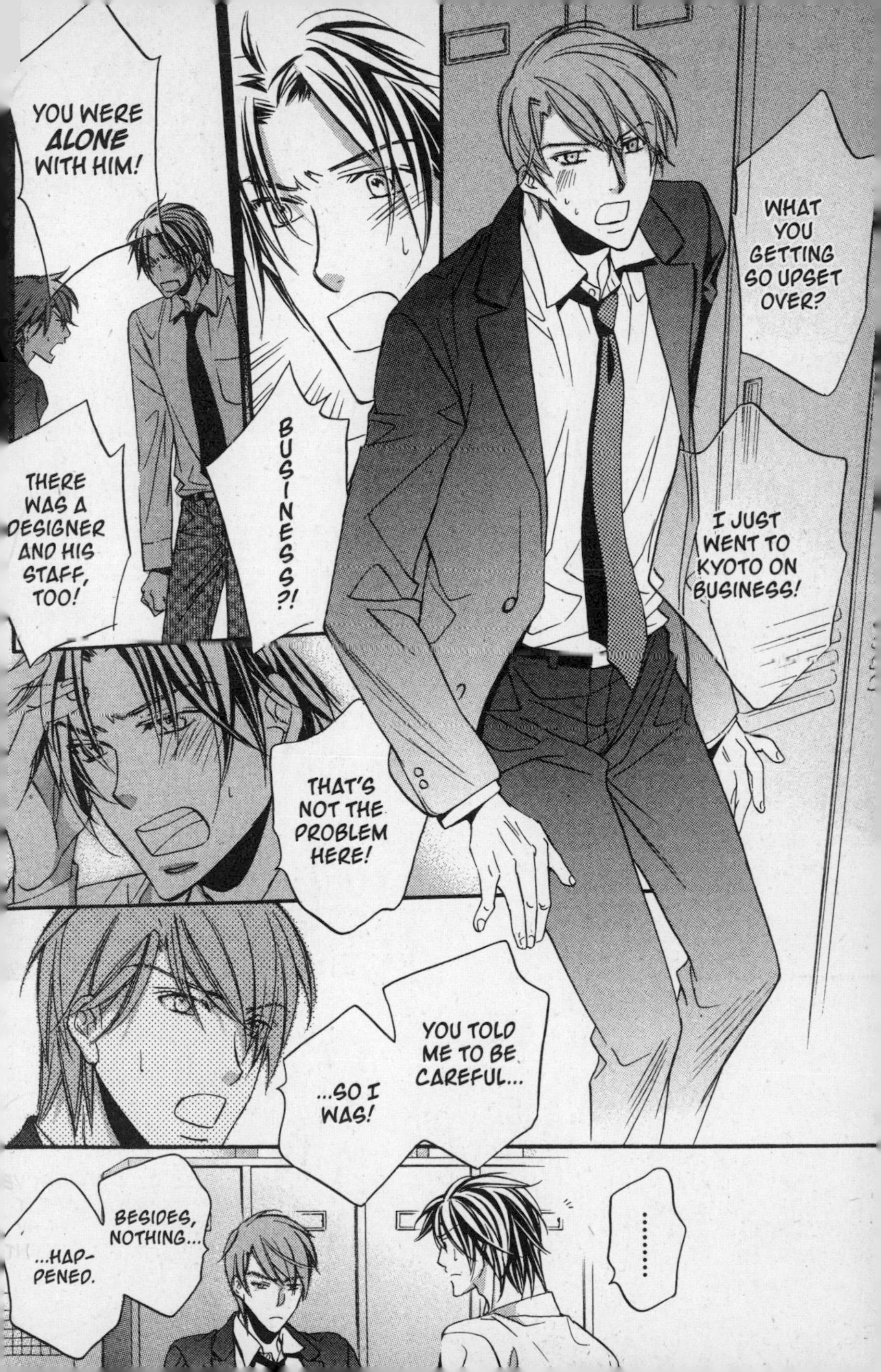
WHAT YOU GETTING SO UPSET OVER?
I JUST WENT TO KYOTO ON BUSINESS!
BUSINESS?!
YOU WERE ALONE WITH HIM!
THERE WAS A DESIGNER AND HIS STAFF, TOO!
THAT'S NOT THE PROBLEM HERE!
YOU TOLD ME TO BE CAREFUL...
...SO I WAS!
....
BESIDES, NOTHING...
...HAP-PENED.

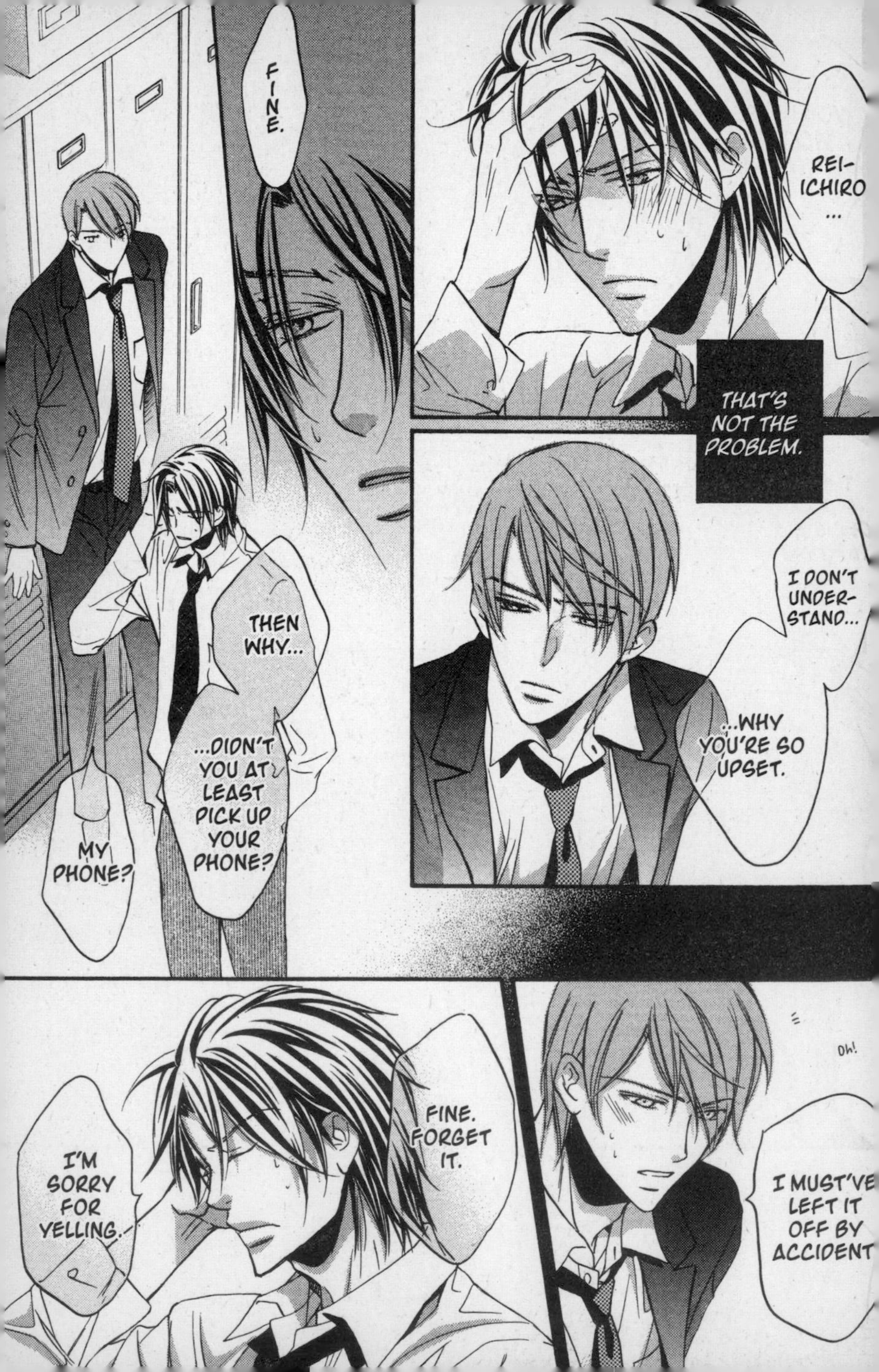
REI-ICHIRO...
THAT'S NOT THE PROBLEM.
I DON'T UNDER-STAND...
...WHY YOU'RE SO UPSET.
FINE.
THEN WHY...
...DIDN'T YOU AT LEAST PICK UP YOUR PHONE?
MY PHONE?
OH!
I MUST'VE LEFT IT OFF BY ACCIDENT
FINE. FORGET IT.
I'M SORRY FOR YELLING...

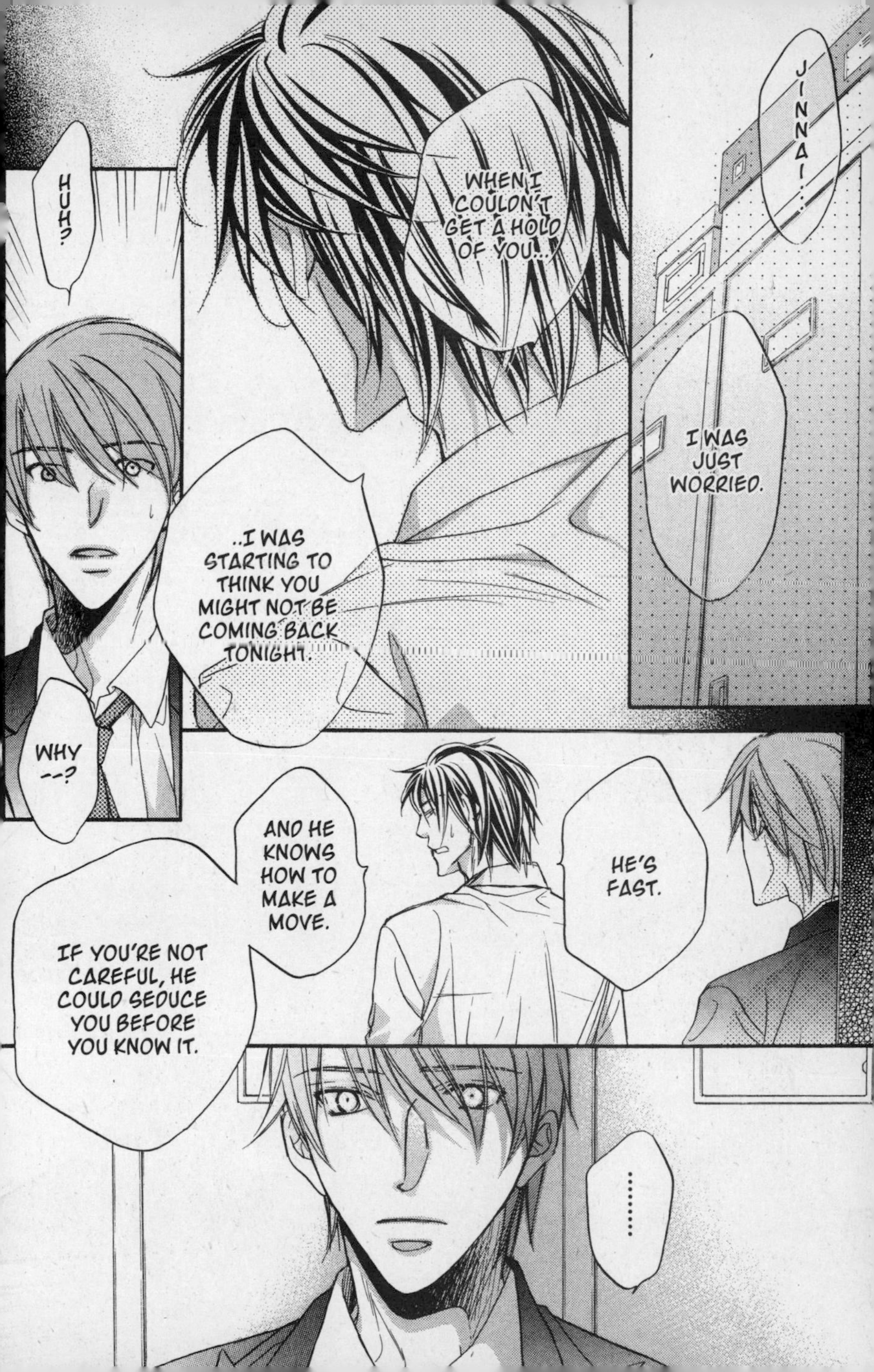
JINNAI...
I WAS JUST WORRIED.
WHEN I COULDN'T GET A HOLD OF YOU...
..I WAS STARTING TO THINK YOU MIGHT NOT BE COMING BACK TONIGHT.
HUH?
WHY --?
HE'S FAST.
AND HE KNOWS HOW TO MAKE A MOVE.
IF YOU'RE NOT CAREFUL, HE COULD SEDUCE YOU BEFORE YOU KNOW IT.
....

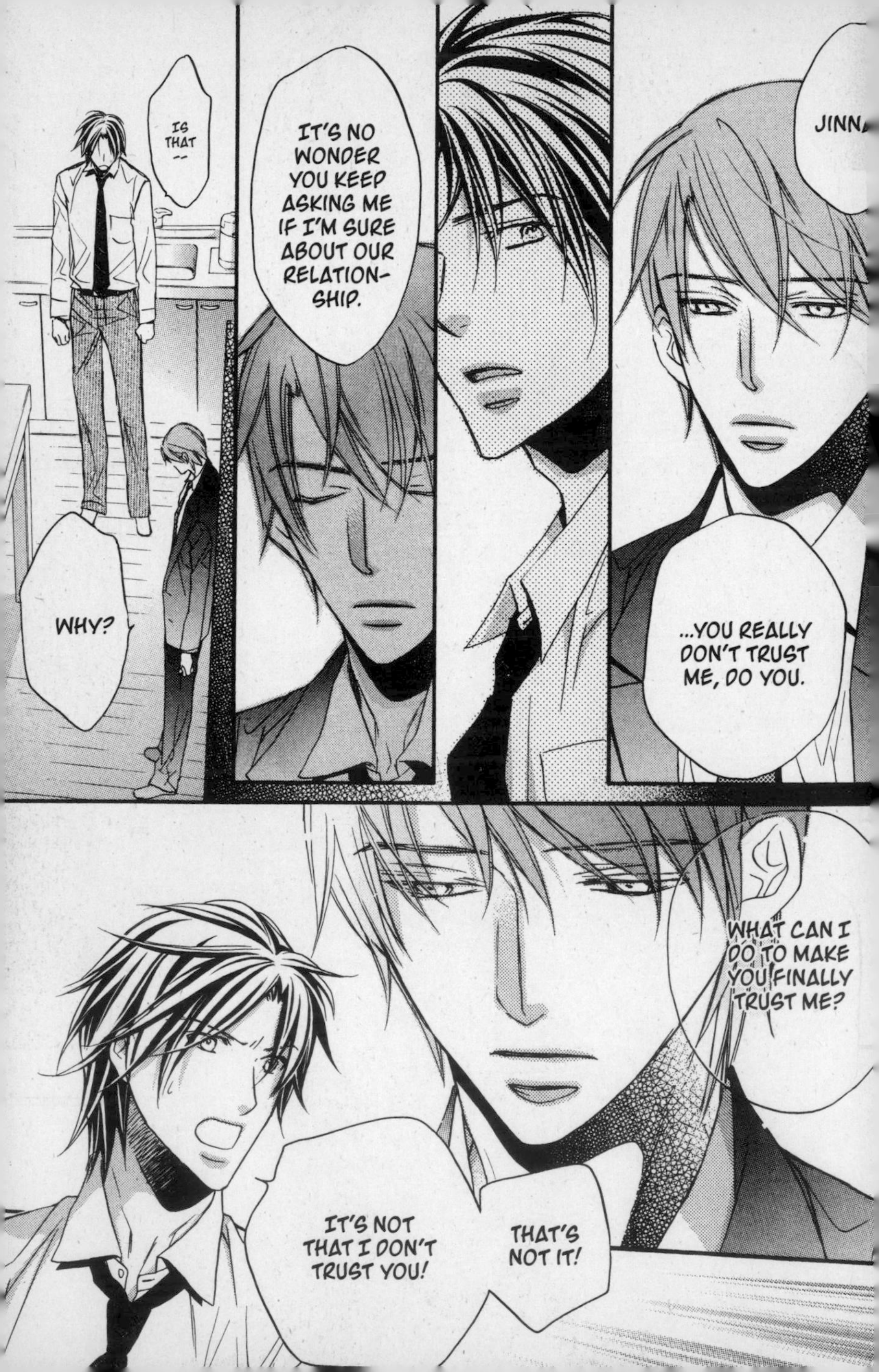
JINNA
...YOU REALLY DON'T TRUST ME, DO YOU.
IT'S NO WONDER YOU KEEP ASKING ME IF I'M SURE ABOUT OUR RELATION-SHIP.
IS THAT --
WHY?
WHAT CAN I DO TO MAKE YOU FINALLY TRUST ME?
THAT'S NOT IT!
IT'S NOT THAT I DON'T TRUST YOU!

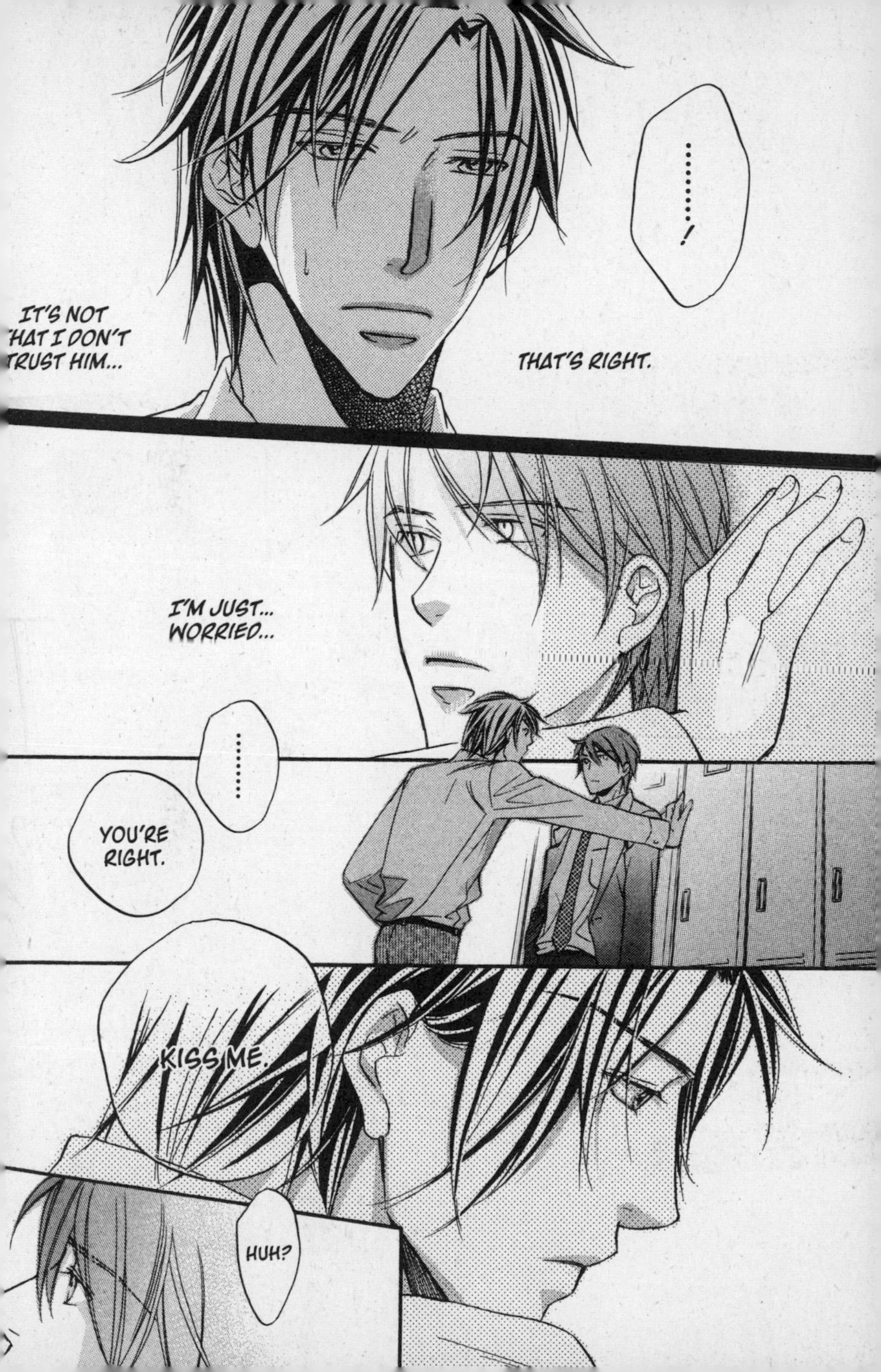
……!
THAT'S RIGHT.
IT'S NOT THAT I DON'T TRUST HIM...
I'M JUST... WORRIED...
……
YOU'RE RIGHT.
KISS ME.
HUH?

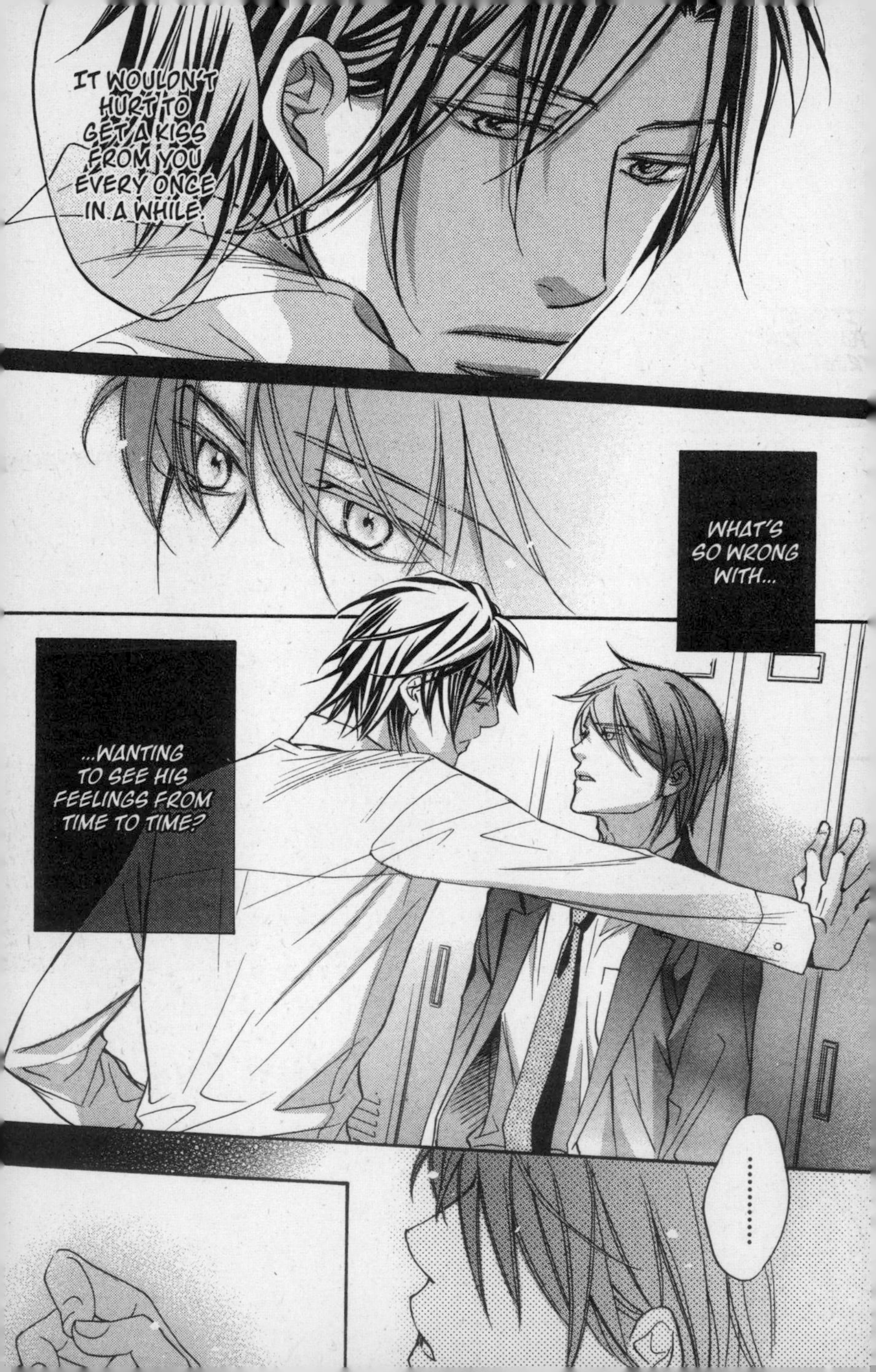

IT WOULDN'T HURT TO GET A KISS FROM YOU EVERY ONCE IN A WHILE.
WHAT'S SO WRONG WITH...
...WANTING TO SEE HIS FEELINGS FROM TIME TO TIME?
......

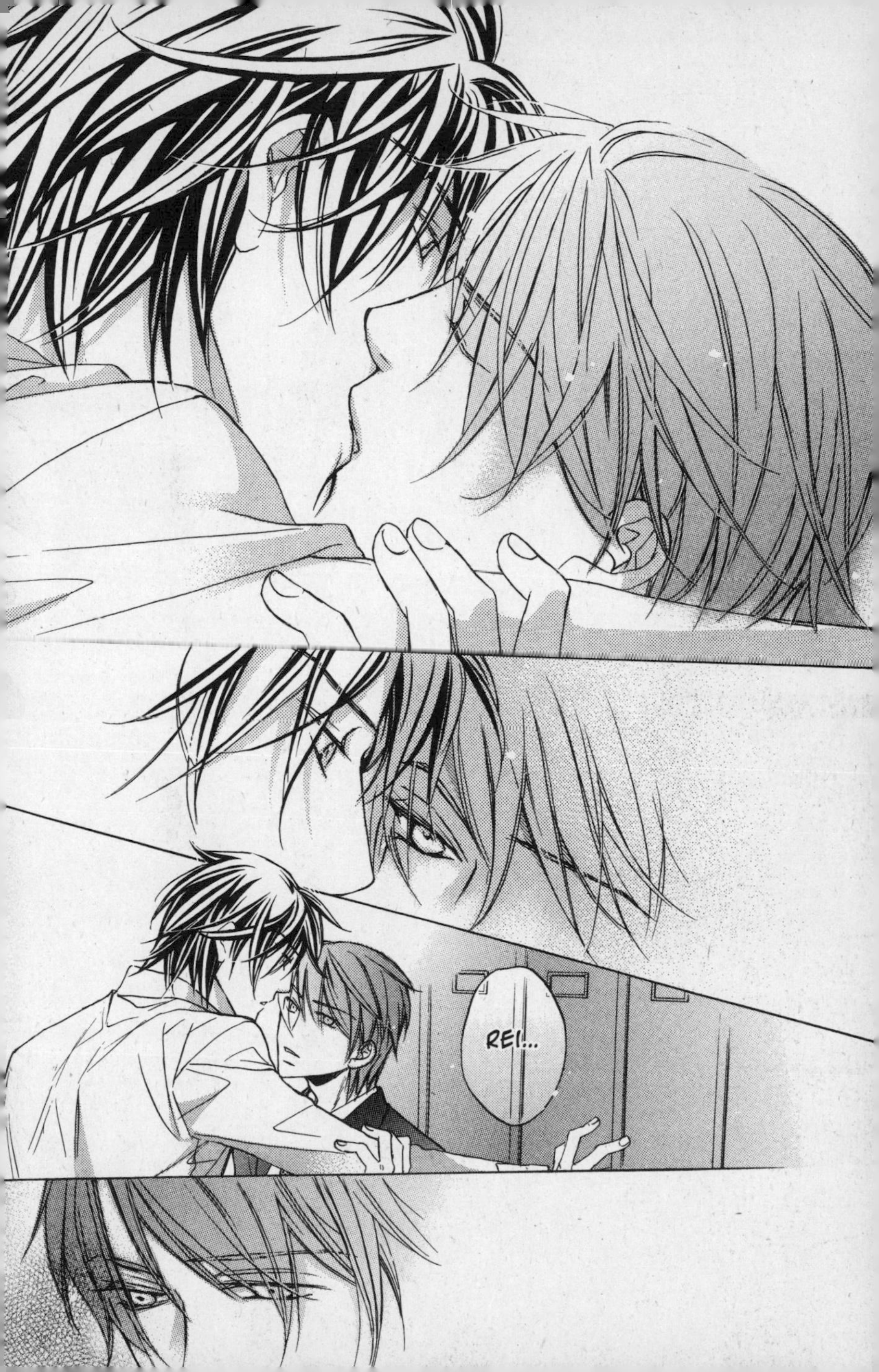
REI...

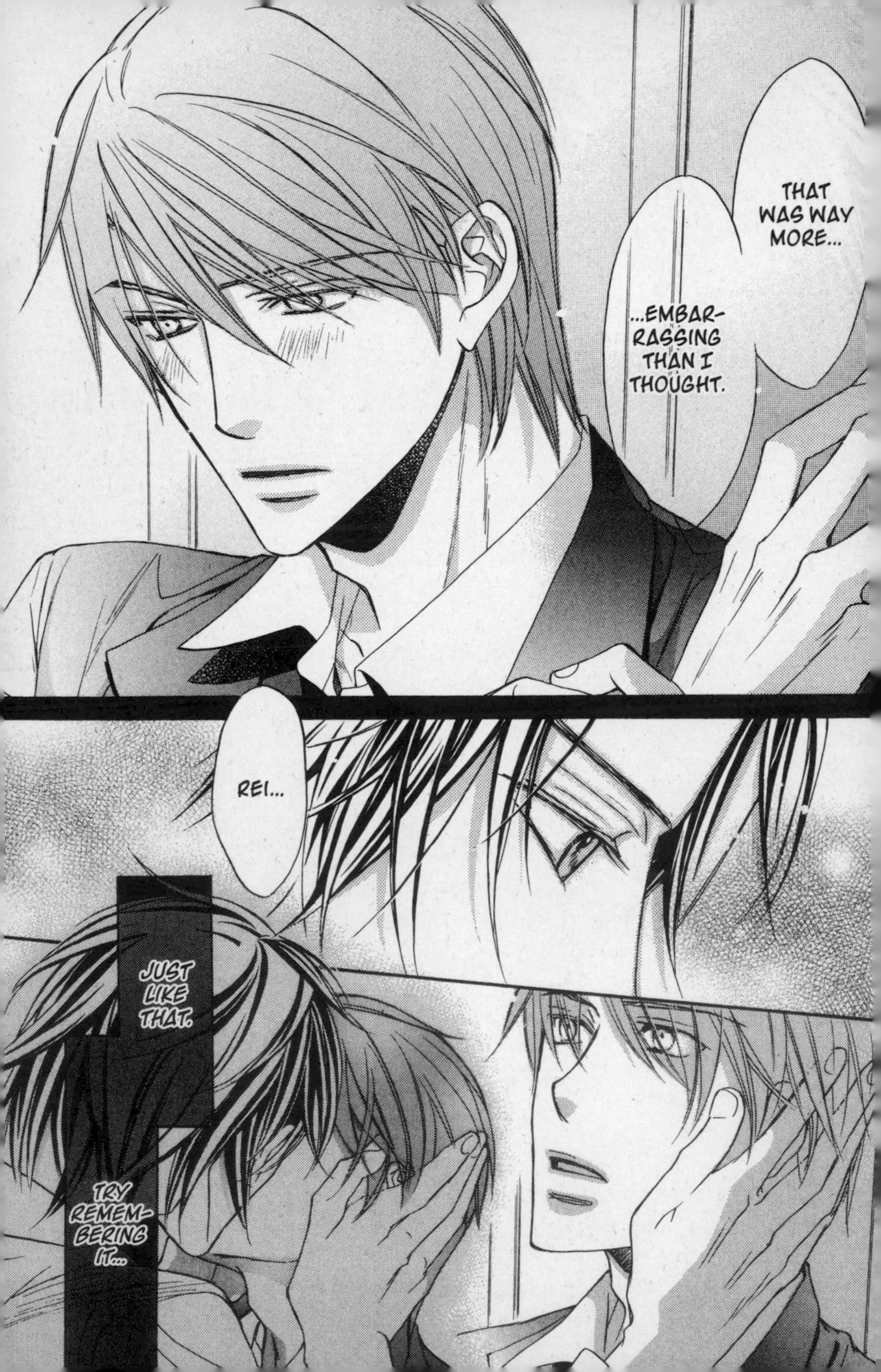
THAT WAS WAY MORE...
...EMBARRASSING THAN I THOUGHT.
REI...
JUST LIKE THAT.
TRY REMEMBERING IT...

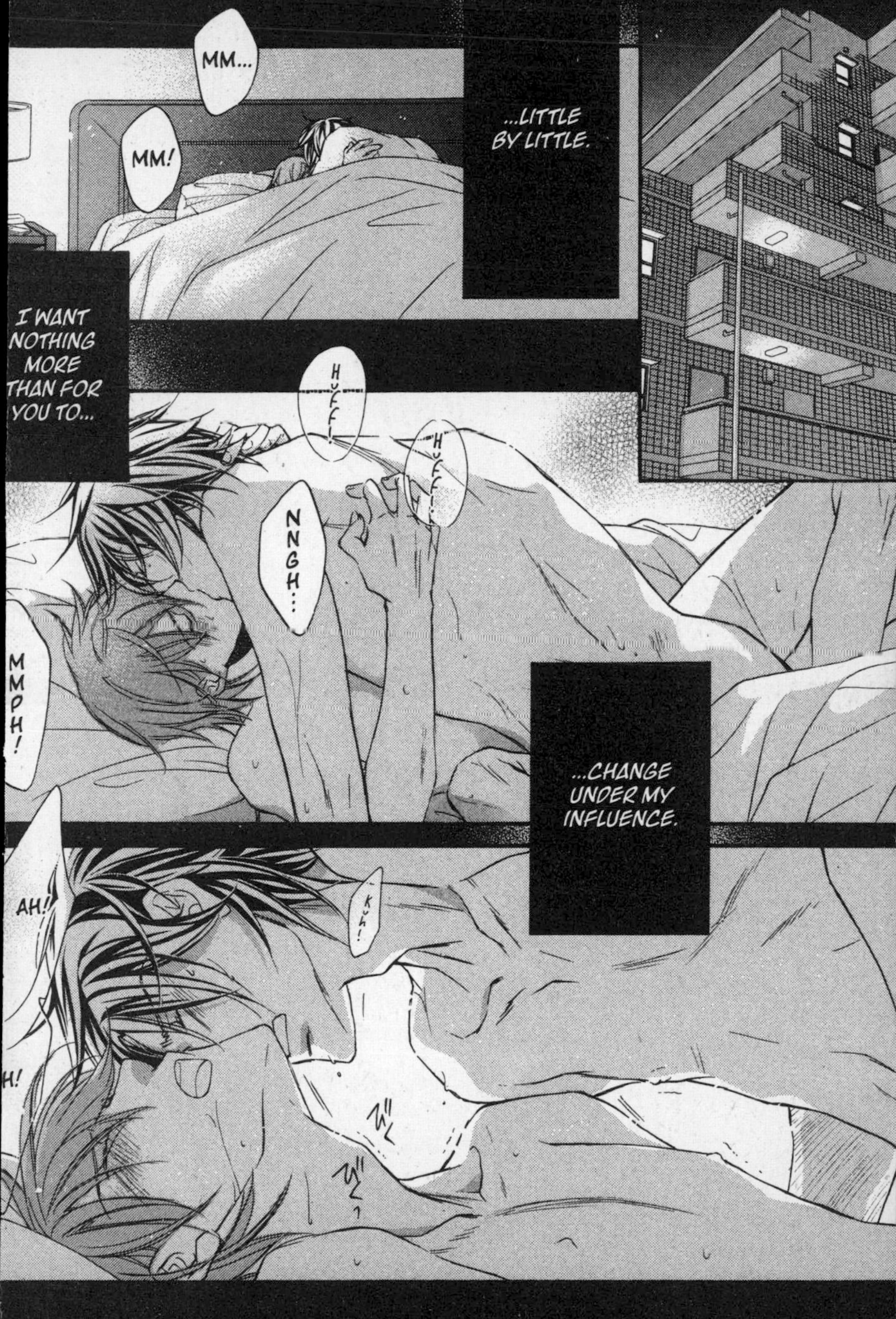

...LITTLE BY LITTLE.
MM...
MM!
I WANT NOTHING MORE THAN FOR YOU TO...
HUFF!
HUFF!
NNGH...
MMPH!
...CHANGE UNDER MY INFLUENCE.
KUH!
AH!

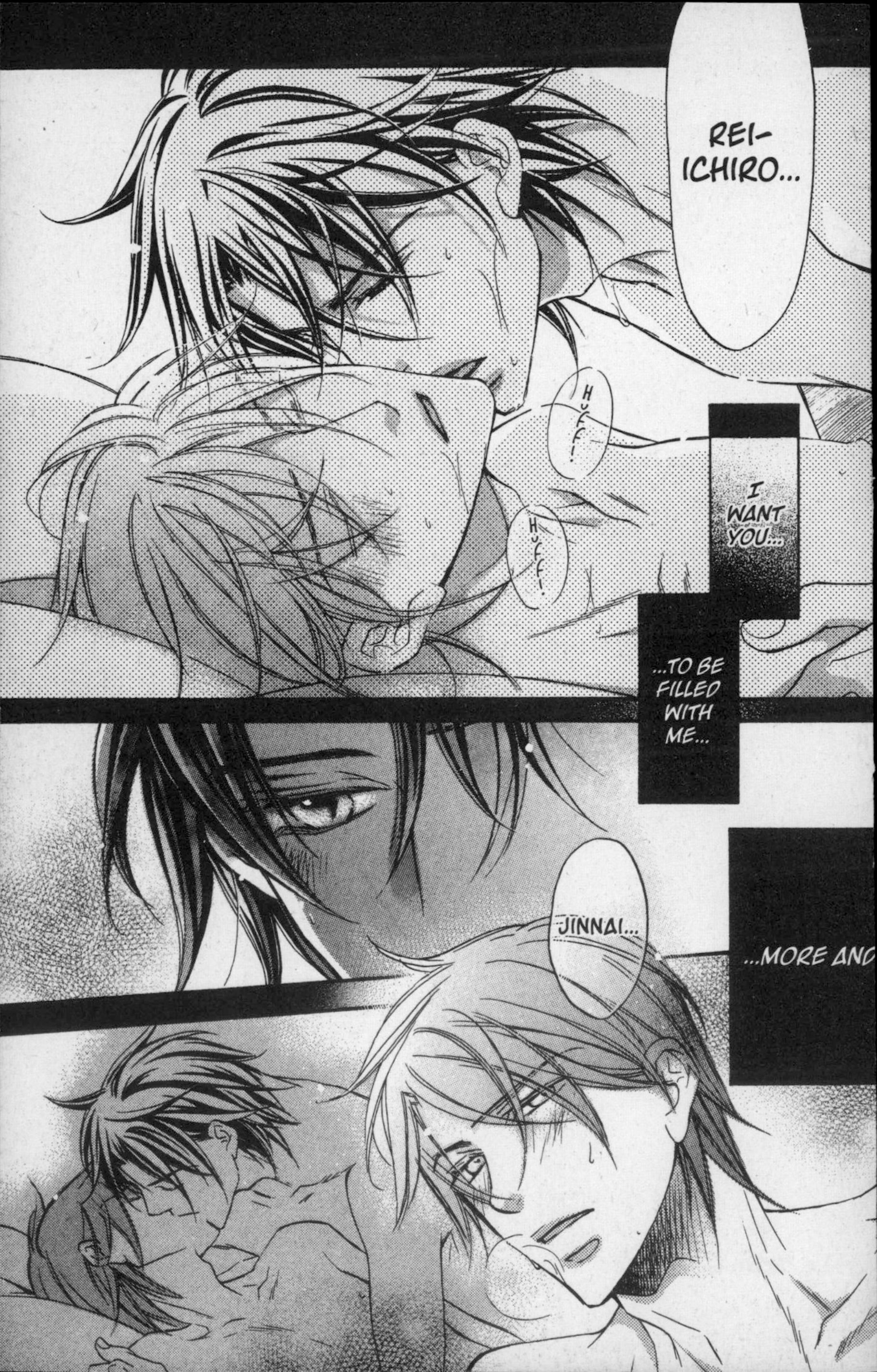
REI-ICHIRO...
HUFF!
HUFF!
I WANT YOU...
...TO BE FILLED WITH ME...
JINNAI...
...MORE AND

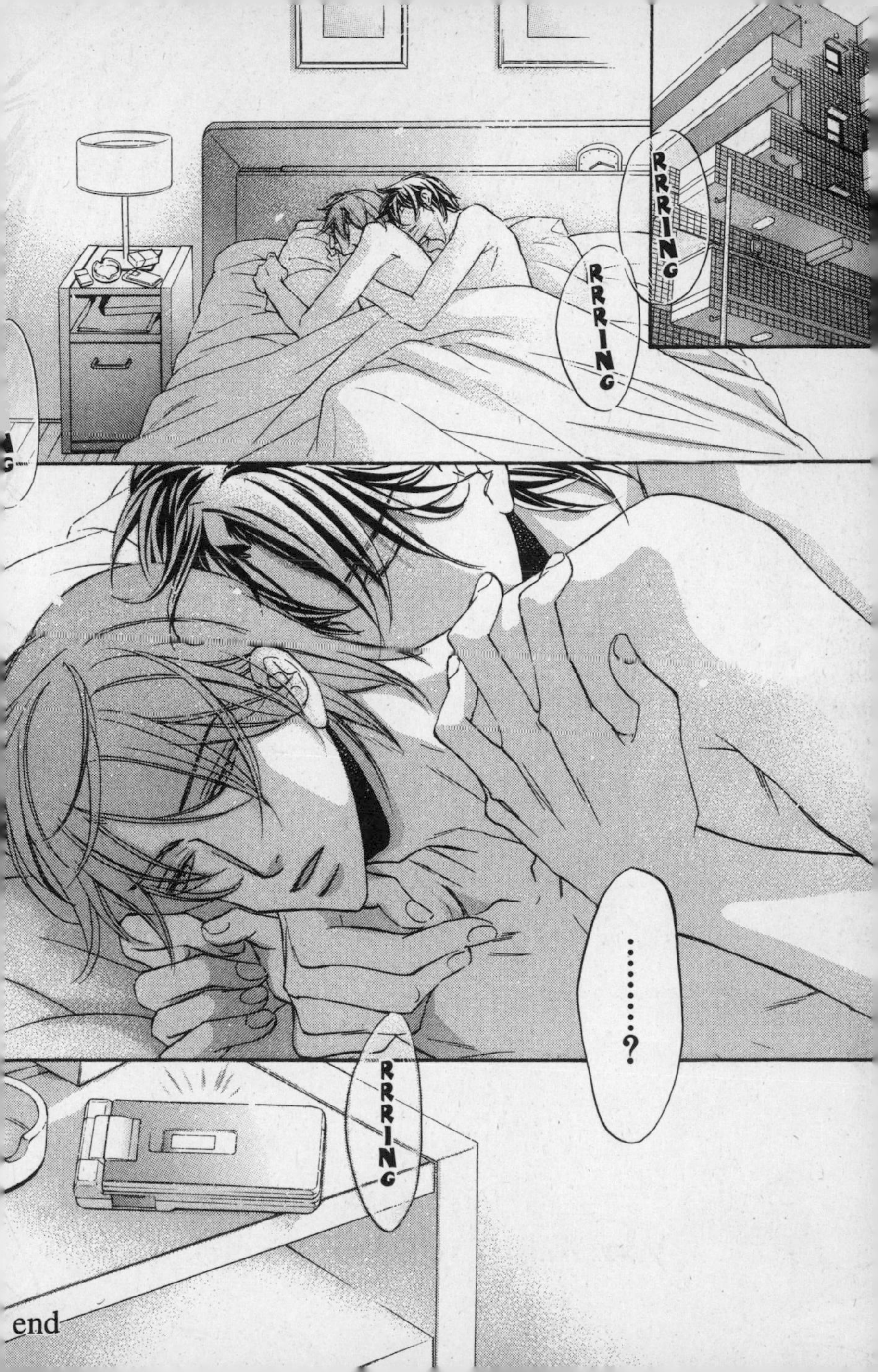
RRRING
RRRING
......?
RRRING
end

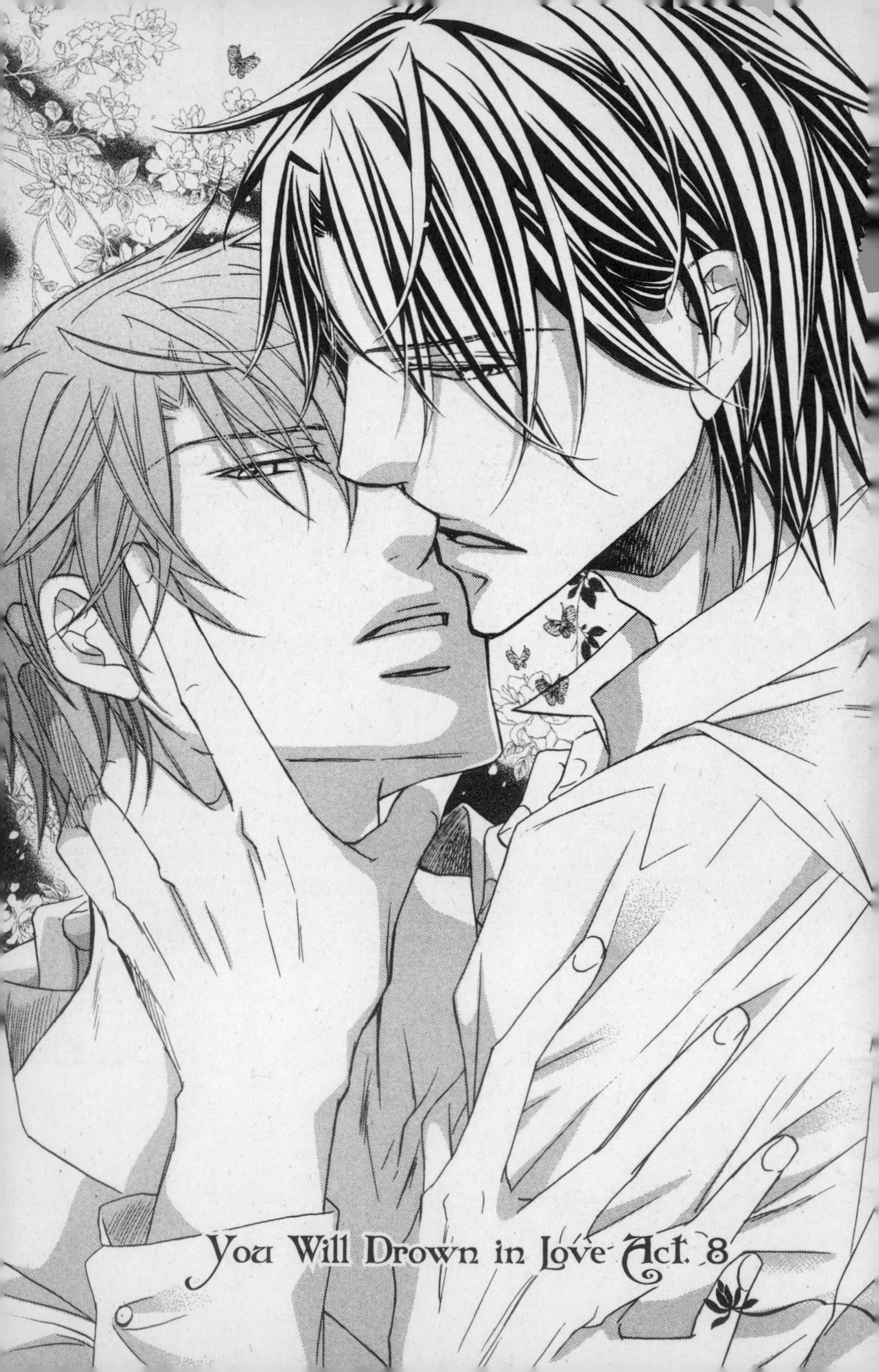
You Will Drown in Love Act. 8

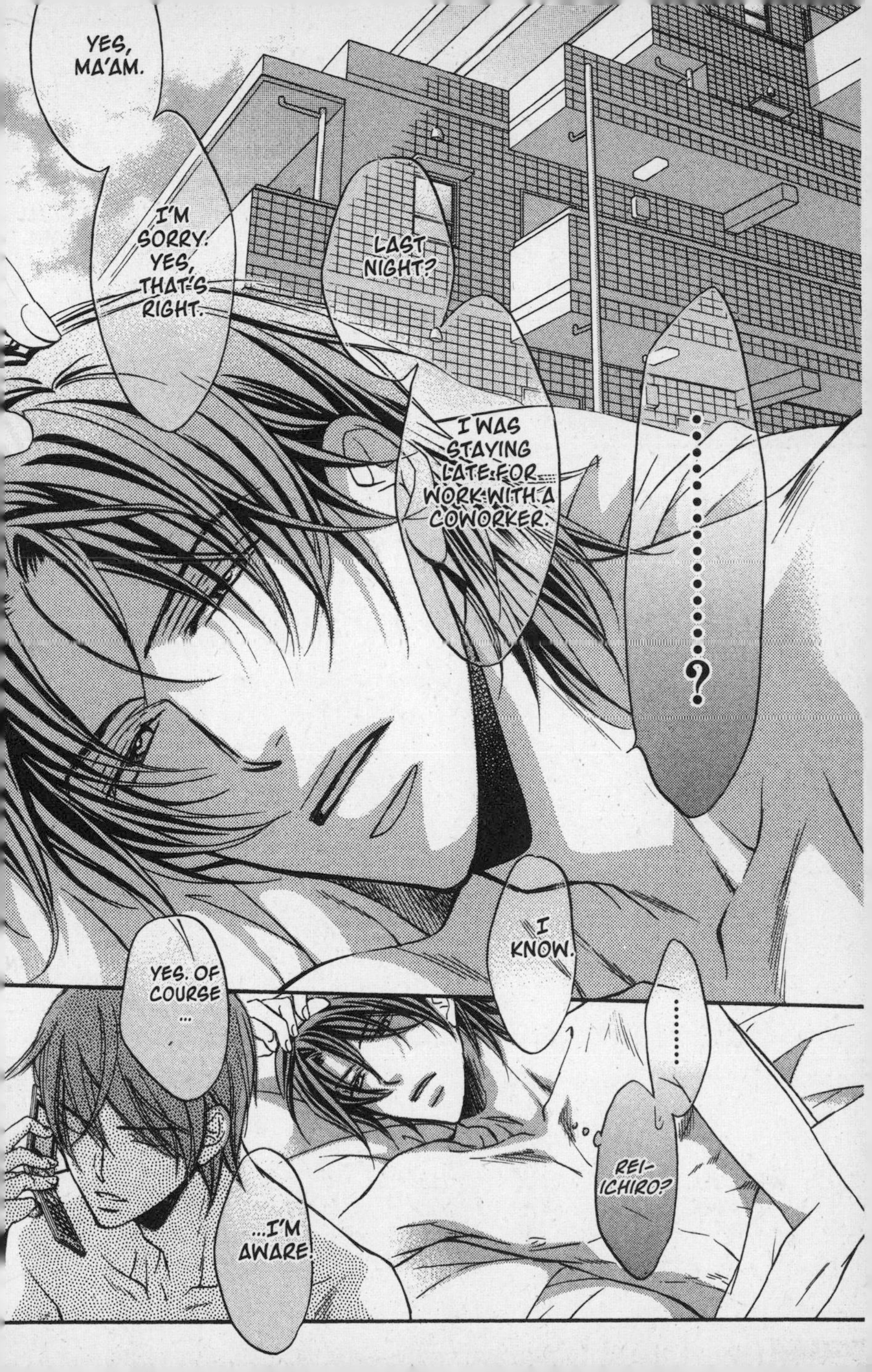
YES, MA'AM.
I'M SORRY. YES, THAT'S RIGHT.
LAST NIGHT?
I WAS STAYING LATE FOR WORK WITH A COWORKER.
..........?
......
I KNOW.
YES. OF COURSE ...
REI-ICHIRO?
...I'M AWARE.

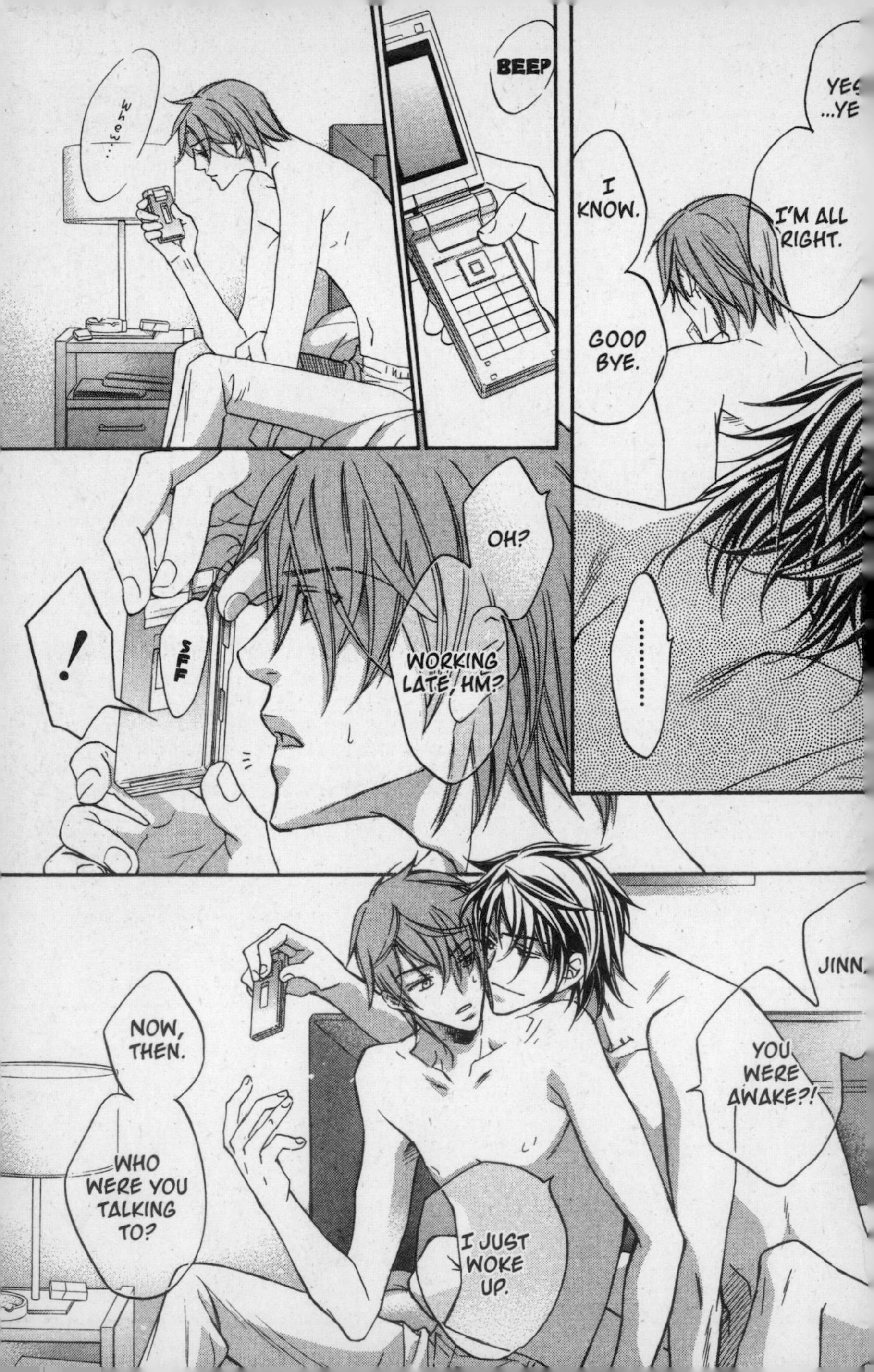
YES ...YE
I'M ALL RIGHT.
I KNOW.
GOOD BYE.
BEEP
whew...
......
OH?
WORKING LATE, HM?
SFF
!
JINN.
YOU WERE AWAKE?!
I JUST WOKE UP.
NOW, THEN.
WHO WERE YOU TALKING TO?

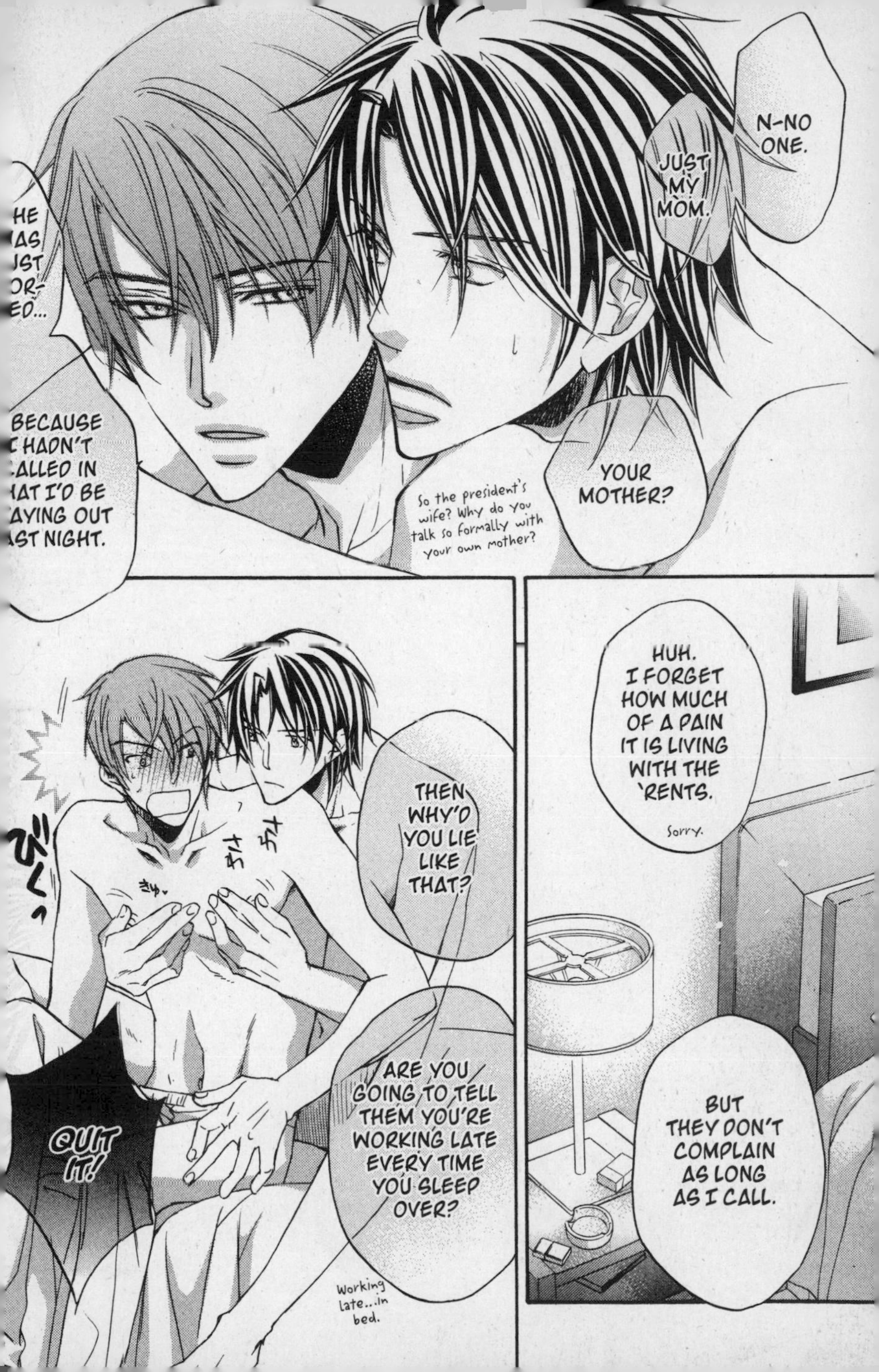
N-NO ONE.
JUST MY MOM.
YOUR MOTHER?
So the president's wife? Why do you talk so formally with your own mother?
HE WAS JUST OR-ED...
BECAUSE I HADN'T CALLED IN THAT I'D BE STAYING OUT LAST NIGHT.
HUH. I FORGET HOW MUCH OF A PAIN IT IS LIVING WITH THE 'RENTS.
Sorry.
BUT THEY DON'T COMPLAIN AS LONG AS I CALL.
THEN WHY'D YOU LIE LIKE THAT?
ARE YOU GOING TO TELL THEM YOU'RE WORKING LATE EVERY TIME YOU SLEEP OVER?
Working late...in bed.
QUIT IT!

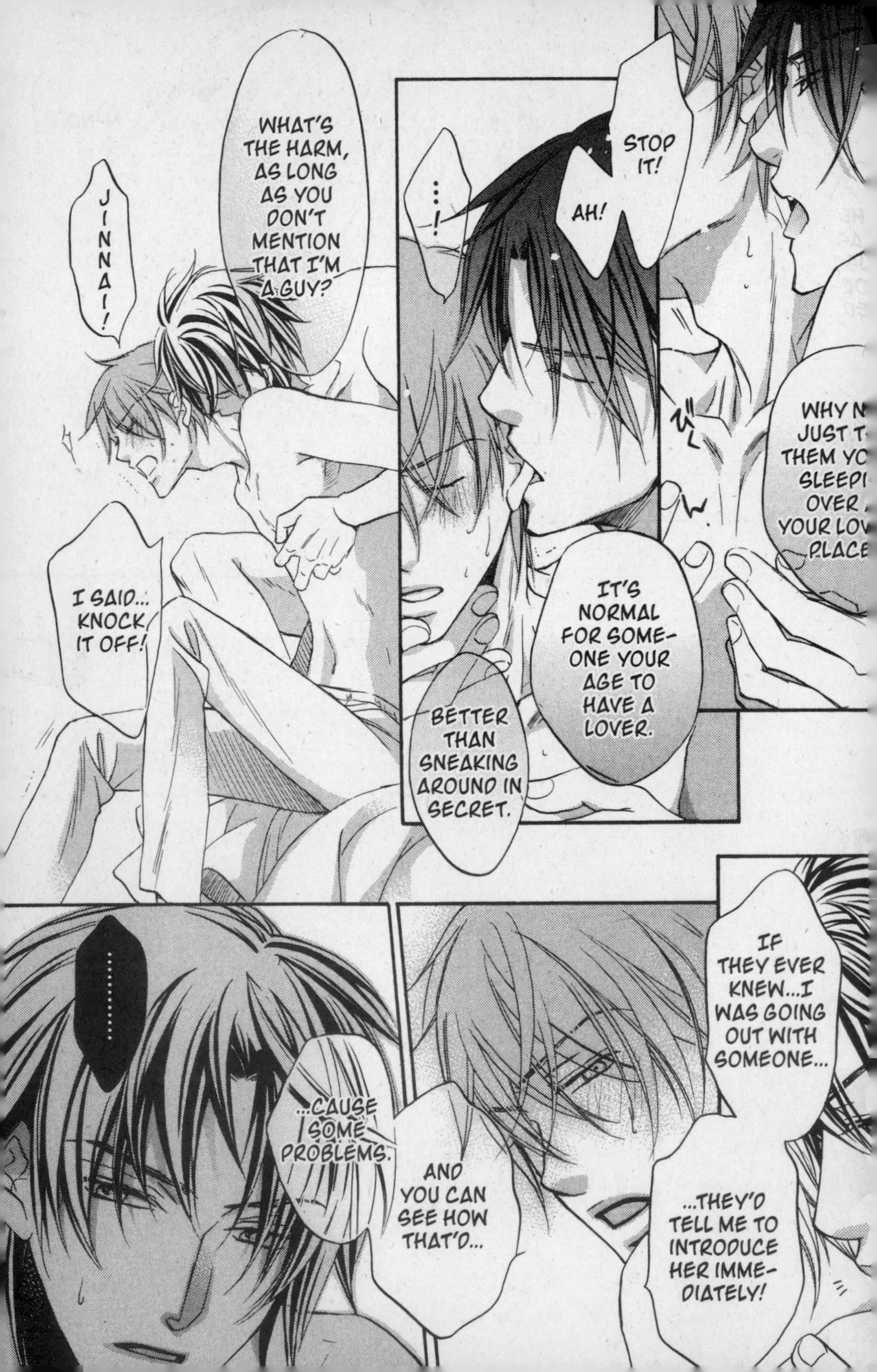
WHY N
JUST T
THEM YO
SLEEPI
OVER
YOUR LOV
PLACE
STOP IT!
AH!
...!
IT'S NORMAL FOR SOME-ONE YOUR AGE TO HAVE A LOVER.
BETTER THAN SNEAKING AROUND IN SECRET.
WHAT'S THE HARM, AS LONG AS YOU DON'T MENTION THAT I'M A GUY?
JINNAI!
I SAID... KNOCK IT OFF!
IF THEY EVER KNEW...I WAS GOING OUT WITH SOMEONE...
...THEY'D TELL ME TO INTRODUCE HER IMME-DIATELY!
AND YOU CAN SEE HOW THAT'D...
...CAUSE SOME PROBLEMS.
....

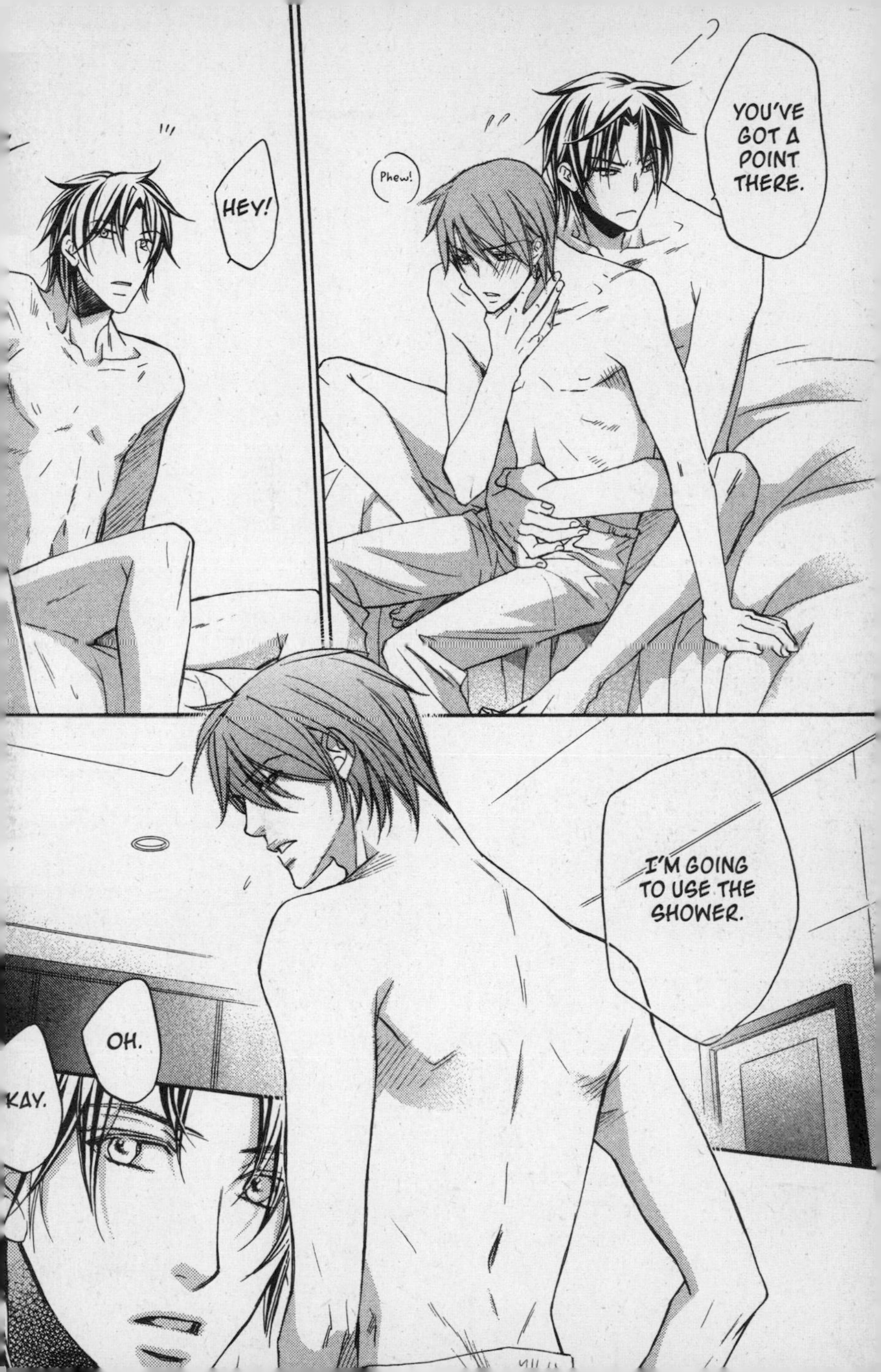
YOU'VE GOT A POINT THERE.
Phew!
HEY!
I'M GOING TO USE THE SHOWER.
OH.
KAY.

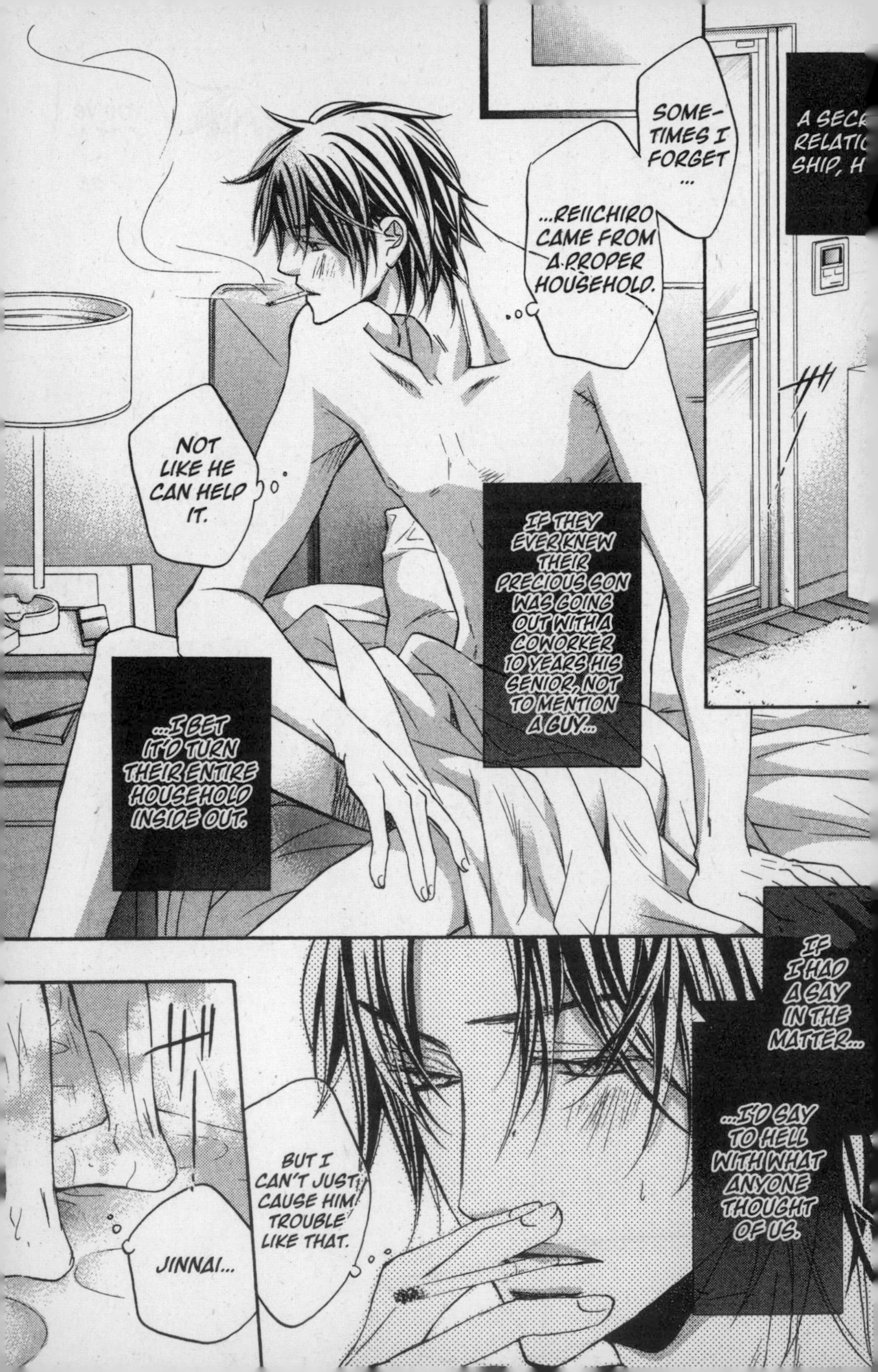
SOME-TIMES I FORGET ...
...REIICHIRO CAME FROM A PROPER HOUSEHOLD.
IF THEY EVER KNEW THEIR PRECIOUS SON WAS GOING OUT WITH A COWORKER 10 YEARS HIS SENIOR, NOT TO MENTION A GUY...
NOT LIKE HE CAN HELP IT.
...I BET IT'D TURN THEIR ENTIRE HOUSEHOLD INSIDE OUT.
IF I HAD A SAY IN THE MATTER...
...I'D SAY TO HELL WITH WHAT ANYONE THOUGHT OF US.
BUT I CAN'T JUST CAUSE HIM TROUBLE LIKE THAT.
JINNAI...

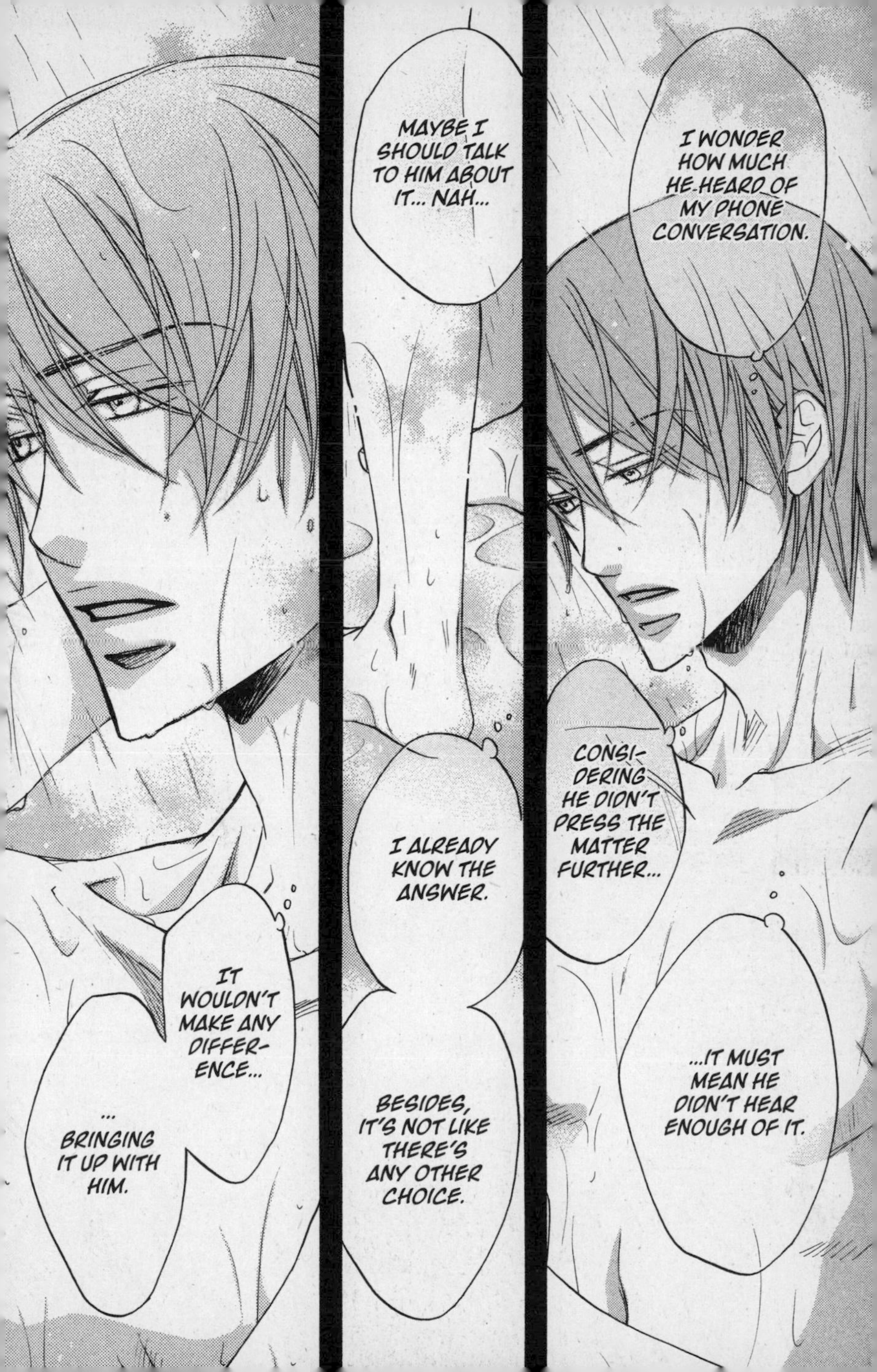
I WONDER HOW MUCH HE HEARD OF MY PHONE CONVERSATION.
CONSI-DERING HE DIDN'T PRESS THE MATTER FURTHER...
...IT MUST MEAN HE DIDN'T HEAR ENOUGH OF IT.
MAYBE I SHOULD TALK TO HIM ABOUT IT... NAH...
I ALREADY KNOW THE ANSWER.
BESIDES, IT'S NOT LIKE THERE'S ANY OTHER CHOICE.
IT WOULDN'T MAKE ANY DIFFER-ENCE...
...BRINGING IT UP WITH HIM.

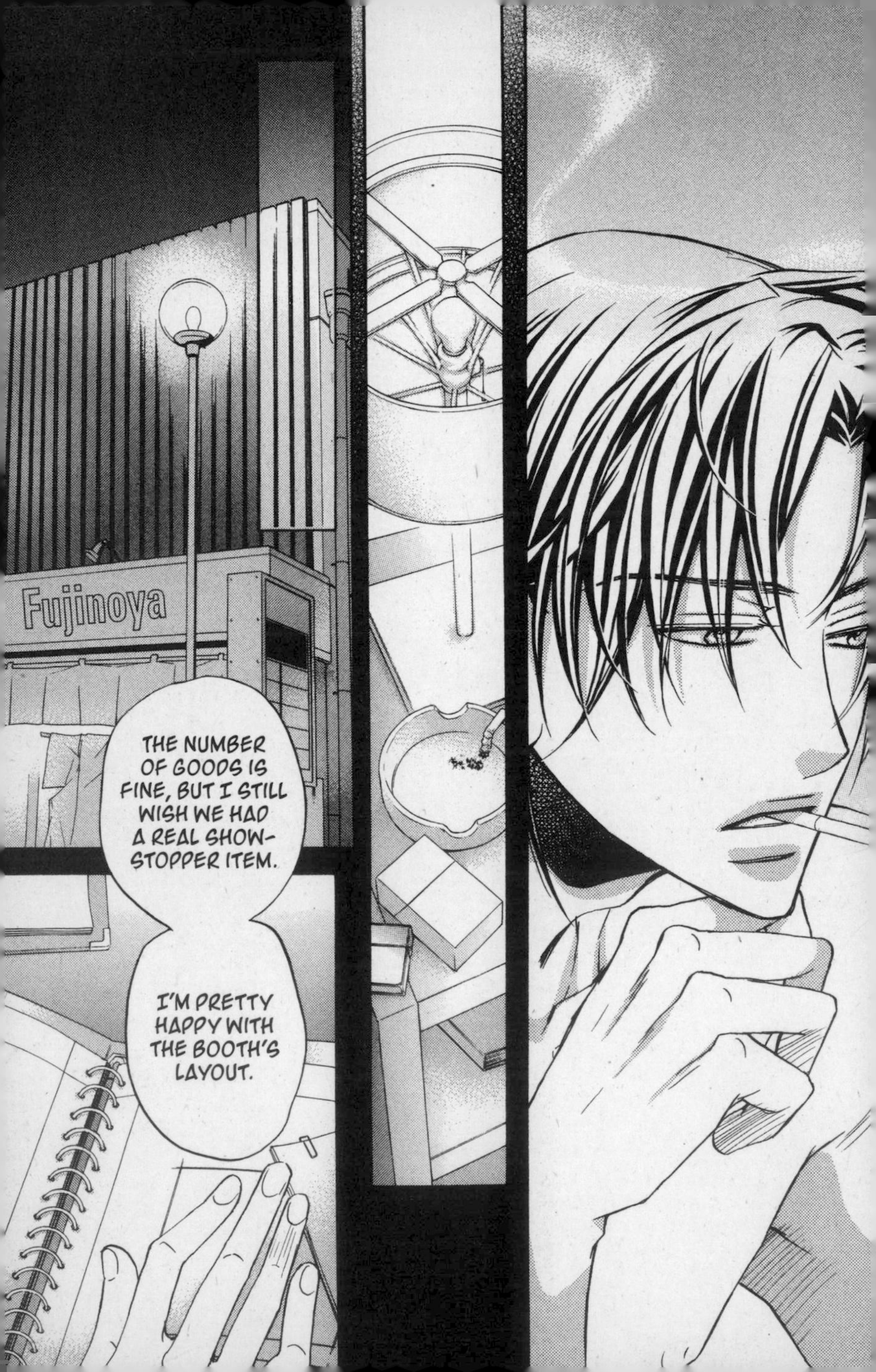
Fujinoya
THE NUMBER OF GOODS IS FINE, BUT I STILL WISH WE HAD A REAL SHOW-STOPPER ITEM.
I'M PRETTY HAPPY WITH THE BOOTH'S LAYOUT.

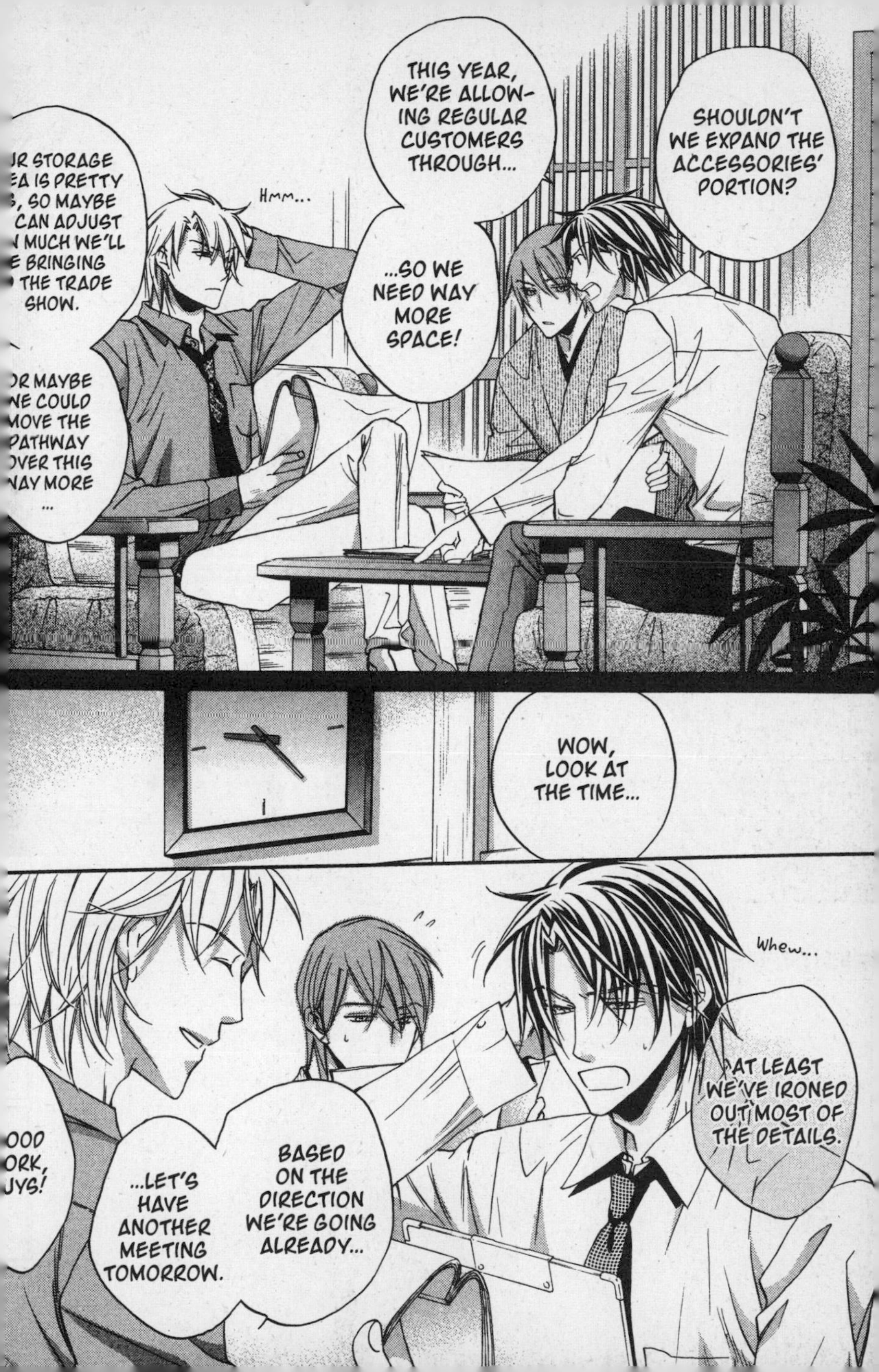
SHOULDN'T WE EXPAND THE ACCESSORIES' PORTION?
THIS YEAR, WE'RE ALLOWING REGULAR CUSTOMERS THROUGH...
...SO WE NEED WAY MORE SPACE!
Hmm...
SHOW.
WAY MORE ...
WOW, LOOK AT THE TIME...
Whew...
AT LEAST WE'VE IRONED OUT MOST OF THE DETAILS.
BASED ON THE DIRECTION WE'RE GOING ALREADY...
...LET'S HAVE ANOTHER MEETING TOMORROW.

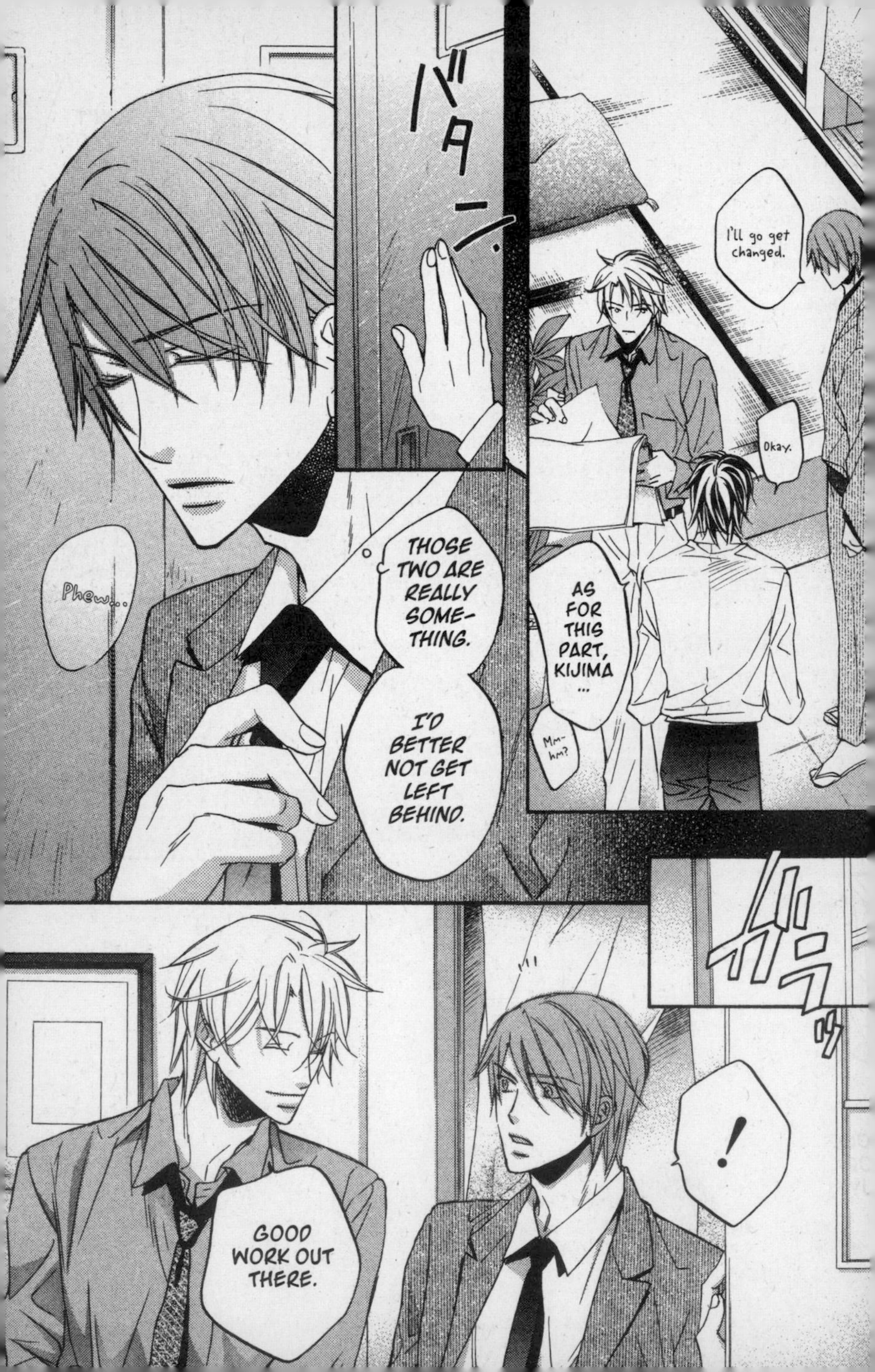
I'll go get changed.
Okay.
AS FOR THIS PART, KIJIMA ...
Mm-hm?
バターン
THOSE TWO ARE REALLY SOME-THING.
I'D BETTER NOT GET LEFT BEHIND.
Phew...
ガラッ
!
GOOD WORK OUT THERE.

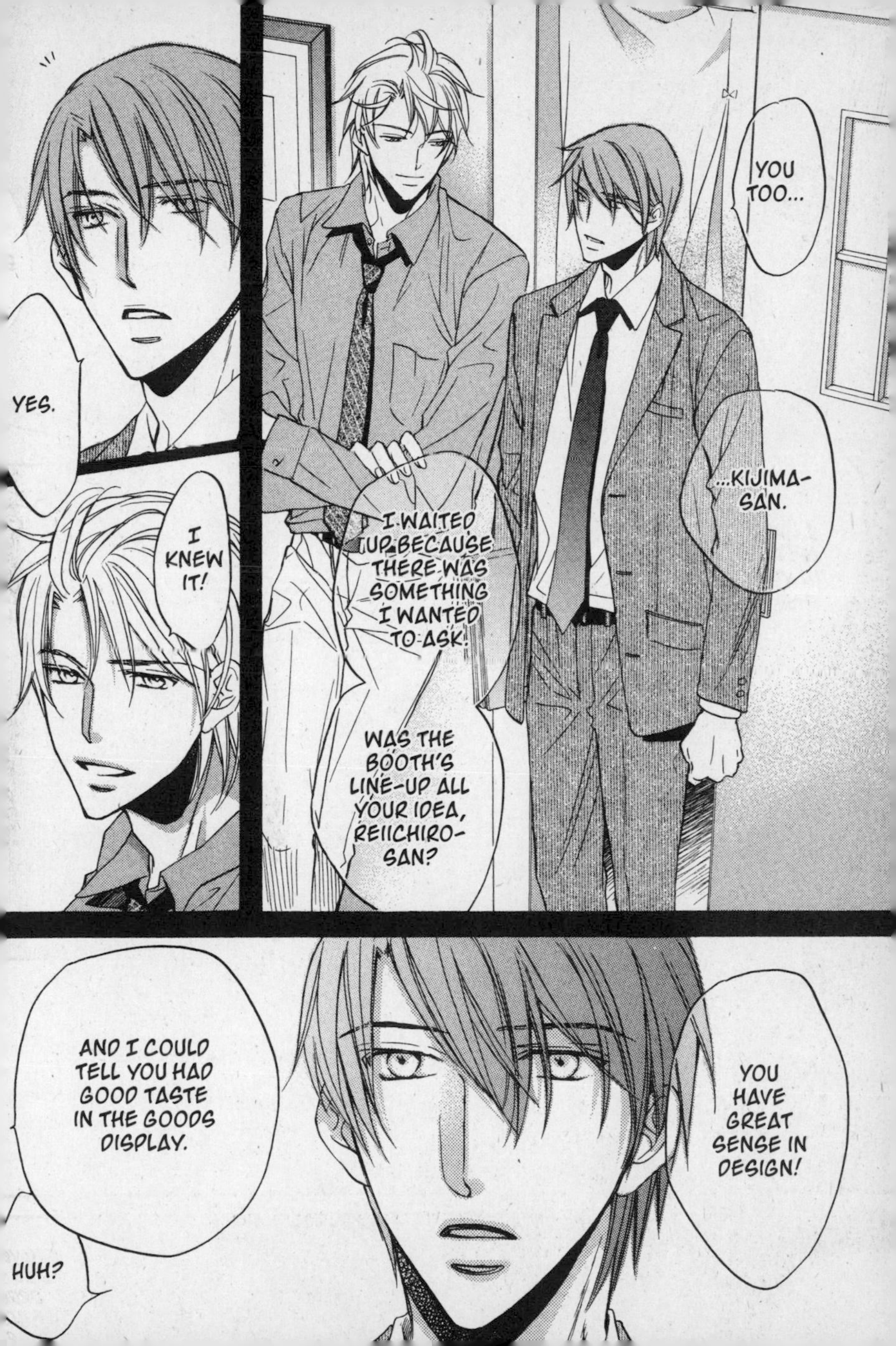
YOU TOO...
...KIJIMA-SAN.
I WAITED UP BECAUSE THERE WAS SOMETHING I WANTED TO ASK.
WAS THE BOOTH'S LINE-UP ALL YOUR IDEA, REIICHIRO-SAN?
YES.
I KNEW IT!
YOU HAVE GREAT SENSE IN DESIGN!
AND I COULD TELL YOU HAD GOOD TASTE IN THE GOODS DISPLAY.
HUH?

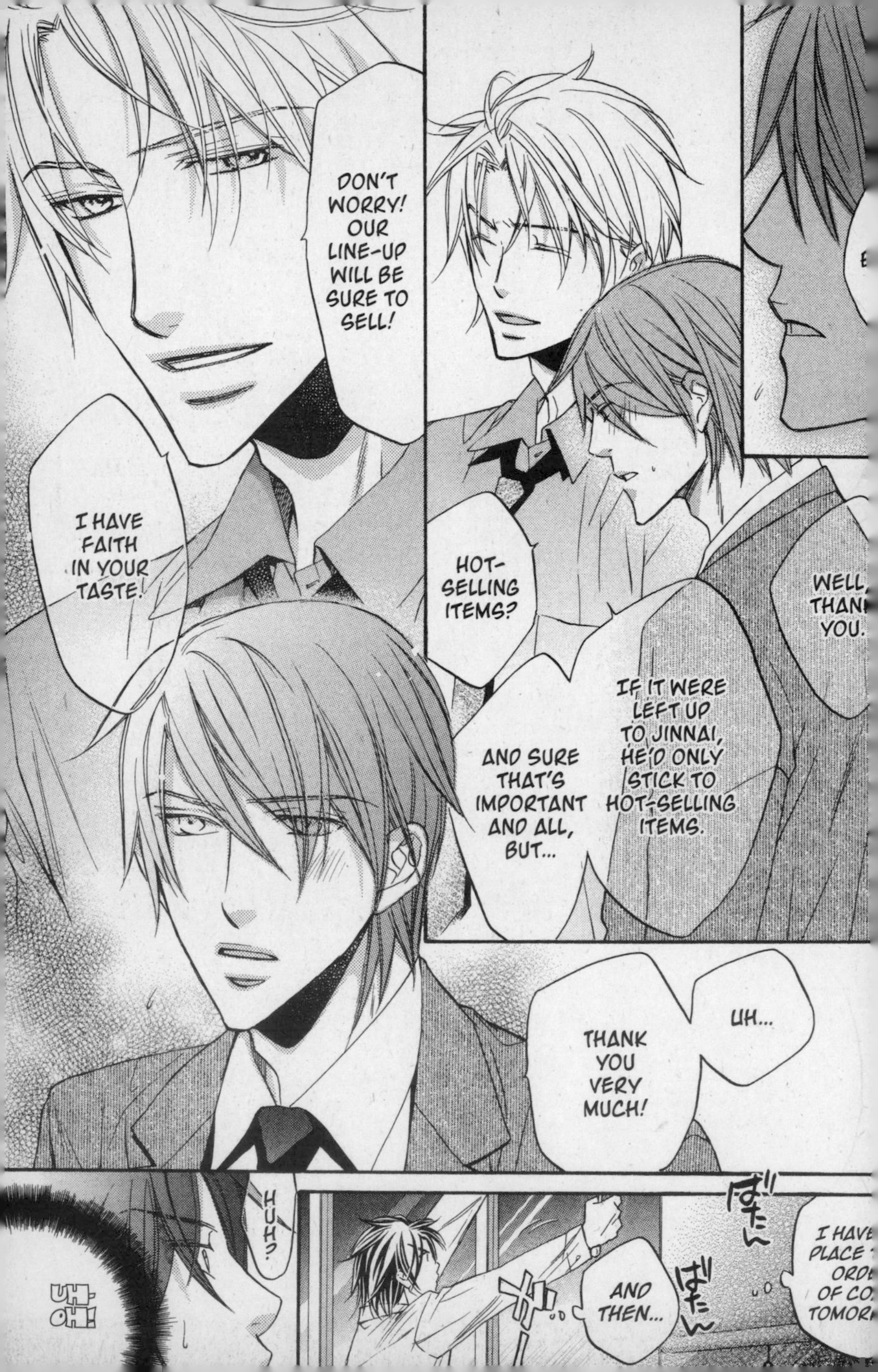
WELL, THAN YOU.
HOT-SELLING ITEMS?
IF IT WERE LEFT UP TO JINNAI, HE'D ONLY STICK TO HOT-SELLING ITEMS.
AND SURE THAT'S IMPORTANT AND ALL, BUT...
DON'T WORRY! OUR LINE-UP WILL BE SURE TO SELL!
I HAVE FAITH IN YOUR TASTE!
UH...
THANK YOU VERY MUCH!
I HAVE PLACE ORDE OF CO TOMOR
ばたん
ばたん
AND THEN...
HUH?
UH-OH!

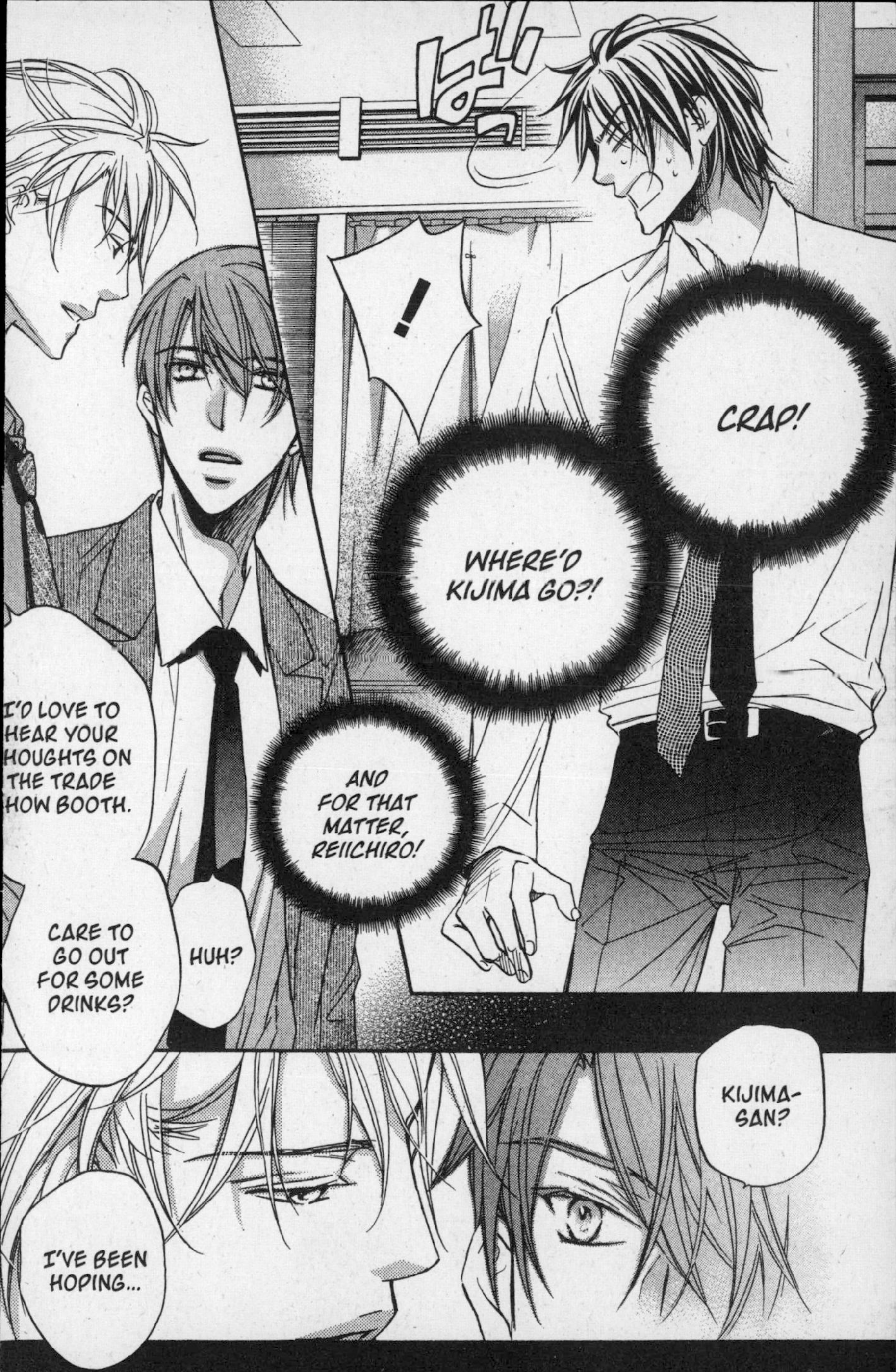
ぱっ
!
CRAP!
WHERE'D KIJIMA GO?!
AND FOR THAT MATTER, REIICHIRO!
I'D LOVE TO HEAR YOUR HOUGHTS ON THE TRADE HOW BOOTH.
HUH?
CARE TO GO OUT FOR SOME DRINKS?
KIJIMA-SAN?
I'VE BEEN HOPING...

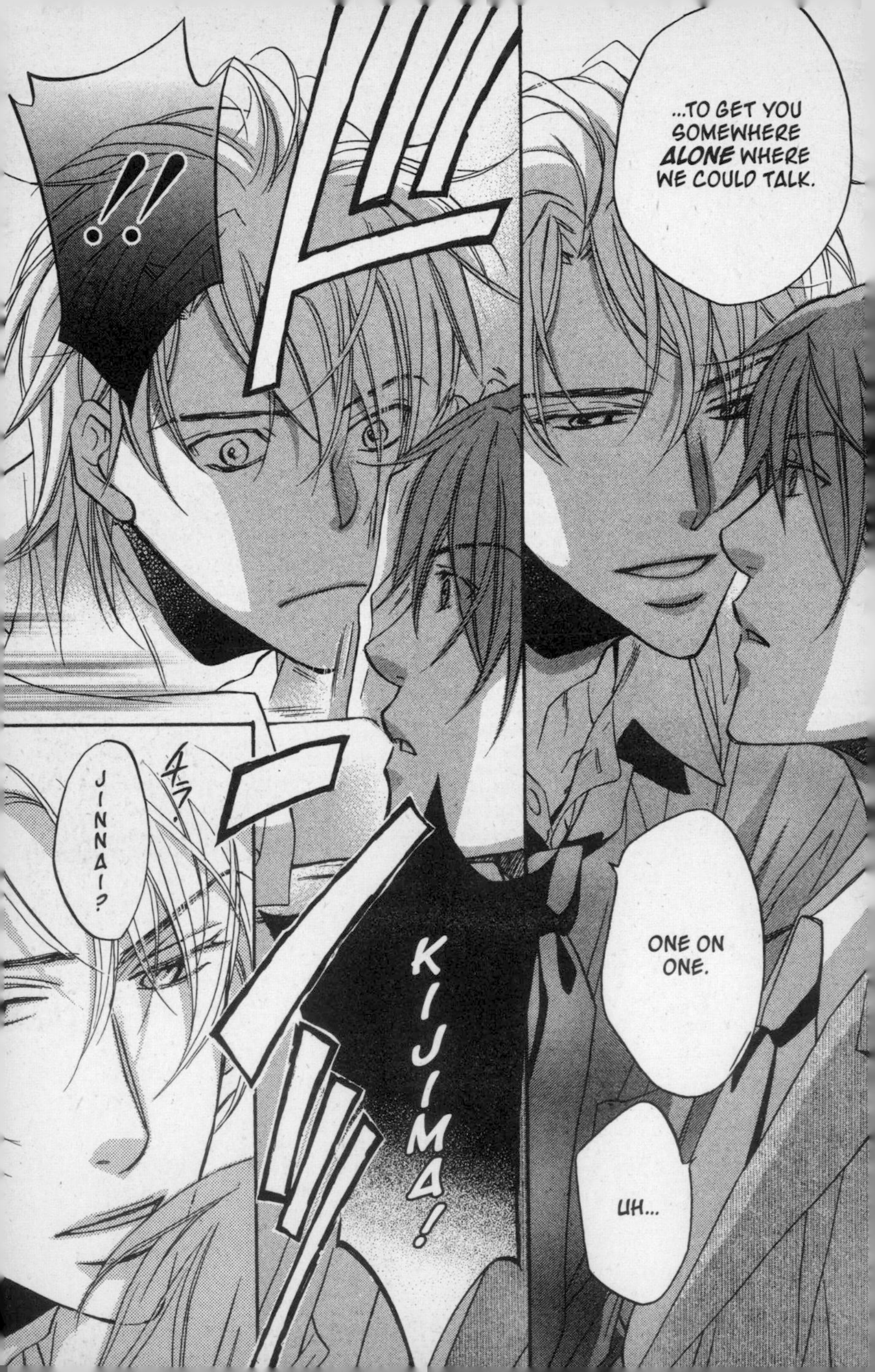
...TO GET YOU SOMEWHERE *ALONE* WHERE WE COULD TALK.
!!
ONE ON ONE.
UH...
KIJIMA!
JINNAI?

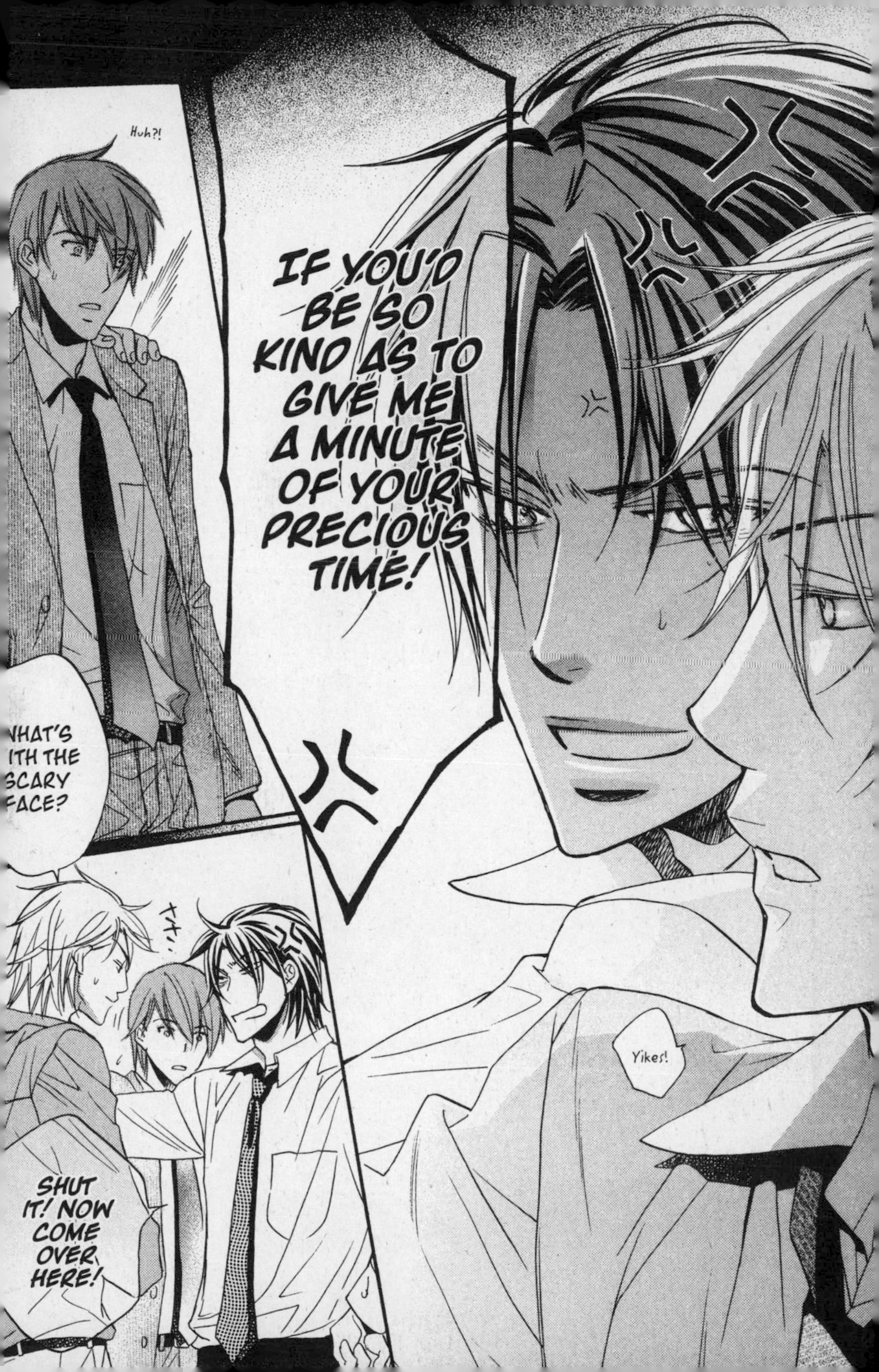
IF YOU'D BE SO KIND AS TO GIVE ME A MINUTE OF YOUR PRECIOUS TIME!
Yikes!
Huh?!
WHAT'S ITH THE SCARY FACE?
SHUT IT! NOW COME OVER HERE!

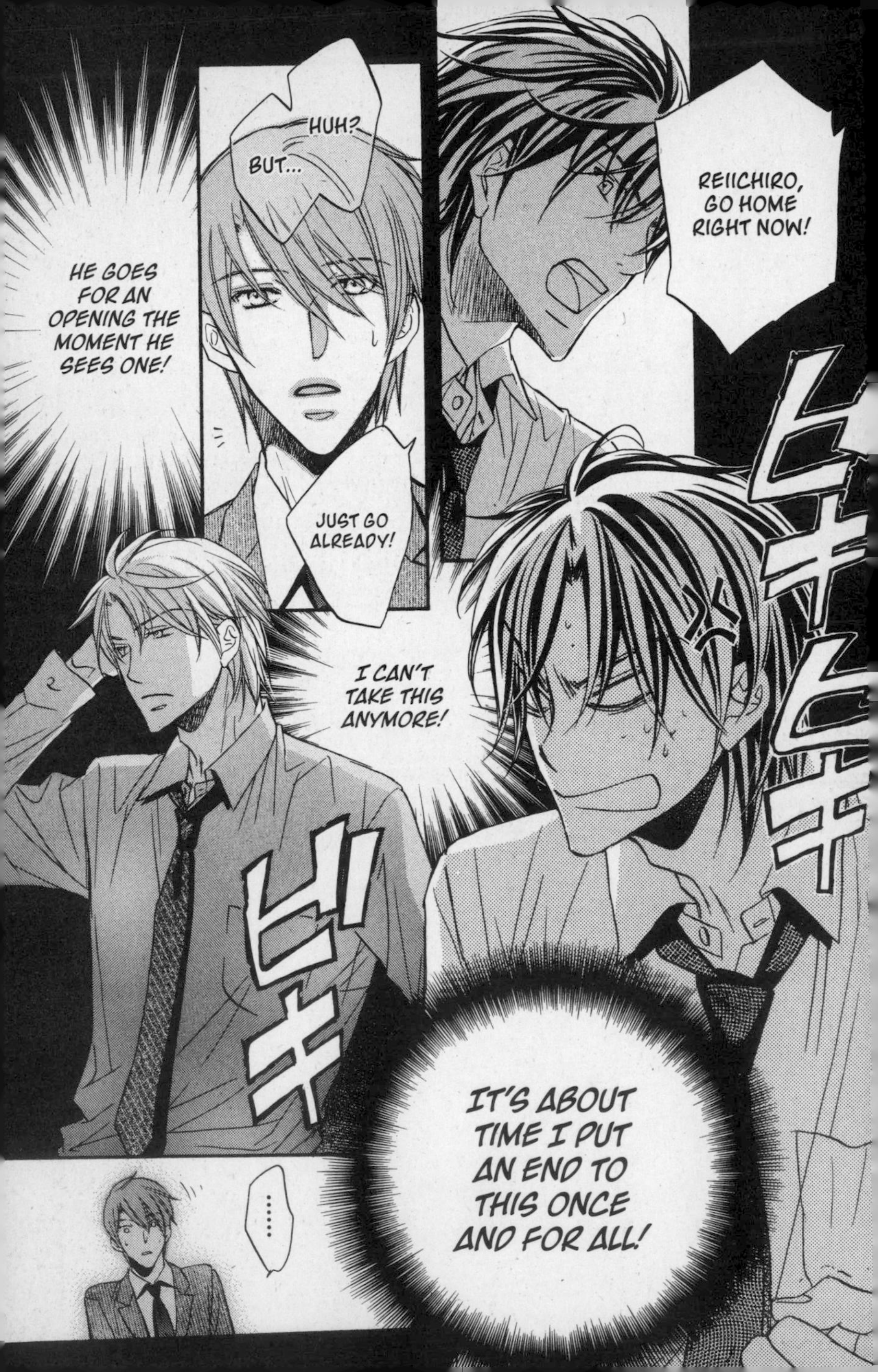
REIICHIRO, GO HOME RIGHT NOW!
HUH?
BUT...
HE GOES FOR AN OPENING THE MOMENT HE SEES ONE!
JUST GO ALREADY!
I CAN'T TAKE THIS ANYMORE!
IT'S ABOUT TIME I PUT AN END TO THIS ONCE AND FOR ALL!
......

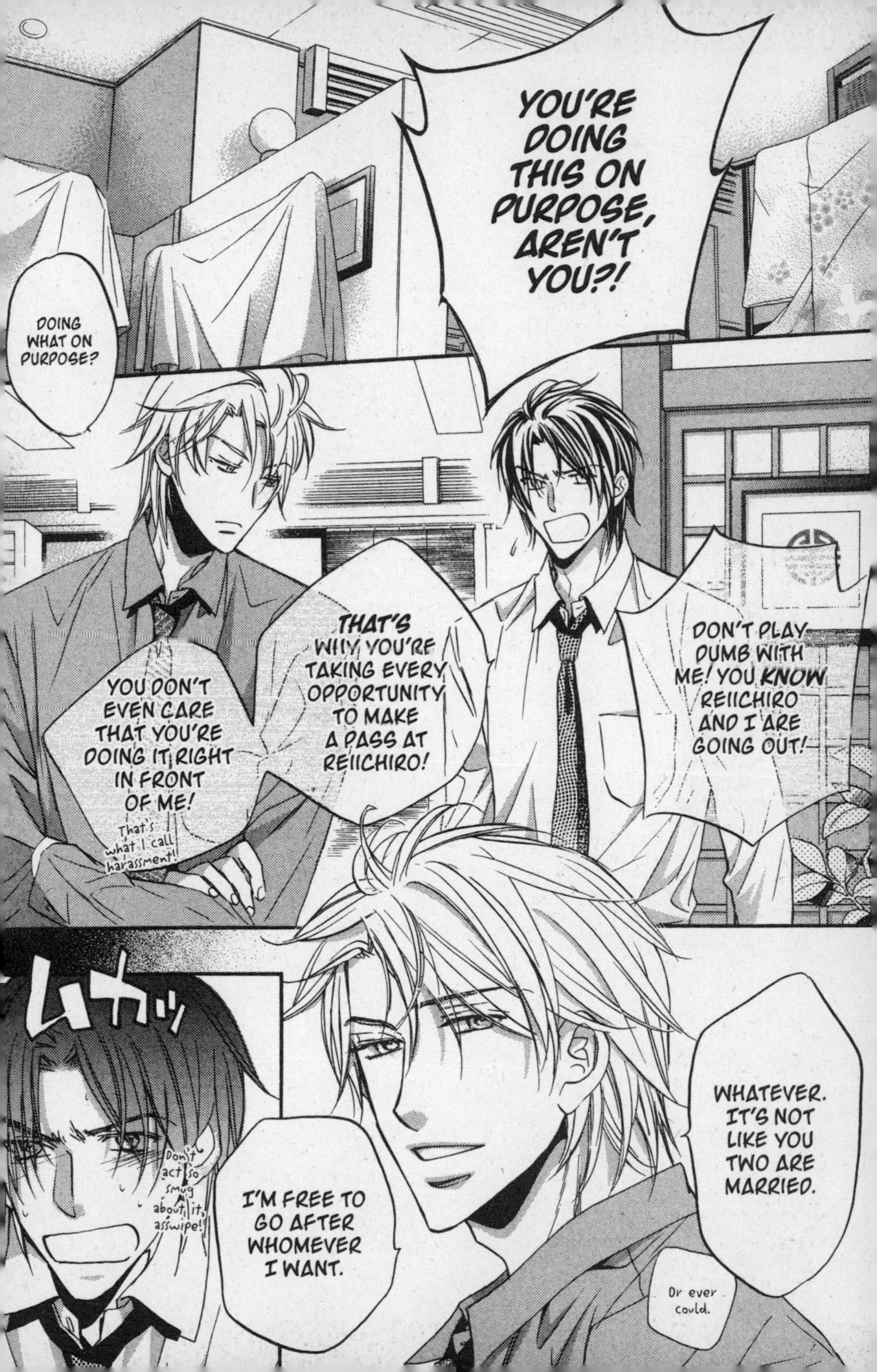
YOU'RE DOING THIS ON PURPOSE, AREN'T YOU?!
DOING WHAT ON PURPOSE?
DON'T PLAY DUMB WITH ME! YOU KNOW REIICHIRO AND I ARE GOING OUT!
THAT'S WHY YOU'RE TAKING EVERY OPPORTUNITY TO MAKE A PASS AT REIICHIRO!
YOU DON'T EVEN CARE THAT YOU'RE DOING IT RIGHT IN FRONT OF ME!
That's what I call harassment!
WHATEVER. IT'S NOT LIKE YOU TWO ARE MARRIED.
Or ever could.
I'M FREE TO GO AFTER WHOMEVER I WANT.
Don't act so smug about it, asswipe!

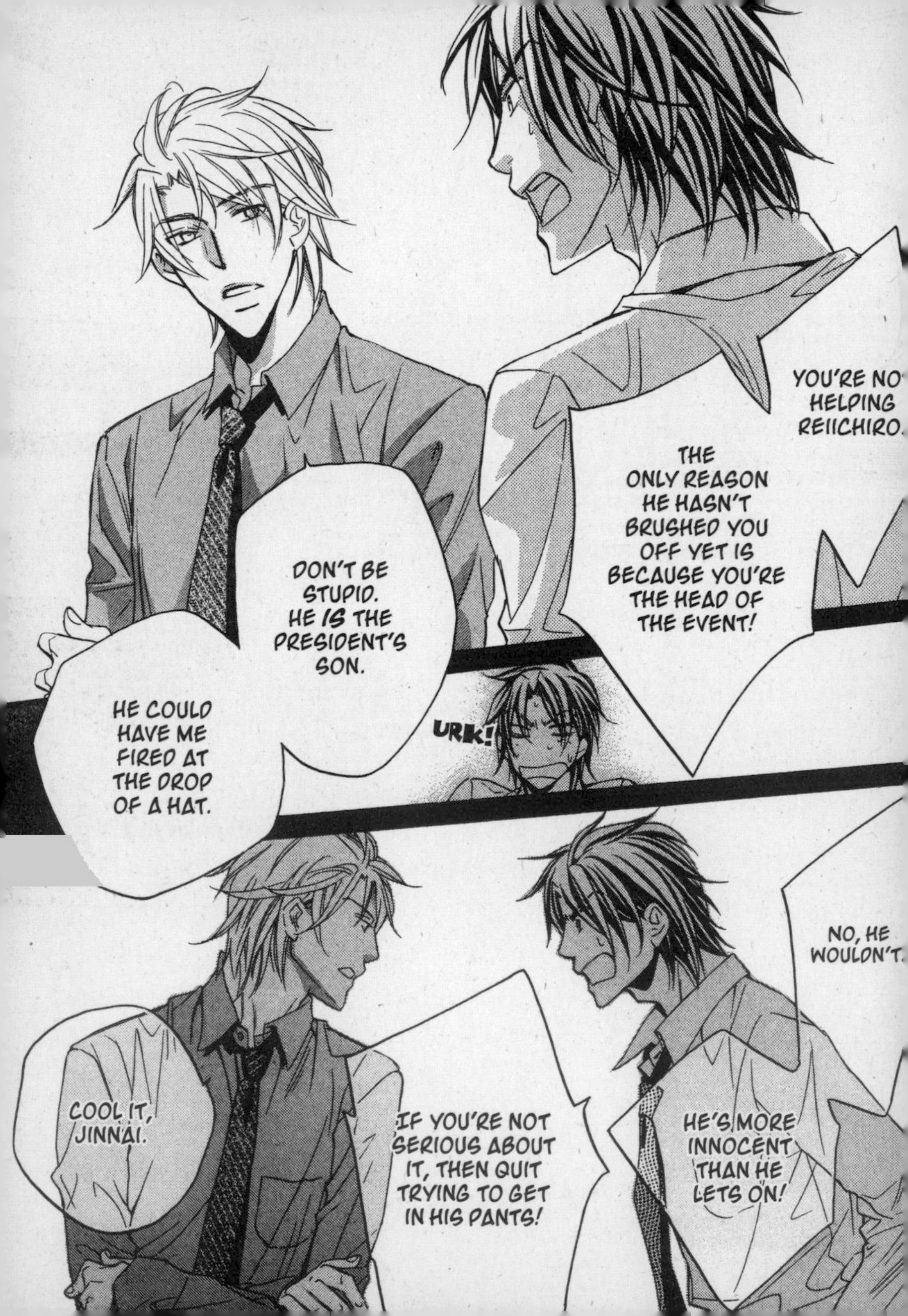
YOU'RE NO HELPING REIICHIRO.
THE ONLY REASON HE HASN'T BRUSHED YOU OFF YET IS BECAUSE YOU'RE THE HEAD OF THE EVENT!
DON'T BE STUPID. HE IS THE PRESIDENT'S SON.
HE COULD HAVE ME FIRED AT THE DROP OF A HAT.
URK!
NO, HE WOULDN'T.
HE'S MORE INNOCENT THAN HE LETS ON!
IF YOU'RE NOT SERIOUS ABOUT IT, THEN QUIT TRYING TO GET IN HIS PANTS!
COOL IT, JINNAI.

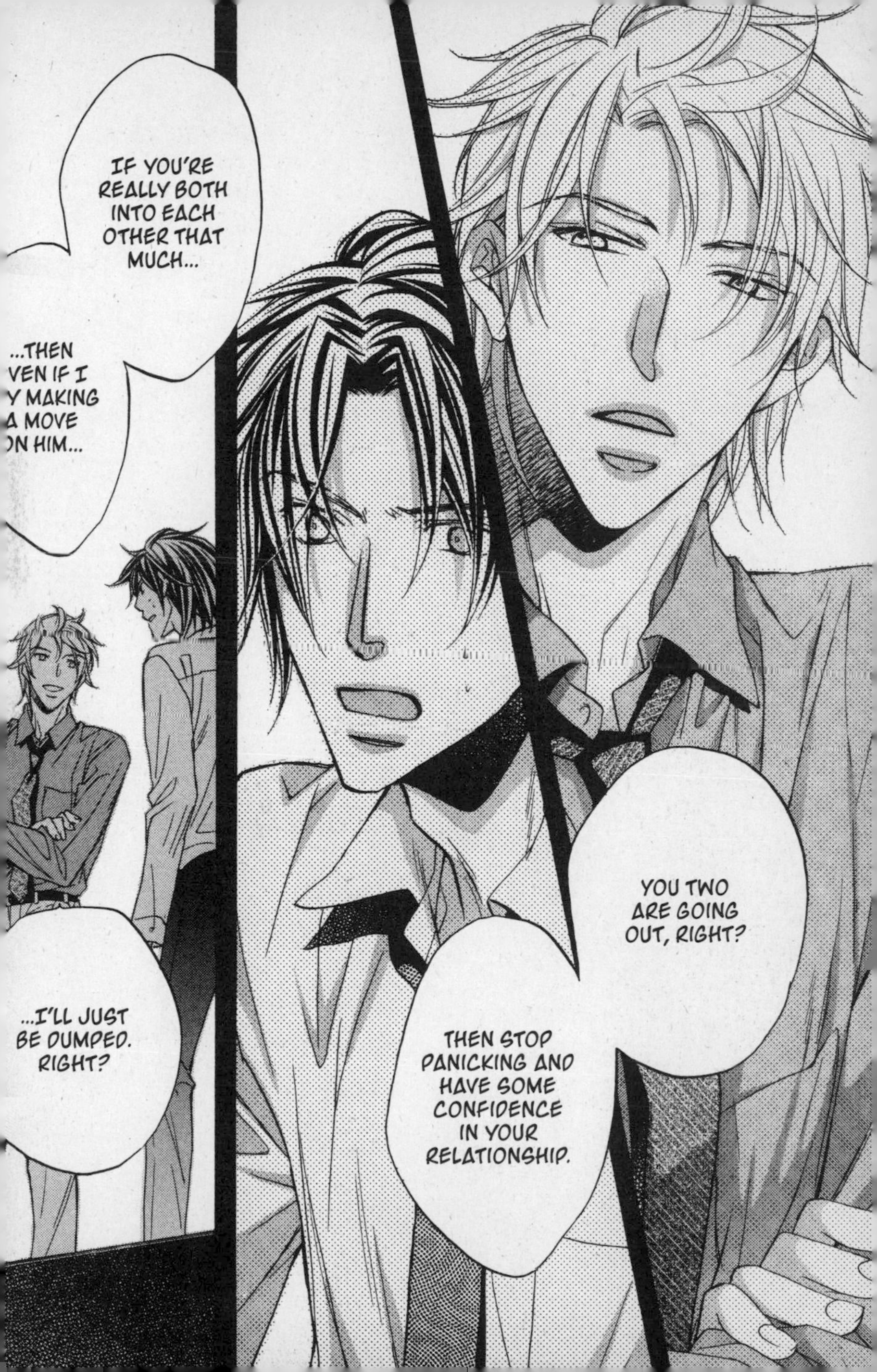

YOU TWO ARE GOING OUT, RIGHT?
THEN STOP PANICKING AND HAVE SOME CONFIDENCE IN YOUR RELATIONSHIP.
IF YOU'RE REALLY BOTH INTO EACH OTHER THAT MUCH...
...THEN VEN IF I Y MAKING A MOVE ON HIM...
...I'LL JUST BE DUMPED. RIGHT?

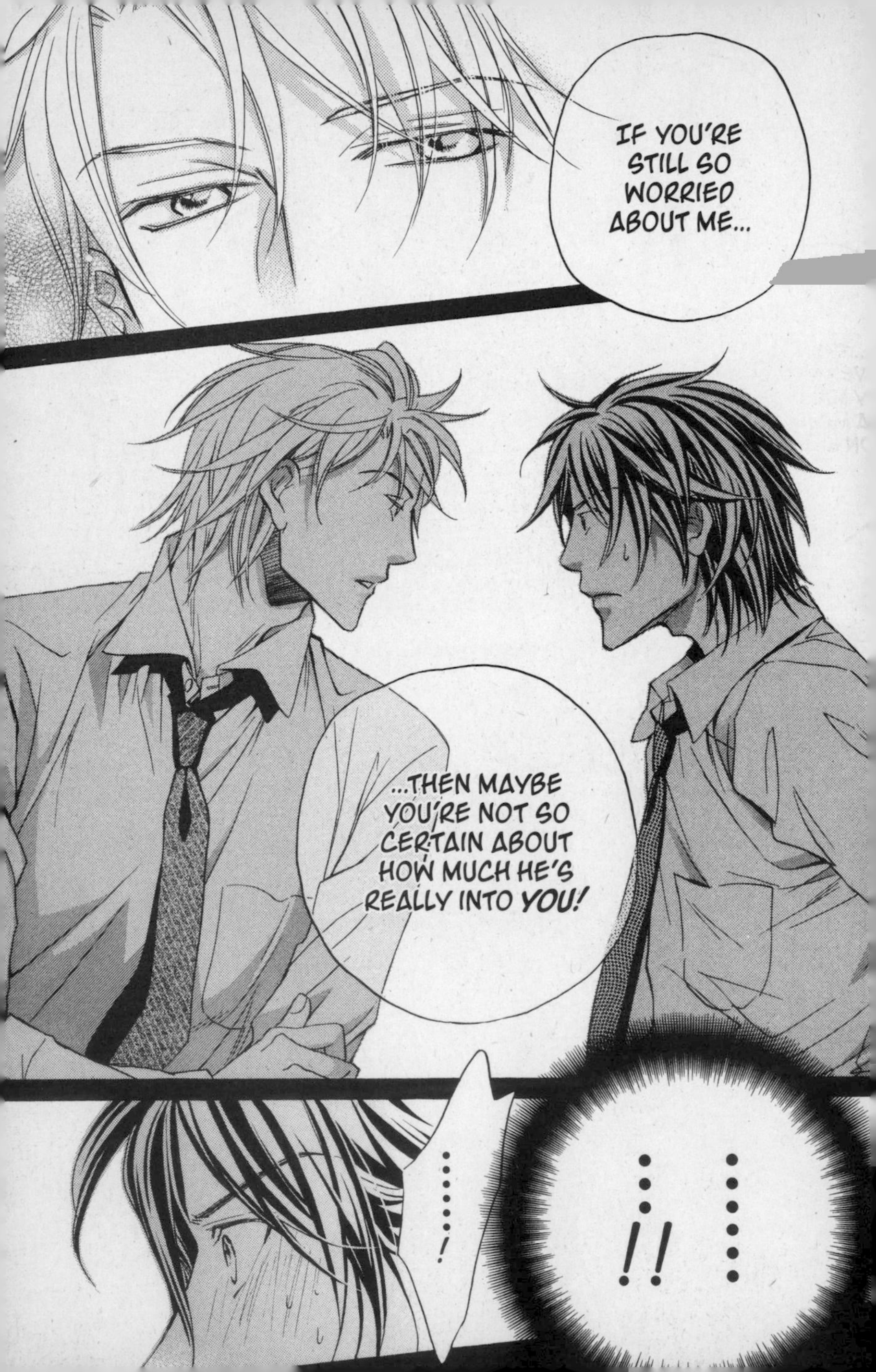
IF YOU'RE STILL SO WORRIED ABOUT ME...
...THEN MAYBE YOU'RE NOT SO CERTAIN ABOUT HOW MUCH HE'S REALLY INTO *YOU*!
......!!
......!

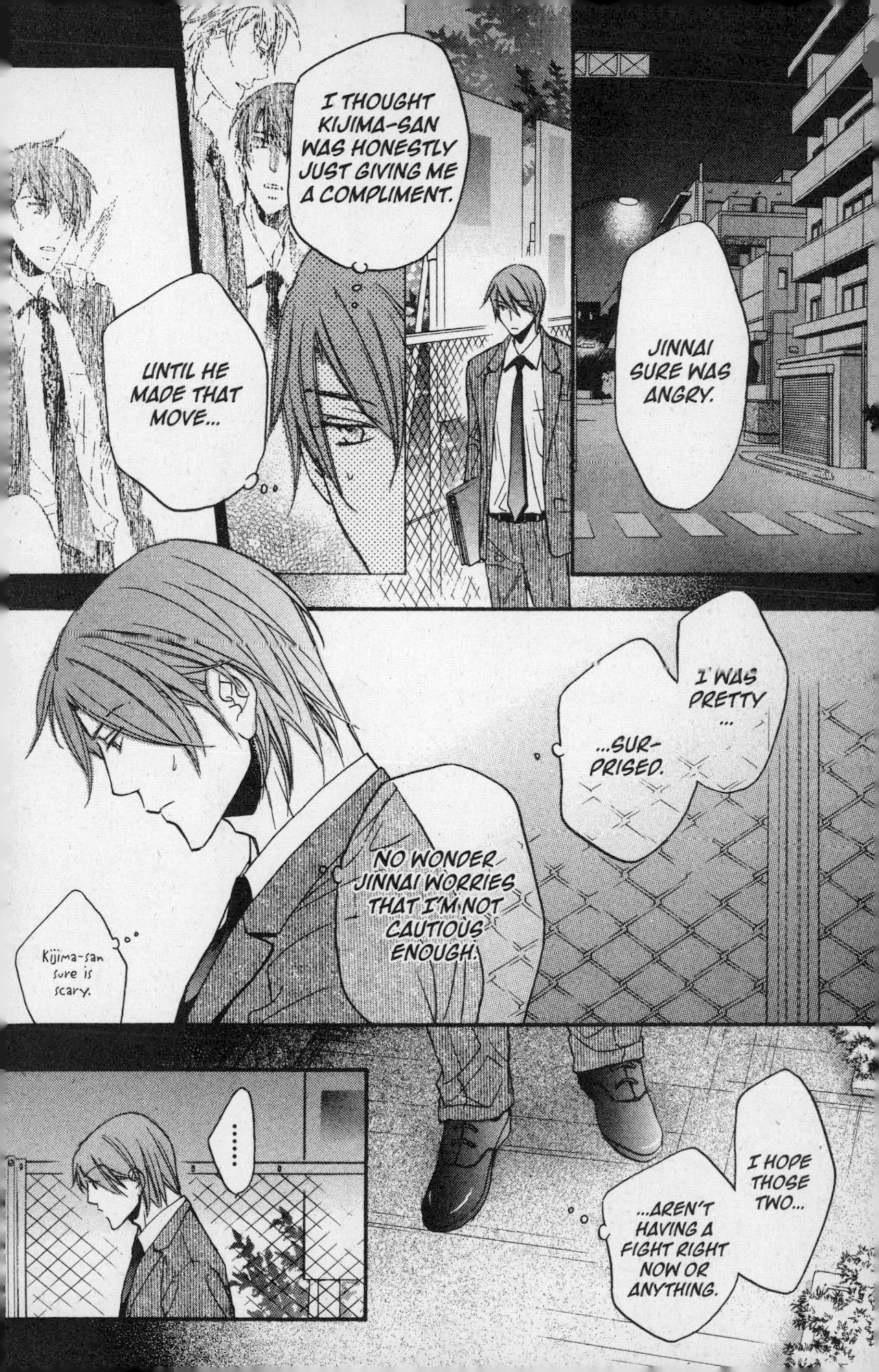
Jinnai sure was angry.
I thought Kijima-san was honestly just giving me a compliment.
Until he made that move...
I was pretty ... ...sur-prised.
No wonder Jinnai worries that I'm not cautious enough.
Kijima-san sure is scary.
I hope those two...
...aren't having a fight right now or anything.
......

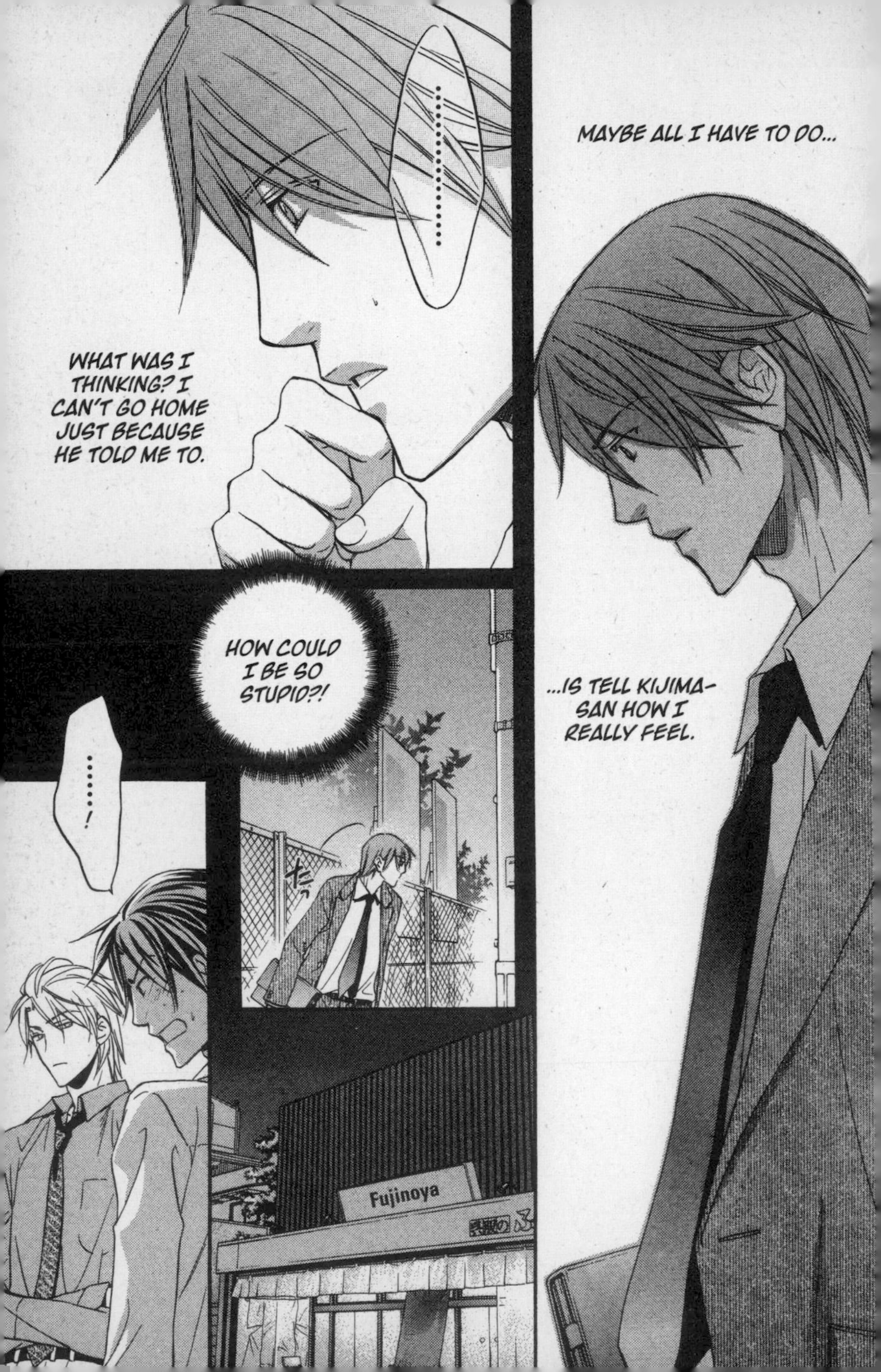
MAYBE ALL I HAVE TO DO...
...IS TELL KIJIMA-SAN HOW I REALLY FEEL.
....
WHAT WAS I THINKING? I CAN'T GO HOME JUST BECAUSE HE TOLD ME TO.
HOW COULD I BE SO STUPID?!
Fujinoya
......!

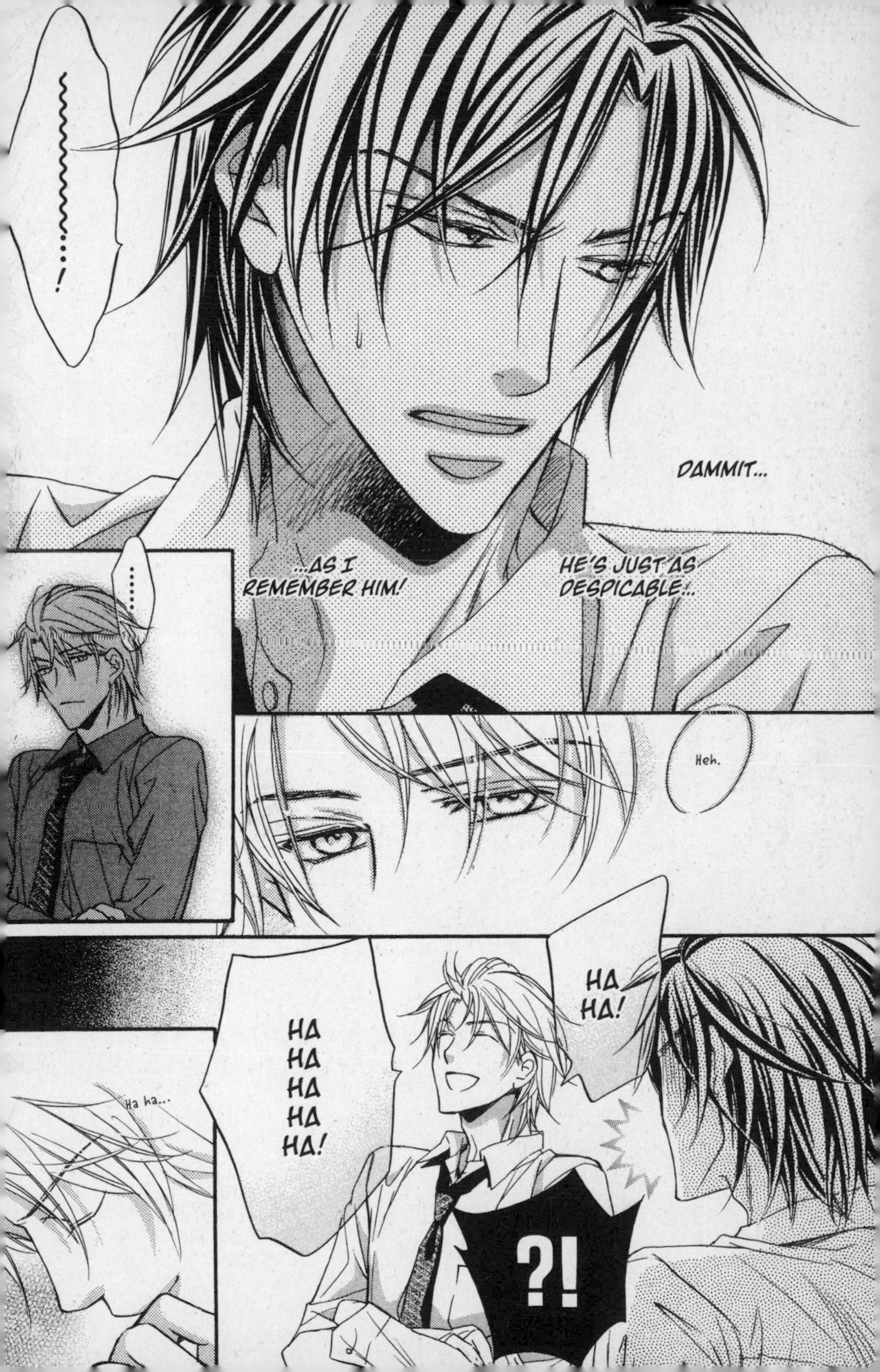
DAMMIT...
HE'S JUST AS DESPICABLE...
...AS I REMEMBER HIM!
......!
Heh.
......
HA HA!
HA HA HA HA HA!
?!
Ha ha...

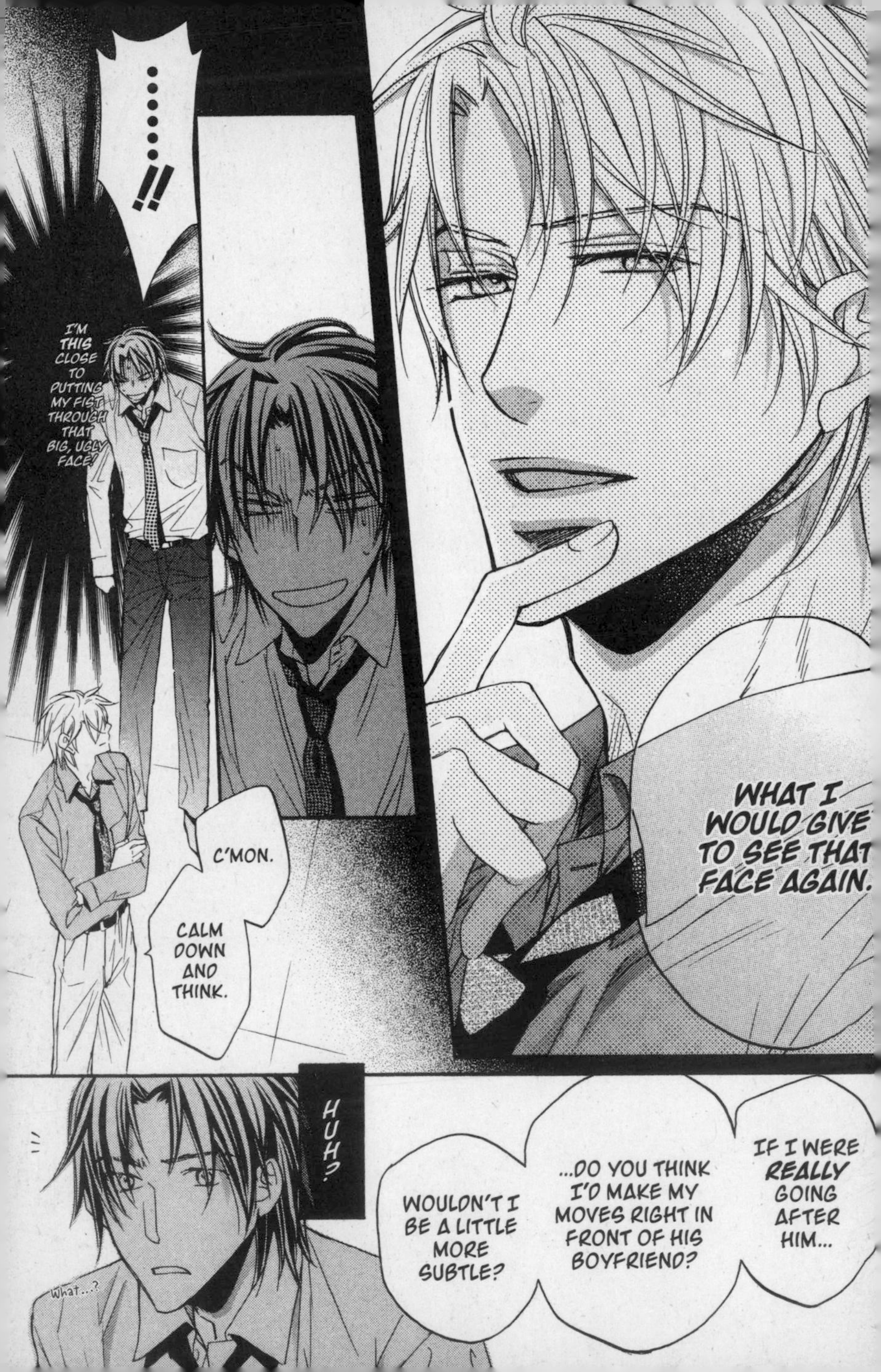
WHAT I WOULD GIVE TO SEE THAT FACE AGAIN.
......!!
I'M THIS CLOSE TO PUTTING MY FIST THROUGH THAT BIG, UGLY FACE!
C'MON.
CALM DOWN AND THINK.
IF I WERE REALLY GOING AFTER HIM...
...DO YOU THINK I'D MAKE MY MOVES RIGHT IN FRONT OF HIS BOYFRIEND?
WOULDN'T I BE A LITTLE MORE SUBTLE?
HUH?
What...?

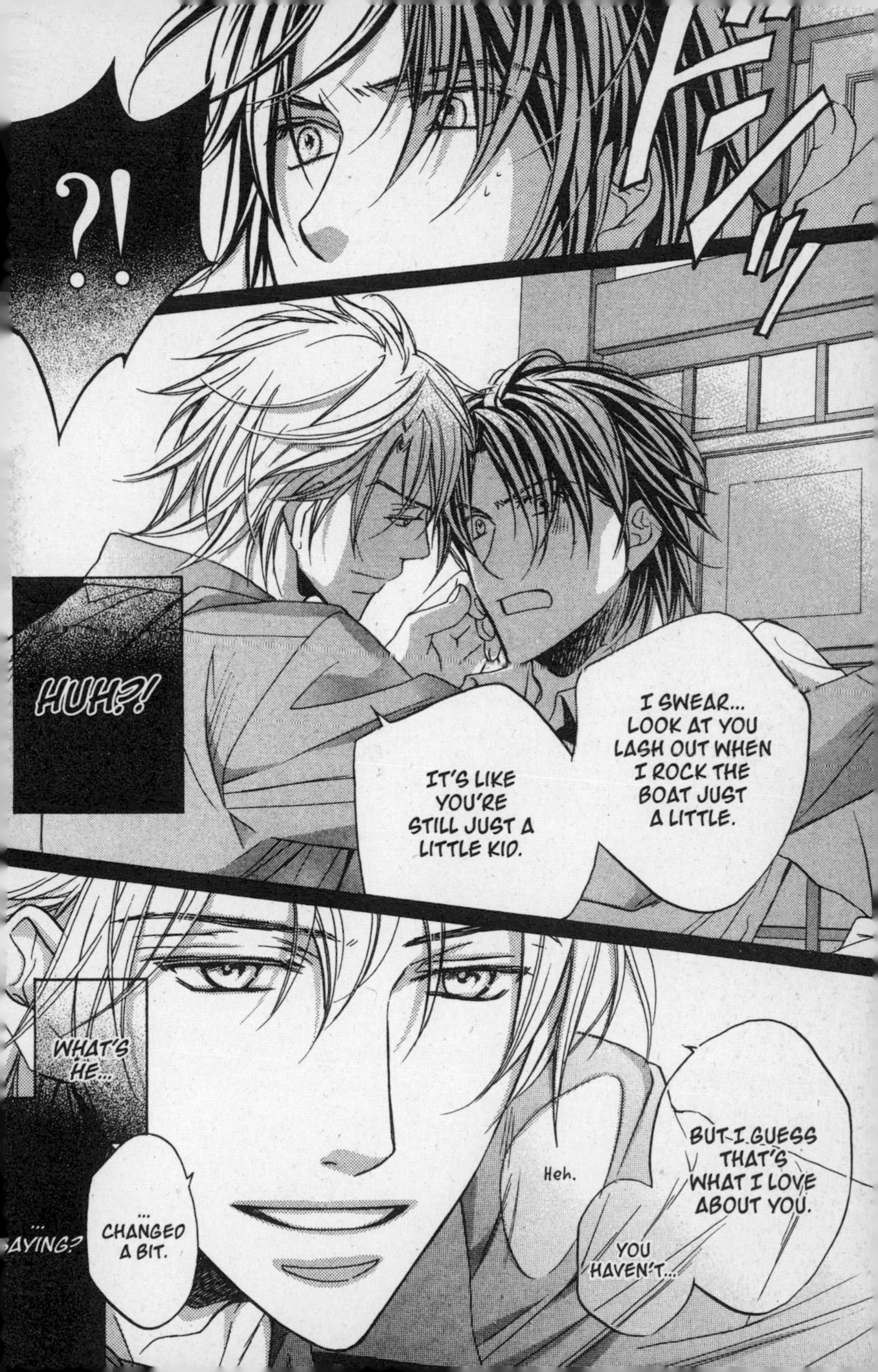
?!
I SWEAR... LOOK AT YOU LASH OUT WHEN I ROCK THE BOAT JUST A LITTLE.
IT'S LIKE YOU'RE STILL JUST A LITTLE KID.
HUH?!
YOU HAVEN'T...
BUT I GUESS THAT'S WHAT I LOVE ABOUT YOU.
Heh.
... CHANGED A BIT.
WHAT'S HE...
... SAYING?

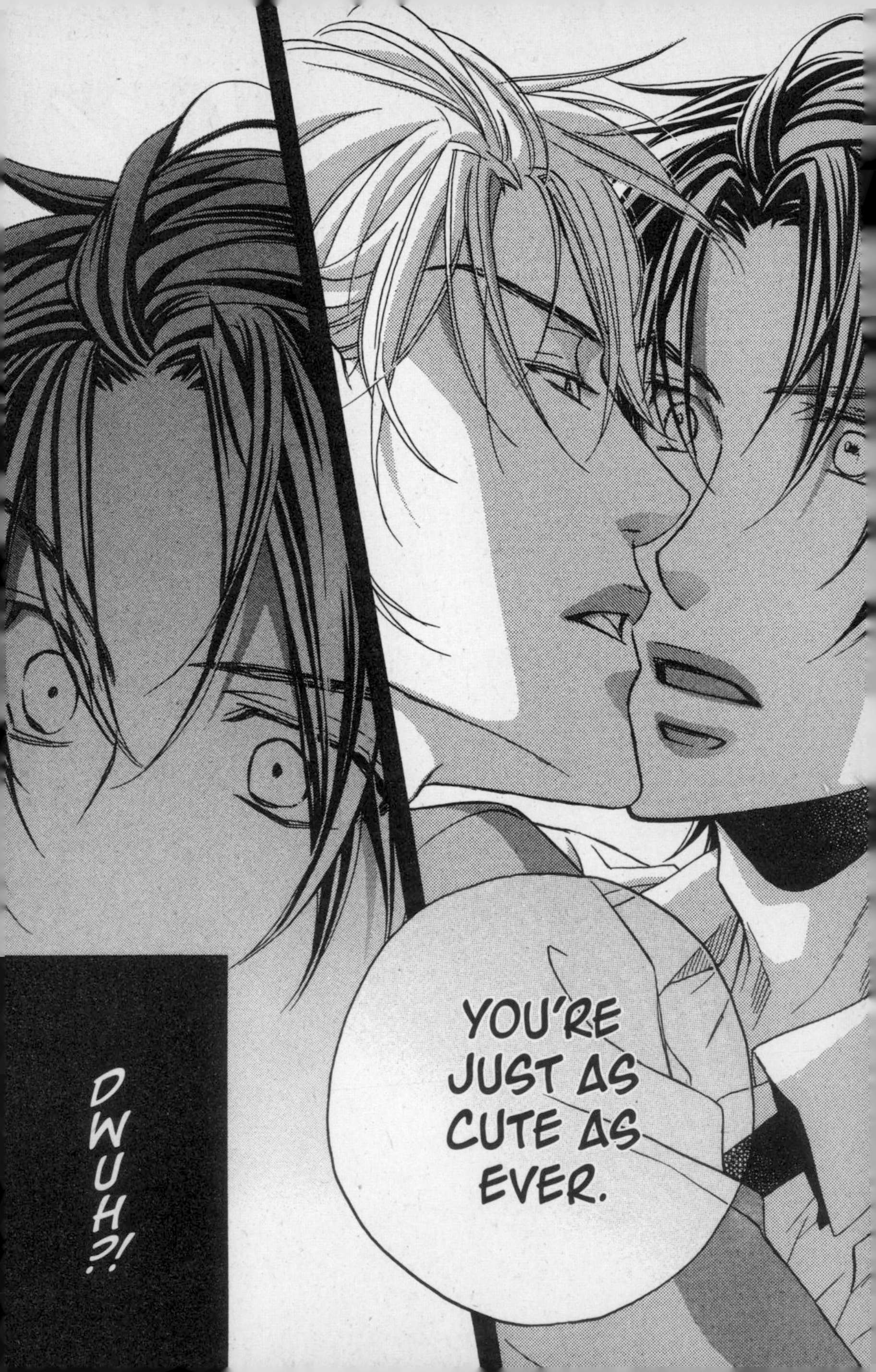
YOU'RE JUST AS CUTE AS EVER.
DWUH?!

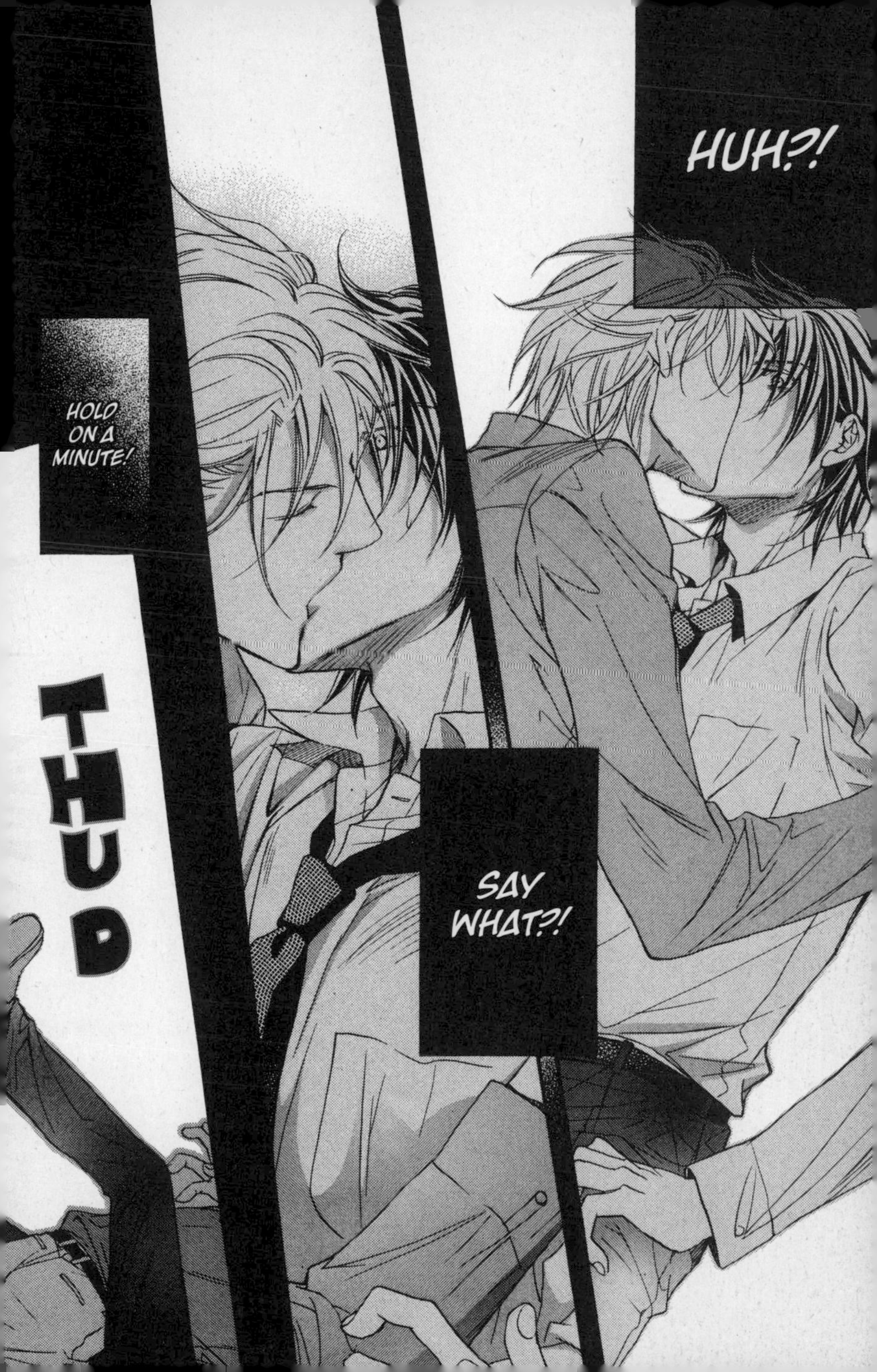
HUH?!
HOLD ON A MINUTE!
SAY WHAT?!
THUD

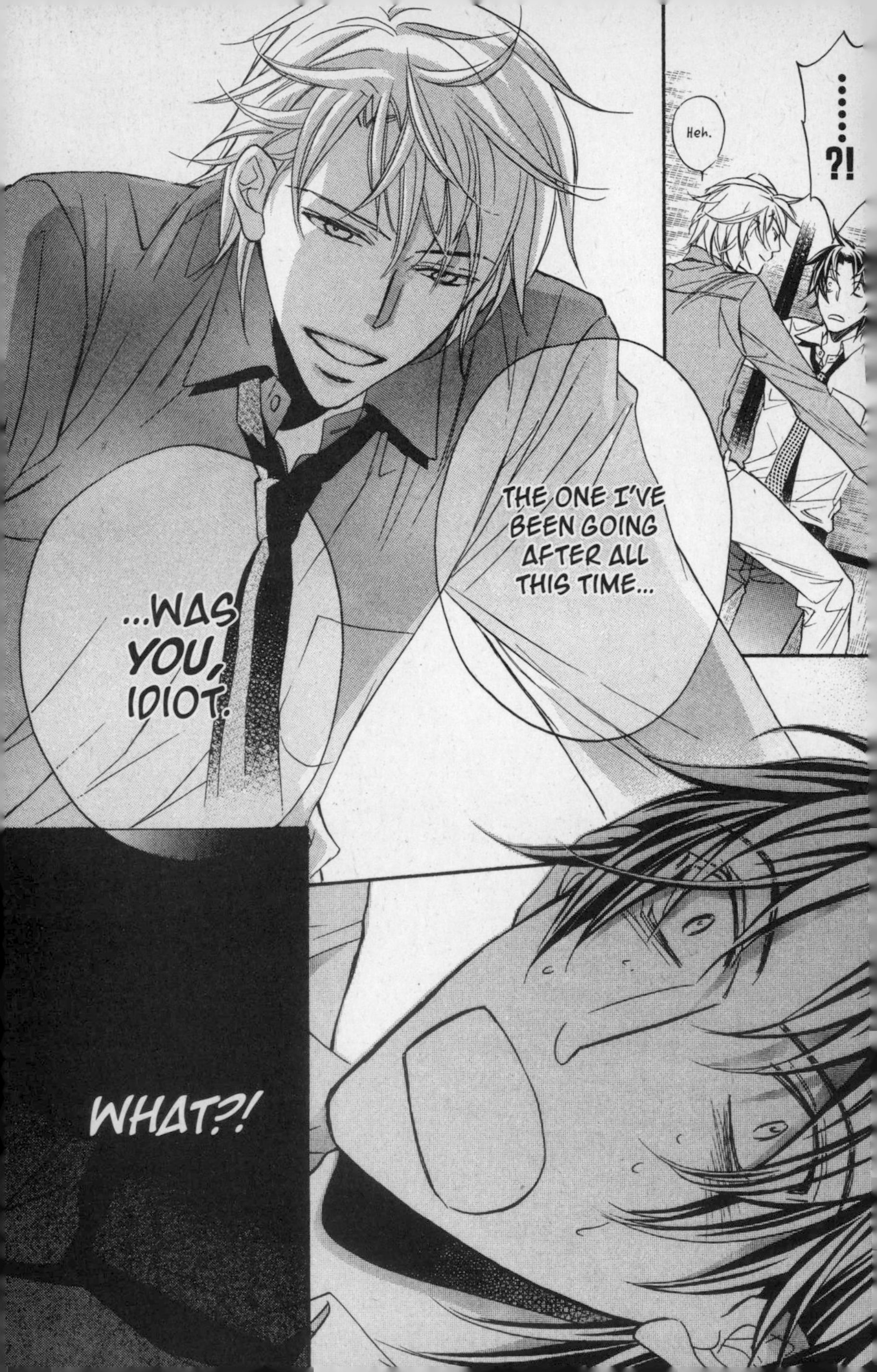
......?!
Heh.
THE ONE I'VE BEEN GOING AFTER ALL THIS TIME...
...WAS YOU, IDIOT.
WHAT?!

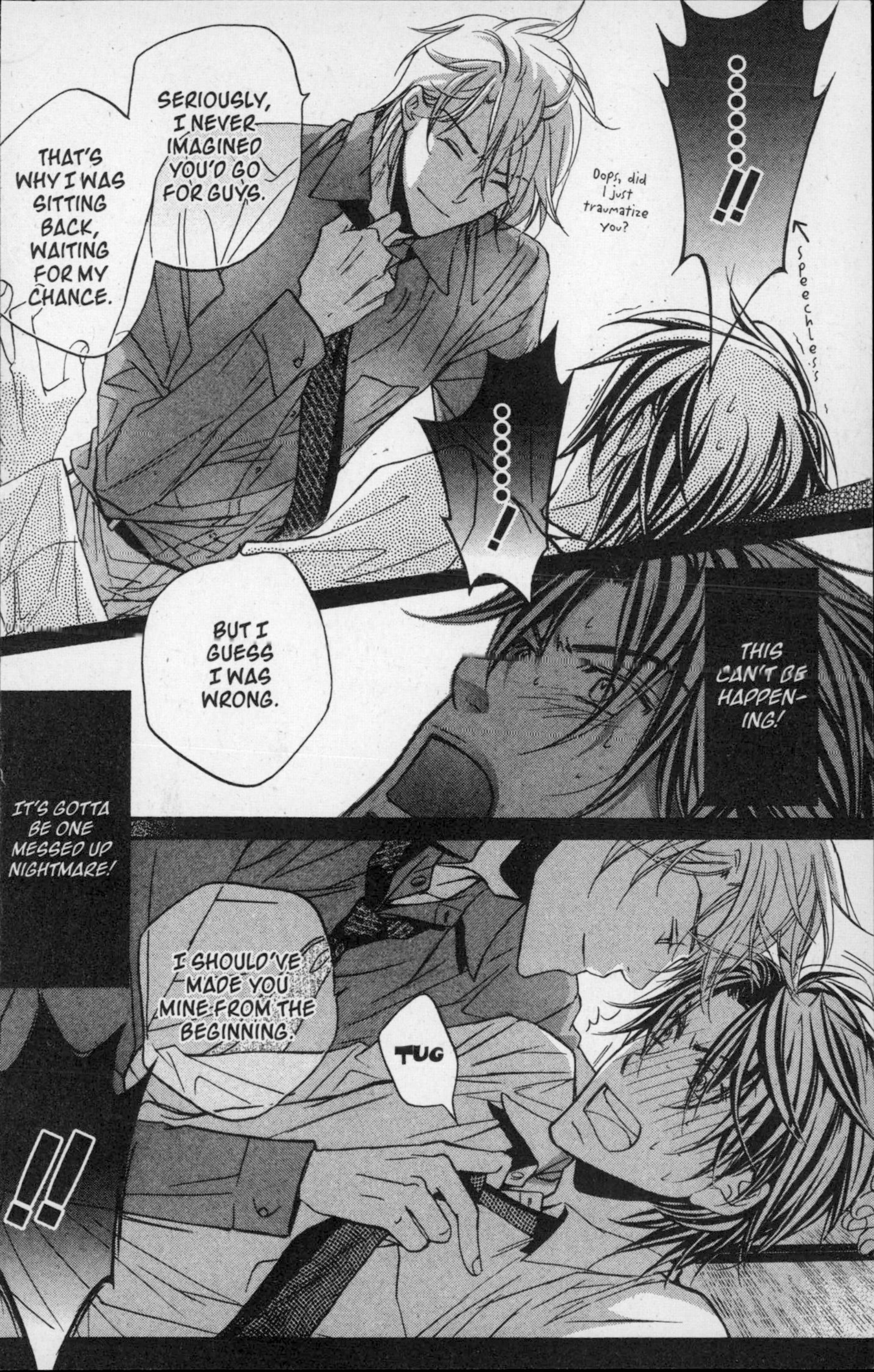
OOOOOO!!
speechless
Oops, did I just traumatize you?
SERIOUSLY, I NEVER IMAGINED YOU'D GO FOR GUYS.
THAT'S WHY I WAS SITTING BACK, WAITING FOR MY CHANCE.
OOOOOO!
THIS CAN'T BE HAPPENING!
BUT I GUESS I WAS WRONG.
IT'S GOTTA BE ONE MESSED UP NIGHTMARE!
I SHOULD'VE MADE YOU MINE FROM THE BEGINNING.
TUG
!!

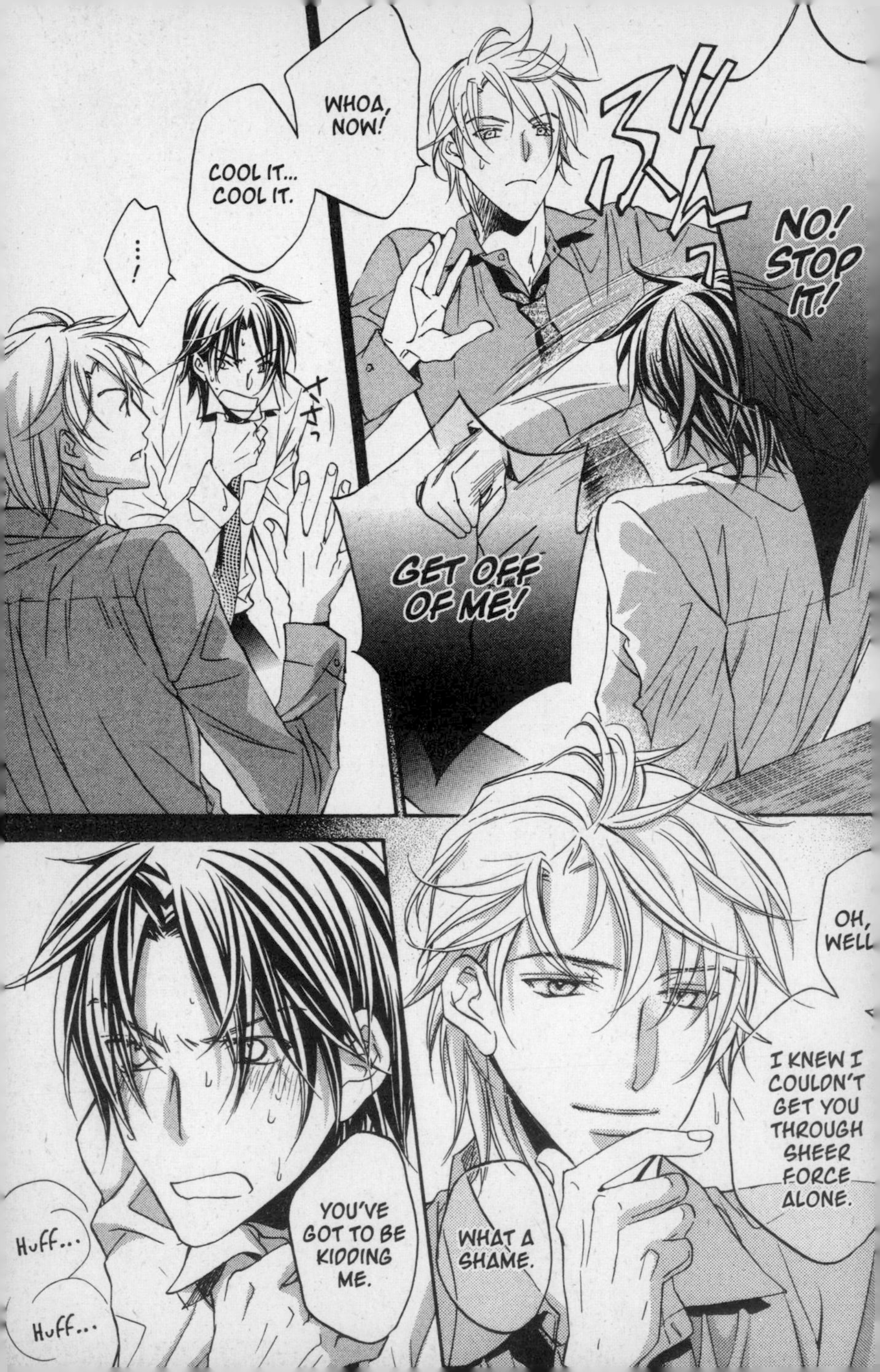
NO! STOP IT!
GET OFF OF ME!
WHOA, NOW!
COOL IT... COOL IT.
...!
OH, WELL
I KNEW I COULDN'T GET YOU THROUGH SHEER FORCE ALONE.
WHAT A SHAME.
YOU'VE GOT TO BE KIDDING ME.
Huff...
Huff...

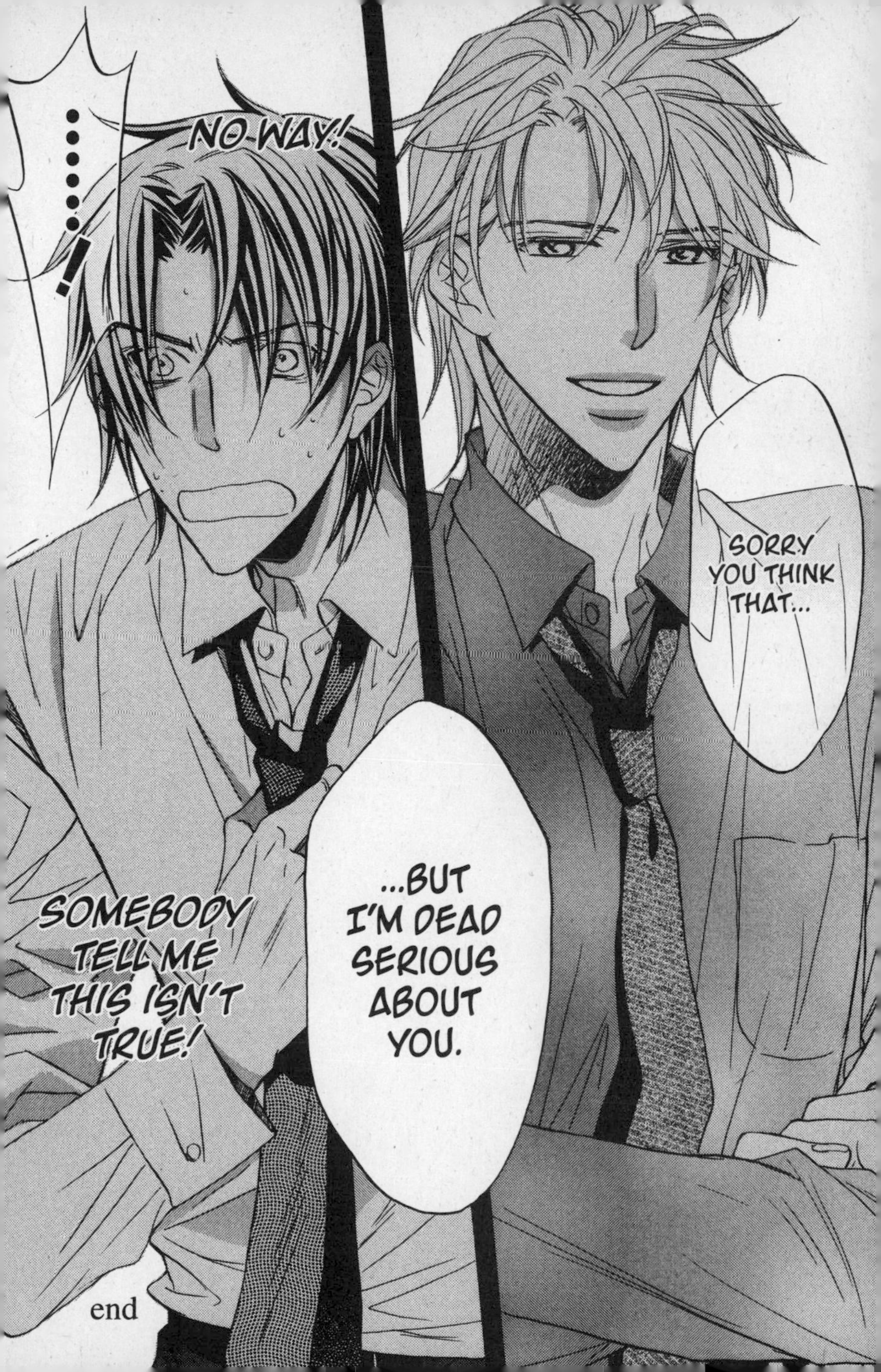
SORRY YOU THINK THAT...
...BUT I'M DEAD SERIOUS ABOUT YOU.
......!
NO WAY!
SOMEBODY TELL ME THIS ISN'T TRUE!

end

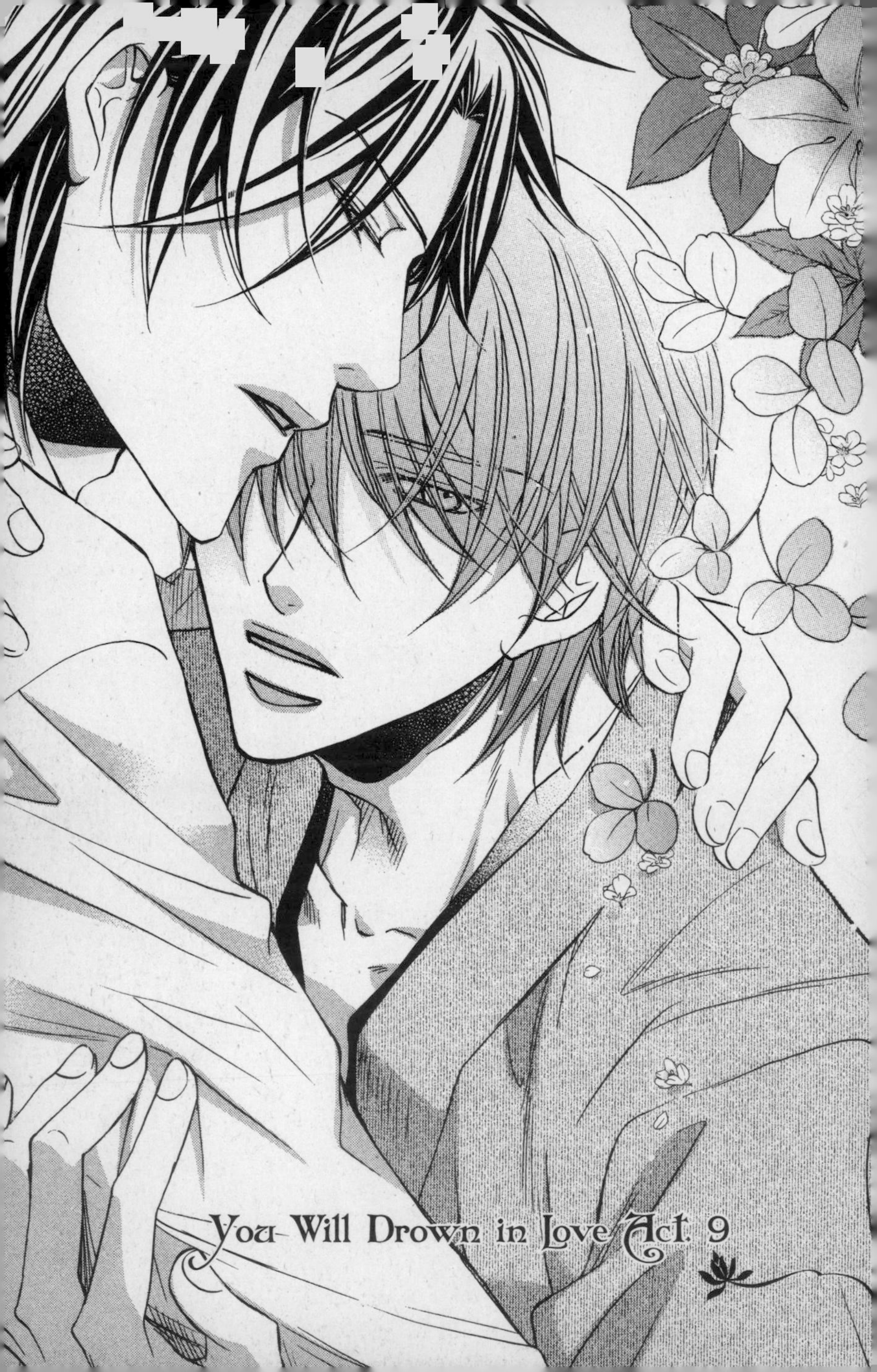
You Will Drown in Love Act. 9

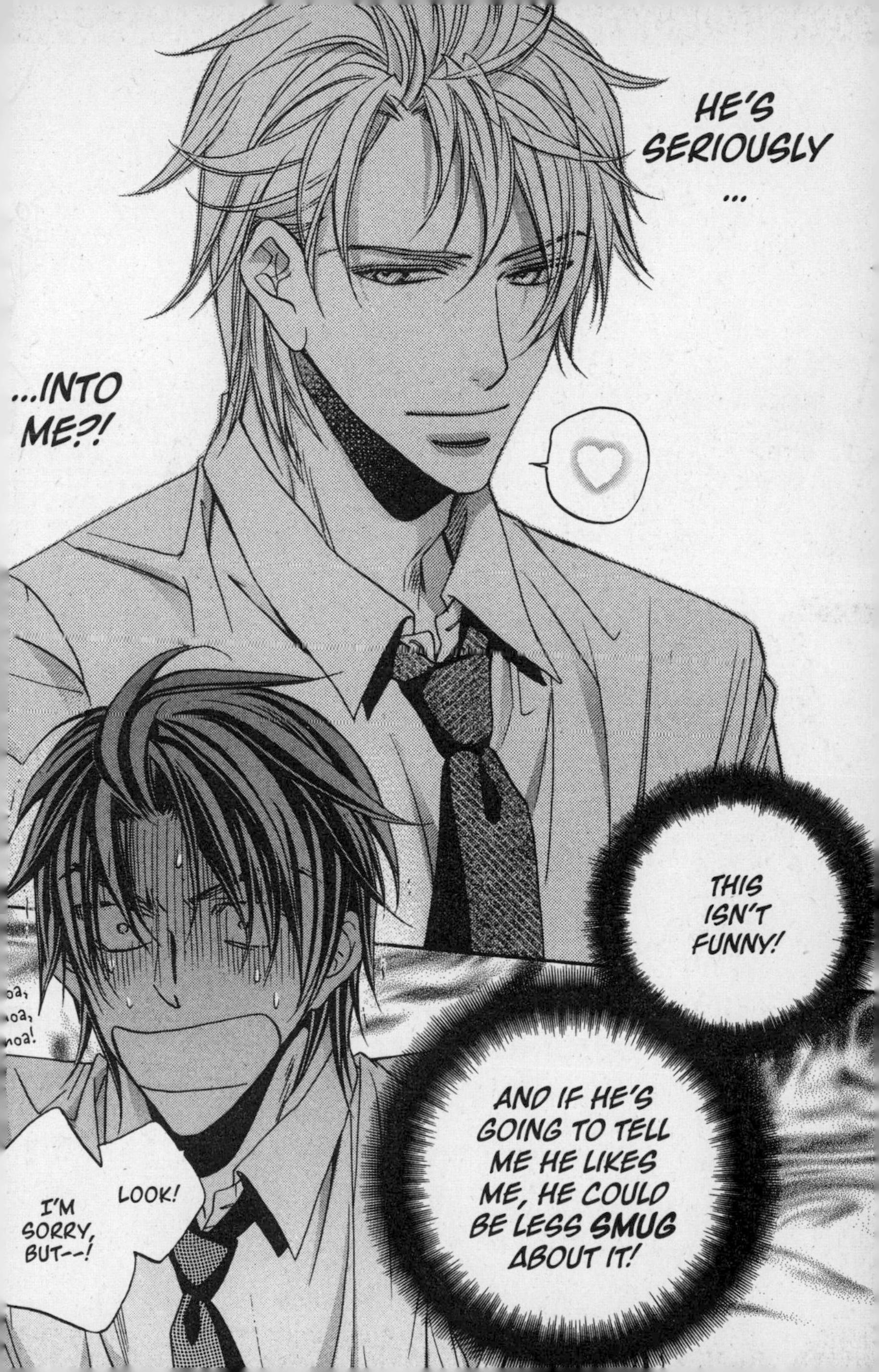
HE'S SERIOUSLY ...
...INTO ME?!
THIS ISN'T FUNNY!
AND IF HE'S GOING TO TELL ME HE LIKES ME, HE COULD BE LESS SMUG ABOUT IT!
LOOK!
I'M SORRY, BUT--!

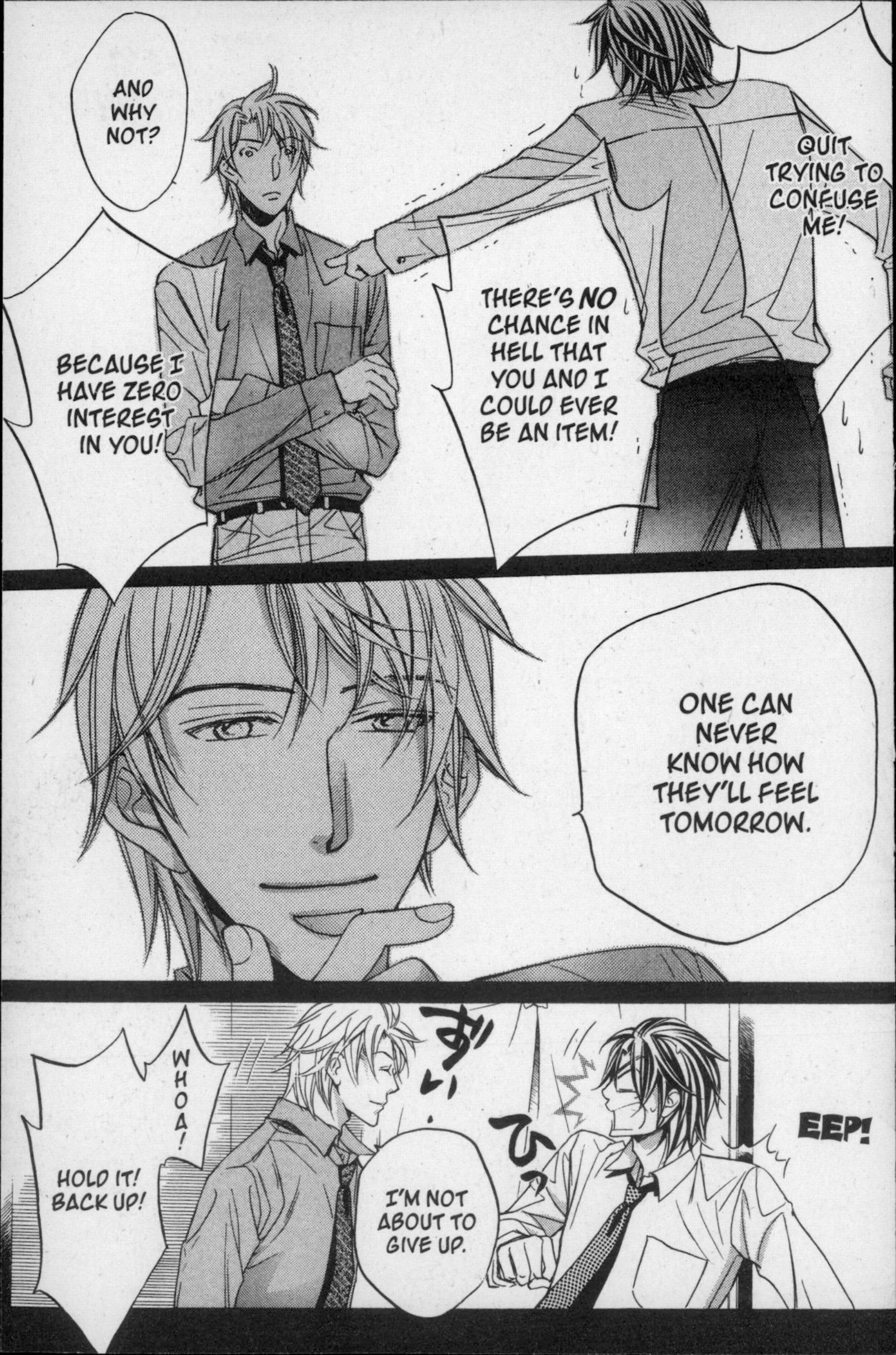
QUIT TRYING TO CONFUSE ME!
THERE'S NO CHANCE IN HELL THAT YOU AND I COULD EVER BE AN ITEM!
AND WHY NOT?
BECAUSE I HAVE ZERO INTEREST IN YOU!
ONE CAN NEVER KNOW HOW THEY'LL FEEL TOMORROW.
EEP!
ひっ
ずい
I'M NOT ABOUT TO GIVE UP.
WHOA!
HOLD IT! BACK UP!

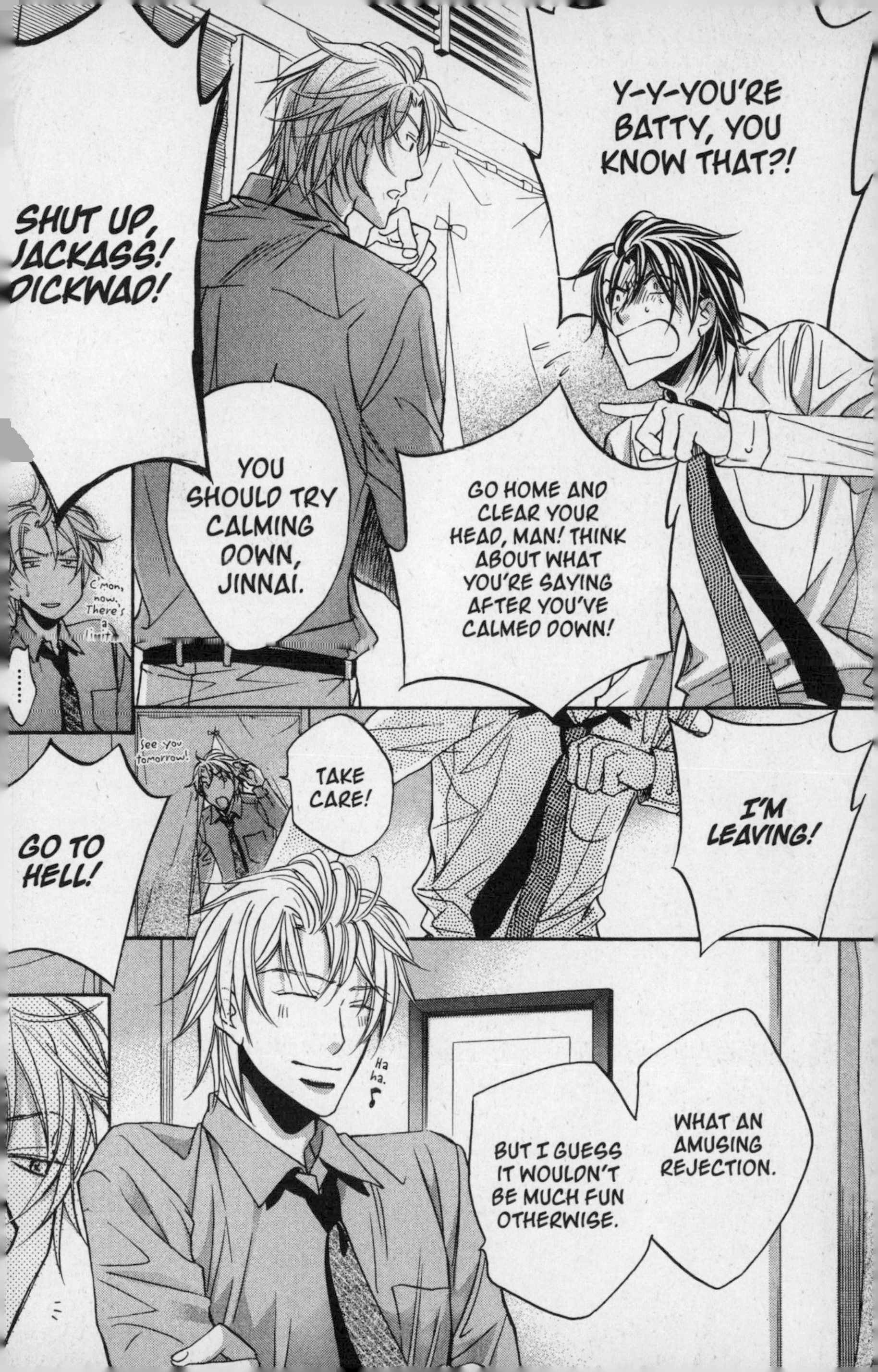
Y-Y-YOU'RE BATTY, YOU KNOW THAT?!
SHUT UP, JACKASS! DICKWAD!
GO HOME AND CLEAR YOUR HEAD, MAN! THINK ABOUT WHAT YOU'RE SAYING AFTER YOU'VE CALMED DOWN!
YOU SHOULD TRY CALMING DOWN, JINNAI.
C'mon, now. There's a limit.
......
I'M LEAVING!
TAKE CARE!
See you tomorrow!
GO TO HELL!
WHAT AN AMUSING REJECTION.
BUT I GUESS IT WOULDN'T BE MUCH FUN OTHERWISE.
Ha ha.

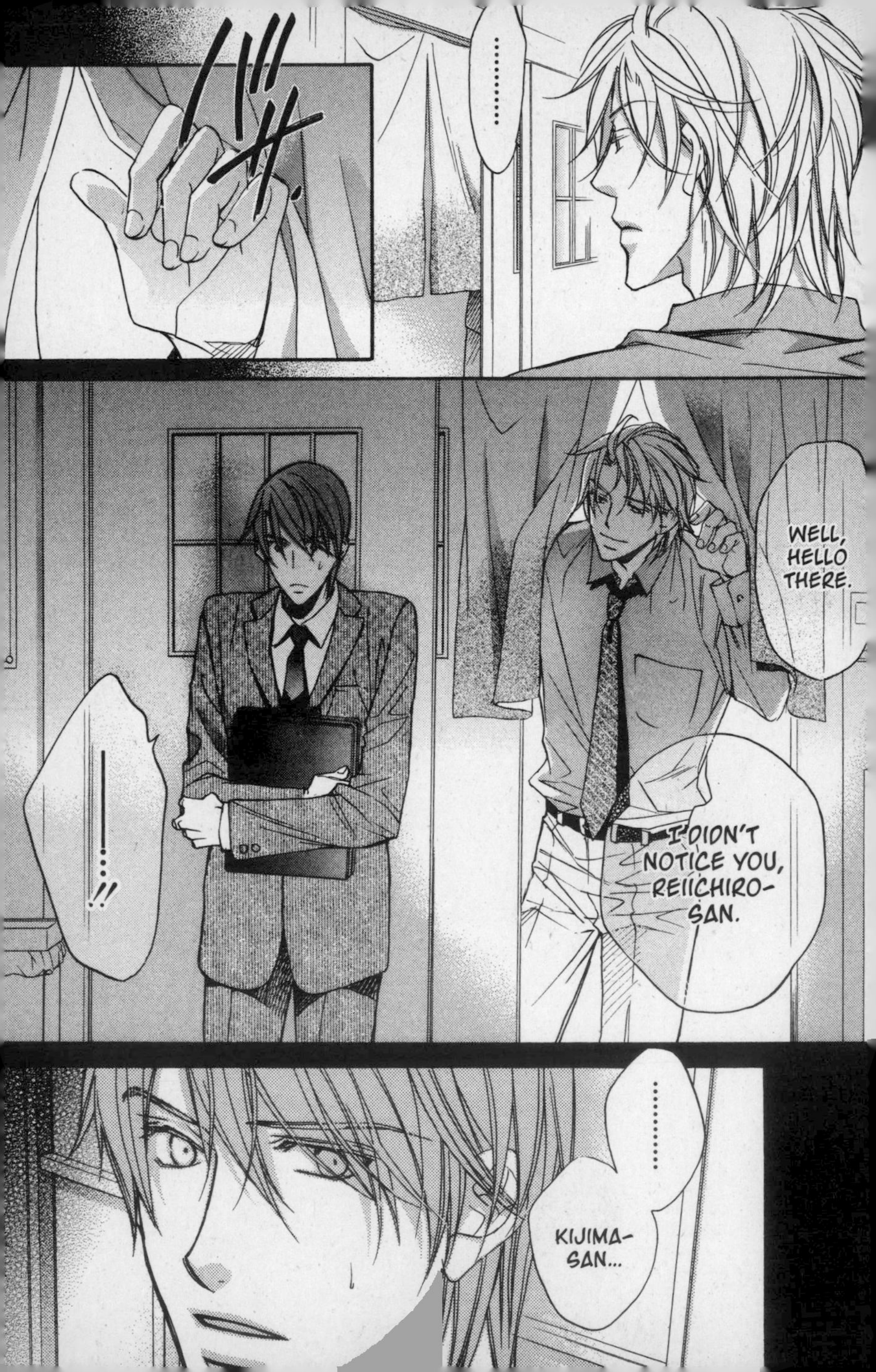
......
WELL, HELLO THERE.
I DIDN'T NOTICE YOU, REIICHIRO-SAN.
......!!
......
KIJIMA-SAN...

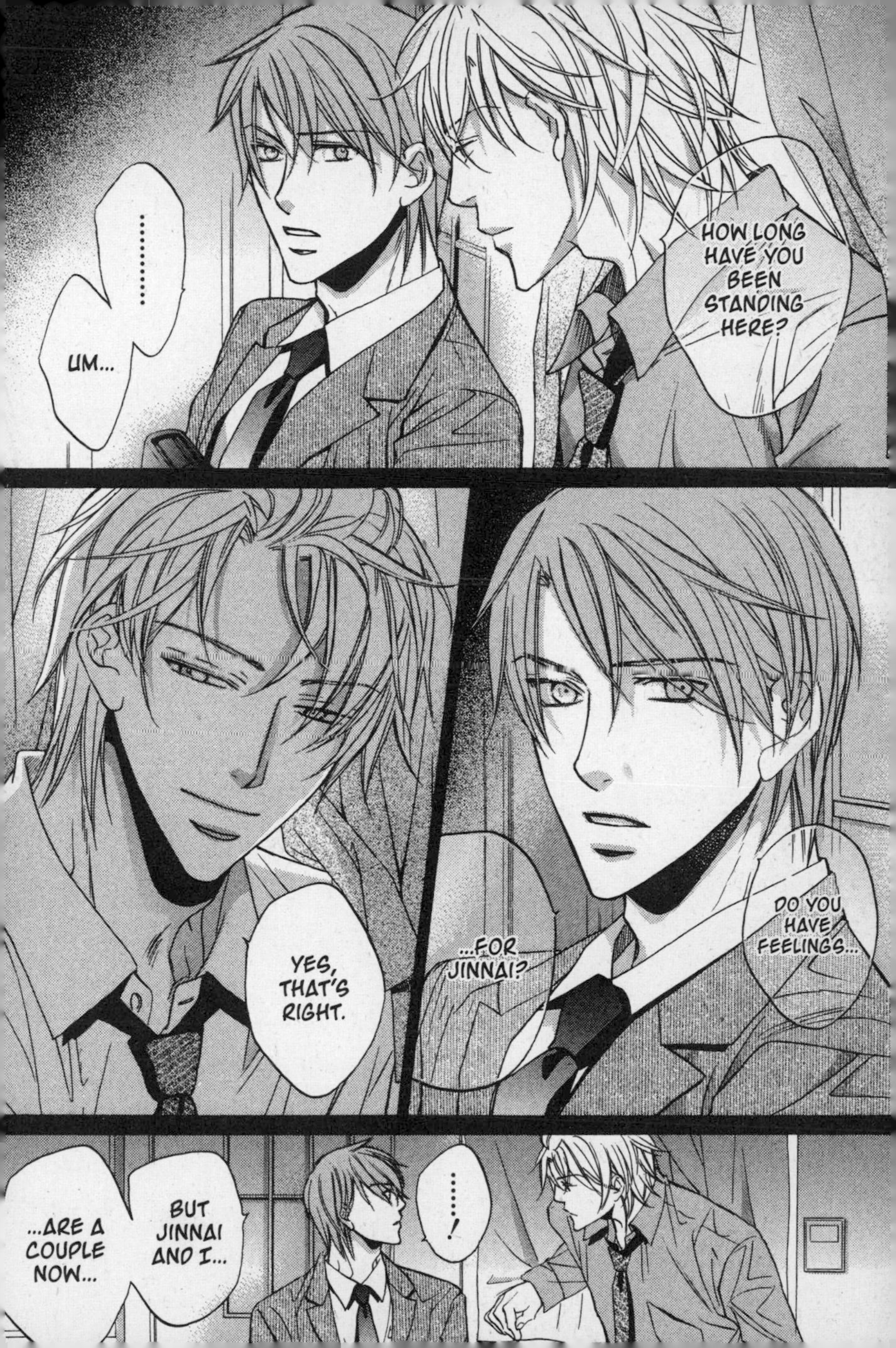
HOW LONG HAVE YOU BEEN STANDING HERE?
......
UM...
DO YOU HAVE FEELINGS...
...FOR JINNAI?
YES, THAT'S RIGHT.
......!
BUT JINNAI AND I...
...ARE A COUPLE NOW...

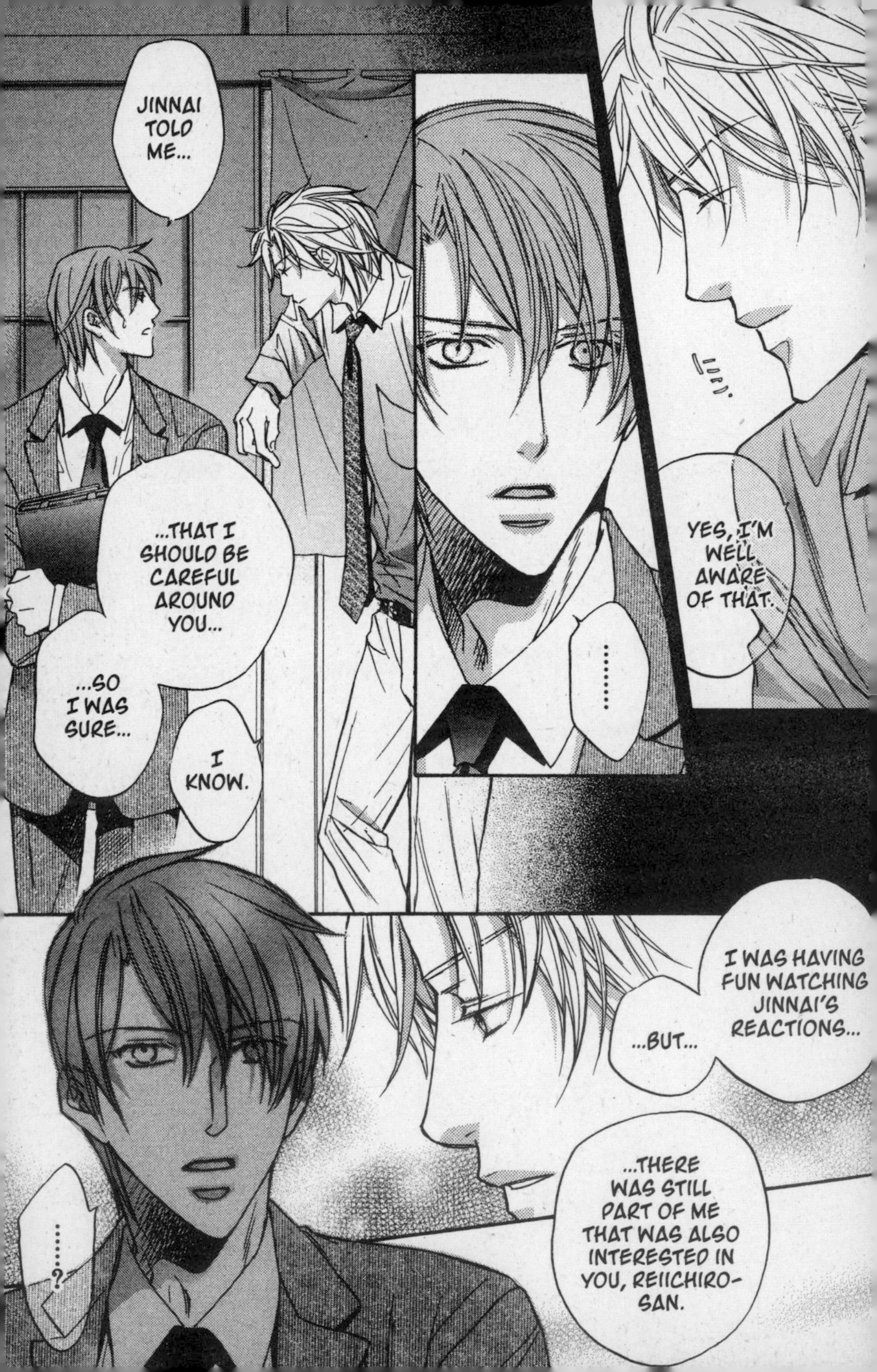
YES, I'M WELL AWARE OF THAT.
......
JINNAI TOLD ME...
...THAT I SHOULD BE CAREFUL AROUND YOU...
...SO I WAS SURE...
I KNOW.
I WAS HAVING FUN WATCHING JINNAI'S REACTIONS...
...BUT...
...THERE WAS STILL PART OF ME THAT WAS ALSO INTERESTED IN YOU, REIICHIRO-SAN.
......?

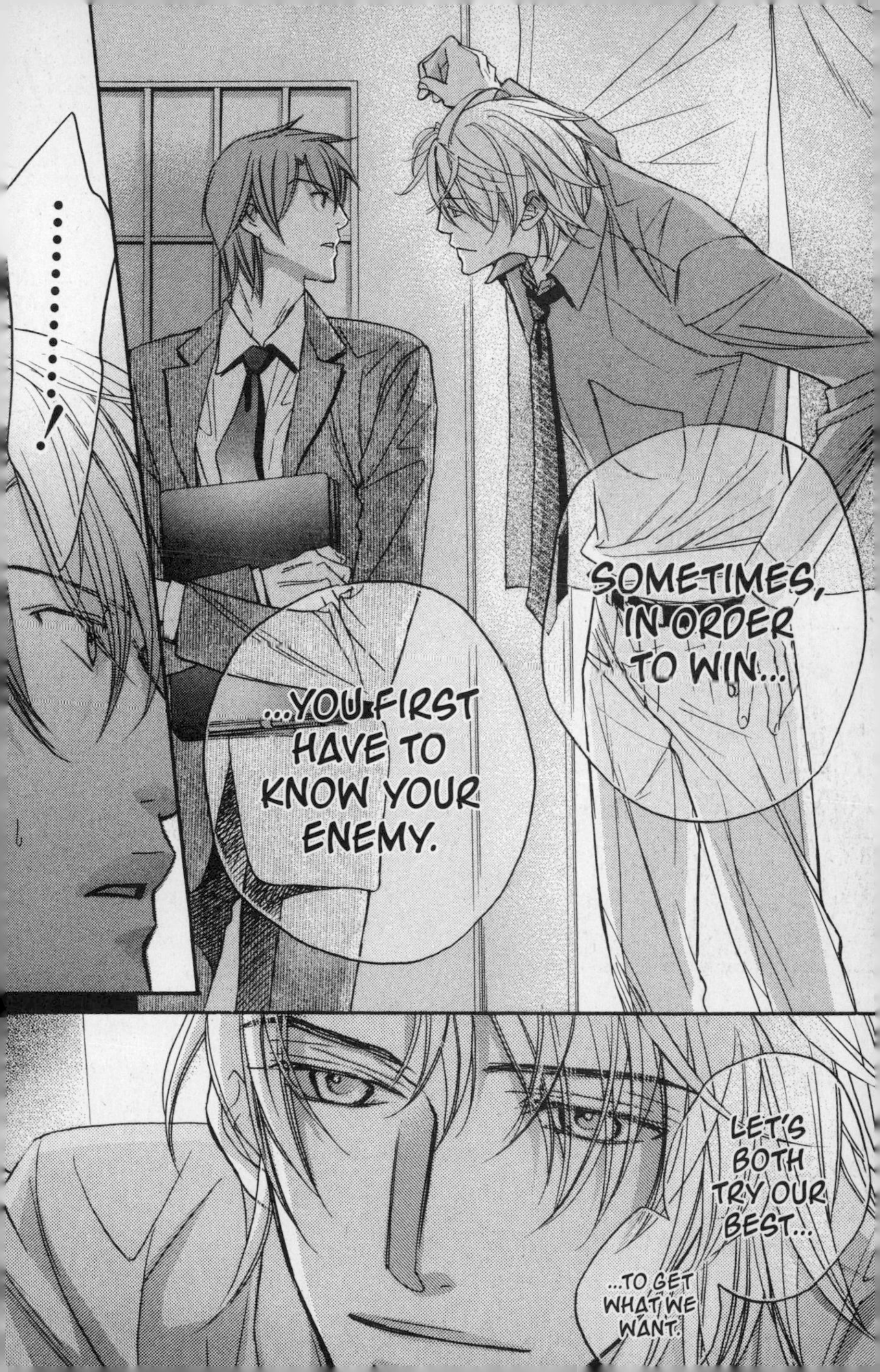
SOMETIMES, IN ORDER TO WIN...
...YOU FIRST HAVE TO KNOW YOUR ENEMY.
......!
LET'S BOTH TRY OUR BEST...
...TO GET WHAT WE WANT.

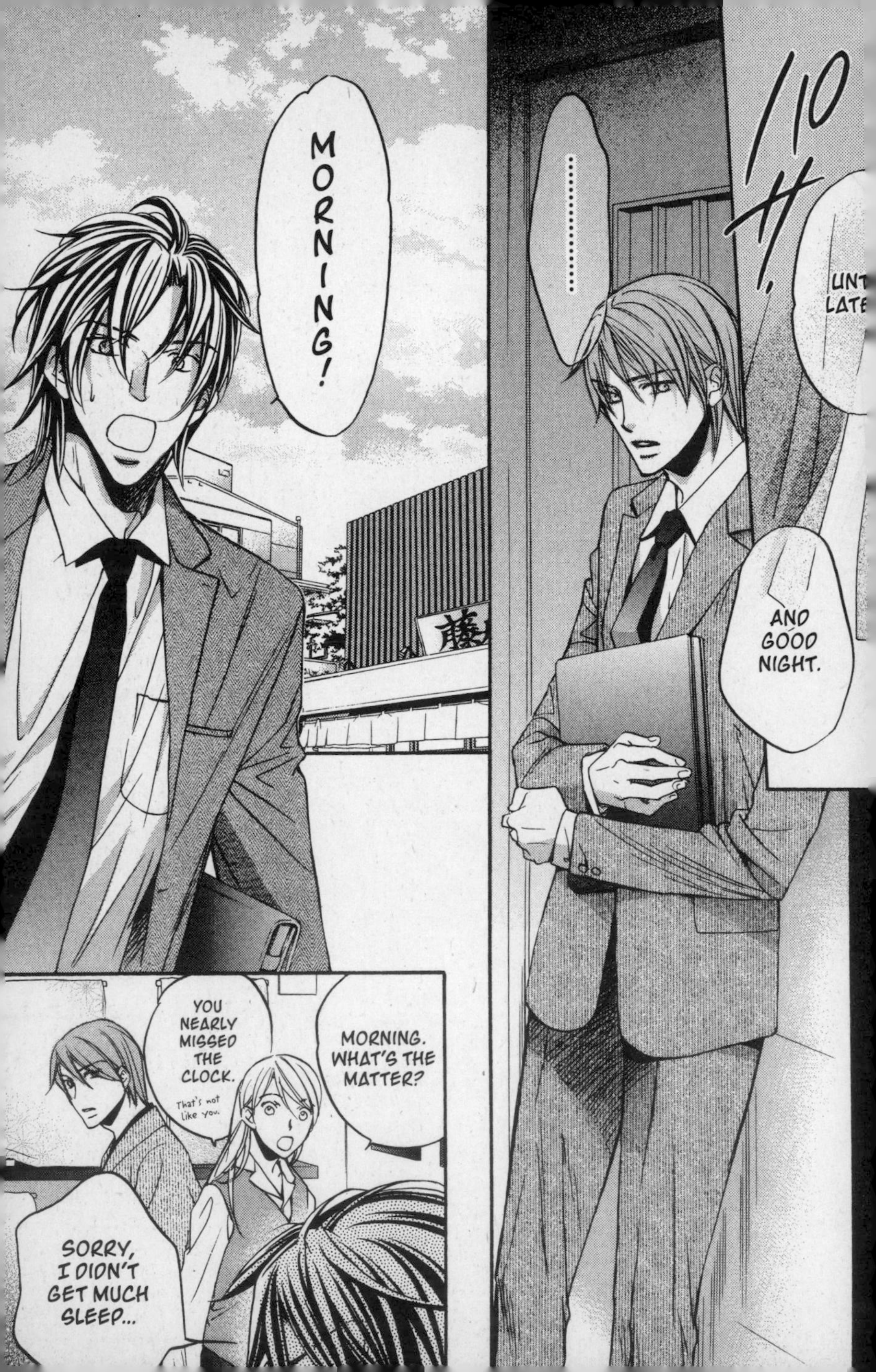
UNT
LATE
AND GOOD NIGHT.
......
MORNING!
MORNING. WHAT'S THE MATTER?
YOU NEARLY MISSED THE CLOCK.
That's not like you.
SORRY, I DIDN'T GET MUCH SLEEP...

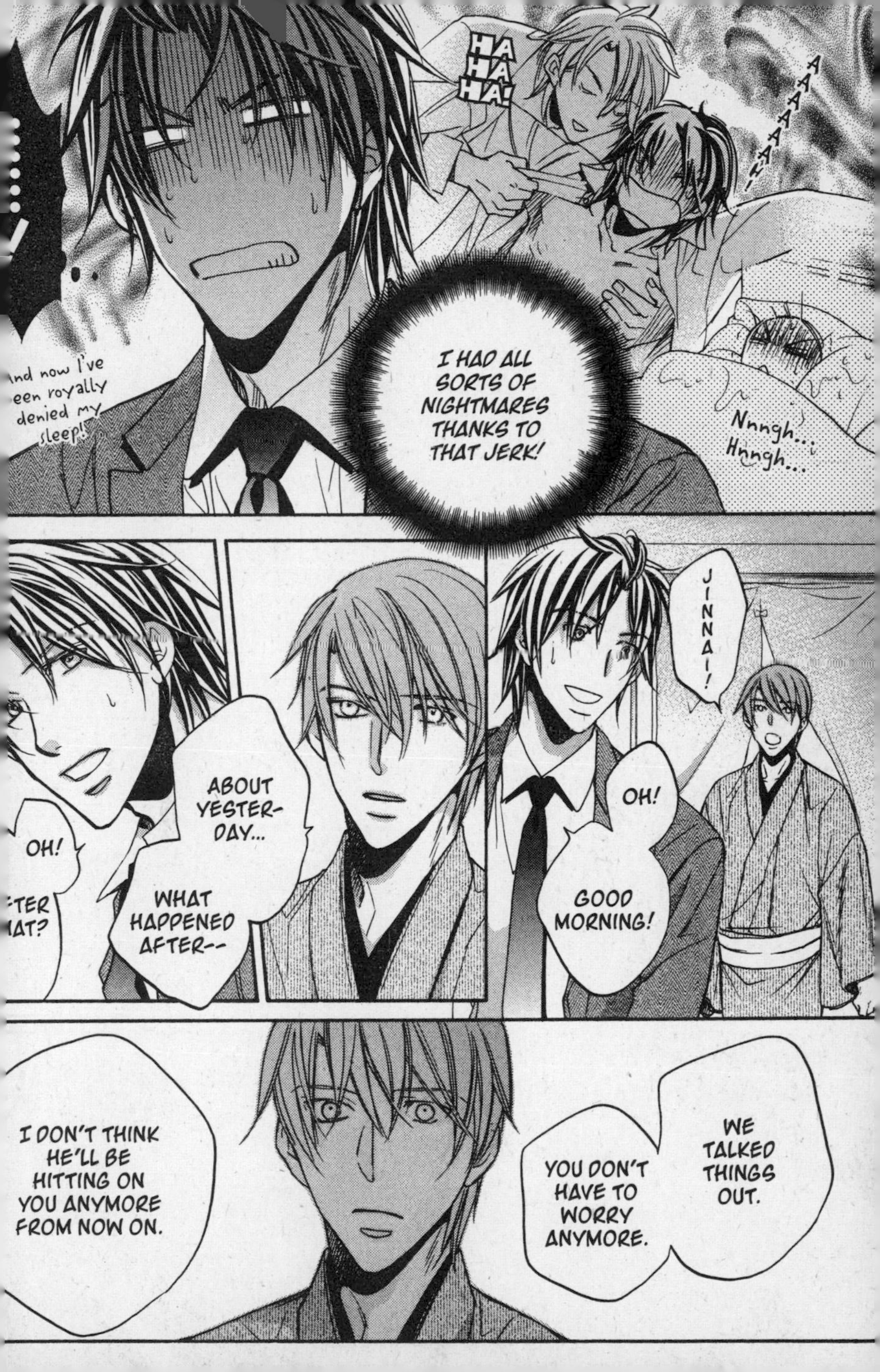
AAAAAAAH!
HA HA HA HA!
Nnngh... Hnngh...
I HAD ALL SORTS OF NIGHTMARES THANKS TO THAT JERK!
And now I've been royally denied my sleep!!
JINNAI!
OH!
GOOD MORNING!
ABOUT YESTERDAY...
WHAT HAPPENED AFTER--
OH!
TER AT?
WE TALKED THINGS OUT.
YOU DON'T HAVE TO WORRY ANYMORE.
I DON'T THINK HE'LL BE HITTING ON YOU ANYMORE FROM NOW ON.

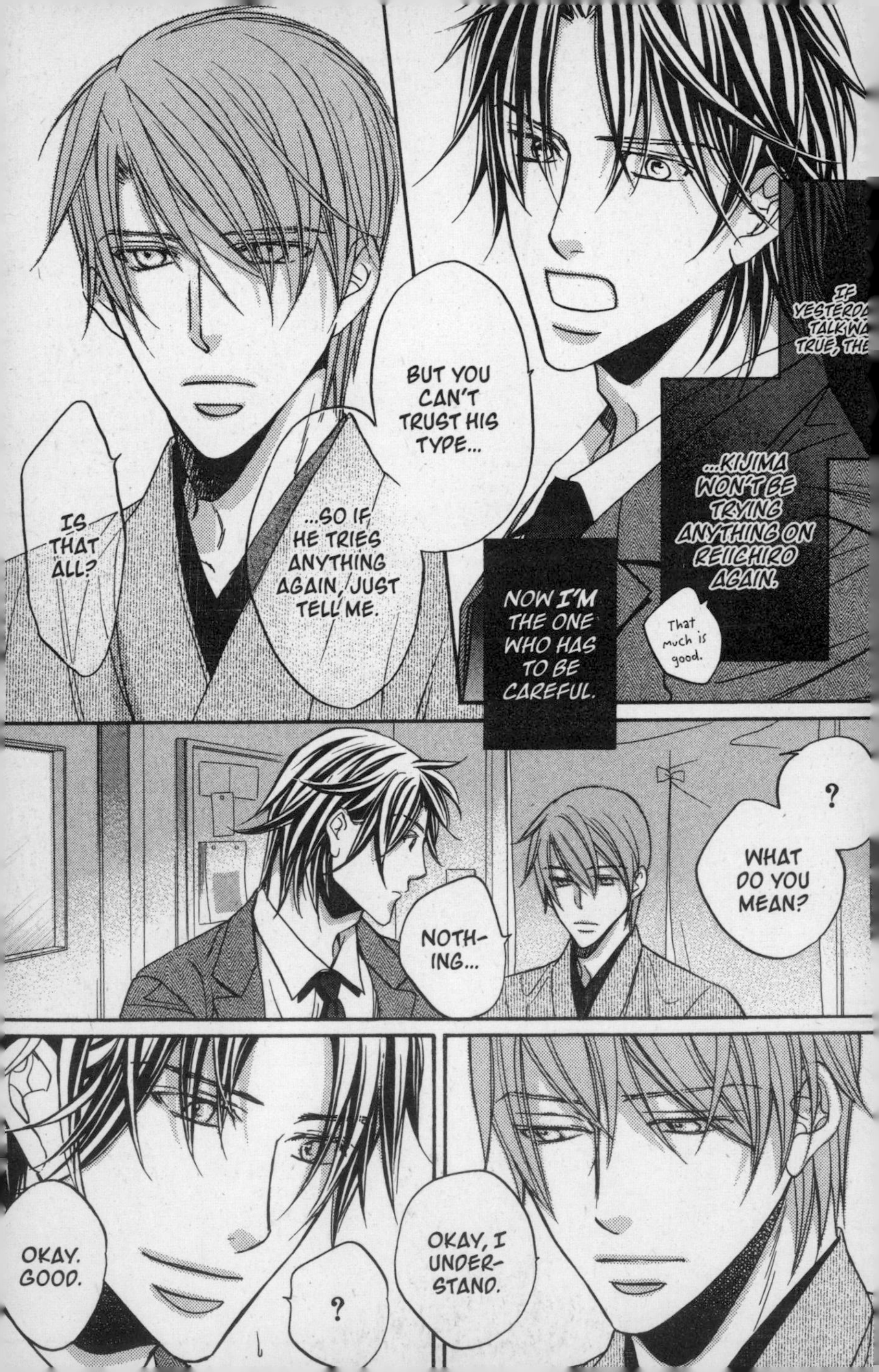
IF YESTERD
TALK WA
TRUE, THE
...KIJIMA WON'T BE TRYING ANYTHING ON REIICHIRO AGAIN.
That much is good.
NOW I'M THE ONE WHO HAS TO BE CAREFUL.
BUT YOU CAN'T TRUST HIS TYPE...
...SO IF HE TRIES ANYTHING AGAIN, JUST TELL ME.
IS THAT ALL?
?
WHAT DO YOU MEAN?
NOTH-ING...
OKAY, I UNDER-STAND.
?
OKAY. GOOD.

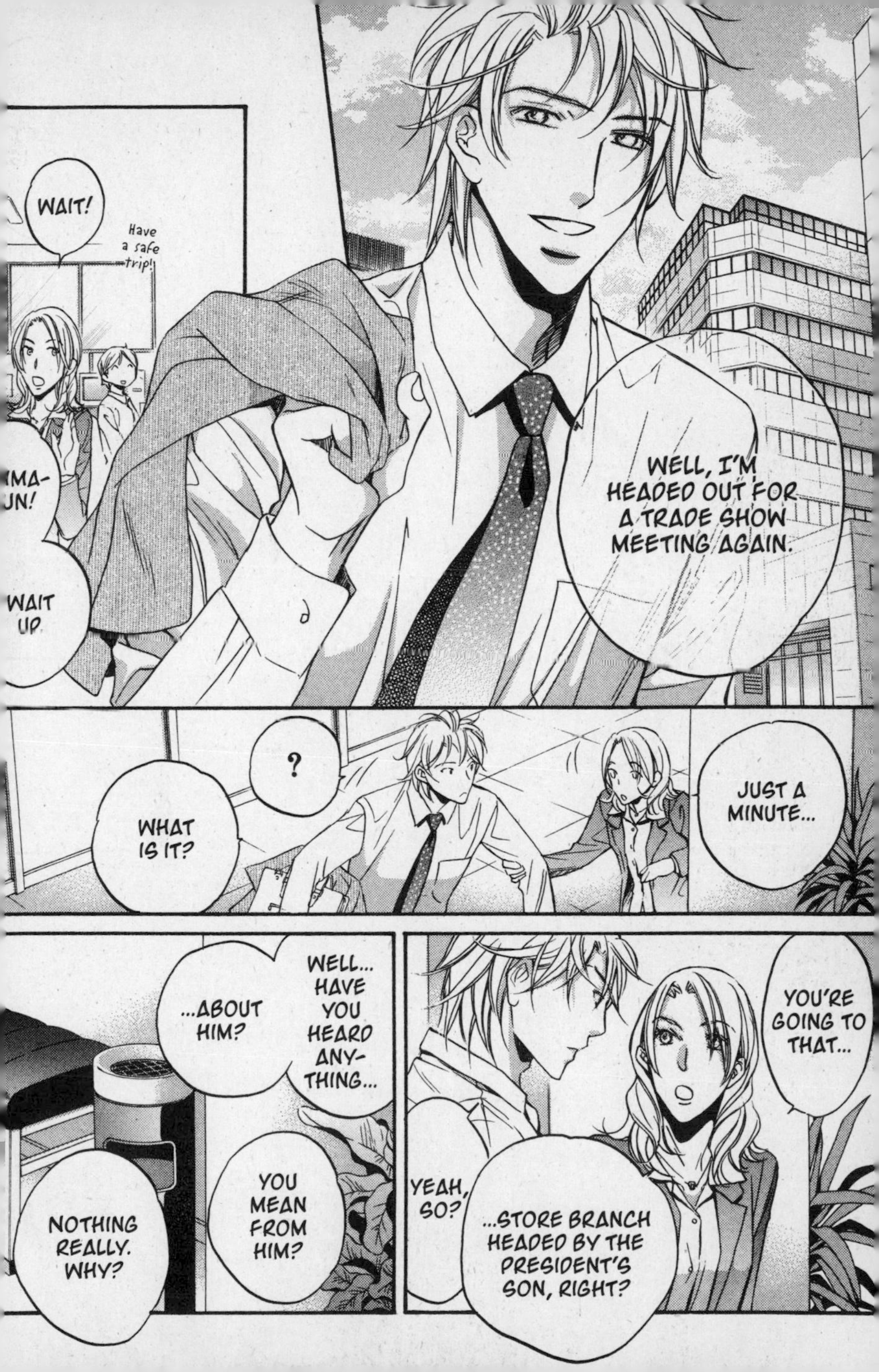
WELL, I'M HEADED OUT FOR A TRADE SHOW MEETING AGAIN.
IMA-UN!
WAIT UP.
WAIT!
Have a safe trip!
JUST A MINUTE...
?
WHAT IS IT?
YOU'RE GOING TO THAT...
...STORE BRANCH HEADED BY THE PRESIDENT'S SON, RIGHT?
YEAH, SO?
WELL... HAVE YOU HEARD ANYTHING...
...ABOUT HIM?
YOU MEAN FROM HIM?
NOTHING REALLY. WHY?

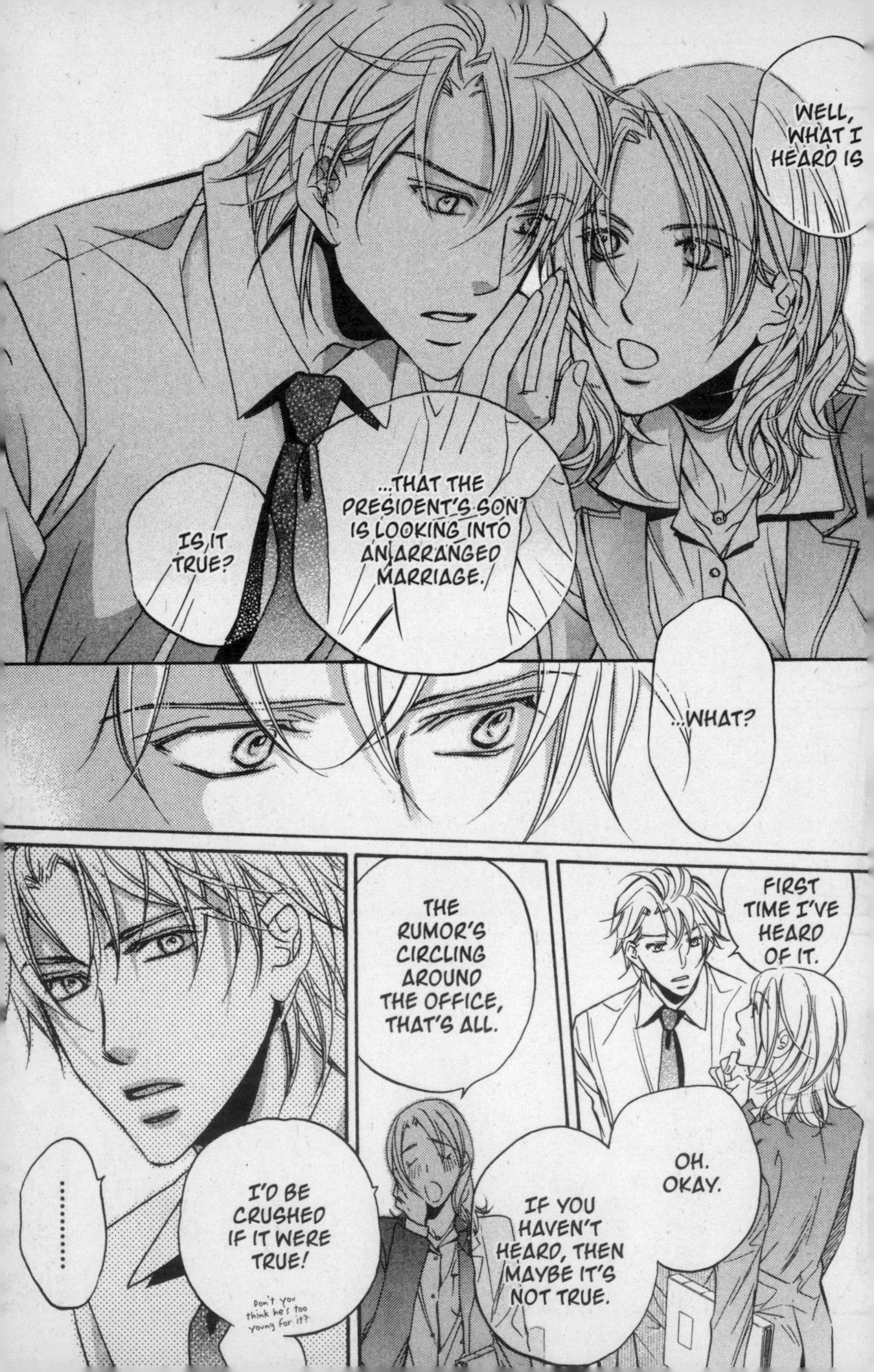
WELL, WHAT I HEARD IS
...THAT THE PRESIDENT'S SON IS LOOKING INTO AN ARRANGED MARRIAGE.
IS IT TRUE?
...WHAT?
FIRST TIME I'VE HEARD OF IT.
THE RUMOR'S CIRCLING AROUND THE OFFICE, THAT'S ALL.
OH. OKAY.
IF YOU HAVEN'T HEARD, THEN MAYBE IT'S NOT TRUE.
I'D BE CRUSHED IF IT WERE TRUE!
Don't you think he's too young for it?
......

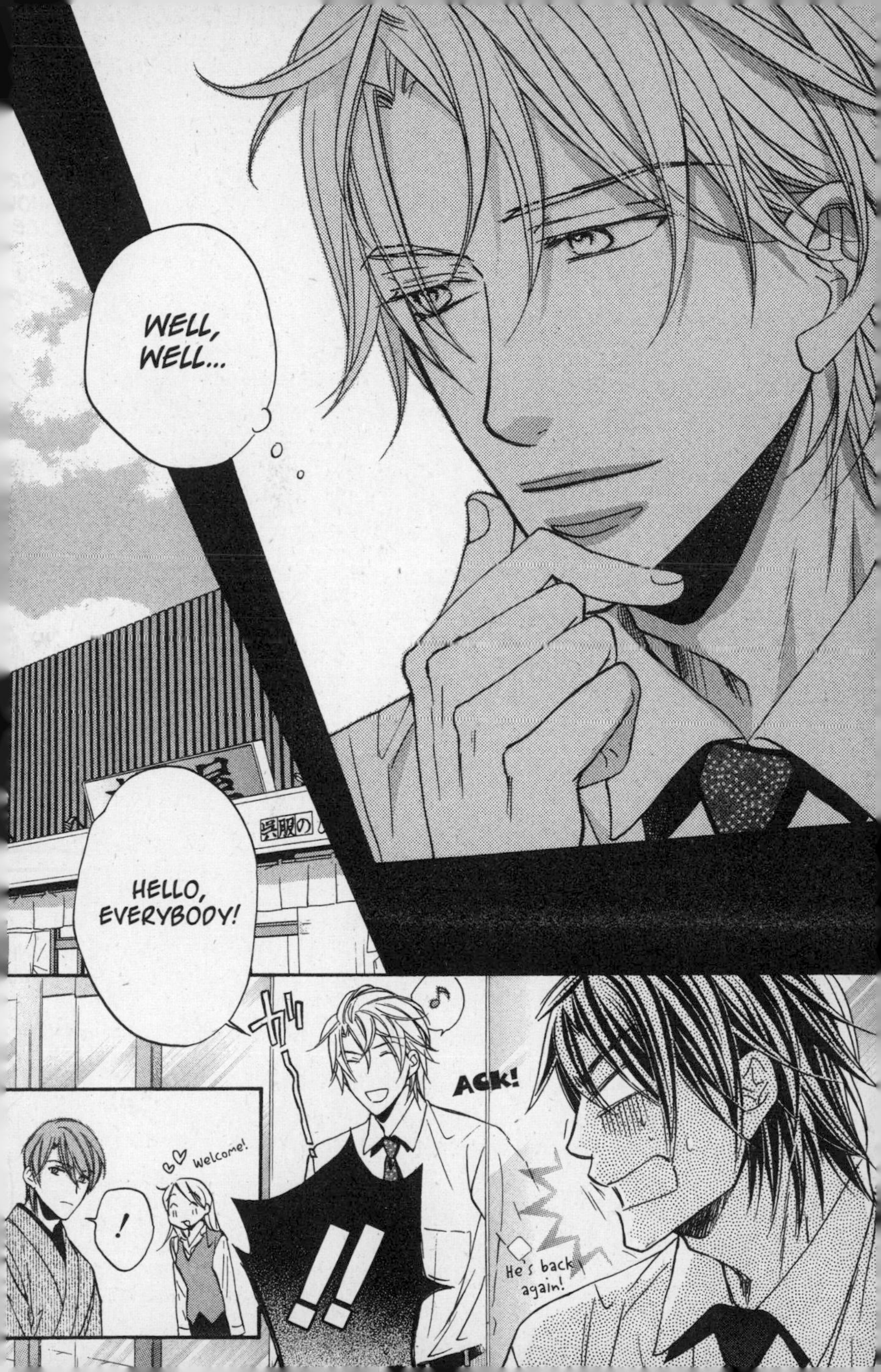
WELL, WELL...
呉服の
HELLO, EVERYBODY!
ACK!
He's back again!
!!
Welcome!
!

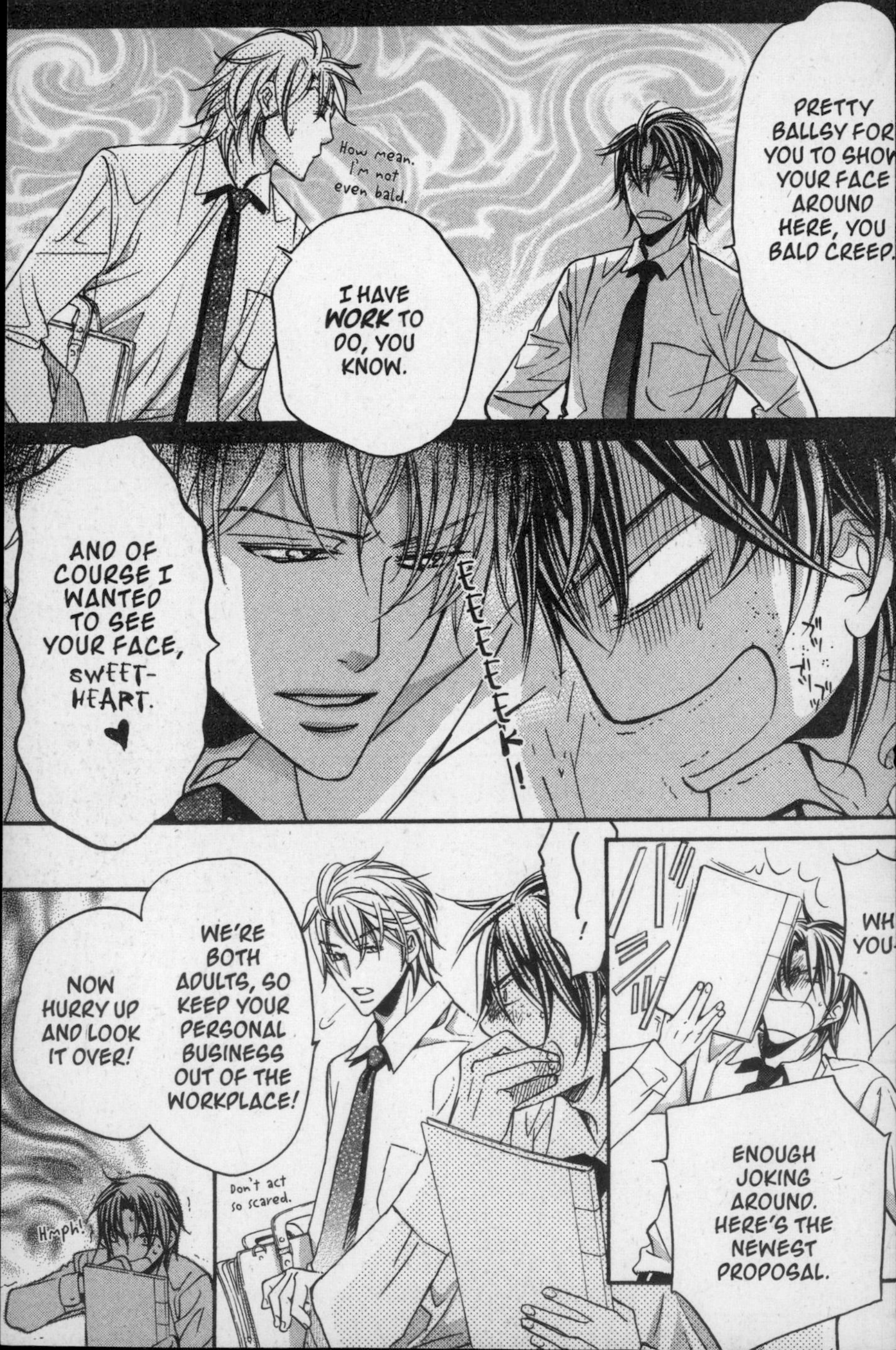
PRETTY BALLSY FOR YOU TO SHOW YOUR FACE AROUND HERE, YOU BALD CREEP.
I HAVE **WORK** TO DO, YOU KNOW.
How mean. I'm not even bald.
AND OF COURSE I WANTED TO SEE YOUR FACE, SWEET-HEART.
EEEEEEEK!
WH- YOU-
!
ENOUGH JOKING AROUND. HERE'S THE NEWEST PROPOSAL.
WE'RE BOTH ADULTS, SO KEEP YOUR PERSONAL BUSINESS OUT OF THE WORKPLACE!
Don't act so scared.
NOW HURRY UP AND LOOK IT OVER!
Hmph!

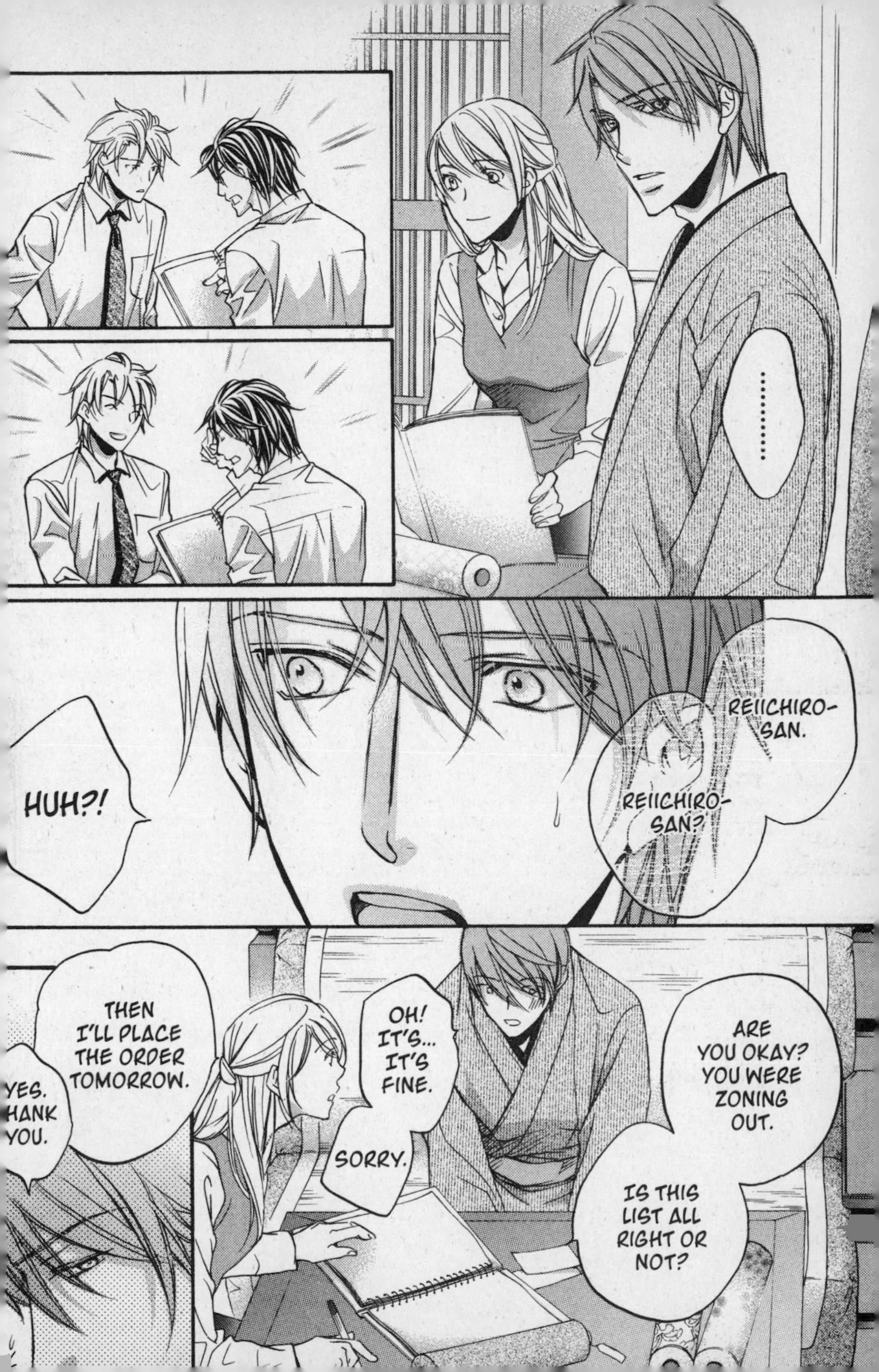
......
REIICHIRO-SAN.
REIICHIRO-SAN?
HUH?!
ARE YOU OKAY? YOU WERE ZONING OUT.
IS THIS LIST ALL RIGHT OR NOT?
OH! IT'S... IT'S FINE.
SORRY.
THEN I'LL PLACE THE ORDER TOMORROW.
YES. HANK YOU.

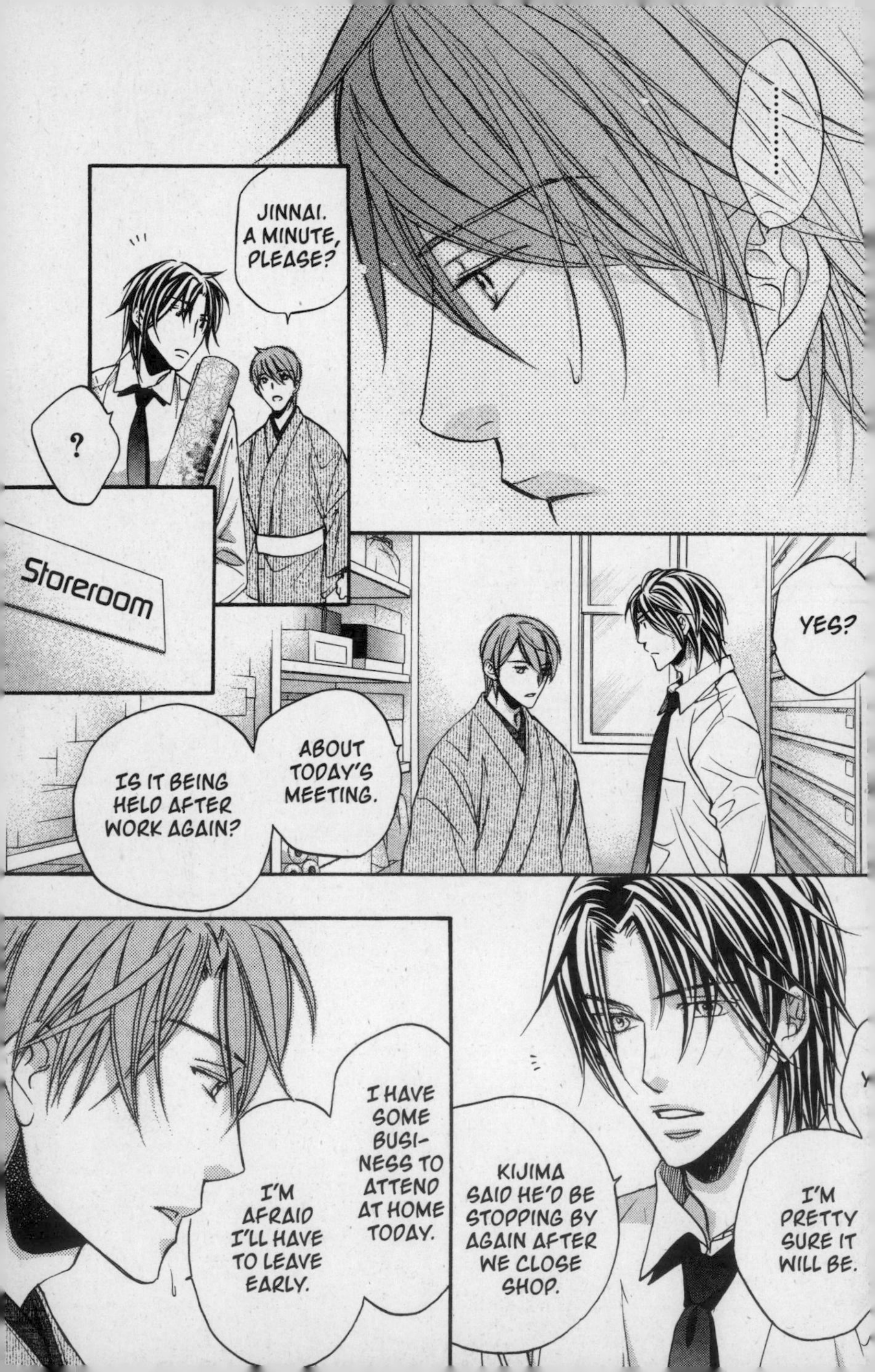
......
JINNAI. A MINUTE, PLEASE?
?
Storeroom
YES?
ABOUT TODAY'S MEETING.
IS IT BEING HELD AFTER WORK AGAIN?
I'M PRETTY SURE IT WILL BE.
KIJIMA SAID HE'D BE STOPPING BY AGAIN AFTER WE CLOSE SHOP.
I HAVE SOME BUSI-NESS TO ATTEND AT HOME TODAY.
I'M AFRAID I'LL HAVE TO LEAVE EARLY.

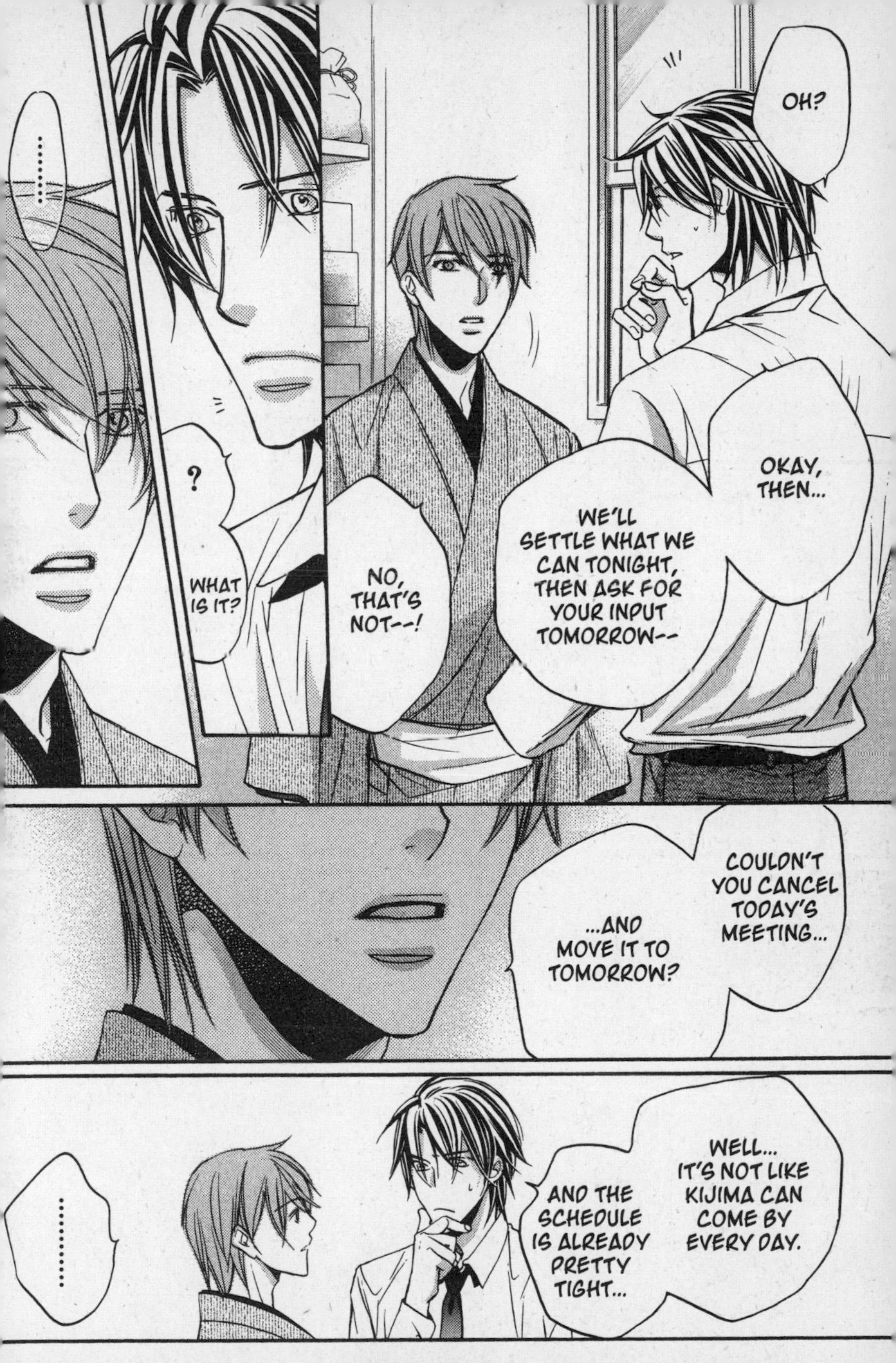
OH?
OKAY, THEN...
WE'LL SETTLE WHAT WE CAN TONIGHT, THEN ASK FOR YOUR INPUT TOMORROW--
NO, THAT'S NOT--!
WHAT IS IT?
?
......
COULDN'T YOU CANCEL TODAY'S MEETING...
...AND MOVE IT TO TOMORROW?
WELL... IT'S NOT LIKE KIJIMA CAN COME BY EVERY DAY.
AND THE SCHEDULE IS ALREADY PRETTY TIGHT...
......

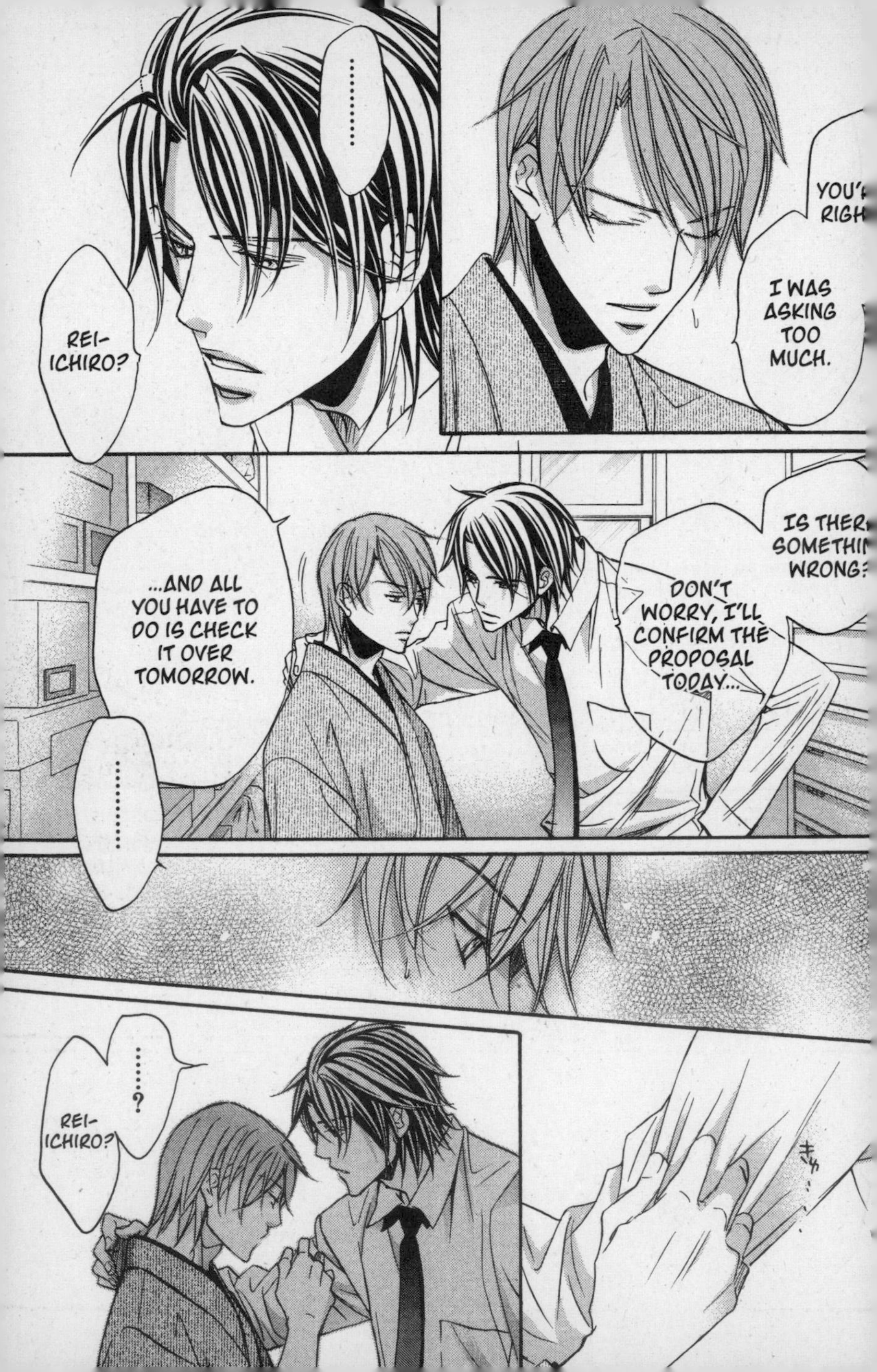
YOU'
RIGH
I WAS ASKING TOO MUCH.
......
REI-ICHIRO?
IS THER SOMETHIN WRONG?
DON'T WORRY, I'LL CONFIRM THE PROPOSAL TODAY...
...AND ALL YOU HAVE TO DO IS CHECK IT OVER TOMORROW.
......
きゅ…
......?
REI-ICHIRO?

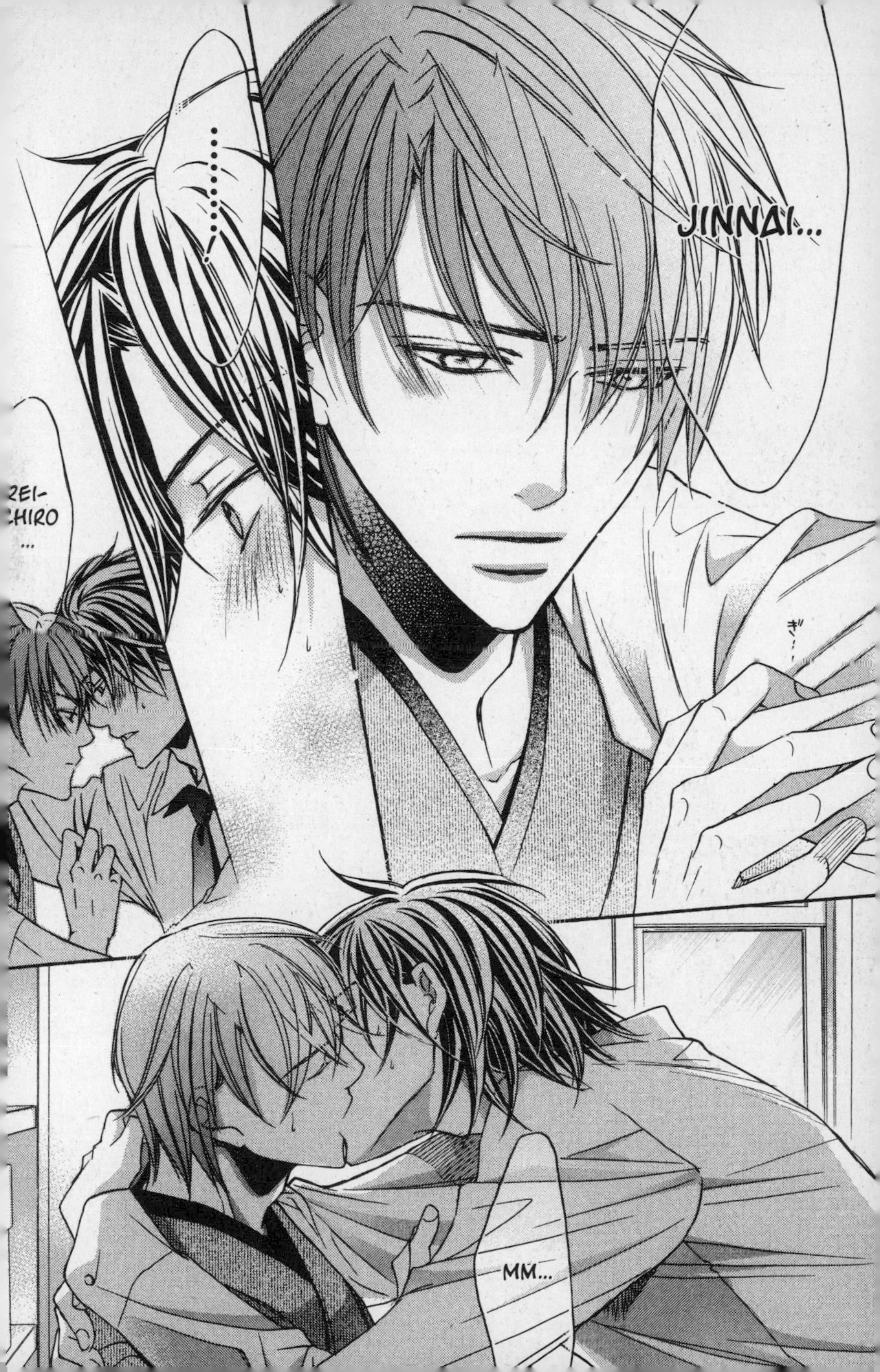
JINNAI...
......!
REI-
CHIRO
...
MM...

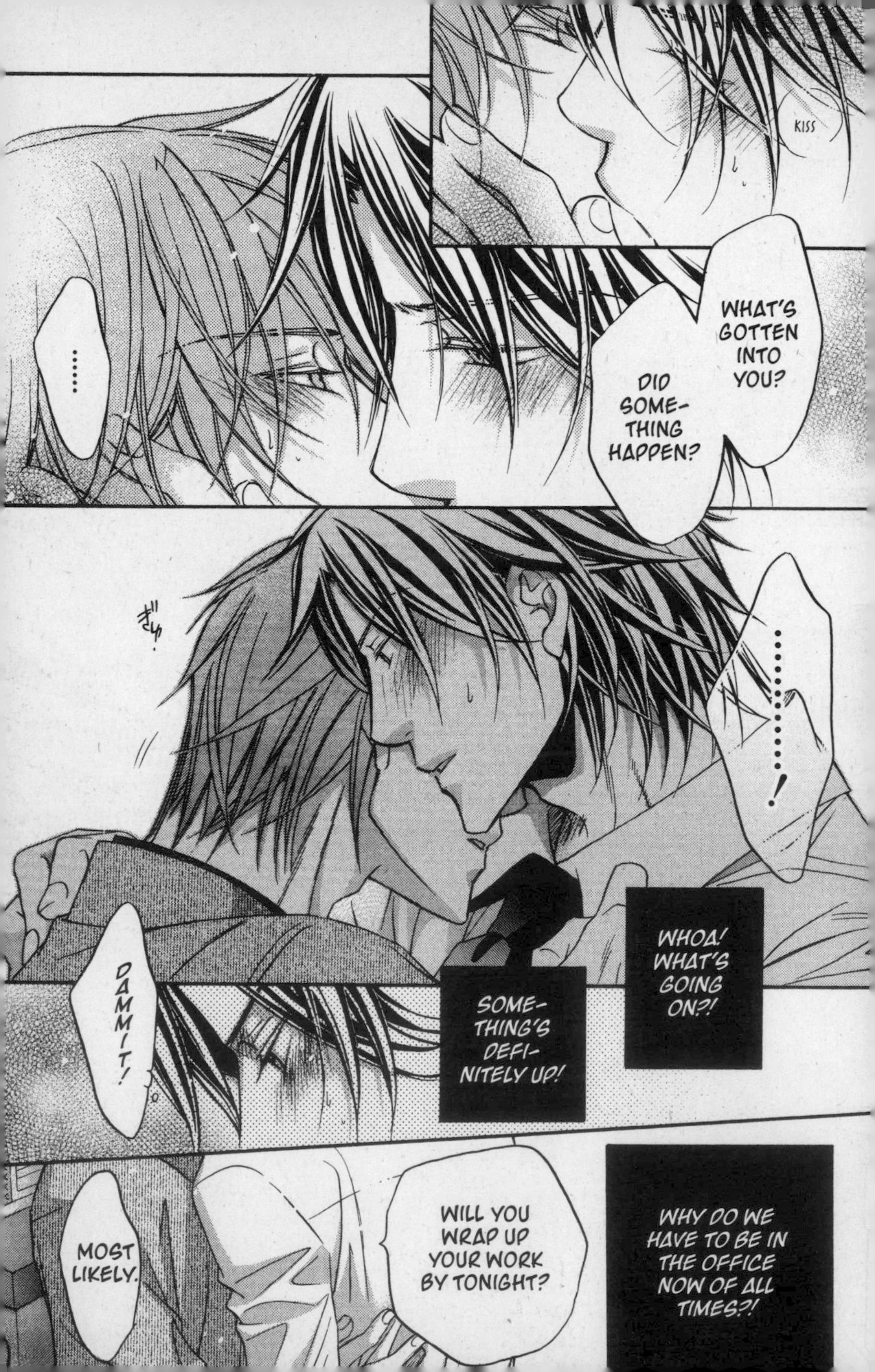
KISS
WHAT'S GOTTEN INTO YOU?
DID SOME-THING HAPPEN?
......
......!
WHOA! WHAT'S GOING ON?!
SOME-THING'S DEFI-NITELY UP!
DAMMIT!
WHY DO WE HAVE TO BE IN THE OFFICE NOW OF ALL TIMES?!
WILL YOU WRAP UP YOUR WORK BY TONIGHT?
MOST LIKELY.

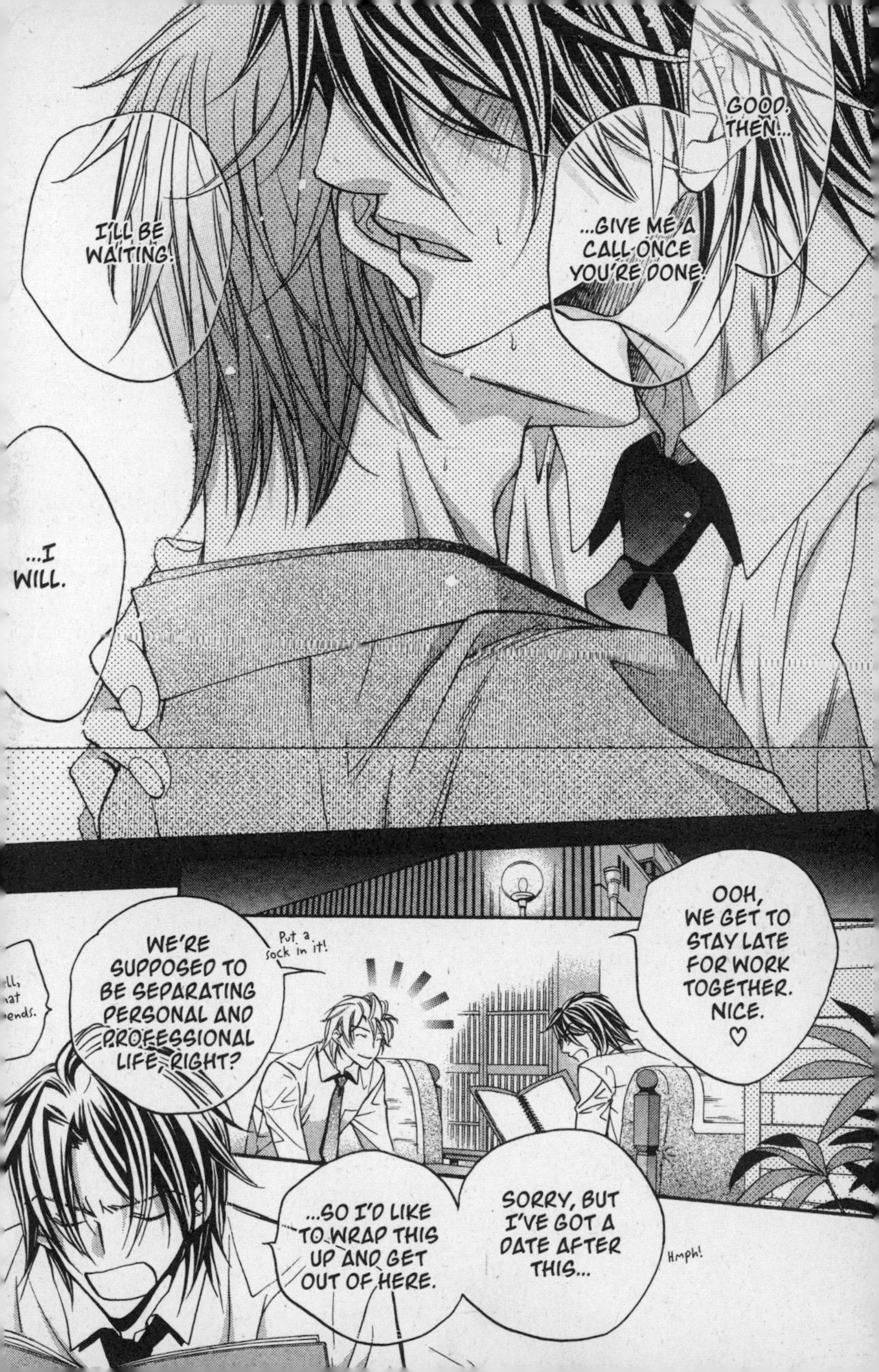
GOOD. THEN...
...GIVE ME A CALL ONCE YOU'RE DONE.
I'LL BE WAITING!
...I WILL.
OOH, WE GET TO STAY LATE FOR WORK TOGETHER. NICE. ♡
WE'RE SUPPOSED TO BE SEPARATING PERSONAL AND PROFESSIONAL LIFE, RIGHT?
Put a sock in it!
SORRY, BUT I'VE GOT A DATE AFTER THIS...
Hmph!
...SO I'D LIKE TO WRAP THIS UP AND GET OUT OF HERE.

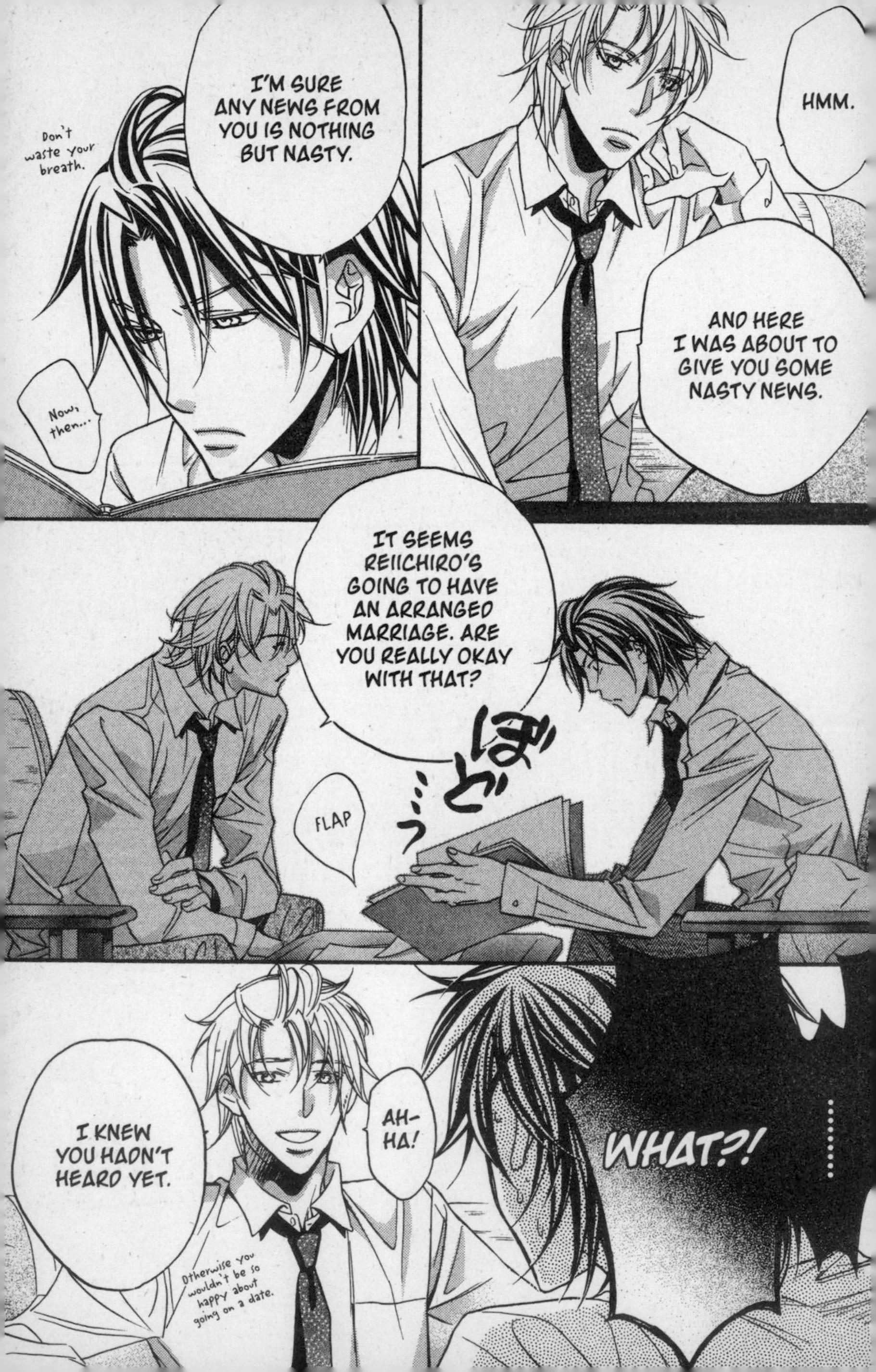
HMM.
AND HERE I WAS ABOUT TO GIVE YOU SOME NASTY NEWS.
I'M SURE ANY NEWS FROM YOU IS NOTHING BUT NASTY.
Don't waste your breath.
Now, then...
IT SEEMS REIICHIRO'S GOING TO HAVE AN ARRANGED MARRIAGE. ARE YOU REALLY OKAY WITH THAT?
ぼどっ
FLAP
......
WHAT?!
AH-HA!
I KNEW YOU HADN'T HEARD YET.
Otherwise you wouldn't be so happy about going on a date.

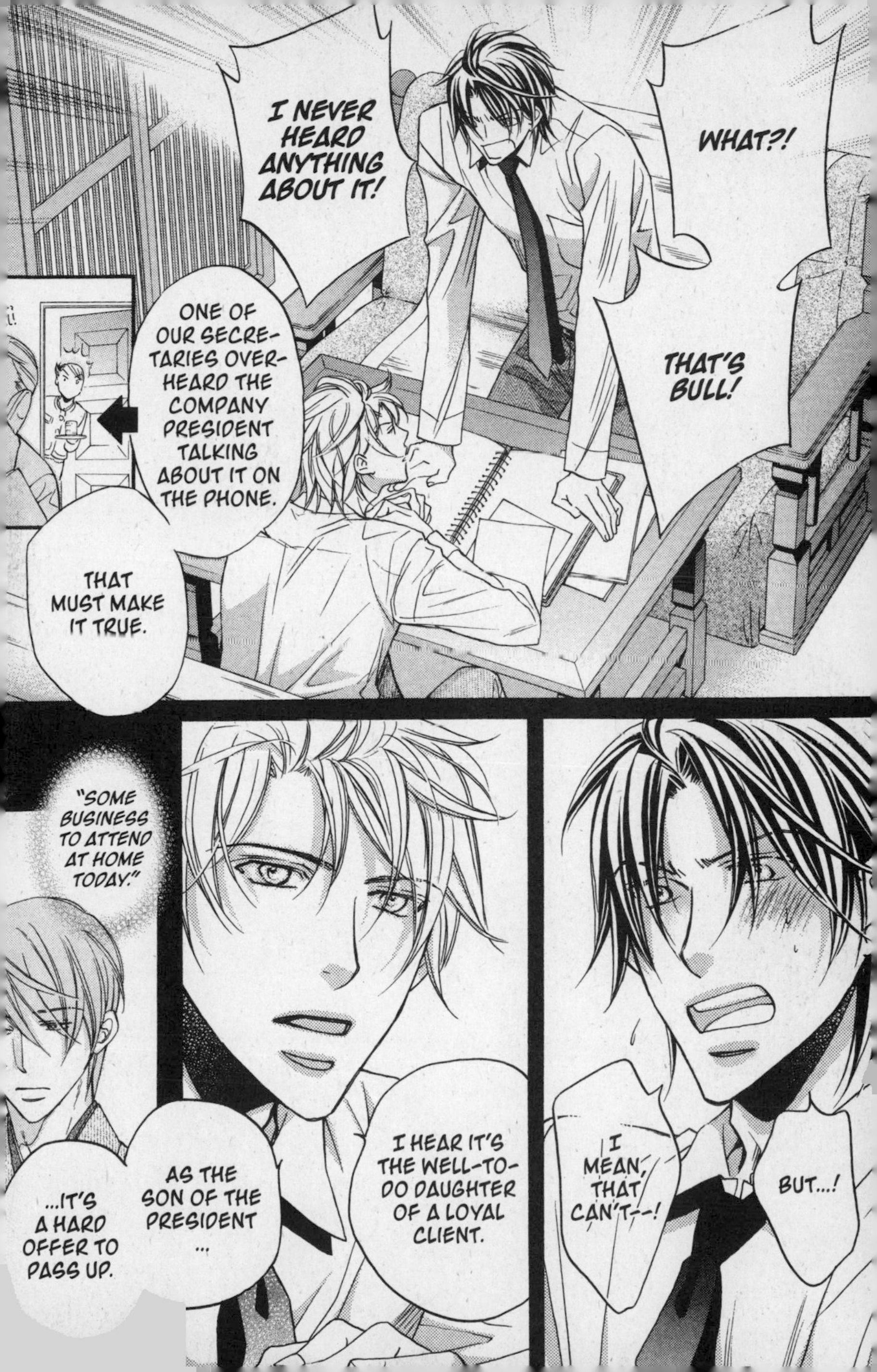
WHAT?!
THAT'S BULL!
I NEVER HEARD ANYTHING ABOUT IT!
ONE OF OUR SECRETARIES OVERHEARD THE COMPANY PRESIDENT TALKING ABOUT IT ON THE PHONE.
THAT MUST MAKE IT TRUE.
BUT...!
I MEAN, THAT CAN'T--!
I HEAR IT'S THE WELL-TO-DO DAUGHTER OF A LOYAL CLIENT.
AS THE SON OF THE PRESIDENT ...
...IT'S A HARD OFFER TO PASS UP.
"SOME BUSINESS TO ATTEND AT HOME TODAY."

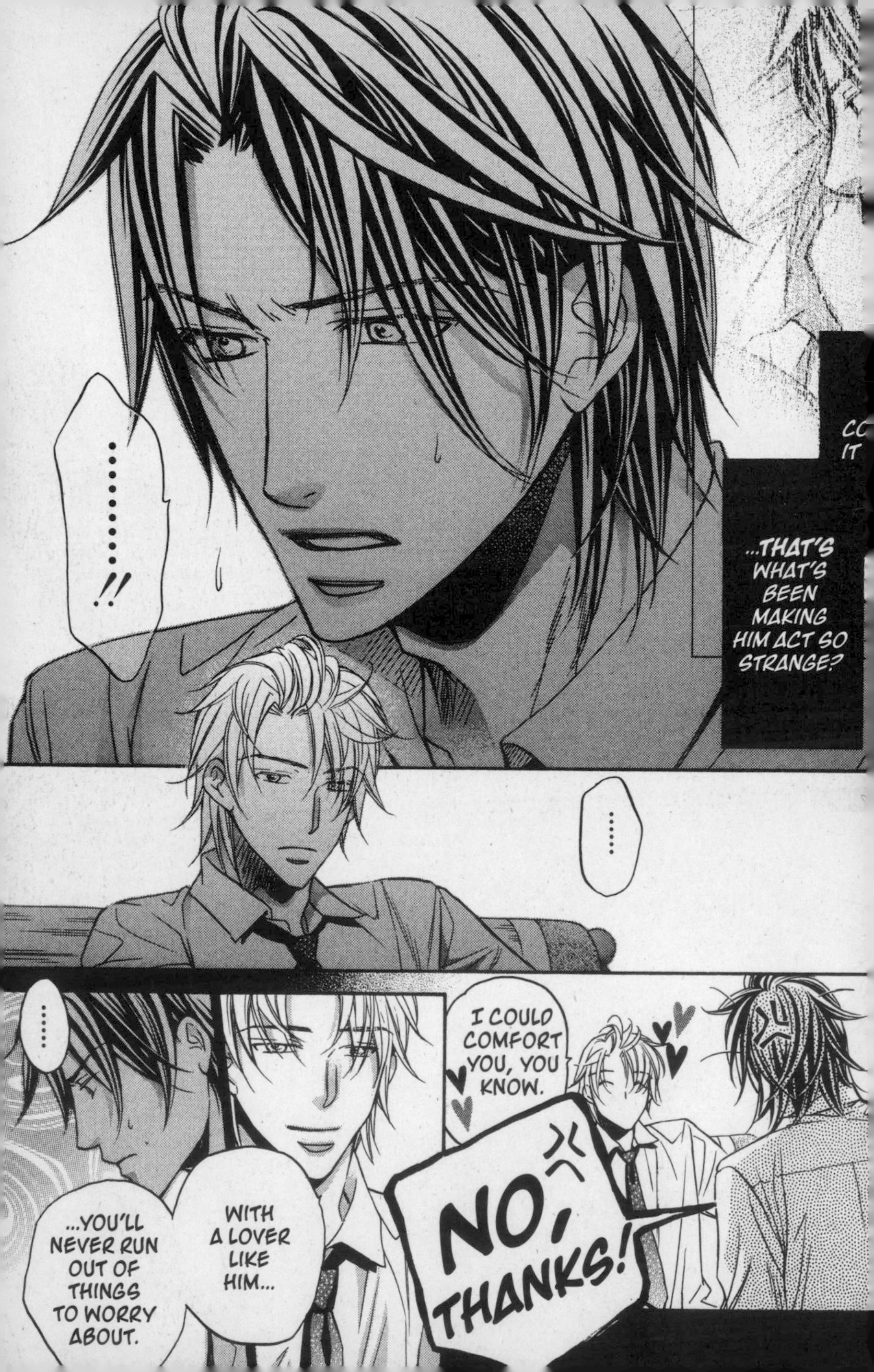
...THAT'S WHAT'S BEEN MAKING HIM ACT SO STRANGE?
........!!
......
I COULD COMFORT YOU, YOU KNOW.
NO, THANKS!
WITH A LOVER LIKE HIM...
...YOU'LL NEVER RUN OUT OF THINGS TO WORRY ABOUT.
......

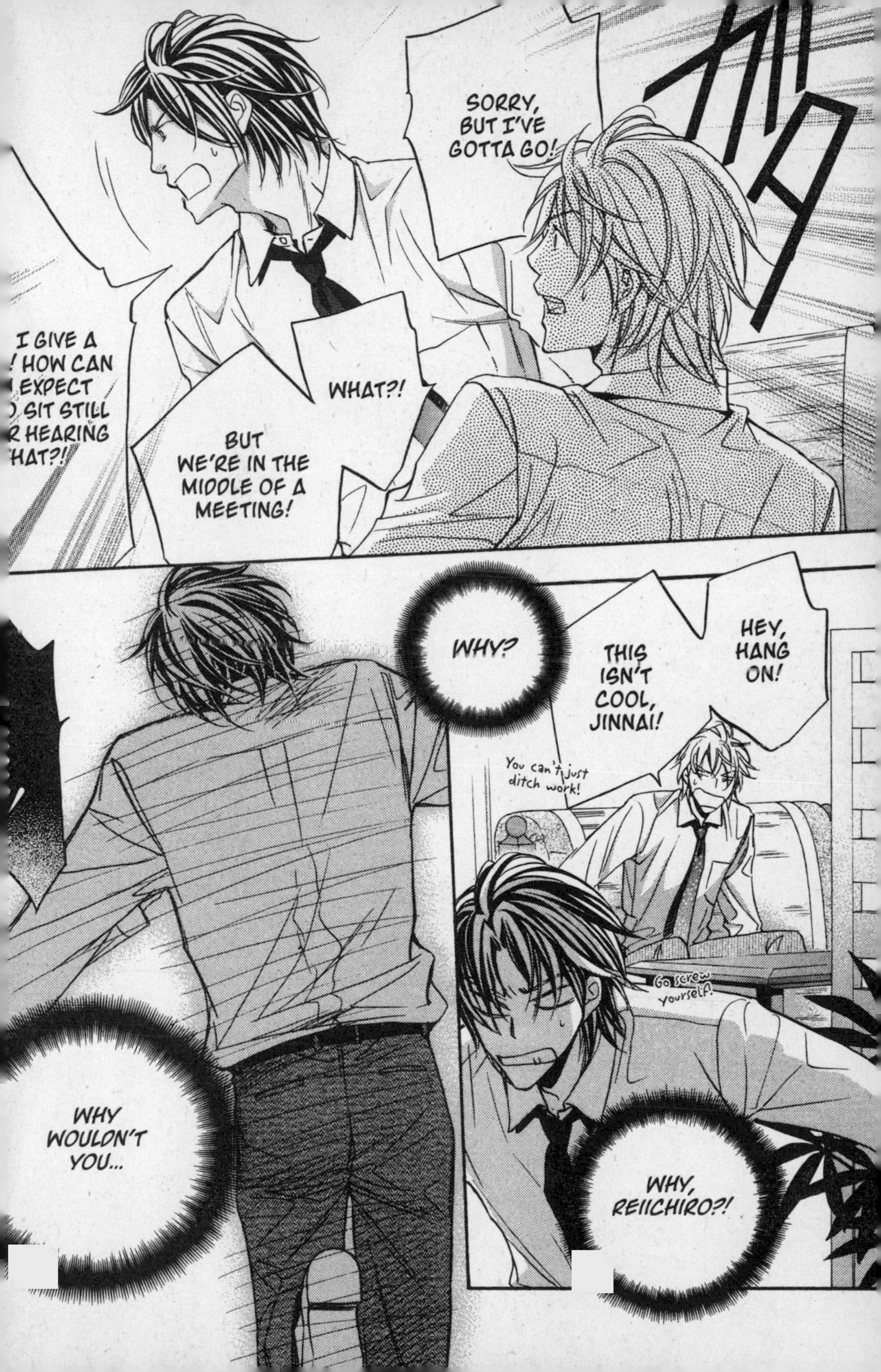
ガタ
SORRY, BUT I'VE GOTTA GO!
WHAT?!
BUT WE'RE IN THE MIDDLE OF A MEETING!
I GIVE A
HOW CAN
EXPECT
SIT STILL
HEARING
HAT?!
HEY, HANG ON!
THIS ISN'T COOL, JINNAI!
You can't just ditch work!
Go screw yourself.
WHY, REIICHIRO?!
WHY?
WHY WOULDN'T YOU...

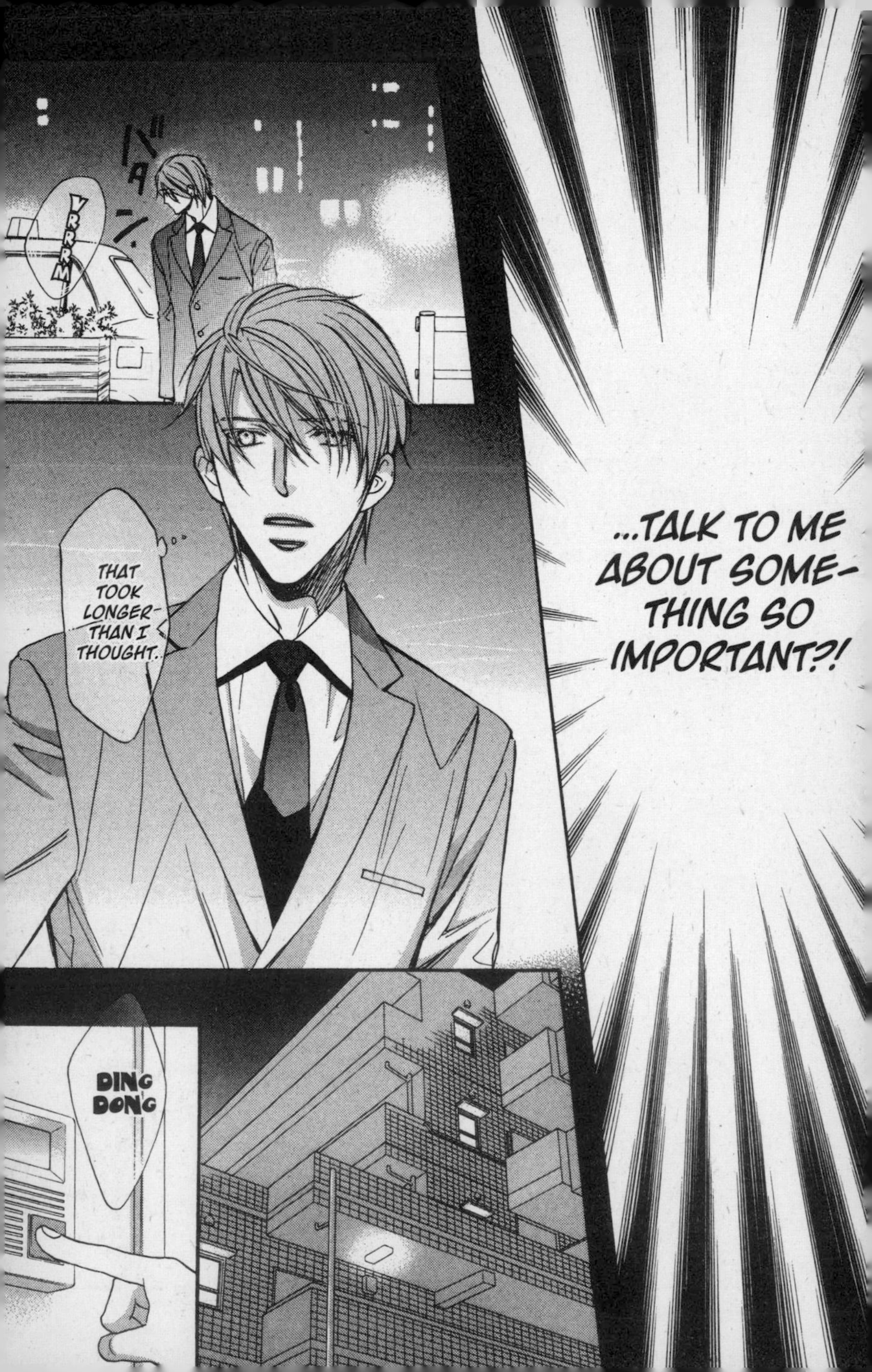
...TALK TO ME ABOUT SOME-THING SO IMPORTANT?!
VRRRM
THAT TOOK LONGER-THAN I THOUGHT...
DING DONG

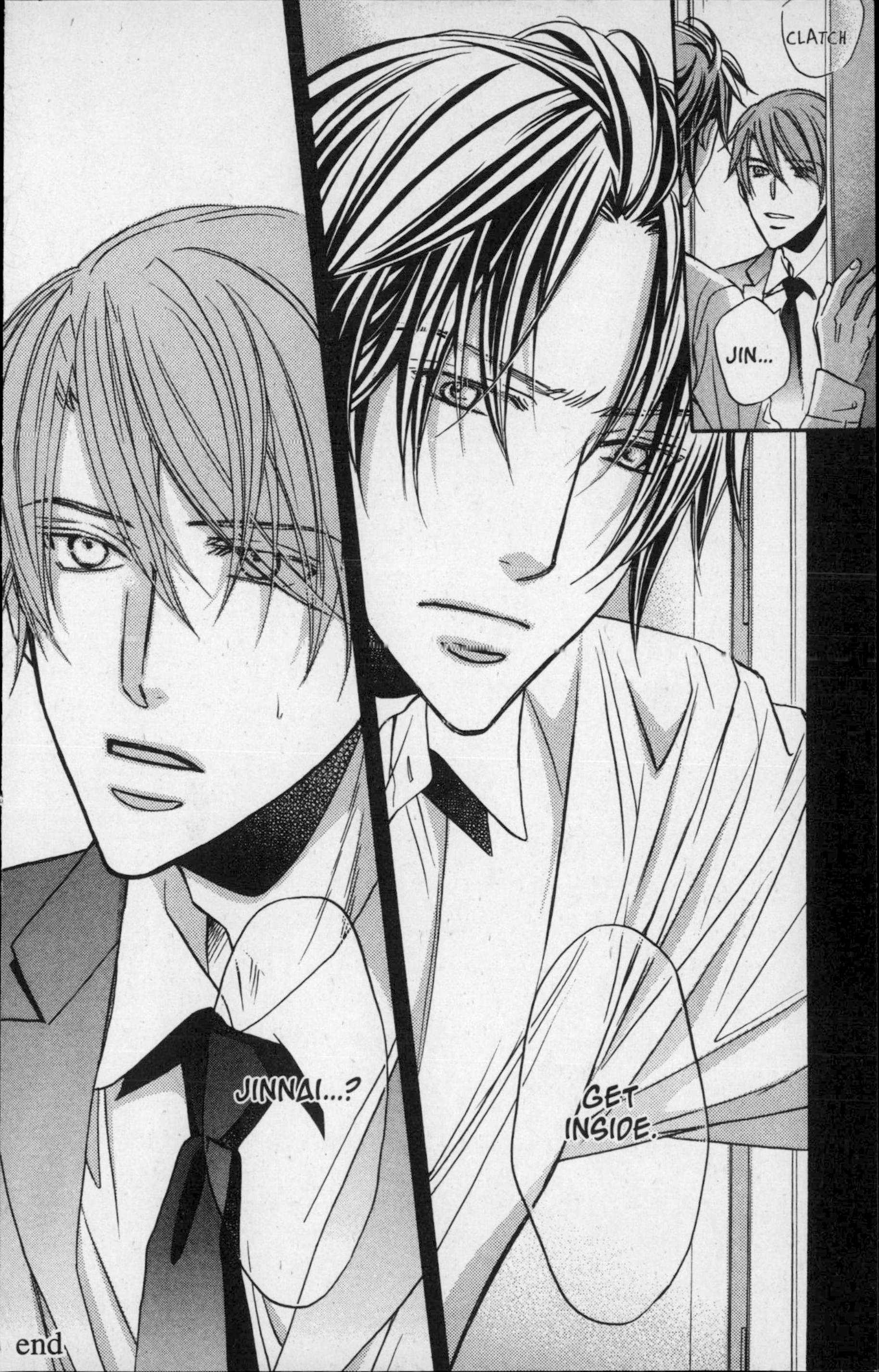
CLATCH
JIN...
GET INSIDE.
JINNAI...?
end

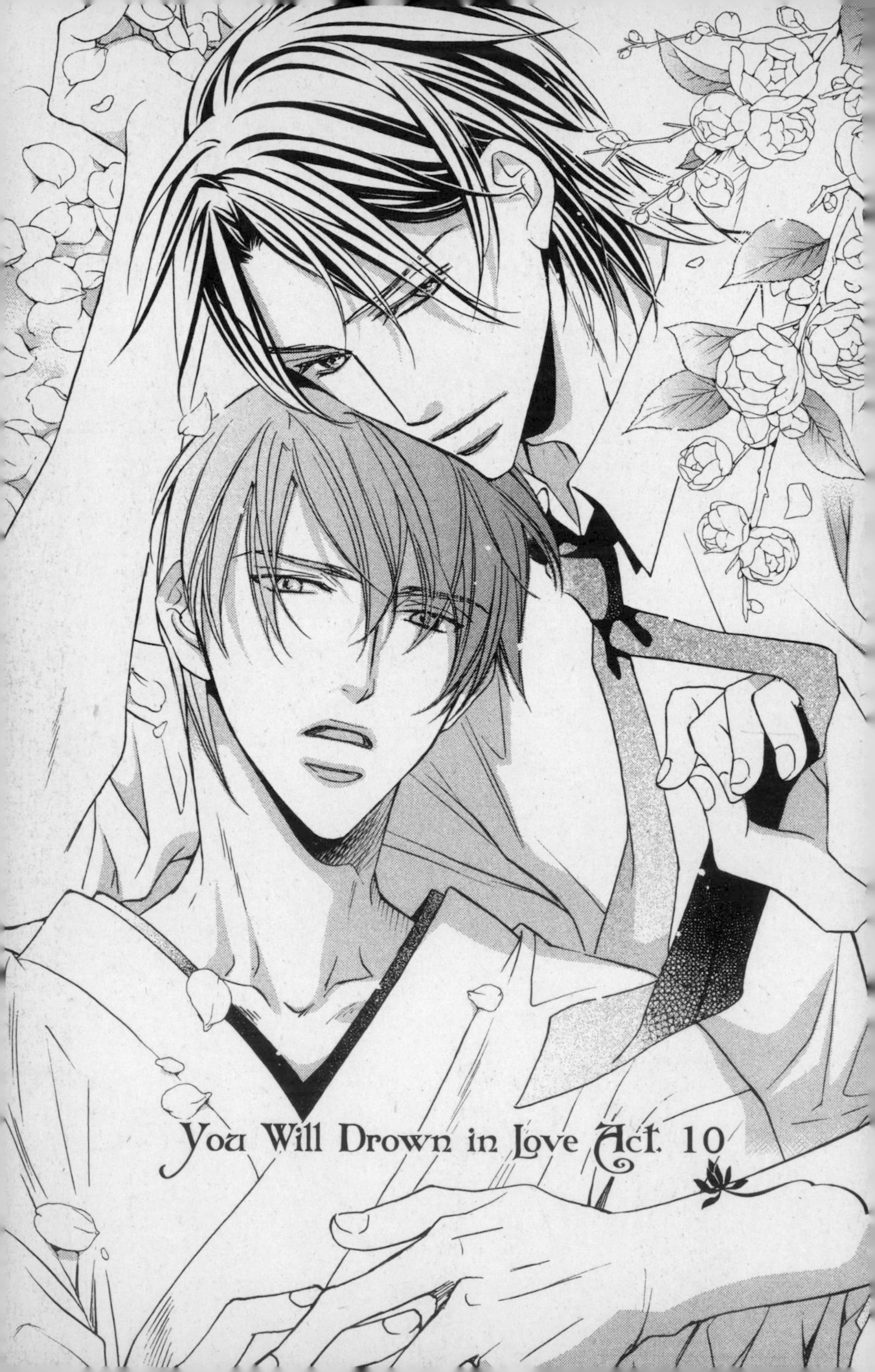
You Will Drown in Love Act. 10

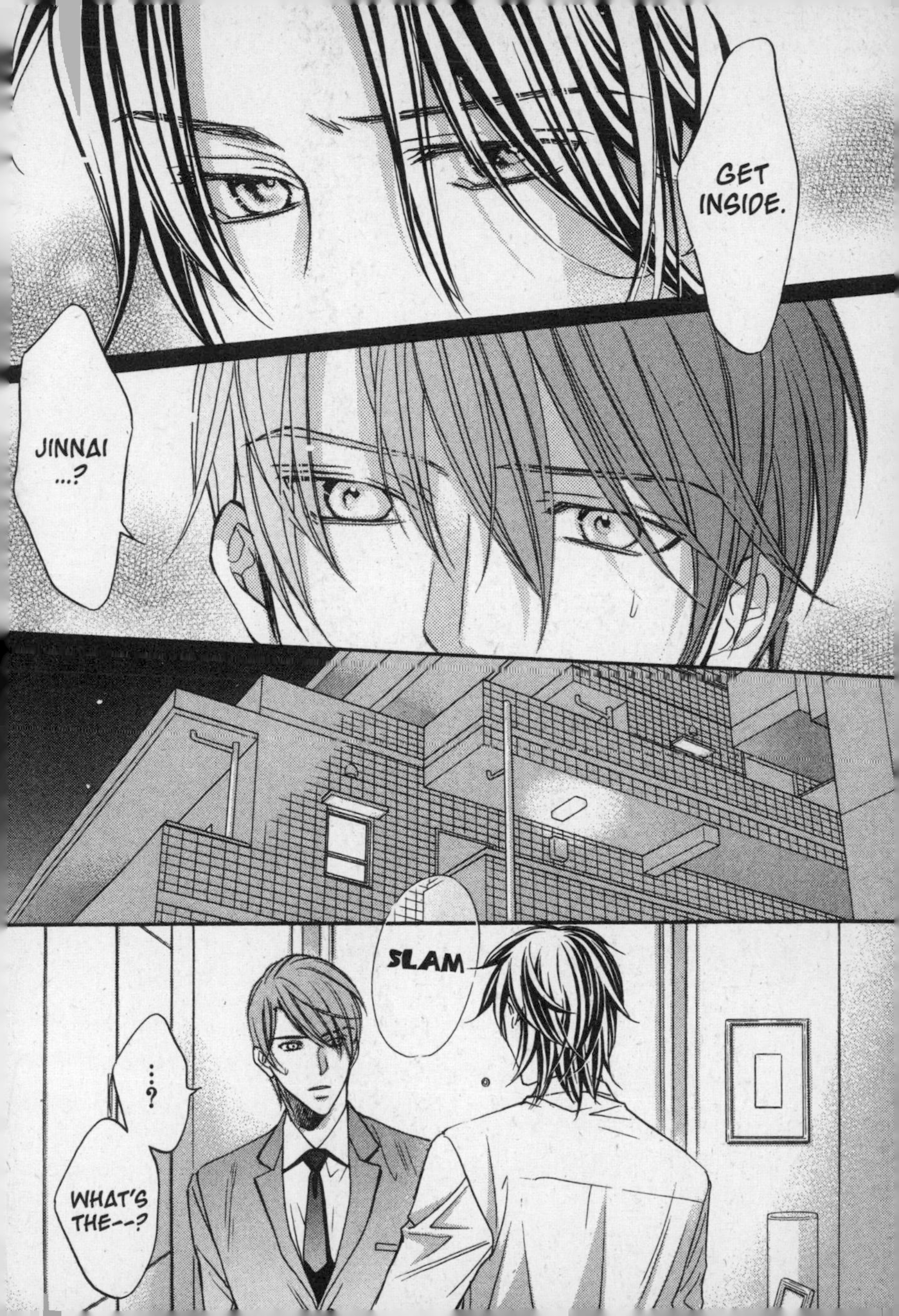
GET INSIDE.
JINNAI ...?
SLAM
...?
WHAT'S THE--?

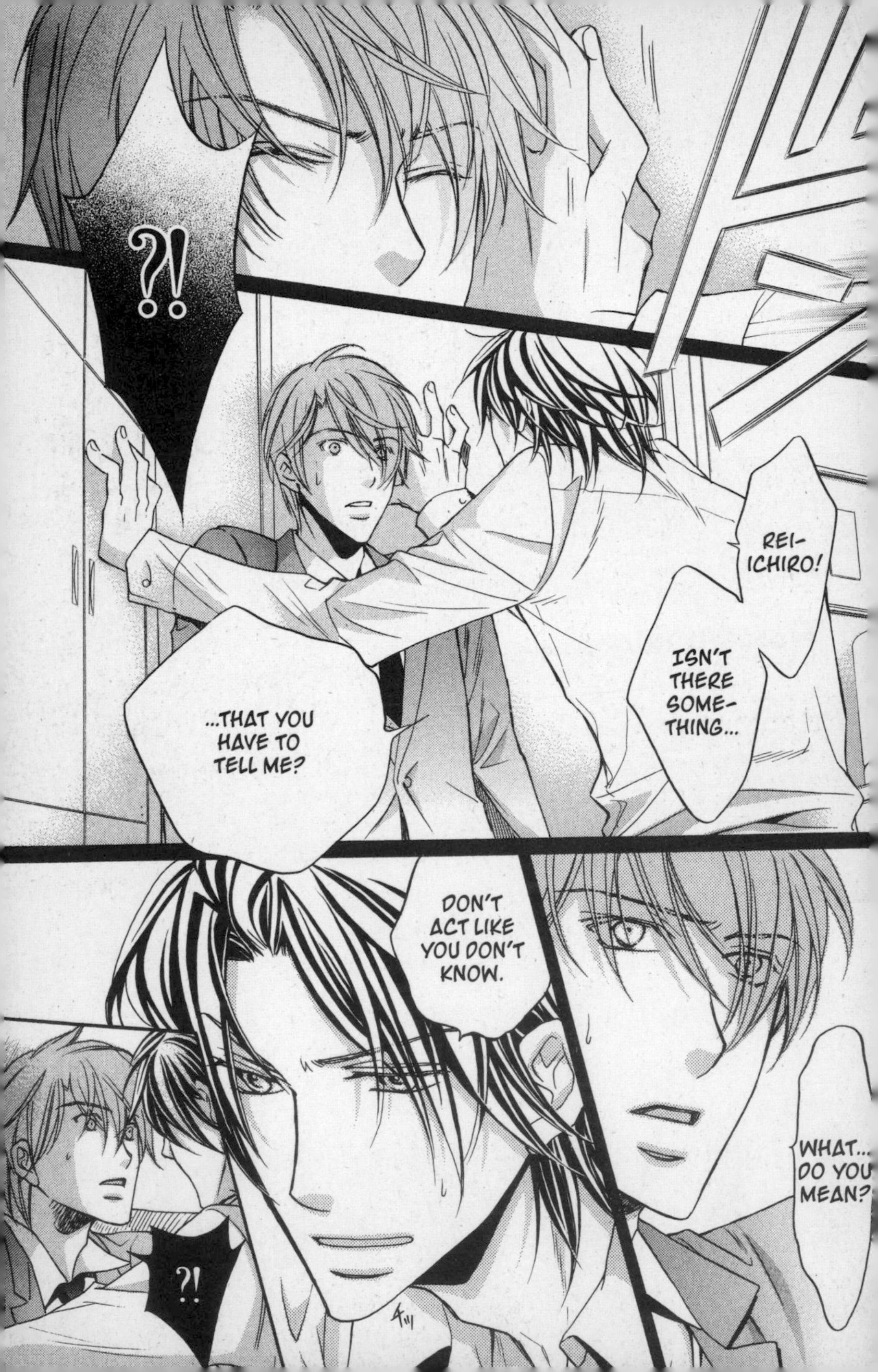
?!
REI-ICHIRO!
ISN'T THERE SOME-THING...
...THAT YOU HAVE TO TELL ME?
WHAT... DO YOU MEAN?
DON'T ACT LIKE YOU DON'T KNOW.
?!

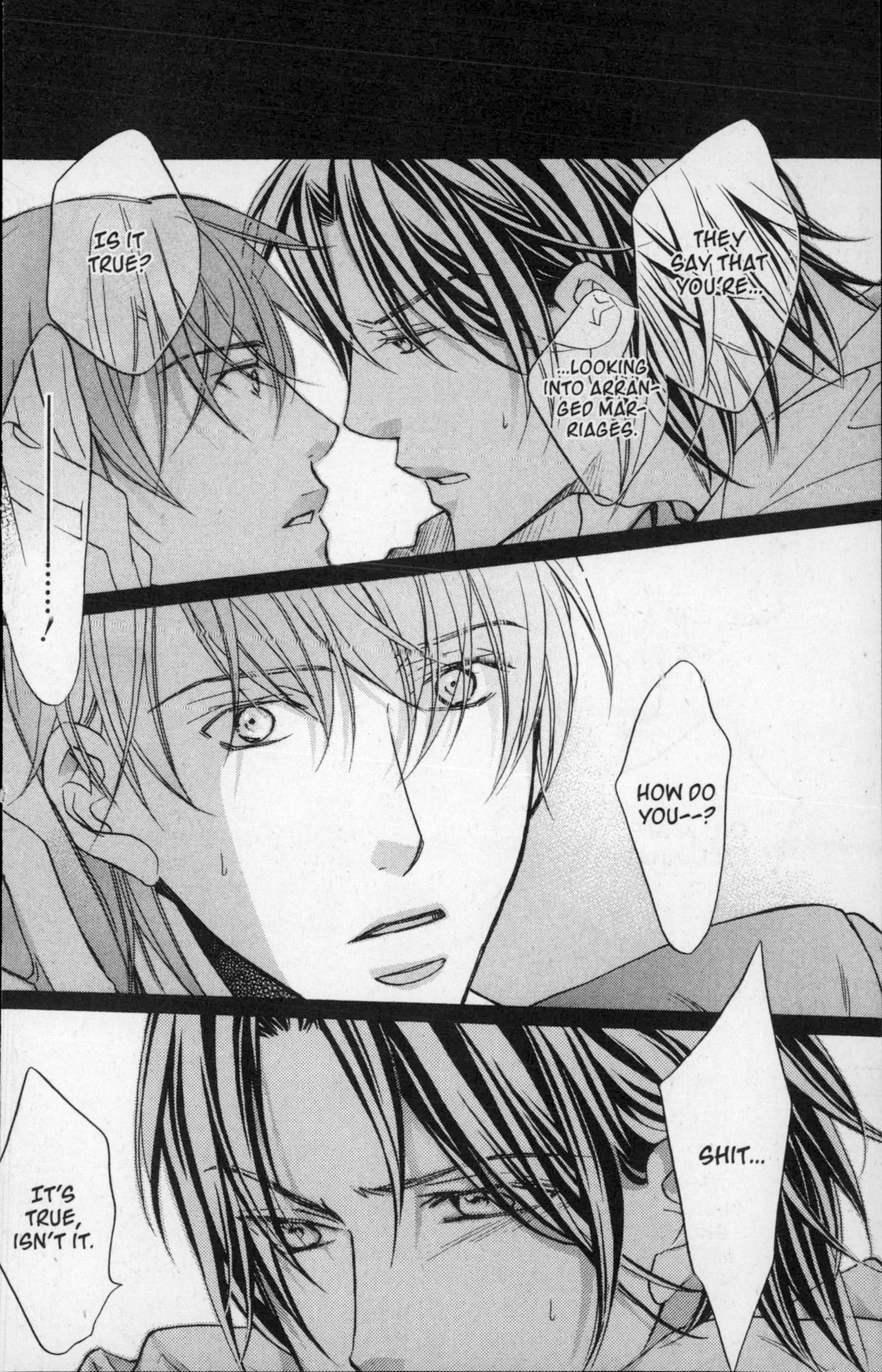
THEY SAY THAT YOU'RE...
...LOOKING INTO ARRANGED MARRIAGES.
IS IT TRUE?
......!
HOW DO YOU--?
SHIT...
IT'S TRUE, ISN'T IT.

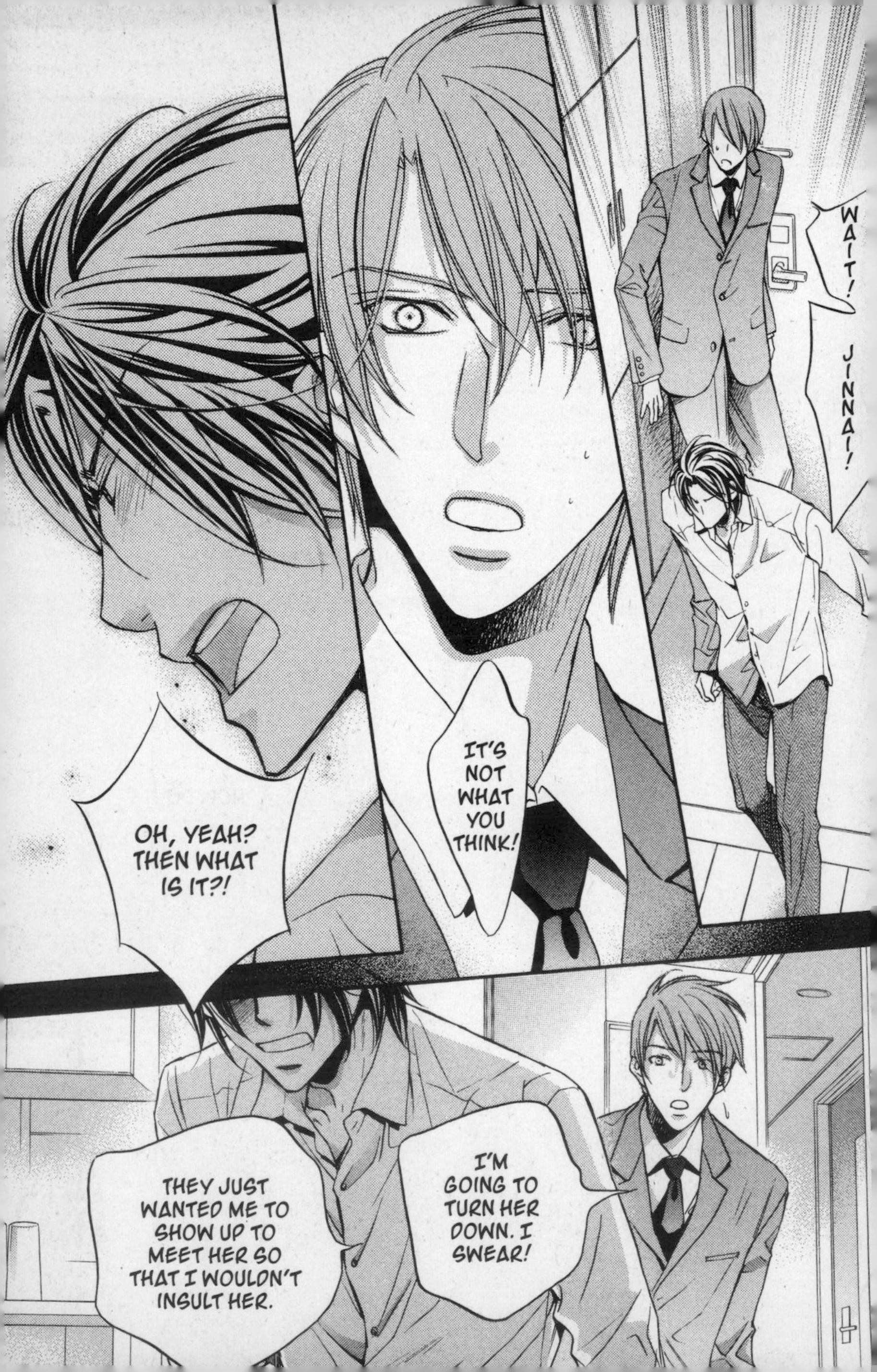
WAIT! JINNAI!
IT'S NOT WHAT YOU THINK!
OH, YEAH? THEN WHAT IS IT?!
I'M GOING TO TURN HER DOWN. I SWEAR!
THEY JUST WANTED ME TO SHOW UP TO MEET HER SO THAT I WOULDN'T INSULT HER.

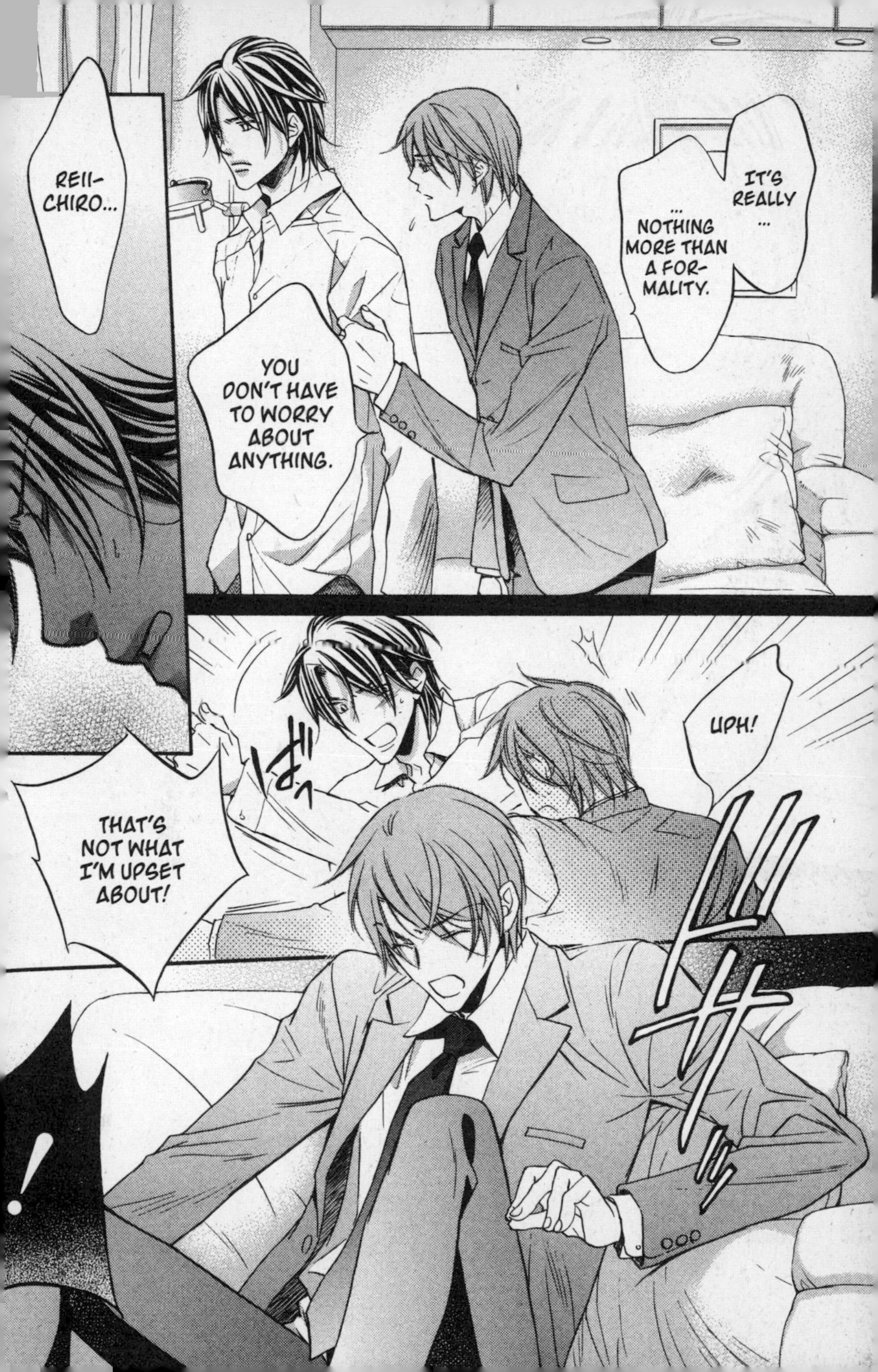
IT'S REALLY ... ... NOTHING MORE THAN A FOR-MALITY.
YOU DON'T HAVE TO WORRY ABOUT ANYTHING.
REII-CHIRO...
ばっ
THAT'S NOT WHAT I'M UPSET ABOUT!
UPH!

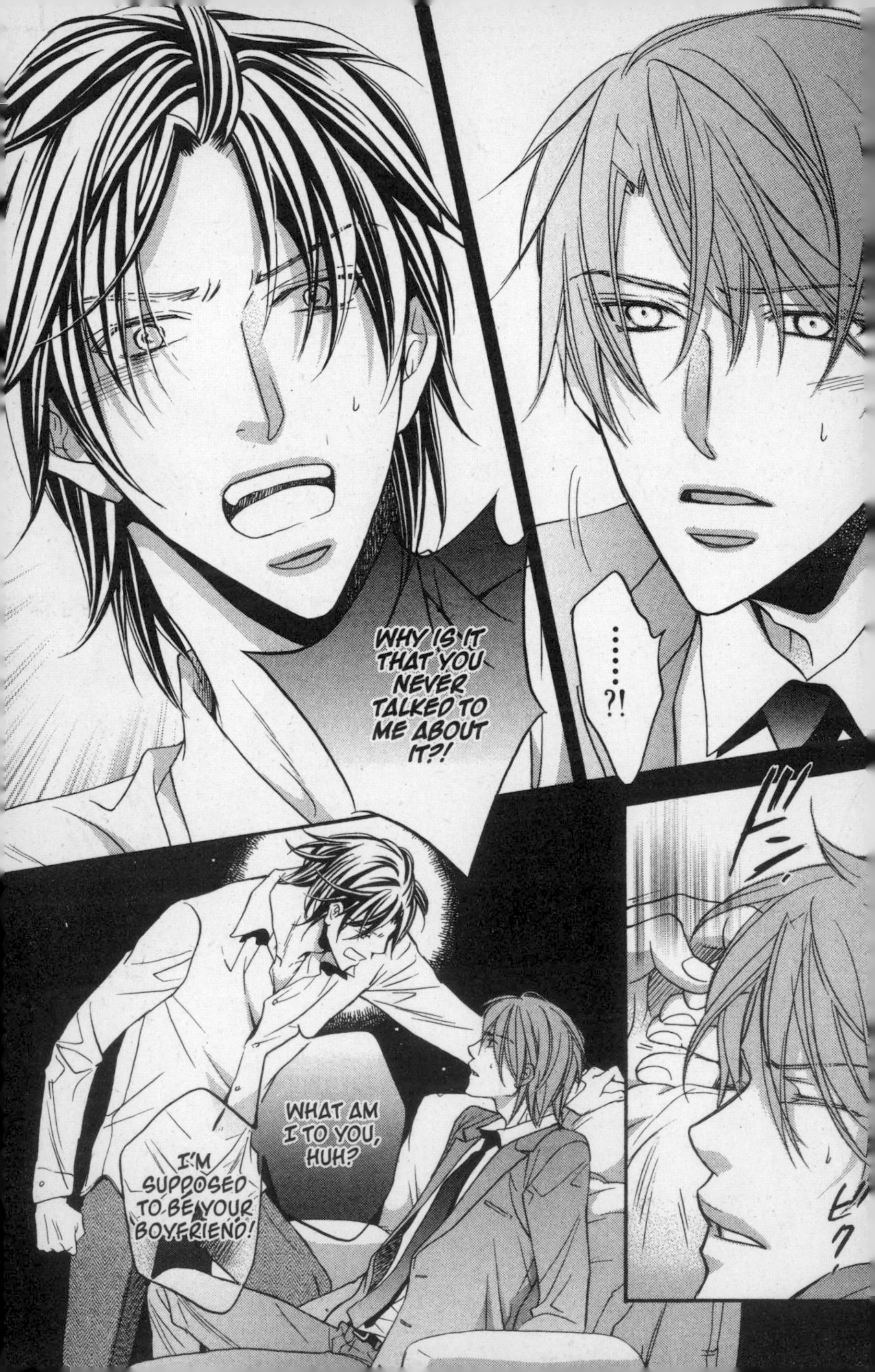
......?!
WHY IS IT THAT YOU NEVER TALKED TO ME ABOUT IT?!
WHAT AM I TO YOU, HUH?
I'M SUPPOSED TO BE YOUR BOYFRIEND!

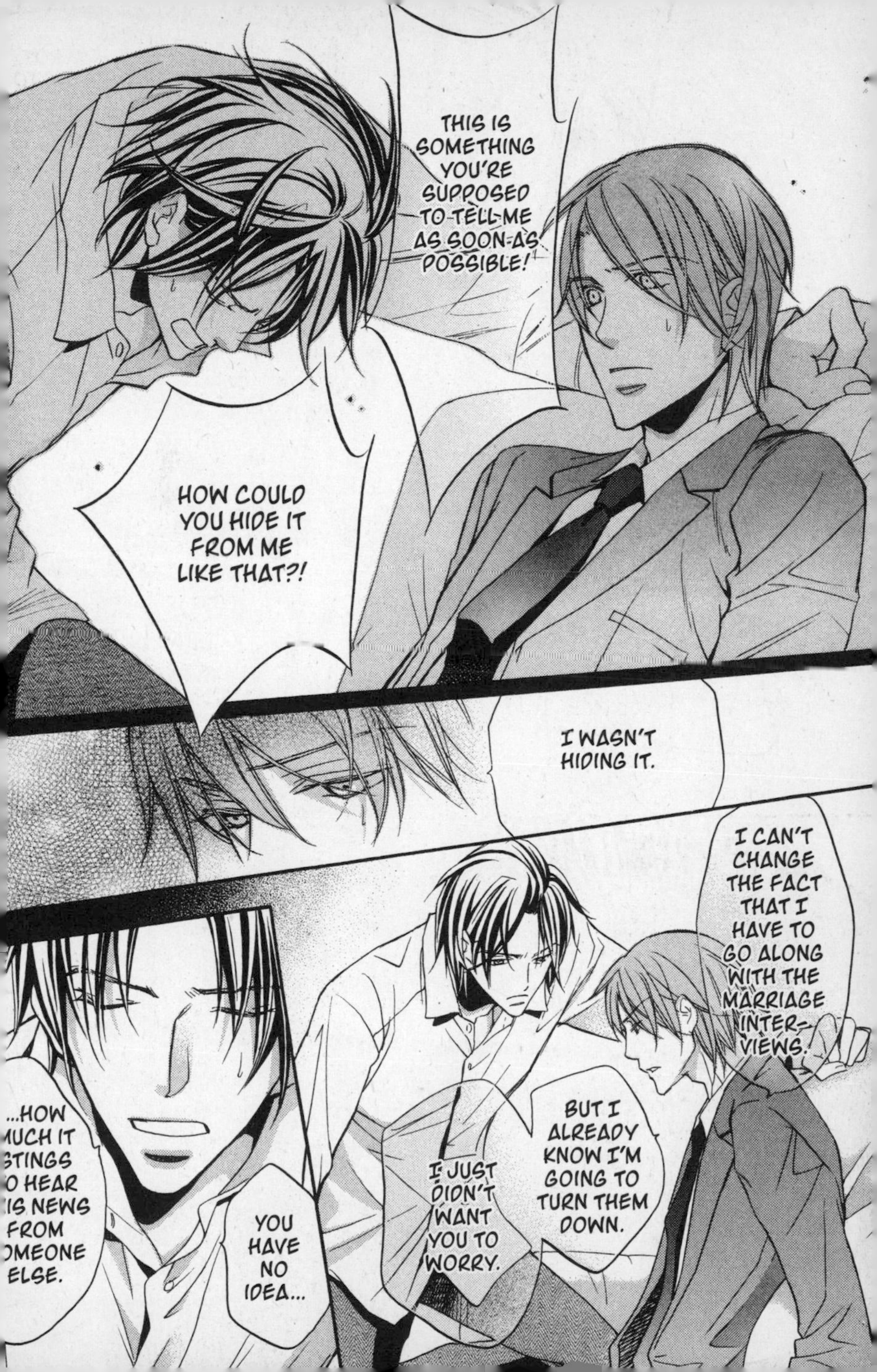
THIS IS SOMETHING YOU'RE SUPPOSED TO TELL ME AS SOON AS POSSIBLE!
HOW COULD YOU HIDE IT FROM ME LIKE THAT?!
I WASN'T HIDING IT.
I CAN'T CHANGE THE FACT THAT I HAVE TO GO ALONG WITH THE MARRIAGE INTER-VIEWS.
BUT I ALREADY KNOW I'M GOING TO TURN THEM DOWN.
I JUST DIDN'T WANT YOU TO WORRY.
YOU HAVE NO IDEA...
...HOW UCH IT TINGS O HEAR IS NEWS FROM OMEONE ELSE.

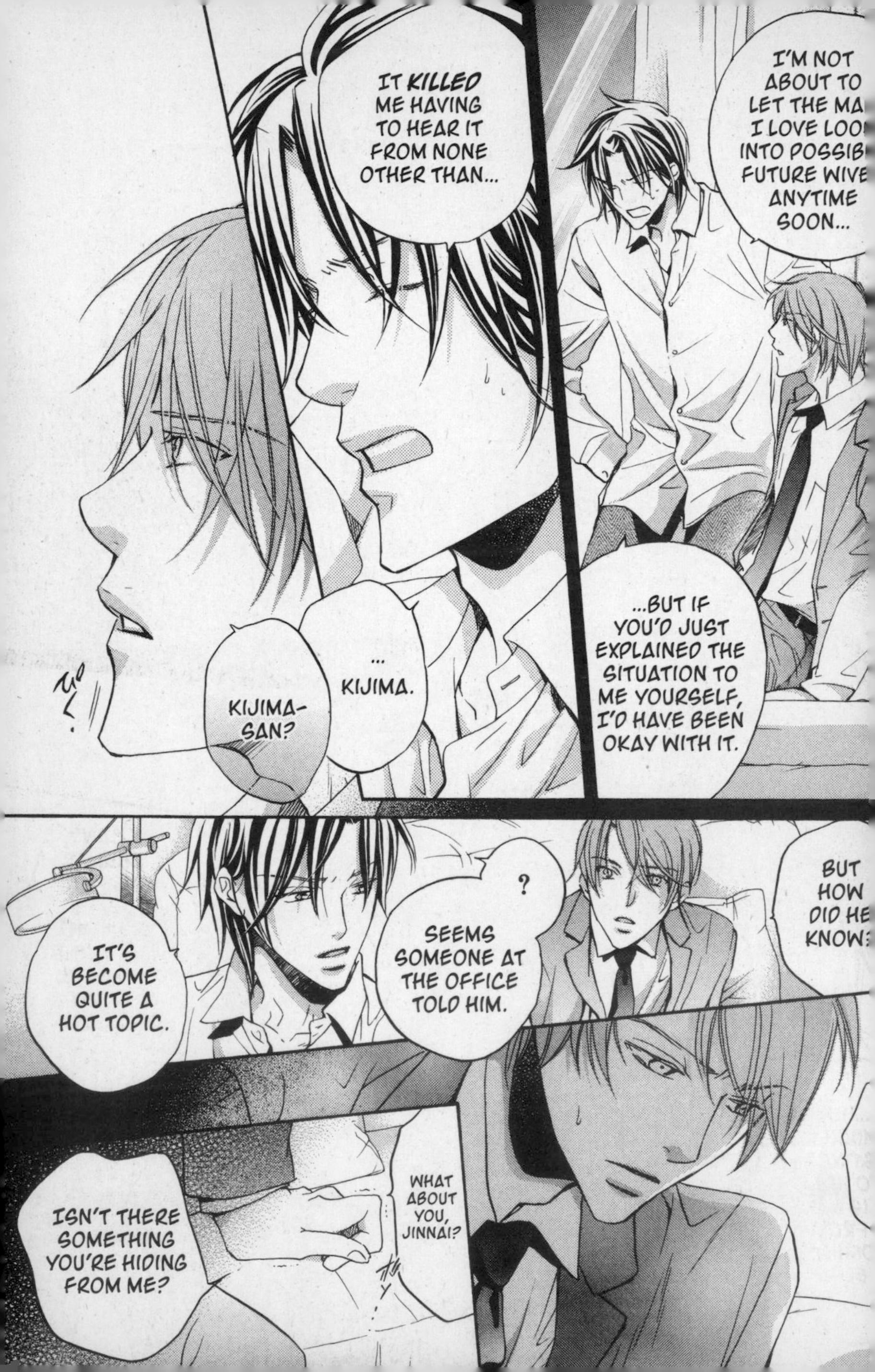
I'M NOT ABOUT TO LET THE MA I LOVE LOO INTO POSSIB FUTURE WIVE ANYTIME SOON...
...BUT IF YOU'D JUST EXPLAINED THE SITUATION TO ME YOURSELF, I'D HAVE BEEN OKAY WITH IT.
IT KILLED ME HAVING TO HEAR IT FROM NONE OTHER THAN...
... KIJIMA.
KIJIMA-SAN?
BUT HOW DID HE KNOW
?
SEEMS SOMEONE AT THE OFFICE TOLD HIM.
IT'S BECOME QUITE A HOT TOPIC.
WHAT ABOUT YOU, JINNAI?
ISN'T THERE SOMETHING YOU'RE HIDING FROM ME?

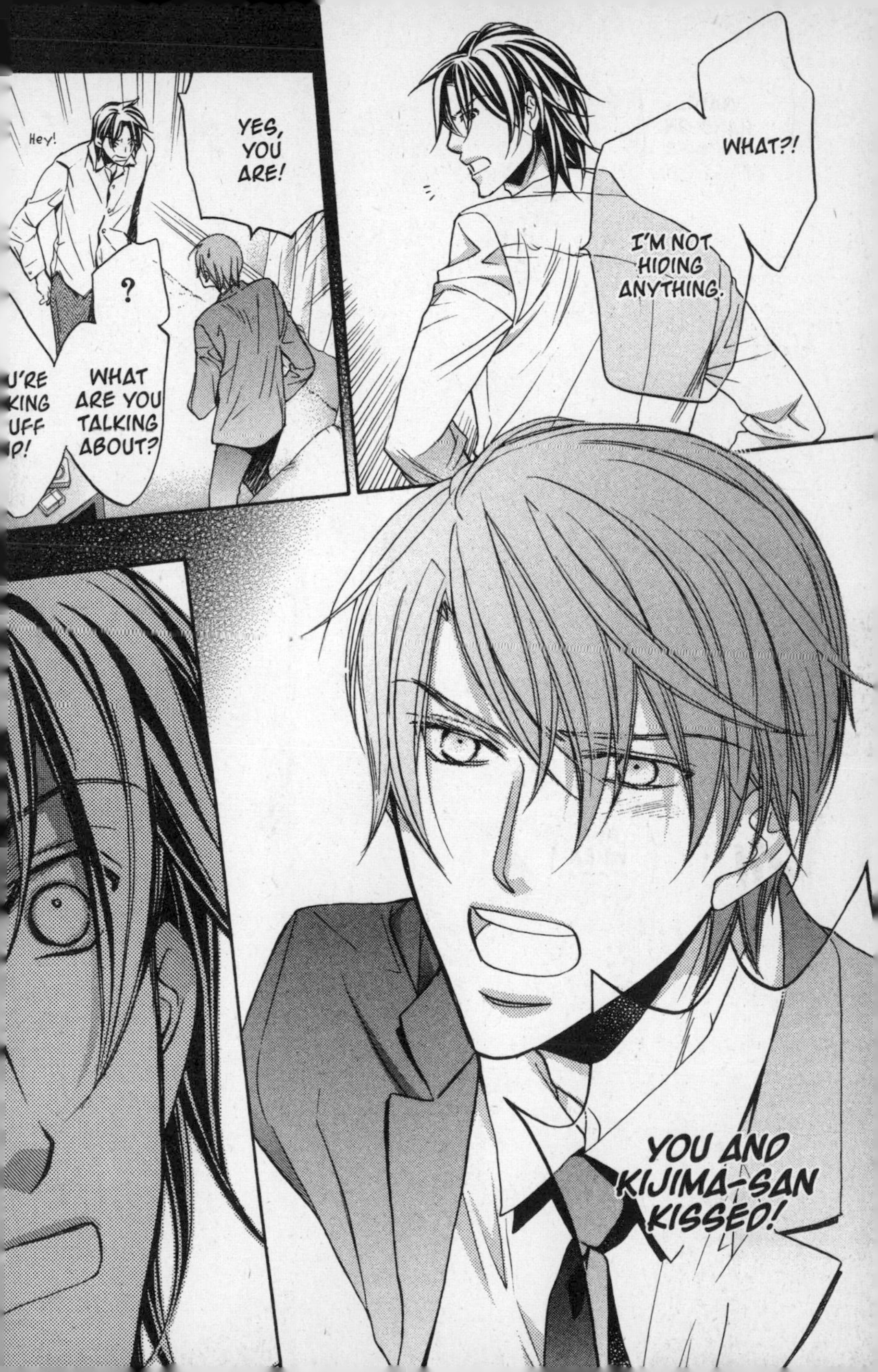
WHAT?!
I'M NOT HIDING ANYTHING.
YES, YOU ARE!
Hey!
?
WHAT ARE YOU TALKING ABOUT?
YOU AND KIJIMA-SAN KISSED!

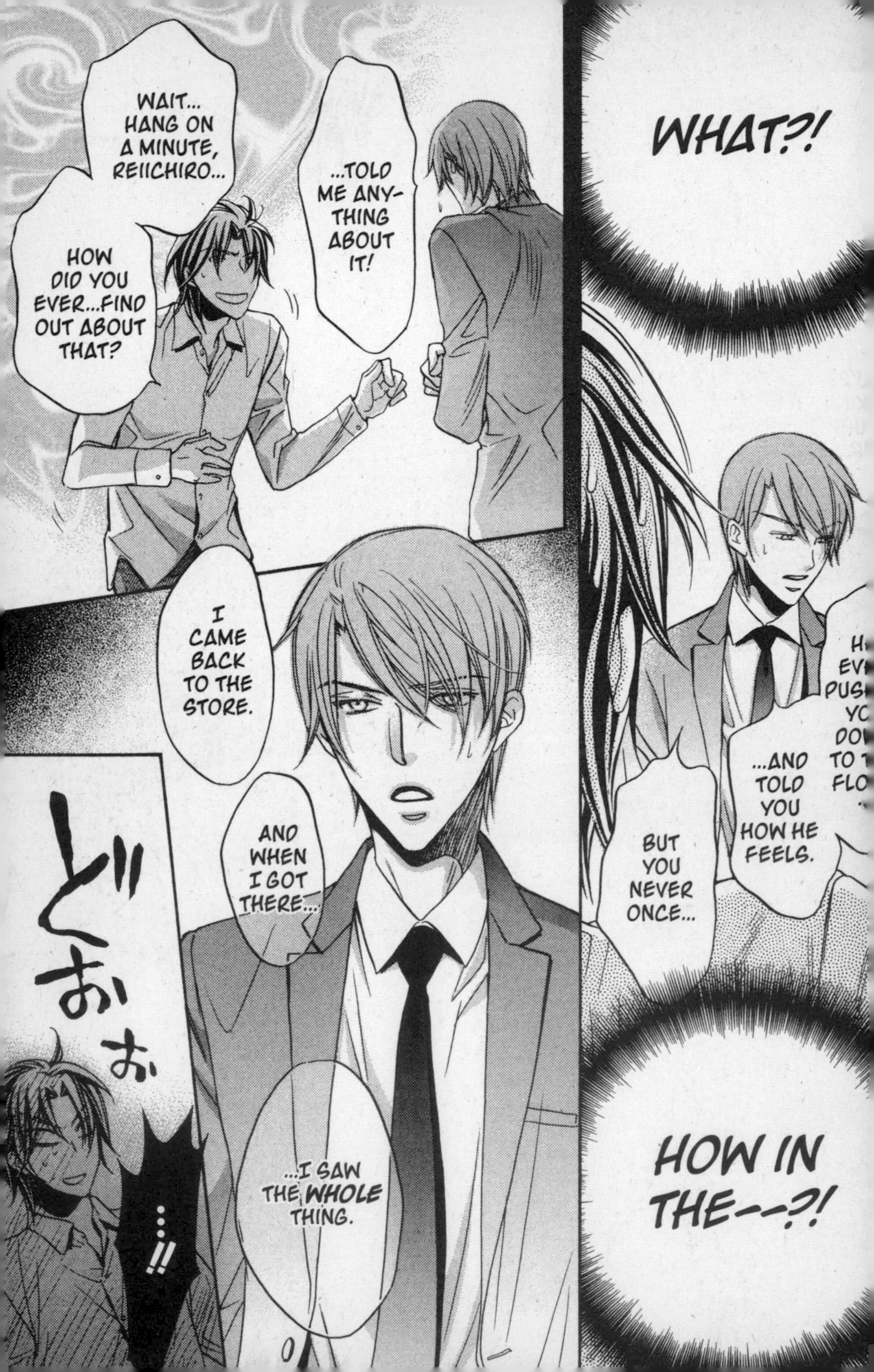
WHAT?!
...AND TOLD YOU HOW HE FEELS.
BUT YOU NEVER ONCE...
HOW IN THE--?!
...TOLD ME ANY-THING ABOUT IT!
WAIT... HANG ON A MINUTE, REIICHIRO...
HOW DID YOU EVER...FIND OUT ABOUT THAT?
I CAME BACK TO THE STORE.
AND WHEN I GOT THERE...
どくぉぉ
...I SAW THE WHOLE THING.
...!!

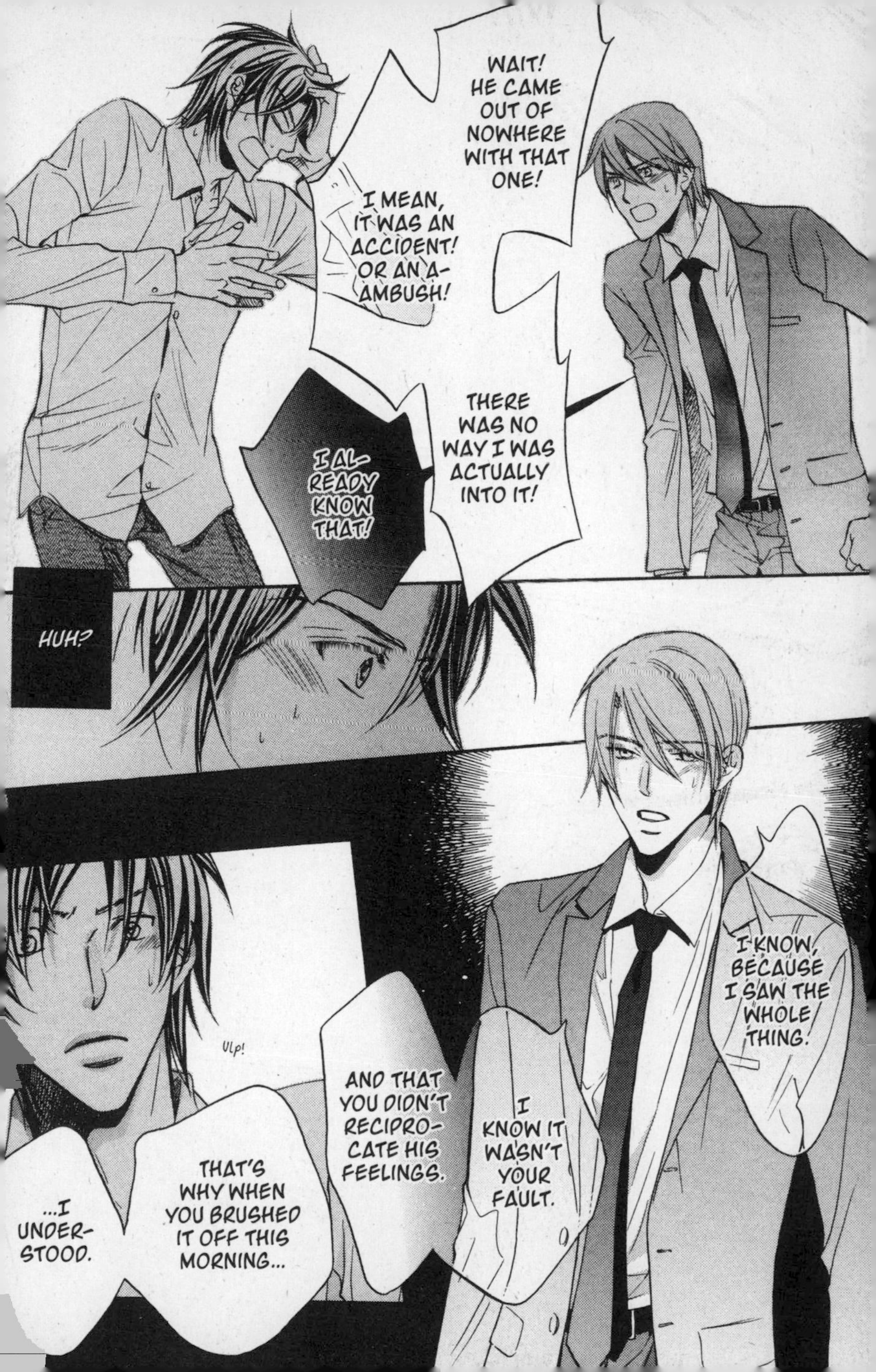
WAIT! HE CAME OUT OF NOWHERE WITH THAT ONE!
I MEAN, IT WAS AN ACCIDENT! OR AN A-AMBUSH!
THERE WAS NO WAY I WAS ACTUALLY INTO IT!
I AL-READY KNOW THAT!
HUH?
I KNOW, BECAUSE I SAW THE WHOLE THING.
I KNOW IT WASN'T YOUR FAULT.
AND THAT YOU DIDN'T RECIPRO-CATE HIS FEELINGS.
THAT'S WHY WHEN YOU BRUSHED IT OFF THIS MORNING...
Ulp!
...I UNDER-STOOD.

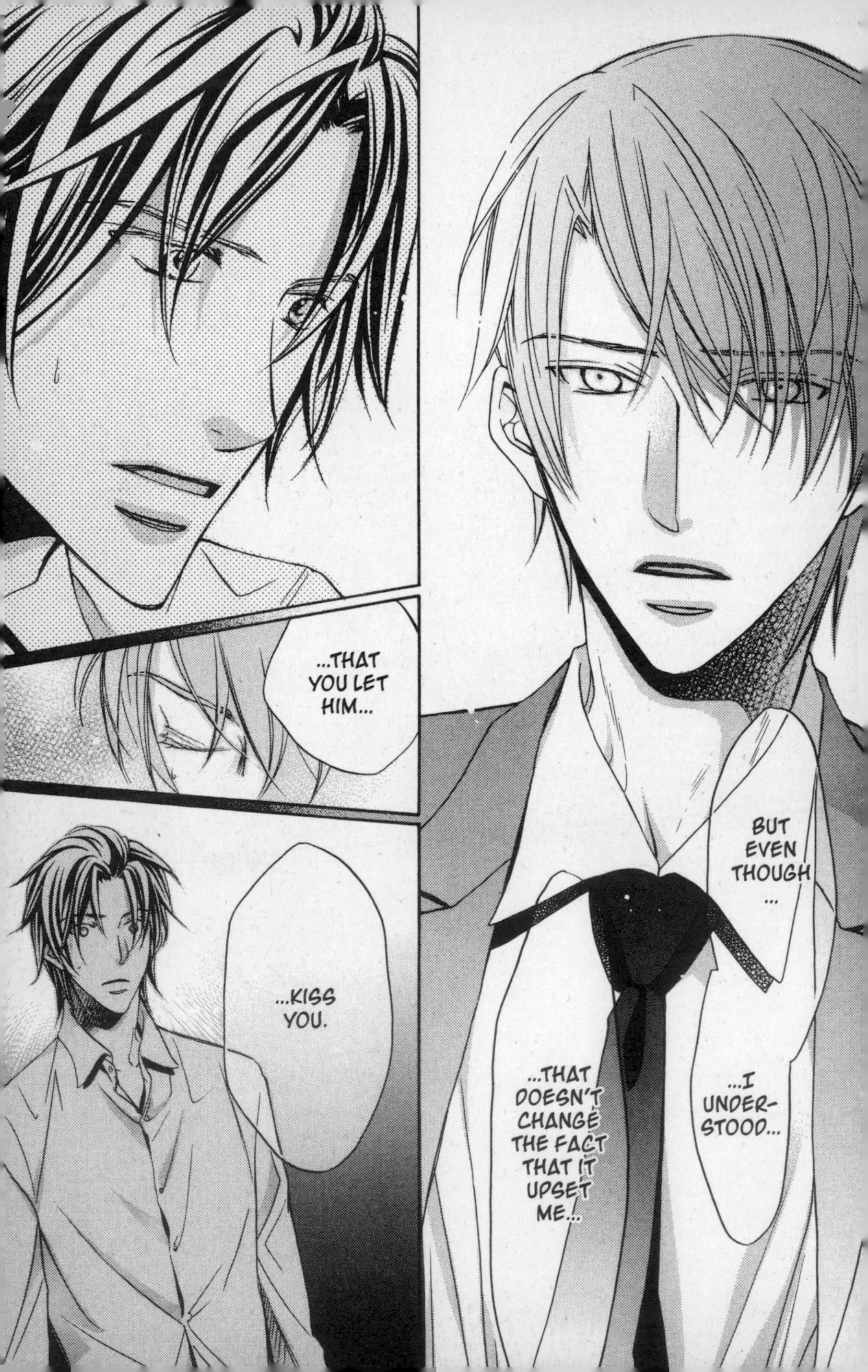
BUT EVEN THOUGH...
...I UNDER-STOOD...
...THAT DOESN'T CHANGE THE FACT THAT IT UPSET ME...
...THAT YOU LET HIM...
...KISS YOU.

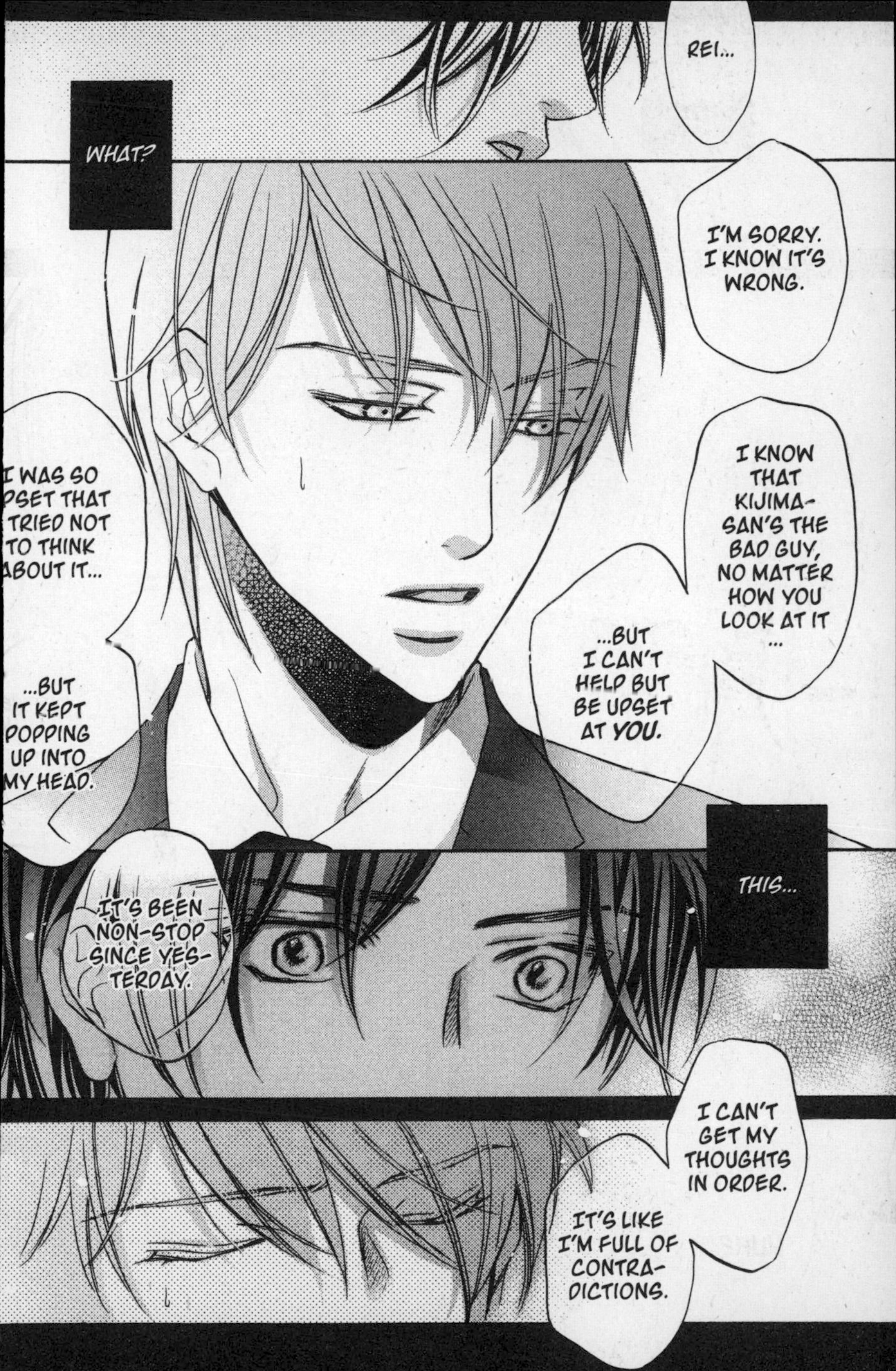
REI...
WHAT?
I'M SORRY. I KNOW IT'S WRONG.
I KNOW THAT KIJIMA-SAN'S THE BAD GUY, NO MATTER HOW YOU LOOK AT IT ...
...BUT I CAN'T HELP BUT BE UPSET AT YOU.
I WAS SO UPSET THAT TRIED NOT TO THINK ABOUT IT...
...BUT IT KEPT POPPING UP INTO MY HEAD.
THIS...
IT'S BEEN NON-STOP SINCE YES-TERDAY.
I CAN'T GET MY THOUGHTS IN ORDER.
IT'S LIKE I'M FULL OF CONTRA-DICTIONS.

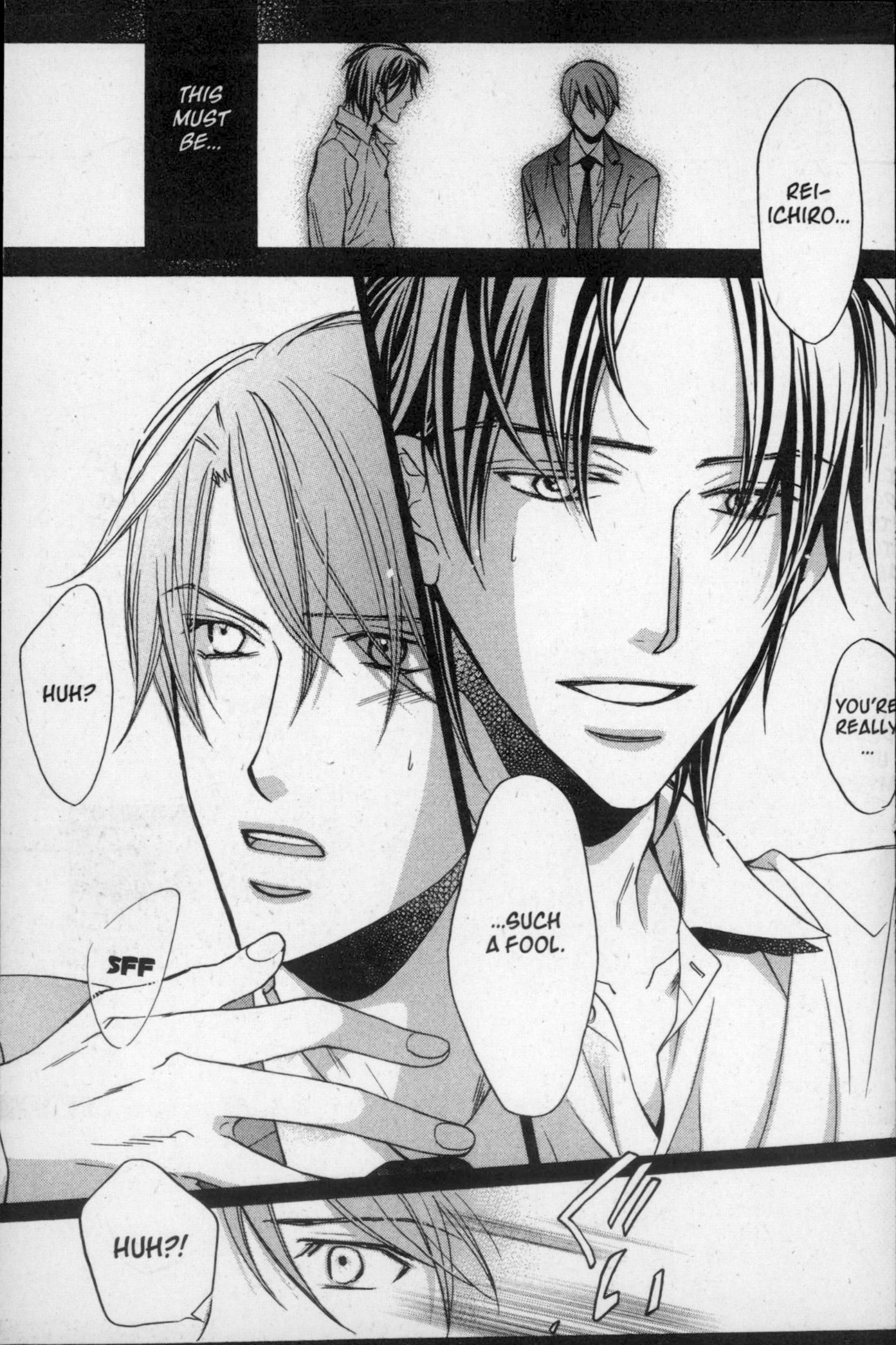
REI-ICHIRO...
THIS MUST BE...
YOU'RE REALLY ...
...SUCH A FOOL.
HUH?
SFF
HUH?!

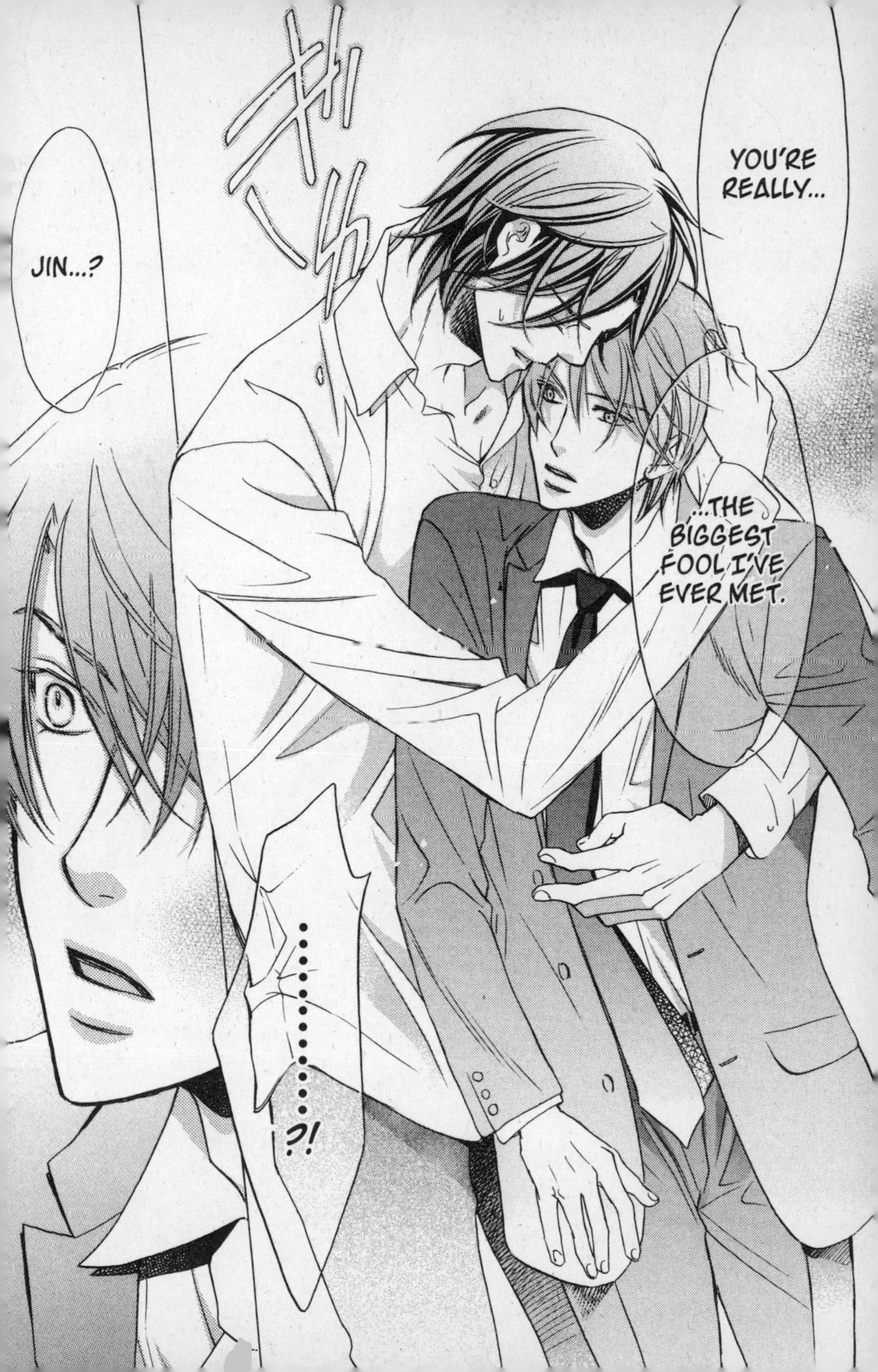
YOU'RE REALLY...
...THE BIGGEST FOOL I'VE EVER MET.
JIN...?
........?!

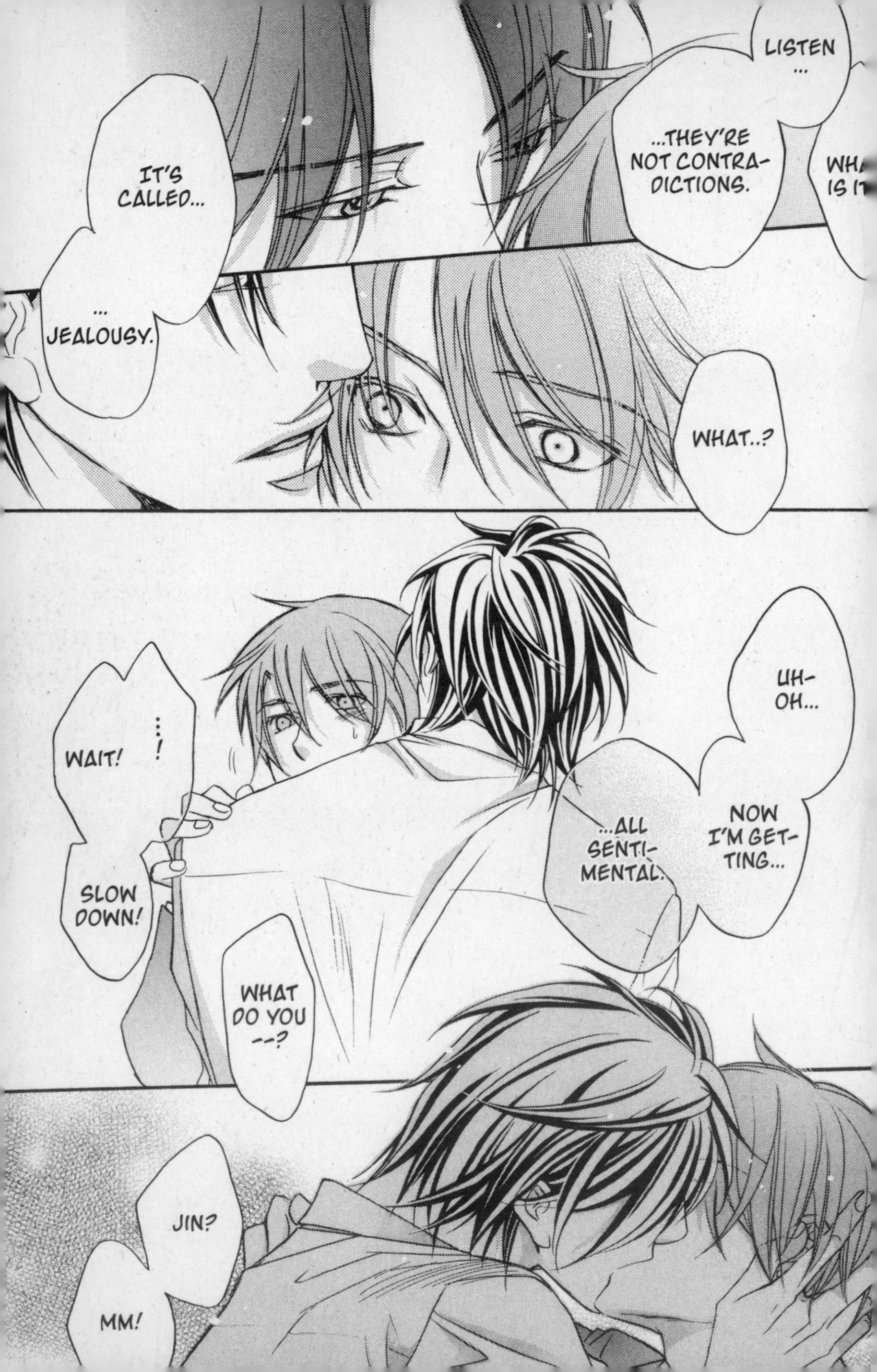
WHA IS I
LISTEN ...
...THEY'RE NOT CONTRA-DICTIONS.
IT'S CALLED...
... JEALOUSY.
WHAT..?
UH-OH...
NOW I'M GET-TING...
...ALL SENTI-MENTAL.
...!
WAIT!
SLOW DOWN!
WHAT DO YOU --?
JIN?
MM!

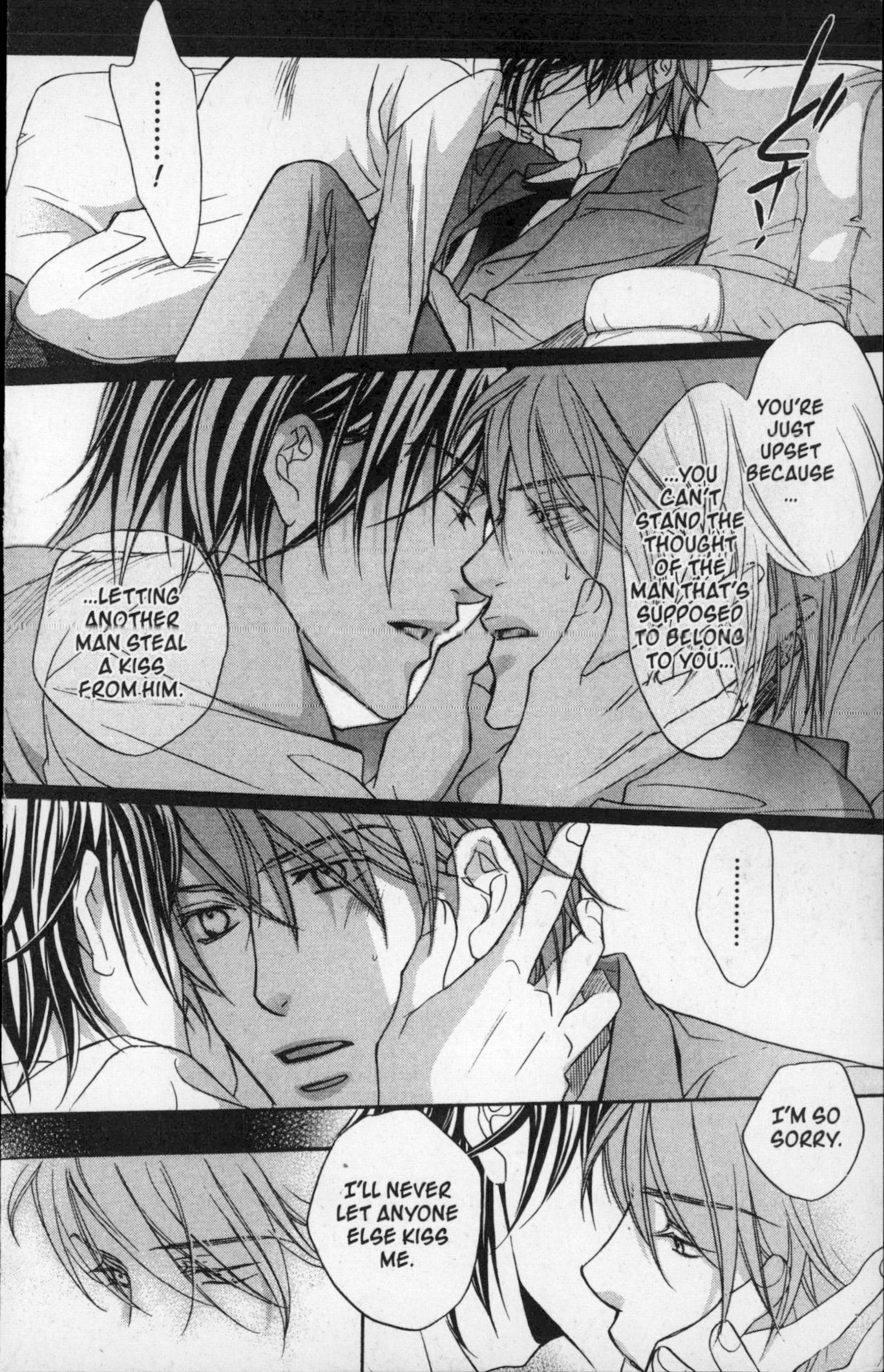
……!
YOU'RE JUST UPSET BECAUSE …
…YOU CAN'T STAND THE THOUGHT OF THE MAN THAT'S SUPPOSED TO BELONG TO YOU…
…LETTING ANOTHER MAN STEAL A KISS FROM HIM.
……
I'M SO SORRY.
I'LL NEVER LET ANYONE ELSE KISS ME.

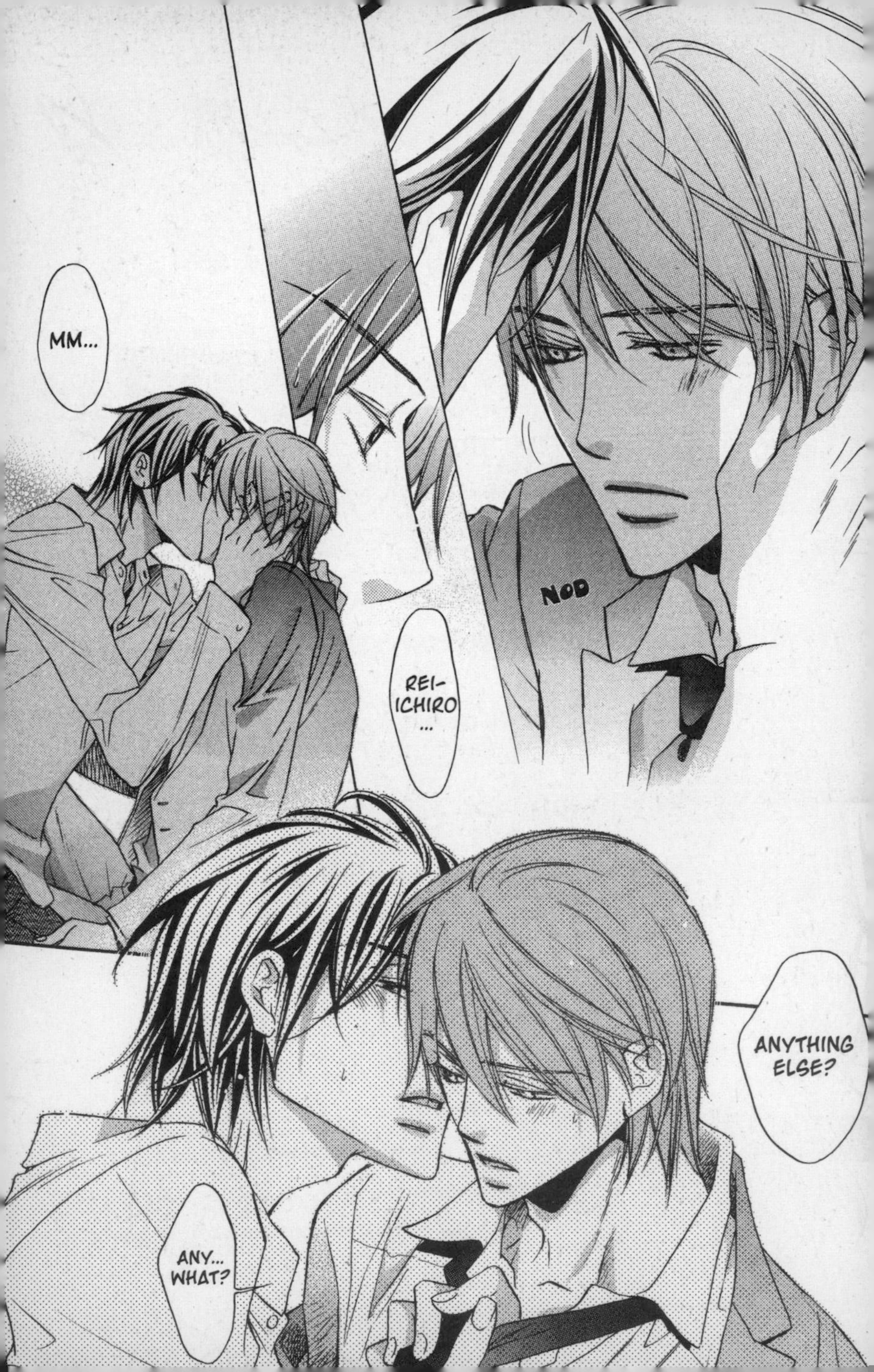
NOD
REI-ICHIRO...
MM...
ANYTHING ELSE?
ANY... WHAT?

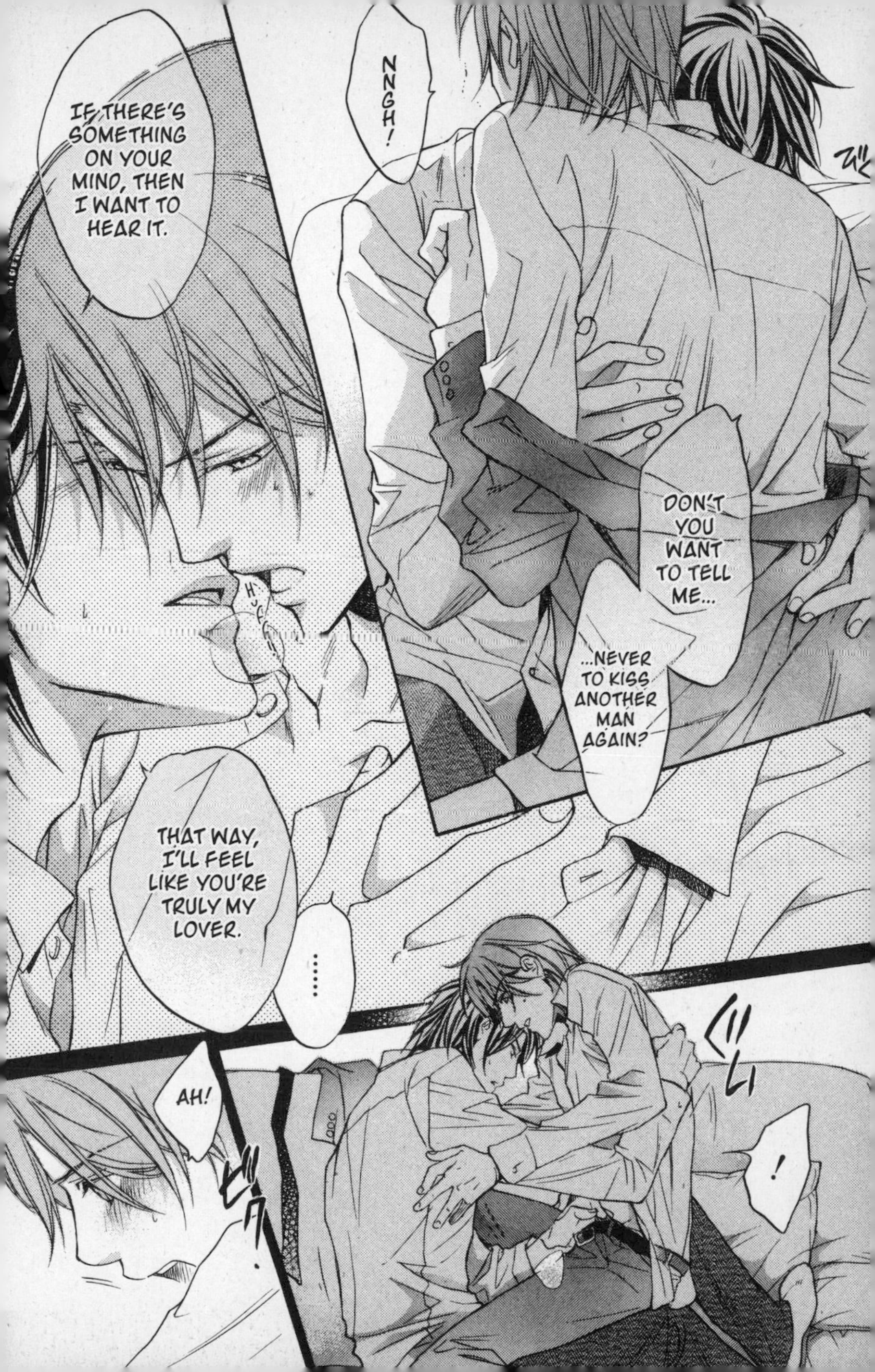
NNGH!
DON'T YOU WANT TO TELL ME...
...NEVER TO KISS ANOTHER MAN AGAIN?
IF THERE'S SOMETHING ON YOUR MIND, THEN I WANT TO HEAR IT.
THAT WAY, I'LL FEEL LIKE YOU'RE TRULY MY LOVER.
......
!
AH!

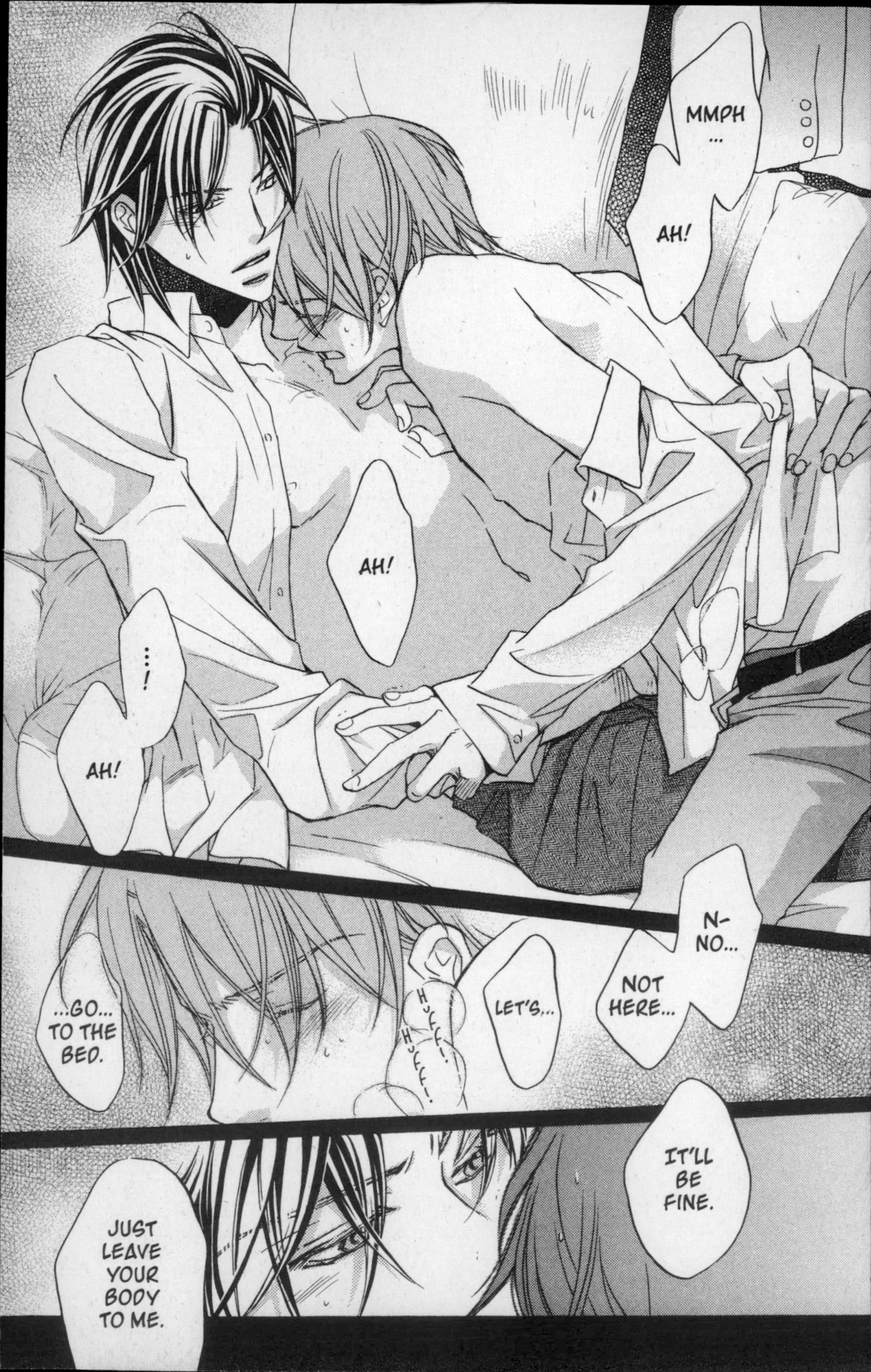
MMPH...
AH!
AH!
...!
AH!
N-NO...
NOT HERE...
LET'S...
HUFF! HUFF!
...GO... TO THE BED.
IT'LL BE FINE.
JUST LEAVE YOUR BODY TO ME.

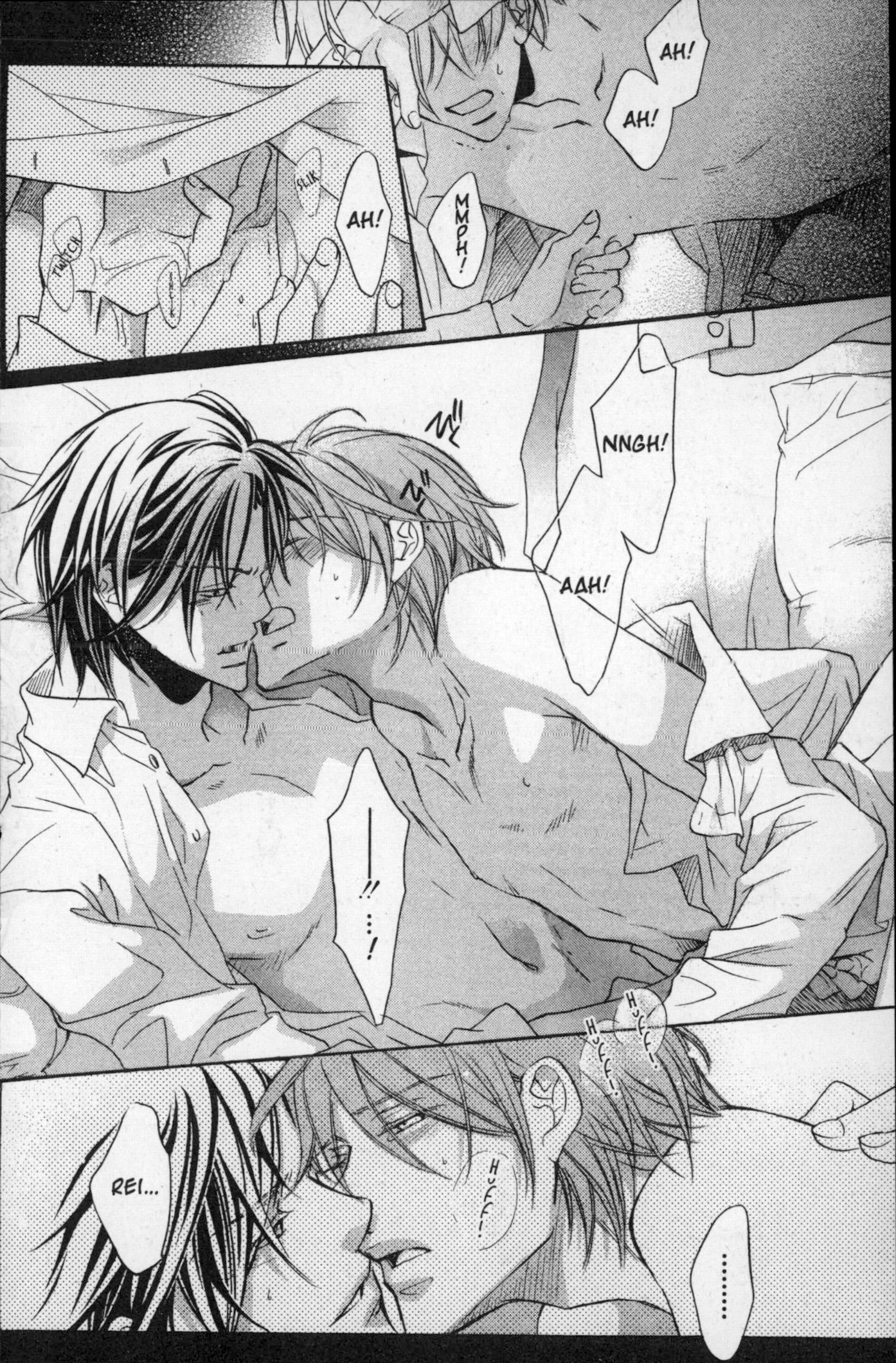
AH!
AH!
MMPH!
AH!
SLIK
TWITCH
NNGH!
AAH!
!! ...!
HUFF!
HUFF!
HUFF!
REI...
......

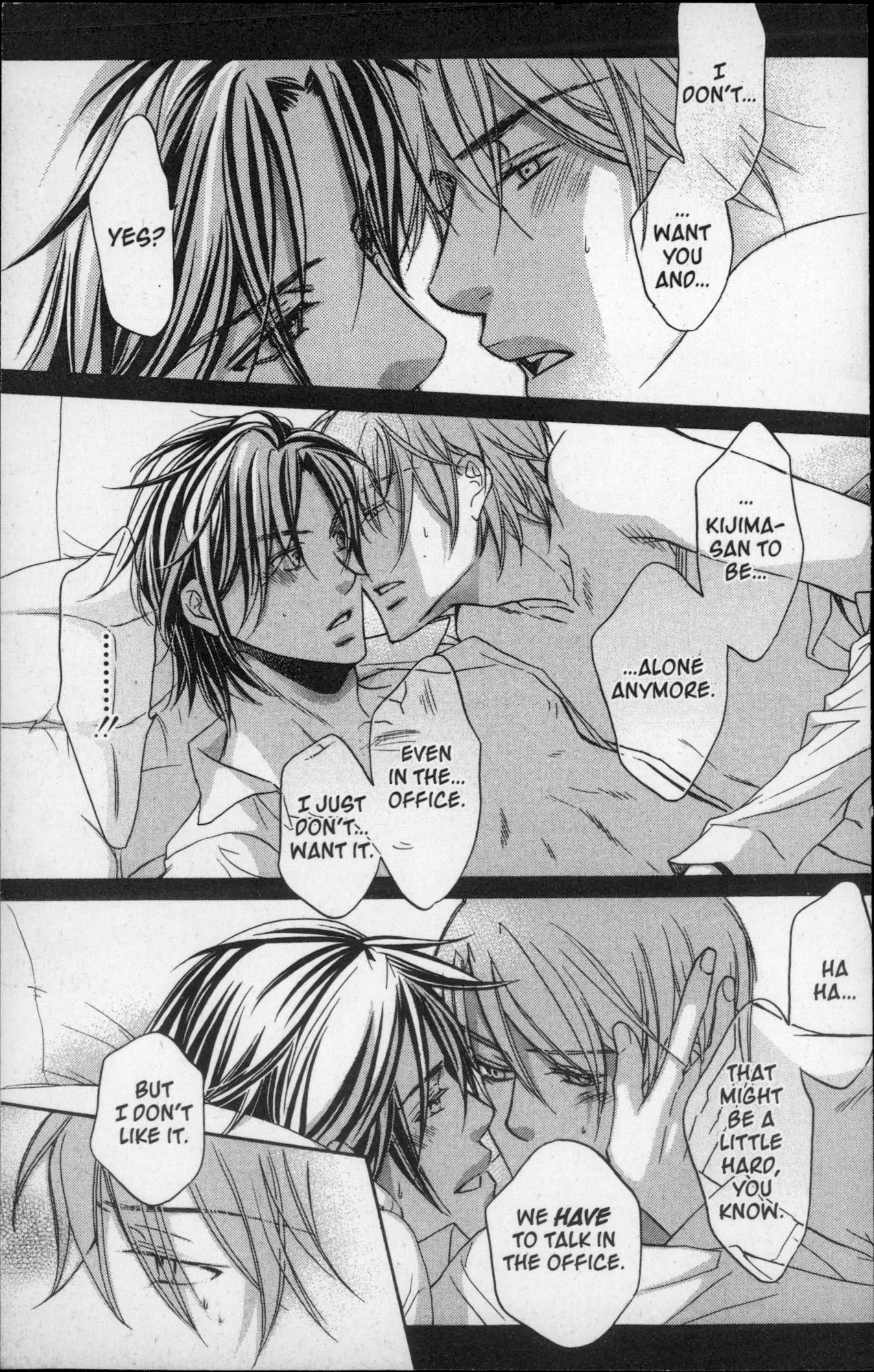
I DON'T...
... WANT YOU AND...
YES?
... KIJIMA-SAN TO BE...
...ALONE ANYMORE.
EVEN IN THE... OFFICE.
I JUST DON'T... WANT IT.
......!!
HA HA...
THAT MIGHT BE A LITTLE HARD, YOU KNOW.
WE *HAVE* TO TALK IN THE OFFICE.
BUT I DON'T LIKE IT.

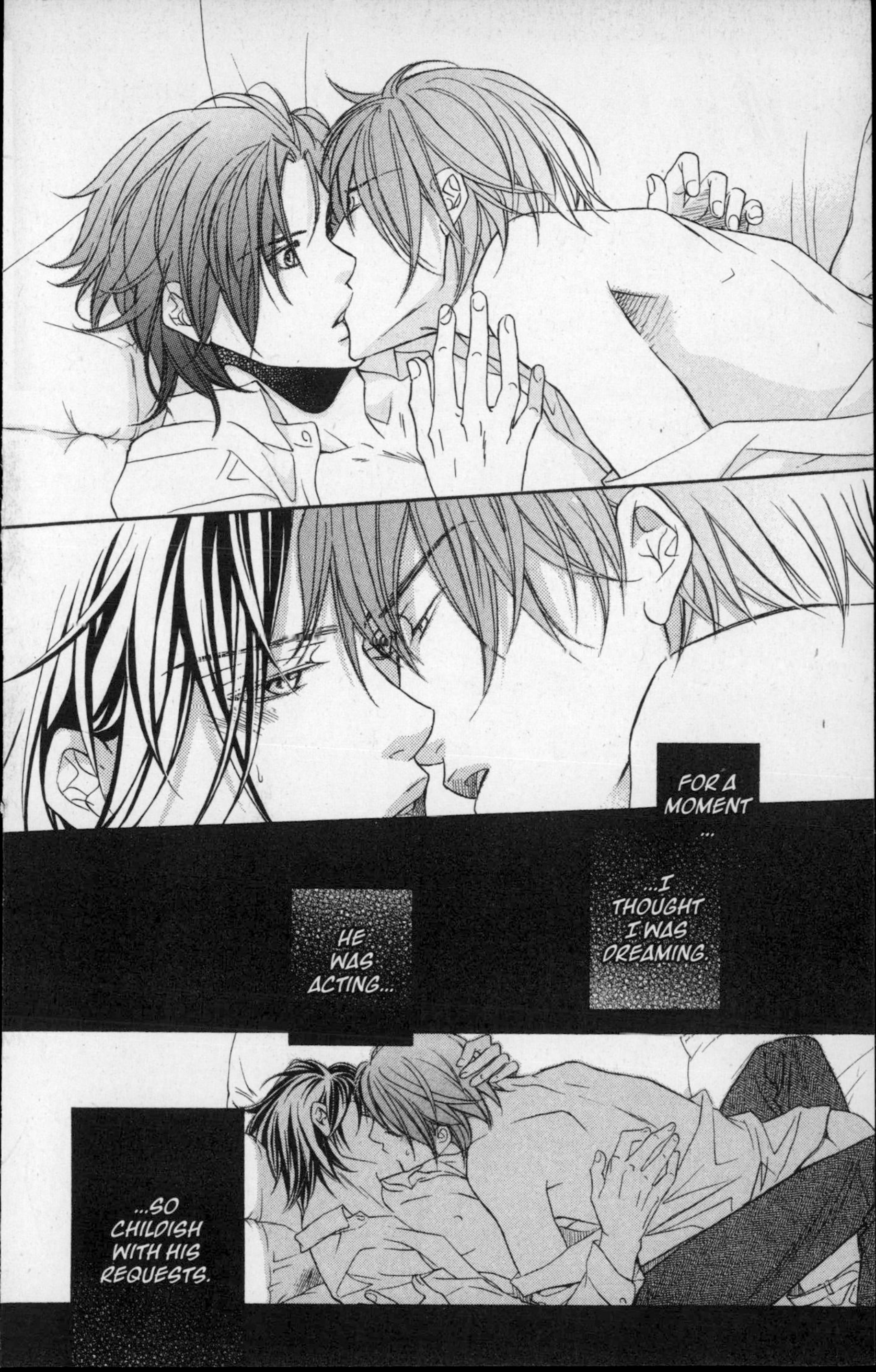
FOR A MOMENT ...
...I THOUGHT I WAS DREAMING.
HE WAS ACTING...
...SO CHILDISH WITH HIS REQUESTS.

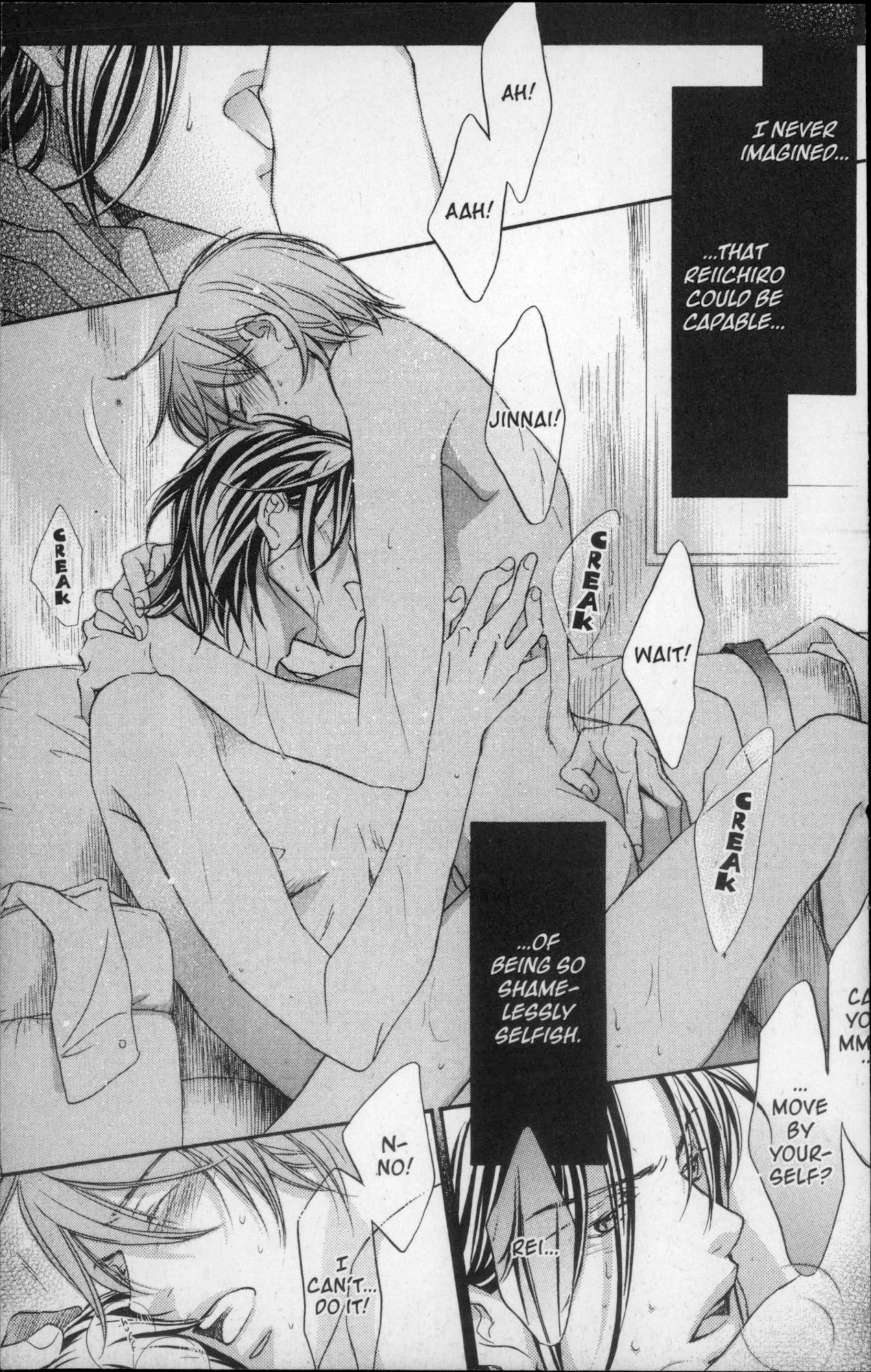
I NEVER IMAGINED...
AH!
AAH!
...THAT REIICHIRO COULD BE CAPABLE...
JINNAI!
CREAK
WAIT!
CREAK
CREAK
...OF BEING SO SHAME-LESSLY SELFISH.
...MOVE BY YOUR-SELF?
REI...
N-NO!
I CAN'T... DO IT!

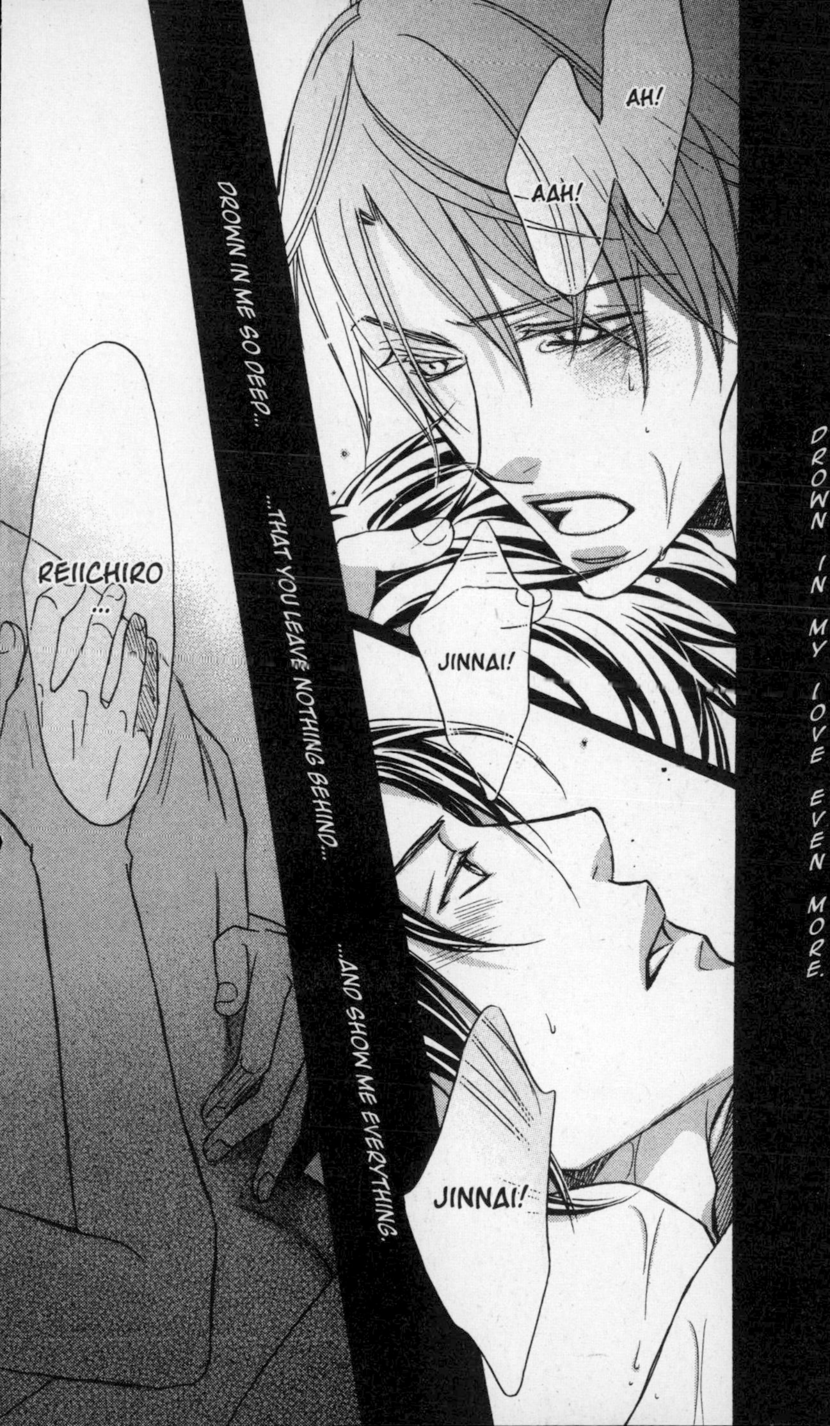
DROWN IN MY LOVE EVEN MORE.
JINNAI!
JINNAI!
...AND SHOW ME EVERYTHING.
...THAT YOU LEAVE NOTHING BEHIND...
AH!
AAH!
DROWN IN ME SO DEEP...
REIICHIRO...

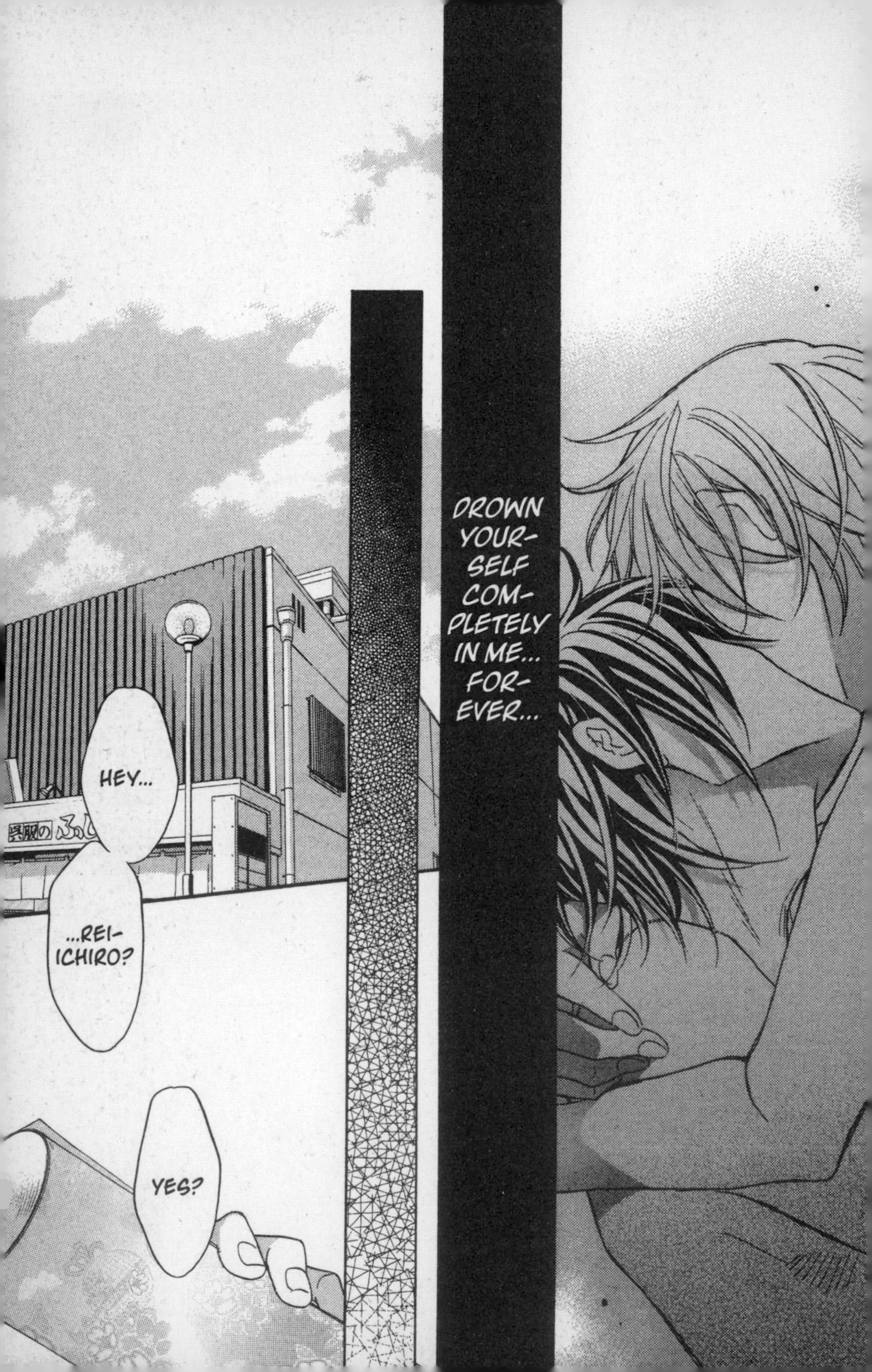
DROWN YOURSELF COMPLETELY IN ME... FOREVER...
HEY...
...REI-ICHIRO?
YES?

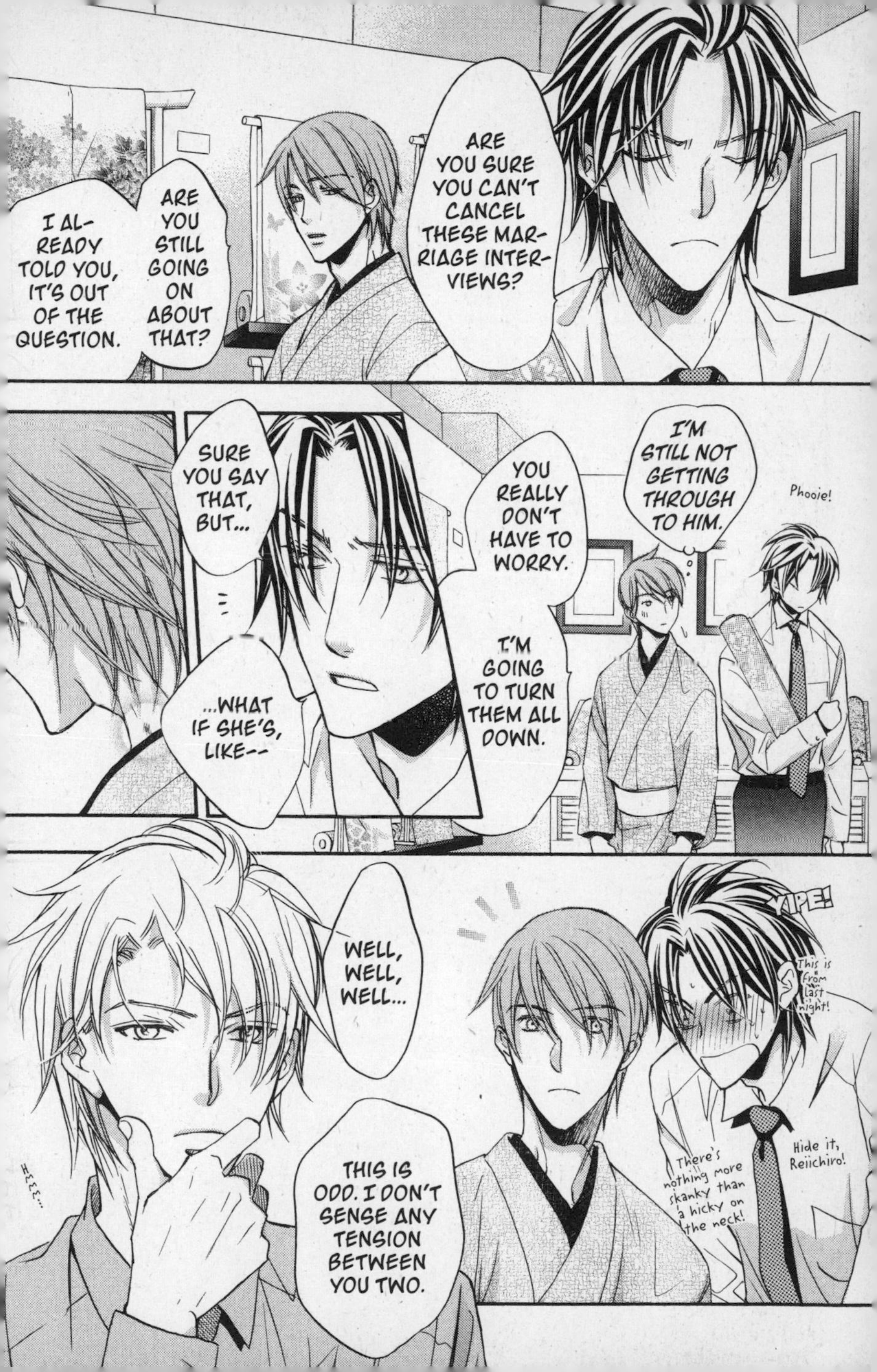
ARE YOU SURE YOU CAN'T CANCEL THESE MAR-RIAGE INTER-VIEWS?
ARE YOU STILL GOING ON ABOUT THAT?
I AL-READY TOLD YOU, IT'S OUT OF THE QUESTION.
Phooie!
I'M STILL NOT GETTING THROUGH TO HIM.
YOU REALLY DON'T HAVE TO WORRY.
I'M GOING TO TURN THEM ALL DOWN.
SURE YOU SAY THAT, BUT...
...WHAT IF SHE'S, LIKE--
YIPE!
This is from last night!
Hide it, Reiichiro!
There's nothing more skanky than a hicky on the neck!
WELL, WELL, WELL...
THIS IS ODD. I DON'T SENSE ANY TENSION BETWEEN YOU TWO.
Hmmm...

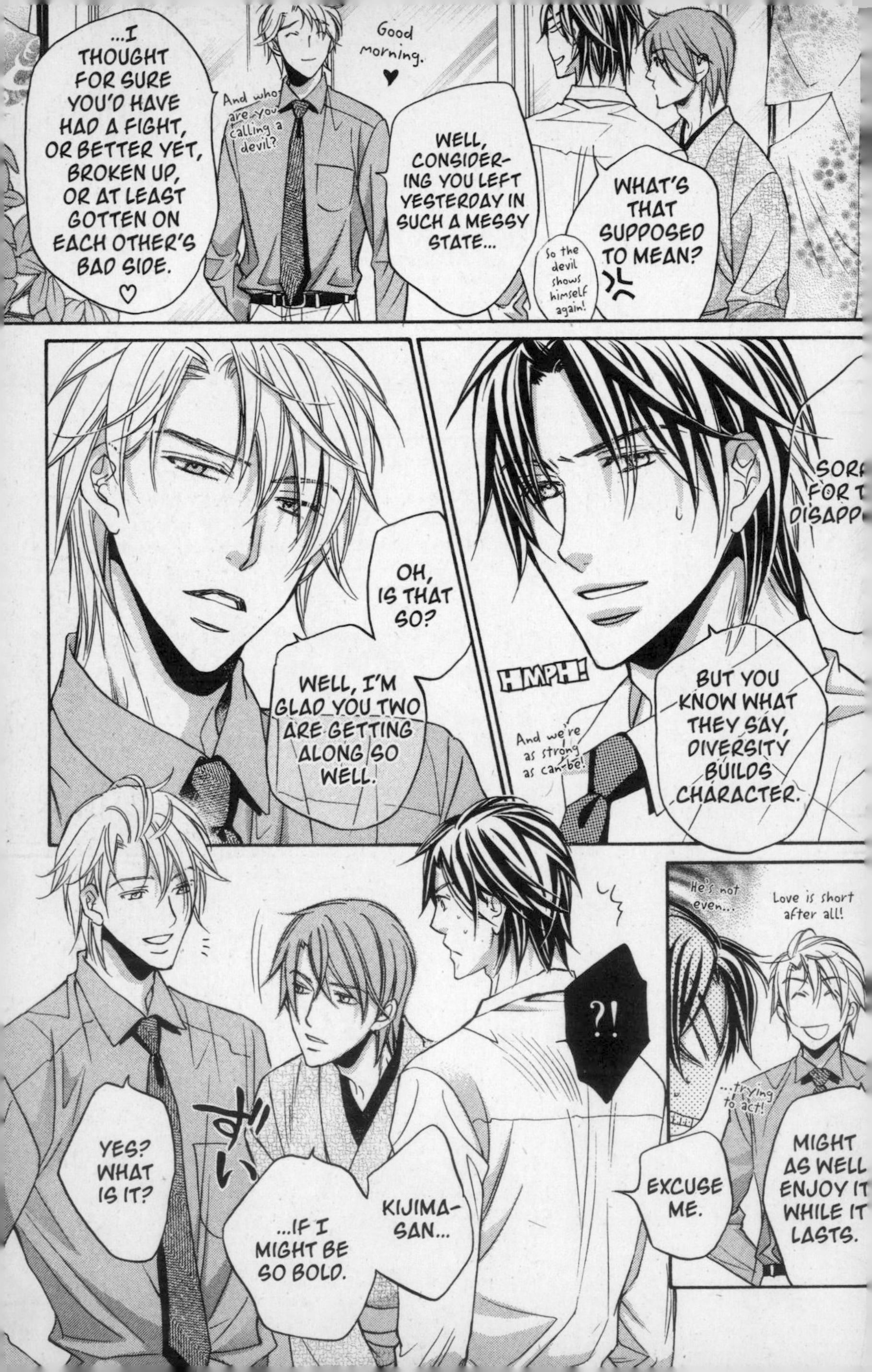
WHAT'S THAT SUPPOSED TO MEAN?
So the devil shows himself again!
WELL, CONSIDERING YOU LEFT YESTERDAY IN SUCH A MESSY STATE...
Good morning. ♥
And who are you calling a devil?
...I THOUGHT FOR SURE YOU'D HAVE HAD A FIGHT, OR BETTER YET, BROKEN UP, OR AT LEAST GOTTEN ON EACH OTHER'S BAD SIDE. ♡
SOR FOR T DISAPP
HMPH!
BUT YOU KNOW WHAT THEY SAY, DIVERSITY BUILDS CHARACTER.
And we're as strong as can be!
OH, IS THAT SO?
WELL, I'M GLAD YOU TWO ARE GETTING ALONG SO WELL.
Love is short after all!
He's not even...
...trying to act!
MIGHT AS WELL ENJOY IT WHILE IT LASTS.
EXCUSE ME.
?!
KIJIMA-SAN...
...IF I MIGHT BE SO BOLD.
ずい
YES? WHAT IS IT?

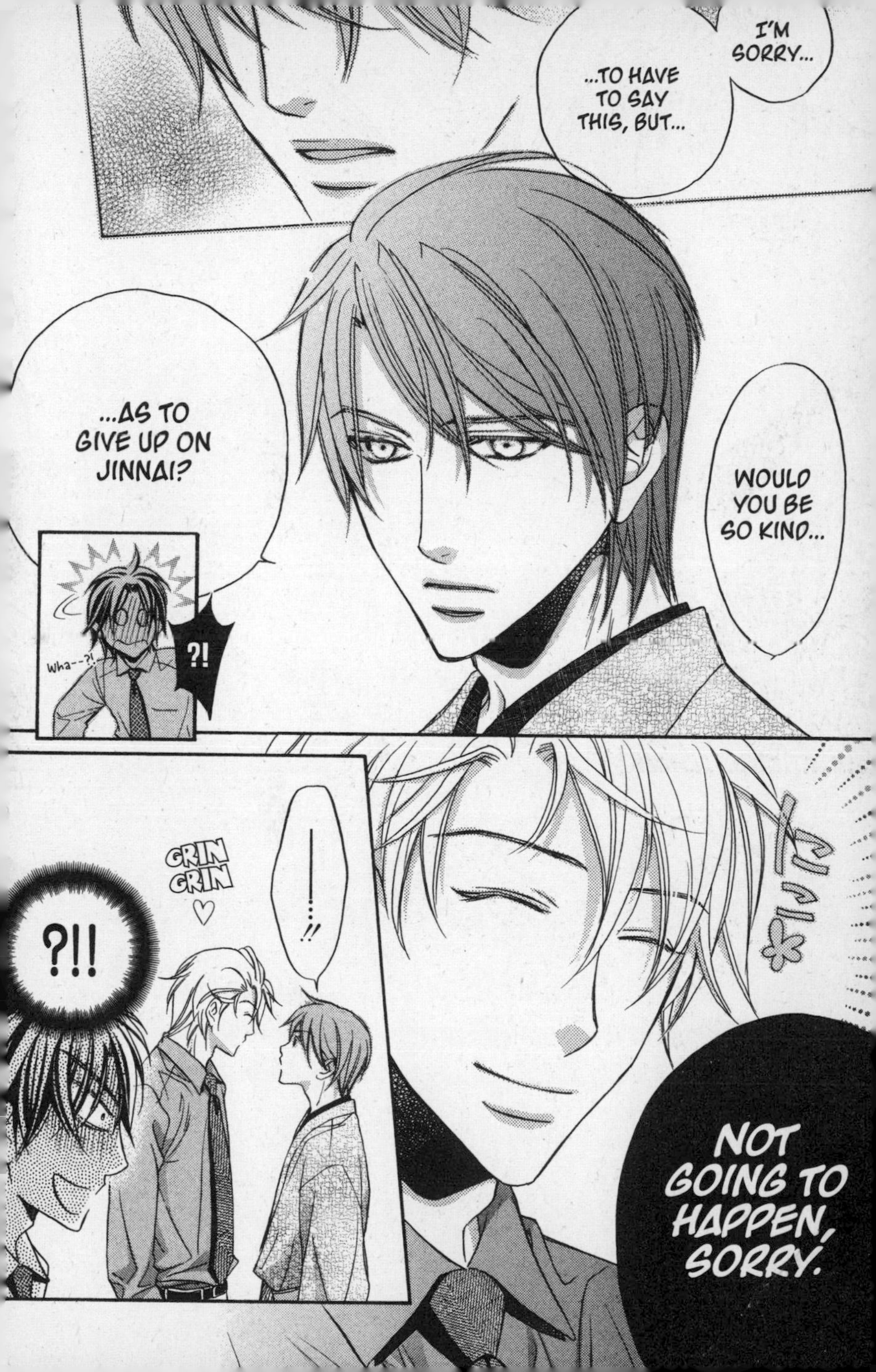
I'M SORRY...
...TO HAVE TO SAY THIS, BUT...
WOULD YOU BE SO KIND...
...AS TO GIVE UP ON JINNAI?
?!
Wha--?!
NOT GOING TO HAPPEN, SORRY.
—...!!
GRIN GRIN ♥
?!!

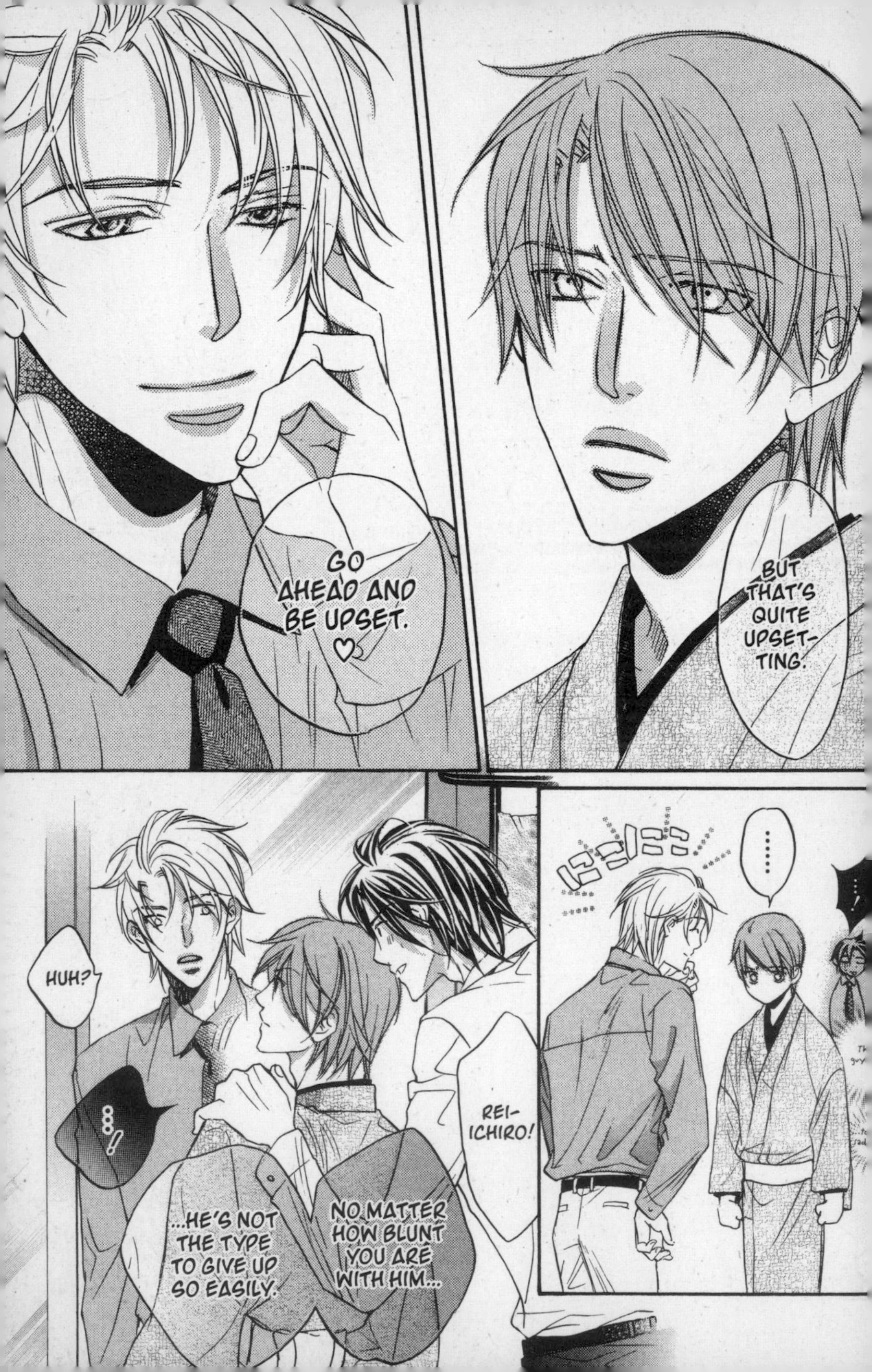
BUT THAT'S QUITE UPSET-TING.
GO AHEAD AND BE UPSET. ♡
......
にこにこ
REI-ICHIRO!
NO MATTER HOW BLUNT YOU ARE WITH HIM...
...HE'S NOT THE TYPE TO GIVE UP SO EASILY.
HUH?

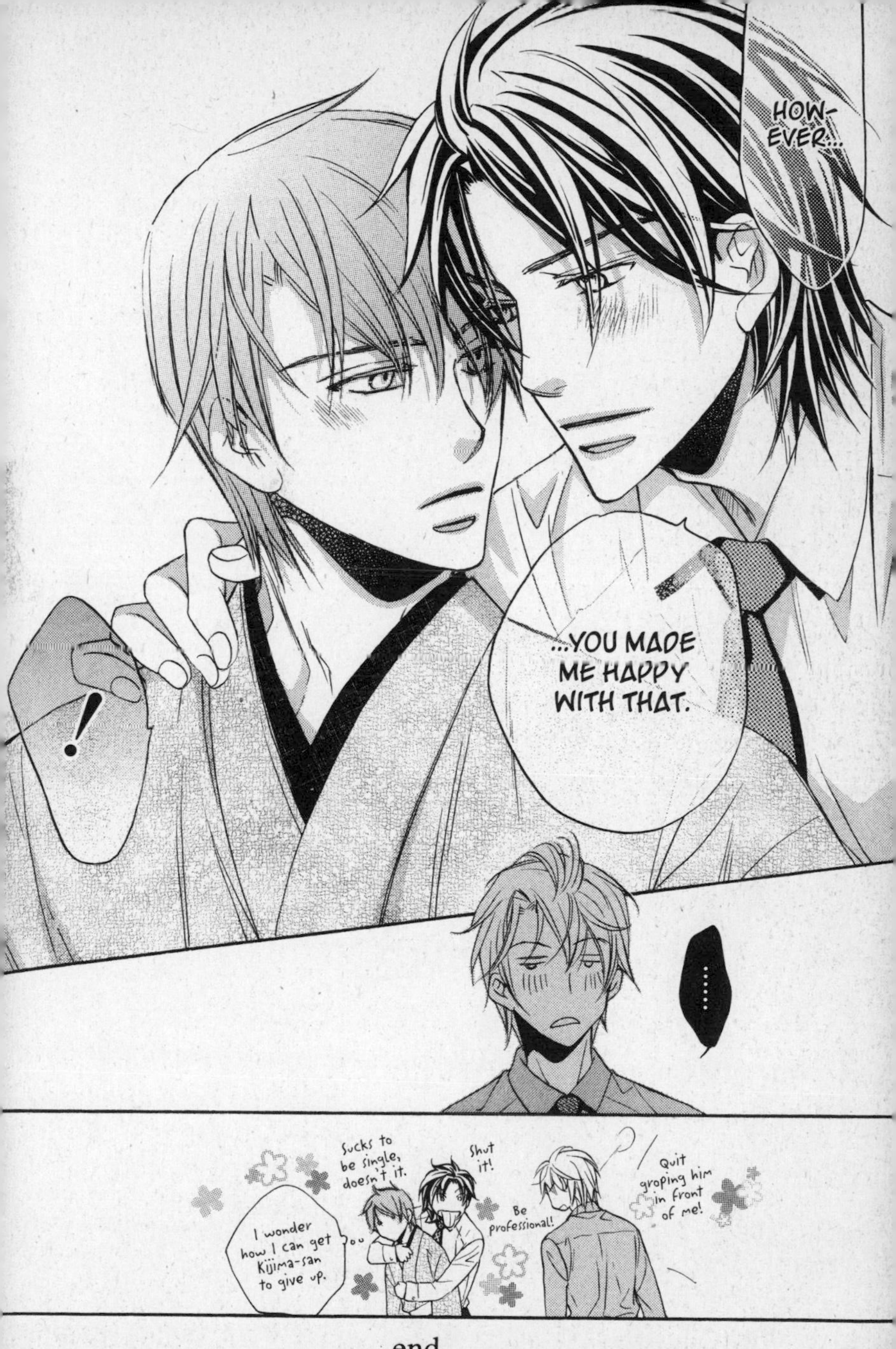
HOW-EVER...
...YOU MADE ME HAPPY WITH THAT.
!
......
Quit groping him in front of me!
Be professional!
Shut it!
Sucks to be single, doesn't it.
I wonder how I can get Kijima-san to give up.

end

You Will Drown in Love

Presented by
Hinako Takanaga
ASUKA COMICS CL-DX

You Will Drown in love

2

Presented by
Hinako Takanaga
ASUKA COMICS CL-DX

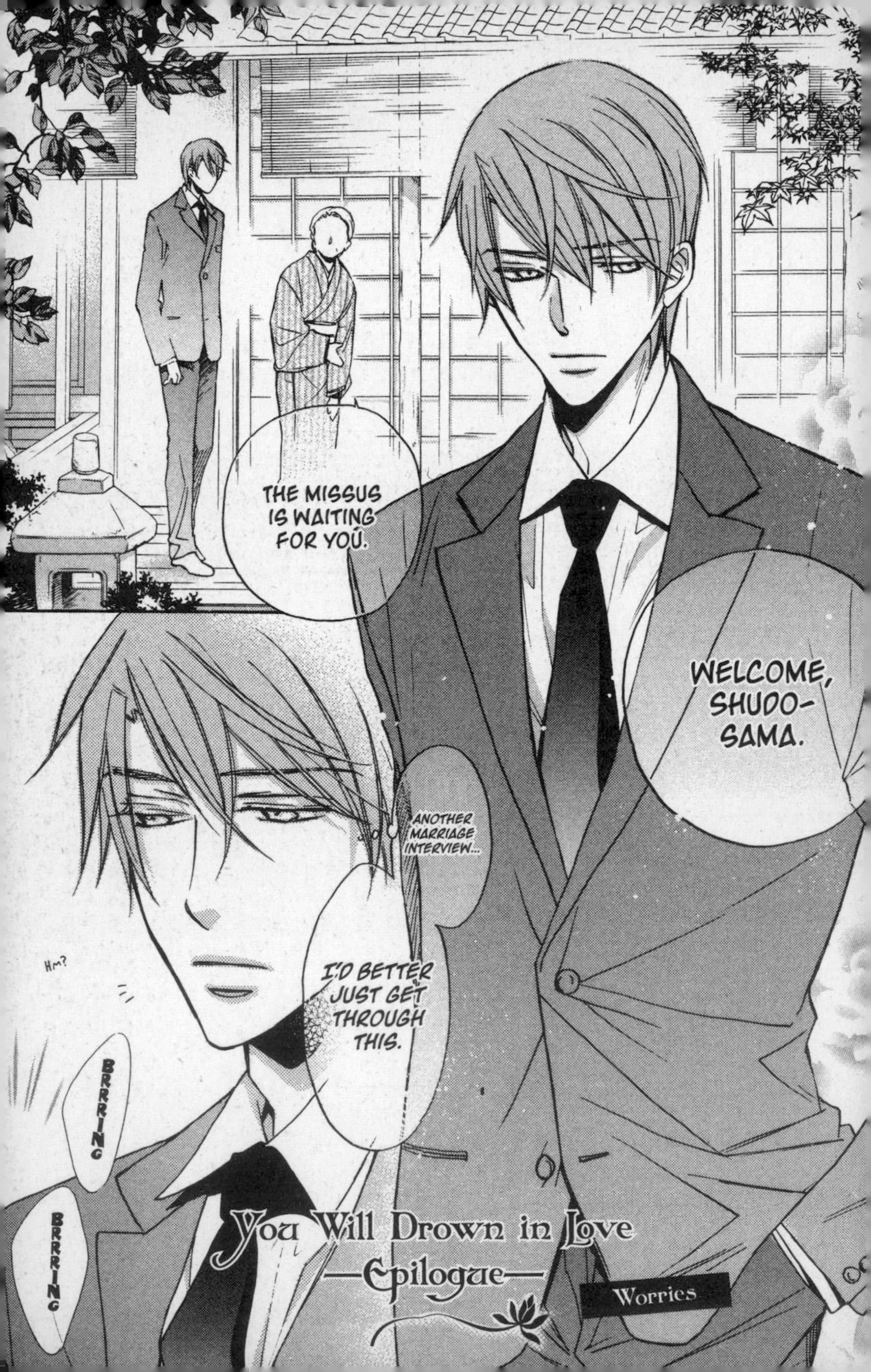
THE MISSUS IS WAITING FOR YOU.
WELCOME, SHUDO-SAMA.
ANOTHER MARRIAGE INTERVIEW...
I'D BETTER JUST GET THROUGH THIS.
HM?
BRRRING
BRRRING
You Will Drown in Love
—Epilogue—
Worries

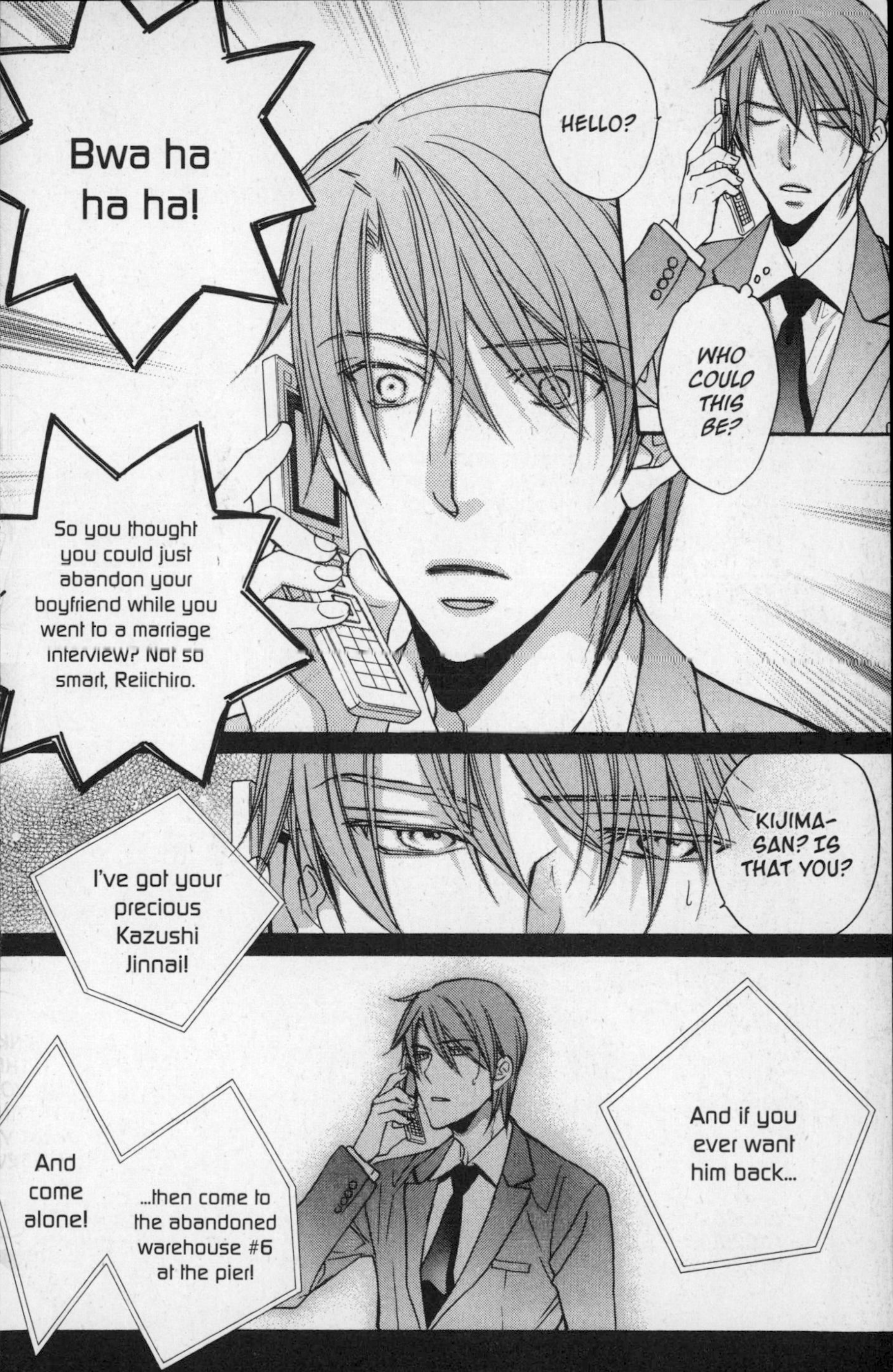
HELLO?
WHO COULD THIS BE?
Bwa ha ha ha!
So you thought you could just abandon your boyfriend while you went to a marriage interview? Not so smart, Reiichiro.
KIJIMA-SAN? IS THAT YOU?
I've got your precious Kazushi Jinnai!
And if you ever want him back...
...then come to the abandoned warehouse #6 at the pier!
And come alone!

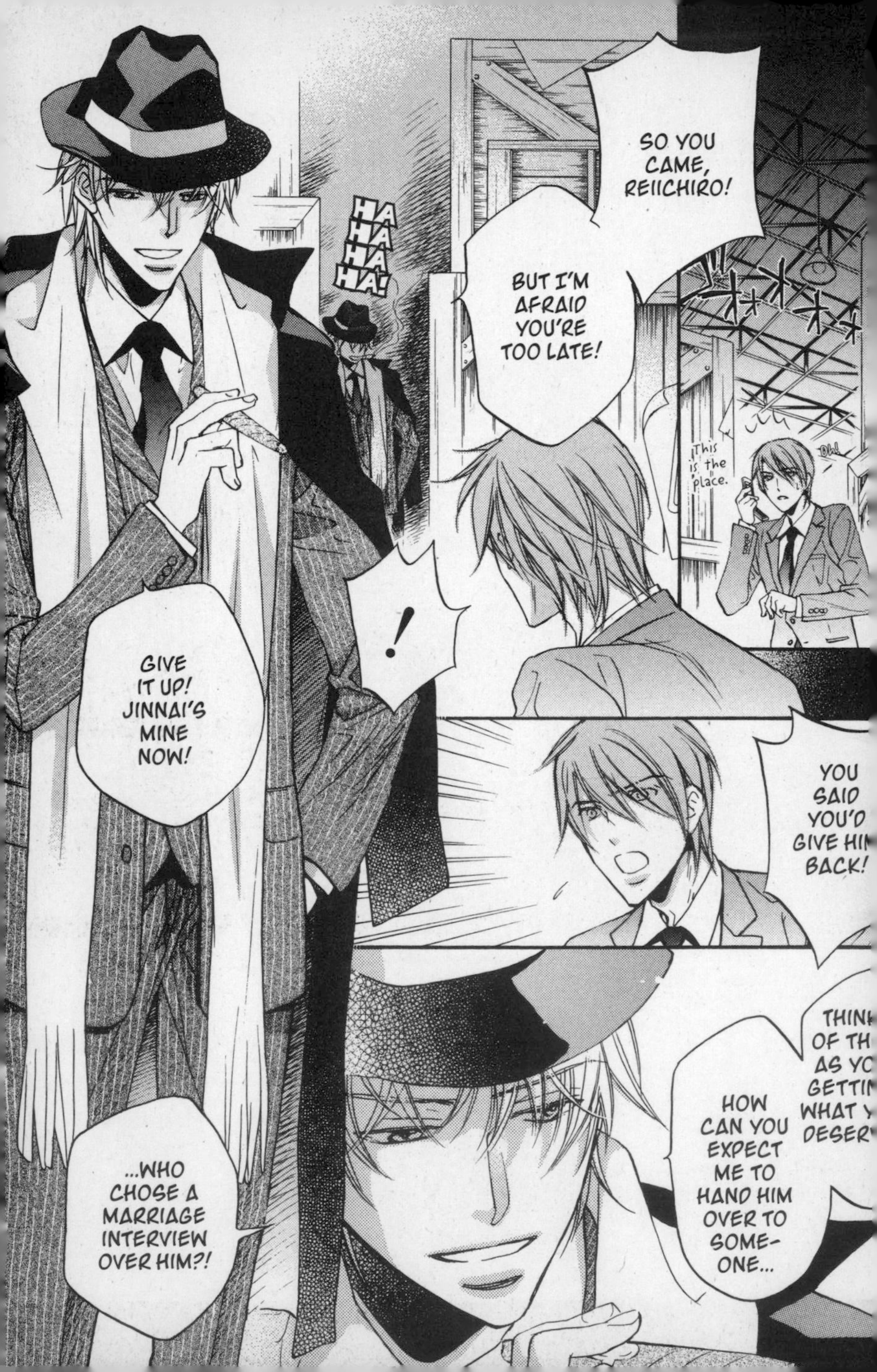
This is the place.
OH!
SO YOU CAME, REIICHIRO!
BUT I'M AFRAID YOU'RE TOO LATE!
HA HA HA HA!
!
YOU SAID YOU'D GIVE HIM BACK!
HOW CAN YOU EXPECT ME TO HAND HIM OVER TO SOME-ONE...
GIVE IT UP! JINNAI'S MINE NOW!
...WHO CHOSE A MARRIAGE INTERVIEW OVER HIM?!

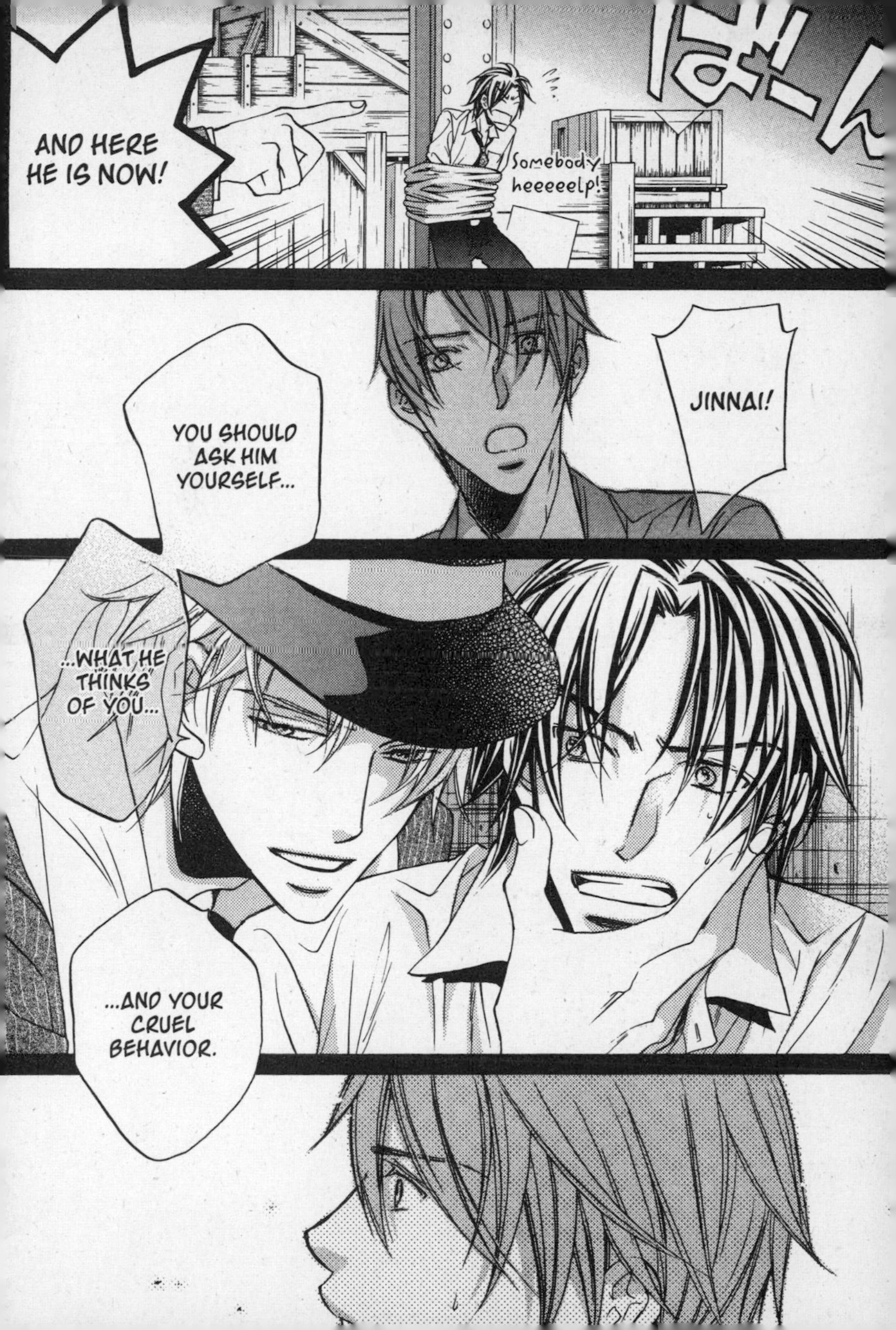
ぱーん
Somebody heeeeelp!
AND HERE HE IS NOW!
JINNAI!
YOU SHOULD ASK HIM YOURSELF...
...WHAT HE THINKS OF YOU...
...AND YOUR CRUEL BEHAVIOR.

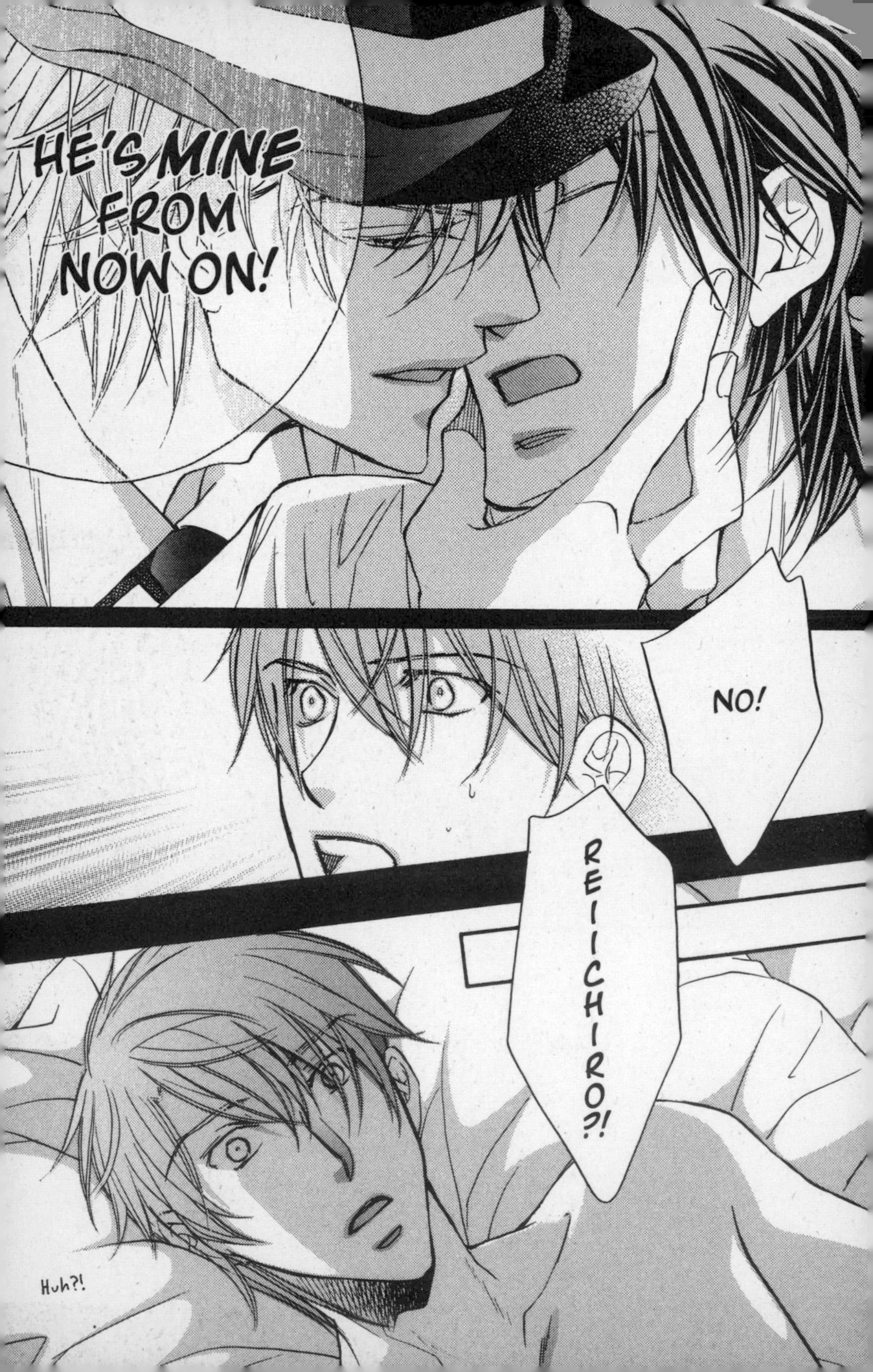
HE'S MINE FROM NOW ON!
NO!
REIICHIRO?!
Huh?!

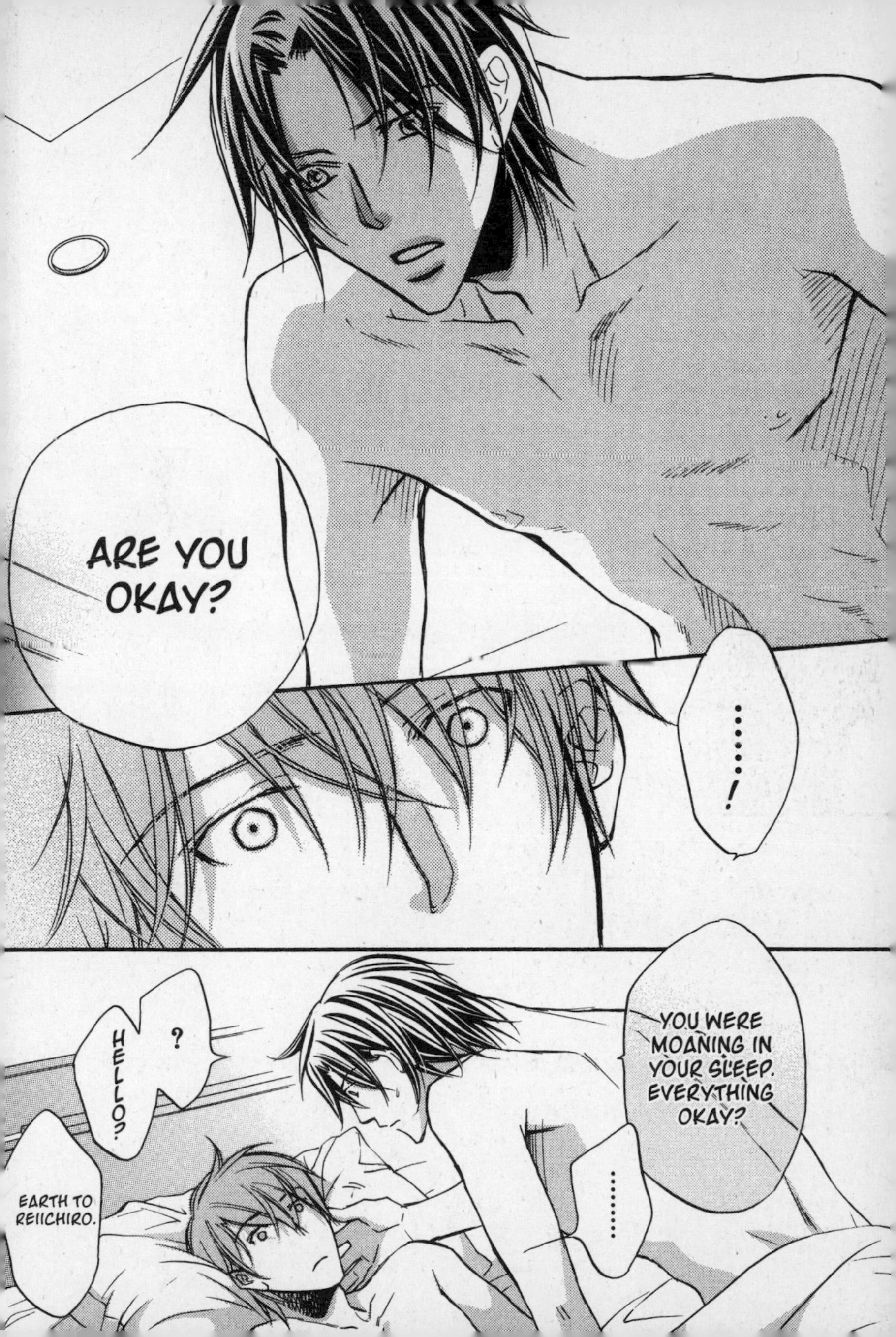
ARE YOU OKAY?
......!
YOU WERE MOANING IN YOUR SLEEP. EVERYTHING OKAY?
......
HELLO?
?
EARTH TO REIICHIRO.

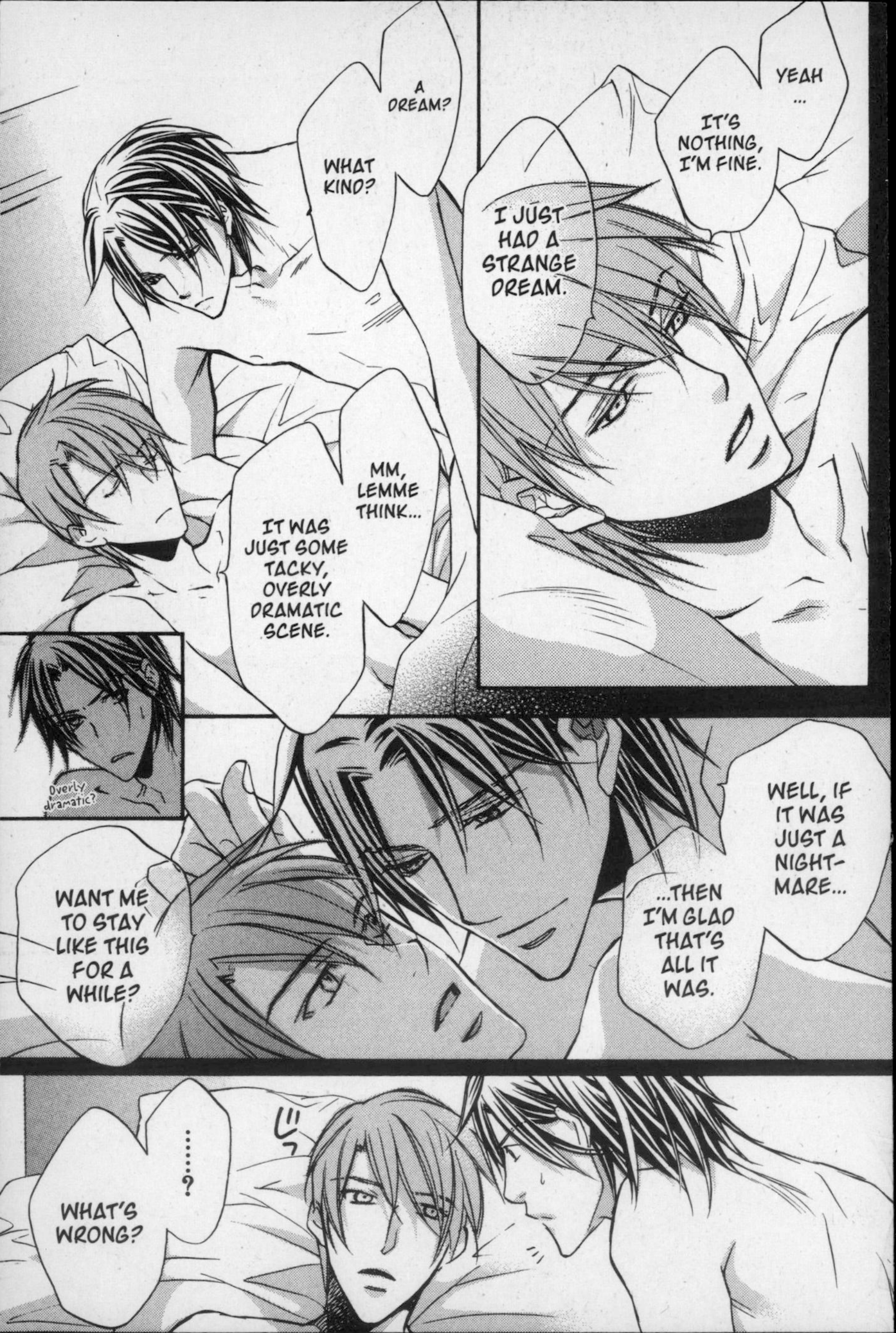
YEAH ...
IT'S NOTHING, I'M FINE.
I JUST HAD A STRANGE DREAM.
A DREAM?
WHAT KIND?
MM, LEMME THINK...
IT WAS JUST SOME TACKY, OVERLY DRAMATIC SCENE.
Overly dramatic?
WELL, IF IT WAS JUST A NIGHT-MARE...
...THEN I'M GLAD THAT'S ALL IT WAS.
WANT ME TO STAY LIKE THIS FOR A WHILE?
......?
WHAT'S WRONG?

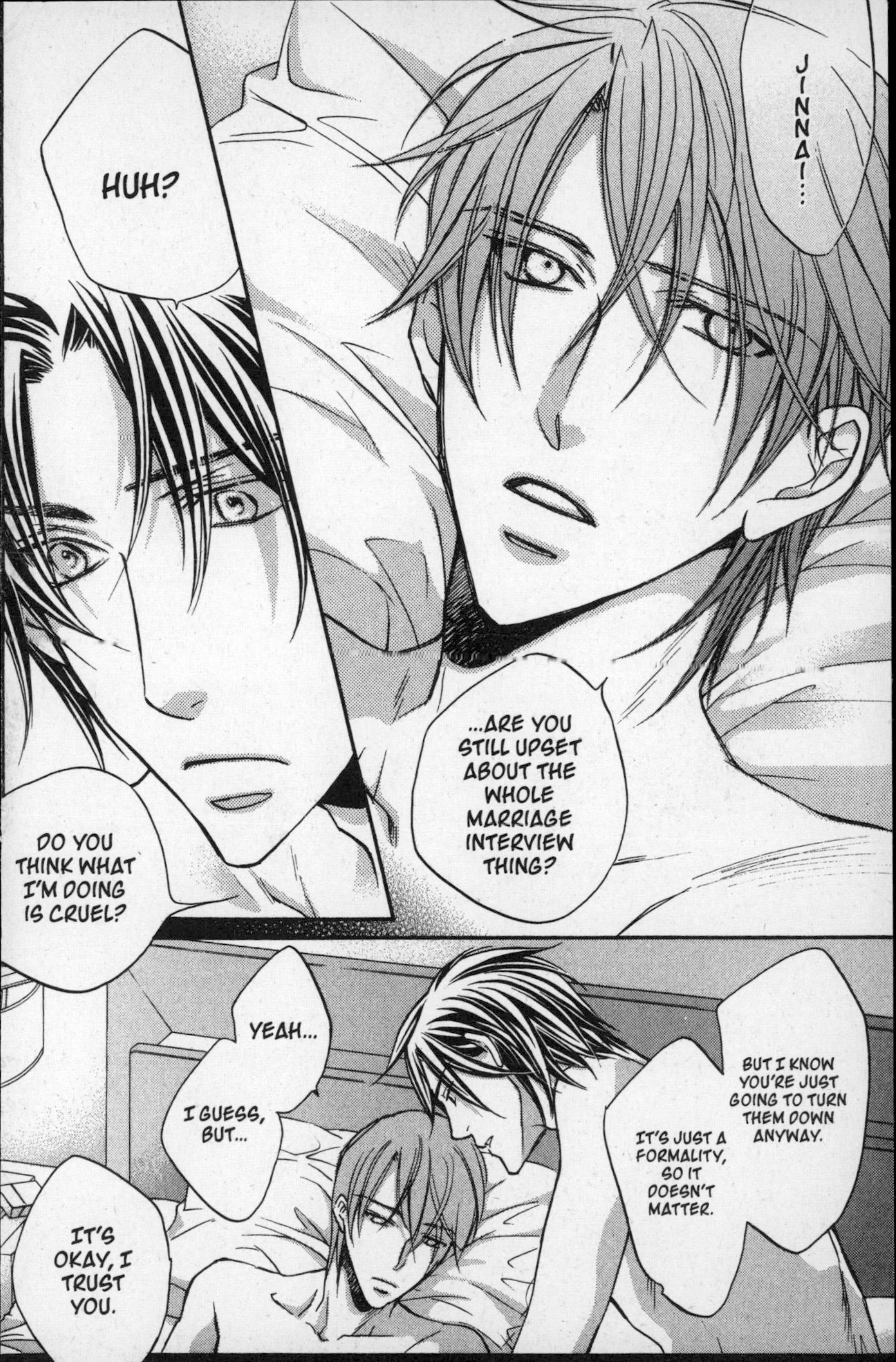
JINNAI...
HUH?
...ARE YOU STILL UPSET ABOUT THE WHOLE MARRIAGE INTERVIEW THING?
DO YOU THINK WHAT I'M DOING IS CRUEL?
BUT I KNOW YOU'RE JUST GOING TO TURN THEM DOWN ANYWAY.
IT'S JUST A FORMALITY, SO IT DOESN'T MATTER.
YEAH...
I GUESS, BUT...
IT'S OKAY, I TRUST YOU.

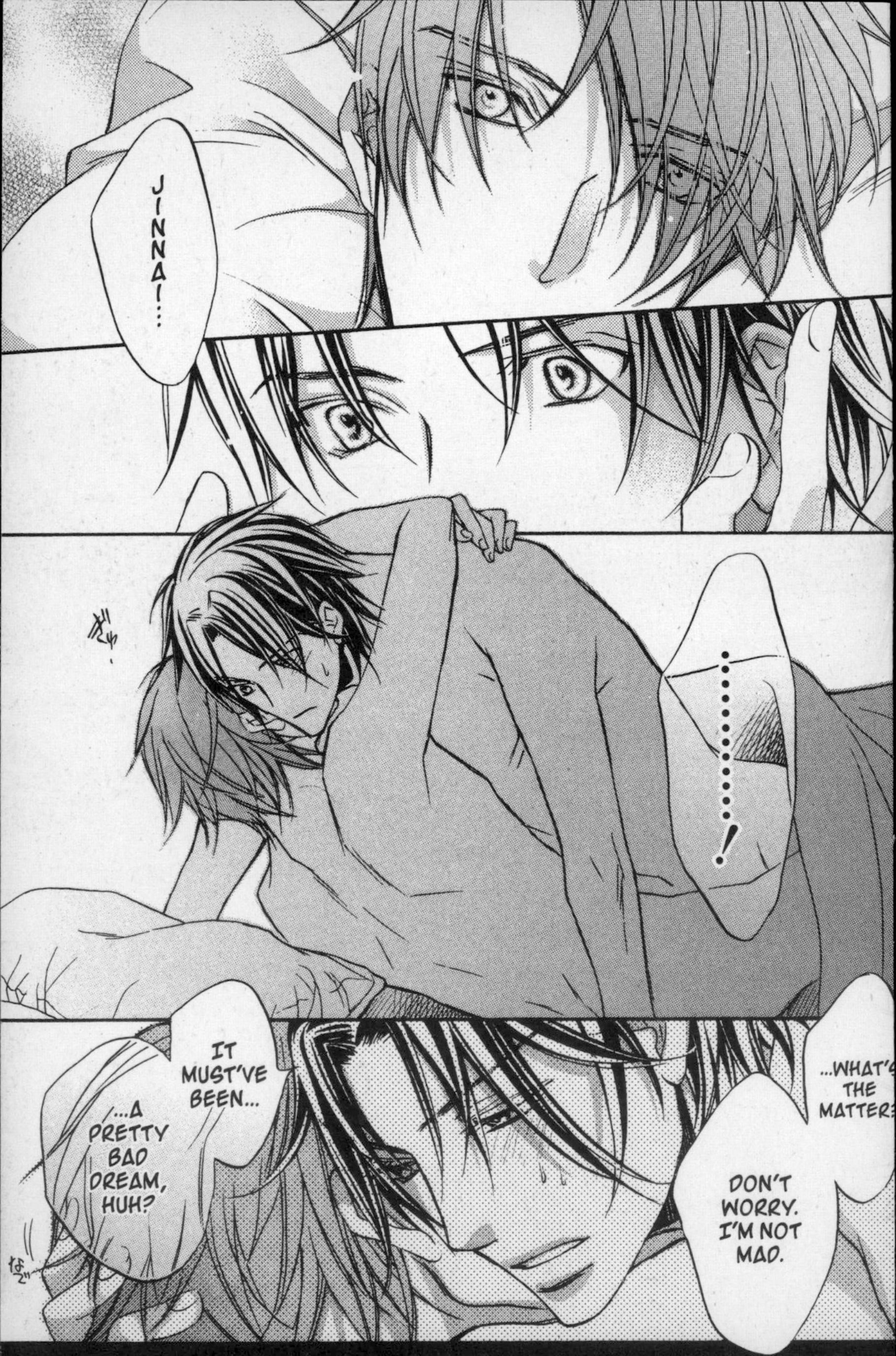
JINNAI...
.........!
...WHAT'S THE MATTER?
DON'T WORRY. I'M NOT MAD.
IT MUST'VE BEEN...
...A PRETTY BAD DREAM, HUH?

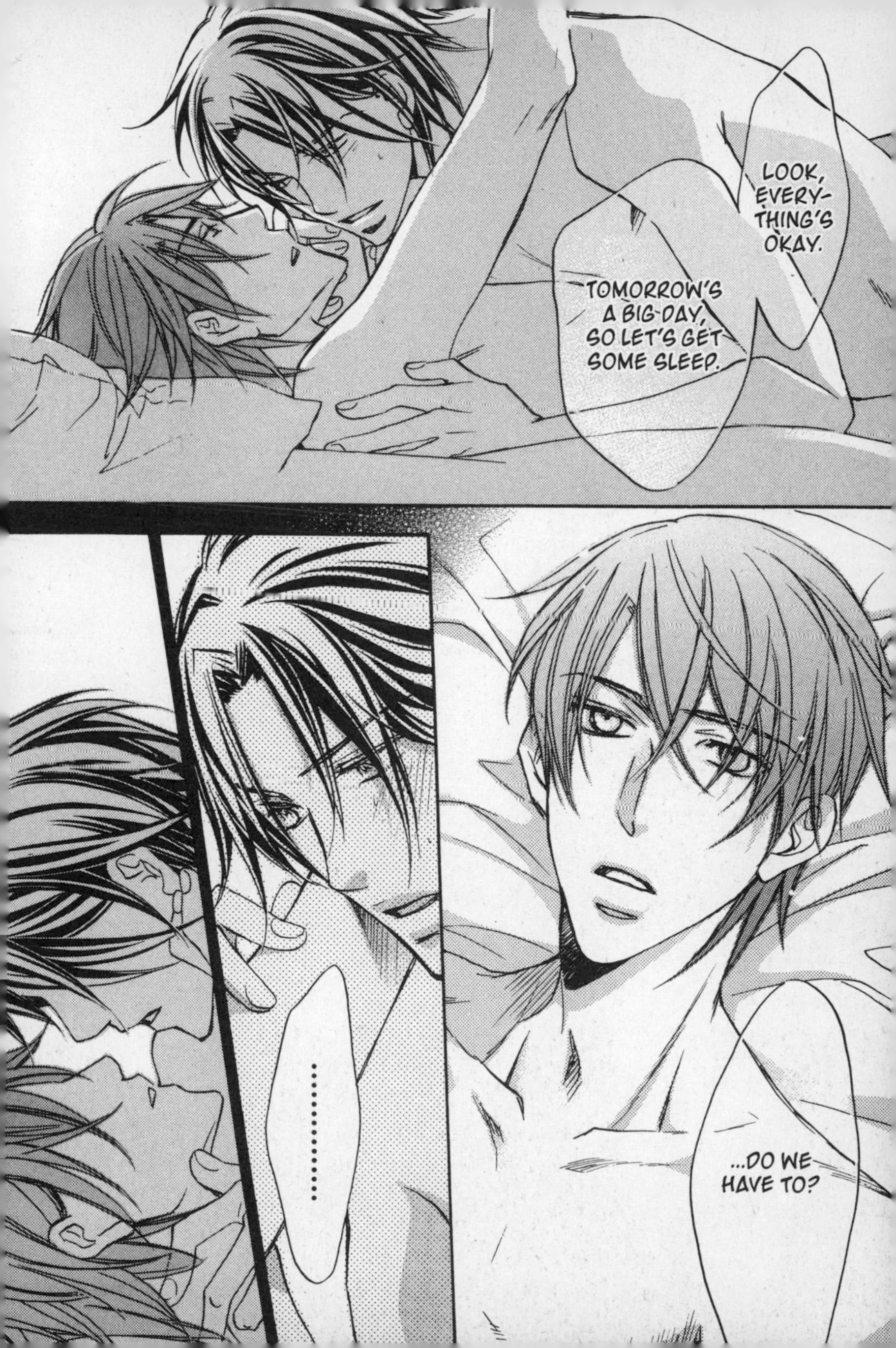
LOOK, EVERY-THING'S OKAY.
TOMORROW'S A BIG-DAY, SO LET'S GET SOME SLEEP.
...DO WE HAVE TO?
....

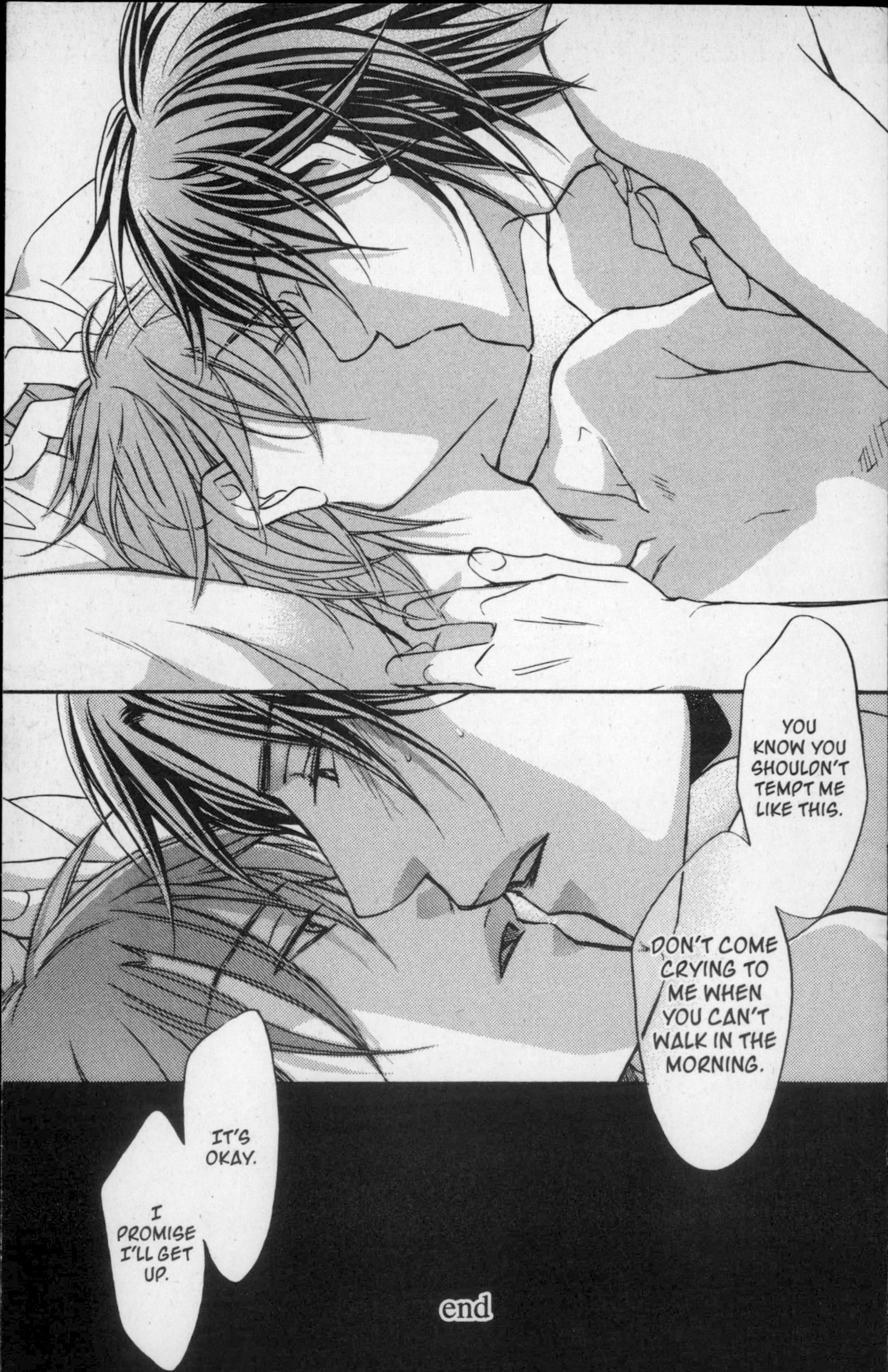
YOU KNOW YOU SHOULDN'T TEMPT ME LIKE THIS.
DON'T COME CRYING TO ME WHEN YOU CAN'T WALK IN THE MORNING.
IT'S OKAY.
I PROMISE I'LL GET UP.
end

Start Here! ⬇

※ Hello! Nice to meet you, to any newbs out there. And thank you to all for picking up this book if this isn't your first time. This is Hinako Takanaga, and this is volume 2 of "You Will Drown in Love." The "2" means there was a first volume before this, so if you've bought this book because you liked the first one, then yippee! But if you picked this one up first, then go right back to the bookstore and get the first volume! Ha ha!

※ For those of you who don't know, I also did a book called "You Will Fall in Love" that's just one volume long before I did the first volume of "You Will Drown in Love." That was the official start of this "You Will~in Love" series. The chapters of "Fall" and "Drown" are connected, so it may be a little difficult to follow if you haven't read "Fall" yet. At least, maybe. Just something for those of you who didn't read it to think about.

※ In other news, I recently moved! I'd been telling myself that I needed to move for a long time now, but once spring came along, it finally happened! I'm now a three-minute walk to the convenience store, close to the park, 100-yen store, and even a cute goods shop. Coming from the countryside, I thought I'd never get used to living here, and I was struck with fear after moving. But then again, the last place I lived didn't have anything at all. I was also worried about my kitty, Choro, who howled during the entire move. I was afraid he'd get stressed out and start losing his fur like last time, but once we arrived at the new place, I was shocked at how quickly he got into scoping the place out. Turns out he got used to the place faster than me! Now he sits on the top bunk like he owns the place, and spends half the day napping peacefully. What about that gorgeous new cage I bought you?! He just stays up there all smug, without a care in the world. I had to buy febreze. (And of course I make him use the cage sometimes. Heh heh.)

↳ cont'd on the left page

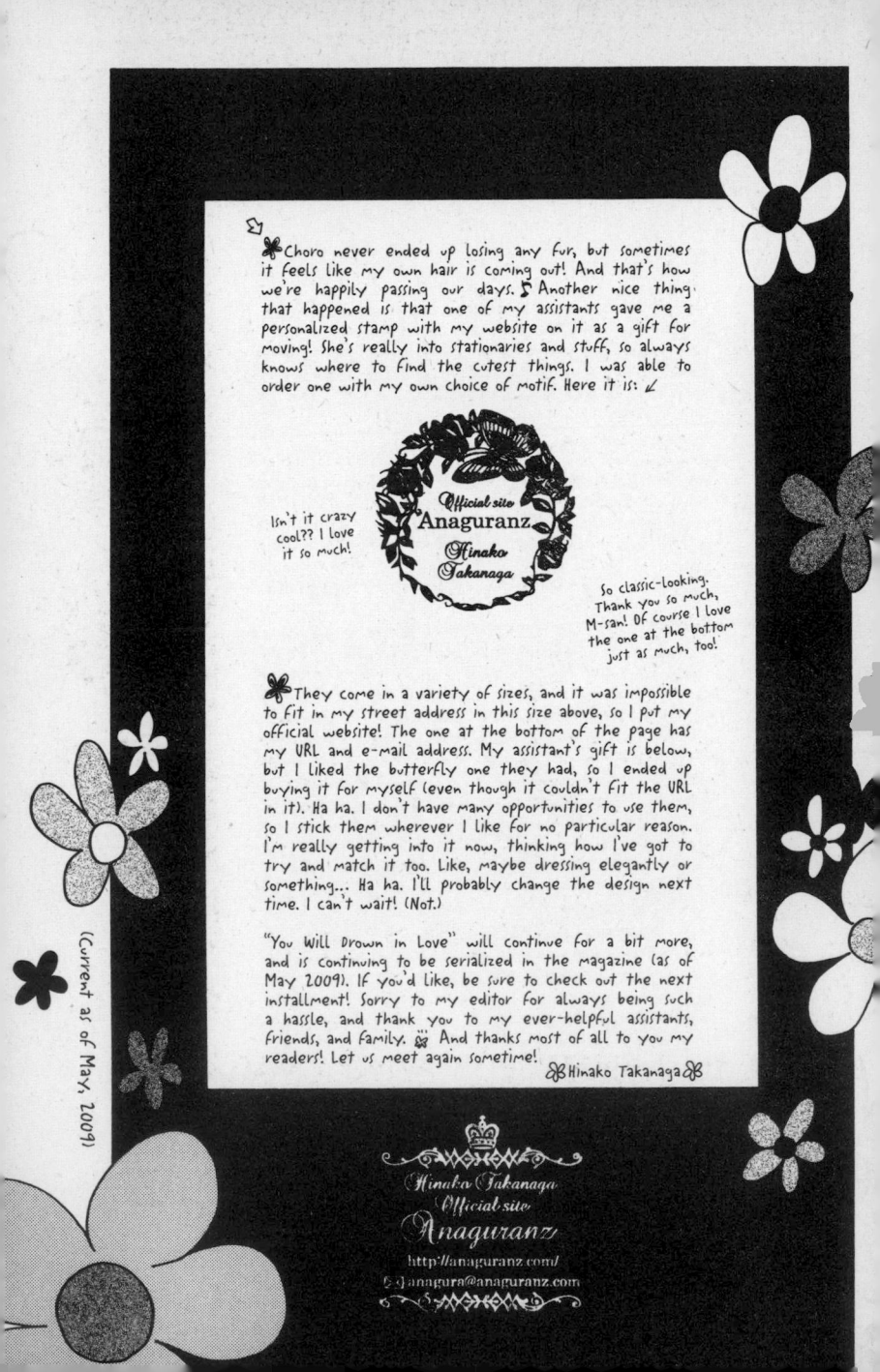

Choro never ended up losing any fur, but sometimes it feels like my own hair is coming out! And that's how we're happily passing our days. Another nice thing that happened is that one of my assistants gave me a personalized stamp with my website on it as a gift for moving! She's really into stationaries and stuff, so always knows where to find the cutest things. I was able to order one with my own choice of motif. Here it is:

Isn't it crazy cool?? I love it so much!

Official site
Anaguranz
Hinako
Takanaga

So classic-looking. Thank you so much, M-san! Of course I love the one at the bottom just as much, too!

They come in a variety of sizes, and it was impossible to fit in my street address in this size above, so I put my official website! The one at the bottom of the page has my URL and e-mail address. My assistant's gift is below, but I liked the butterfly one they had, so I ended up buying it for myself (even though it couldn't fit the URL in it). Ha ha. I don't have many opportunities to use them, so I stick them wherever I like for no particular reason. I'm really getting into it now, thinking how I've got to try and match it too. Like, maybe dressing elegantly or something... Ha ha. I'll probably change the design next time. I can't wait! (Not.)

"You Will Drown in Love" will continue for a bit more, and is continuing to be serialized in the magazine (as of May 2009). If you'd like, be sure to check out the next installment! Sorry to my editor for always being such a hassle, and thank you to my ever-helpful assistants, friends, and family. And thanks most of all to you my readers! Let us meet again sometime!

Hinako Takanaga

Hinako Takanaga
Official site
Anaguranz
http://anaguranz.com/
anagura@anaguranz.com

(Current as of May, 2009)

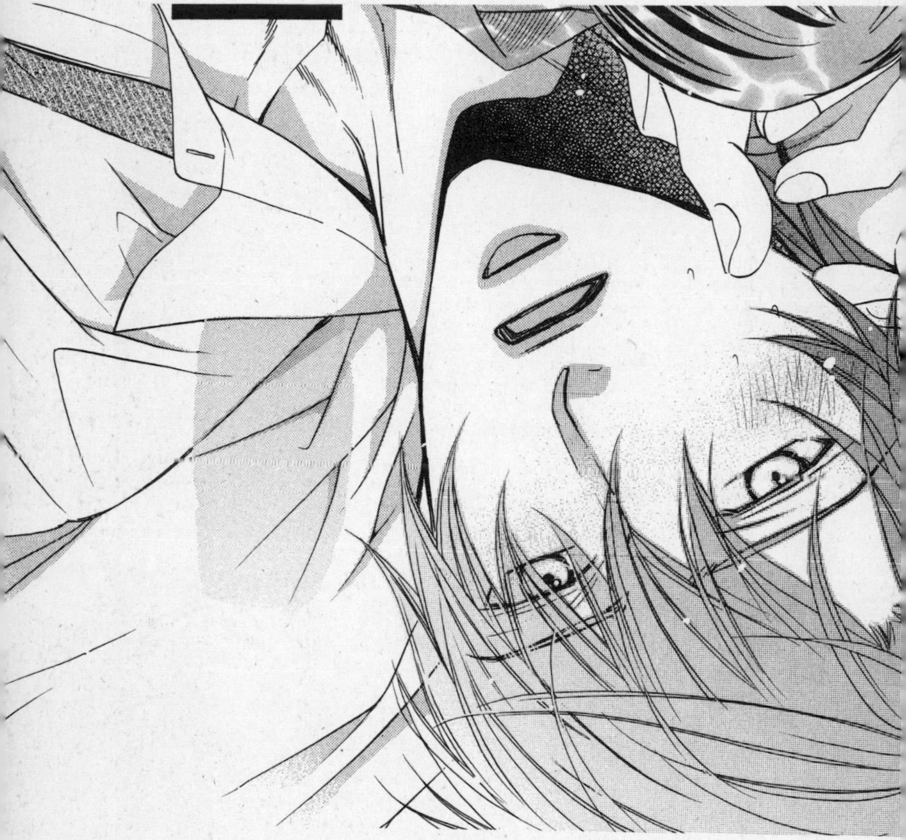

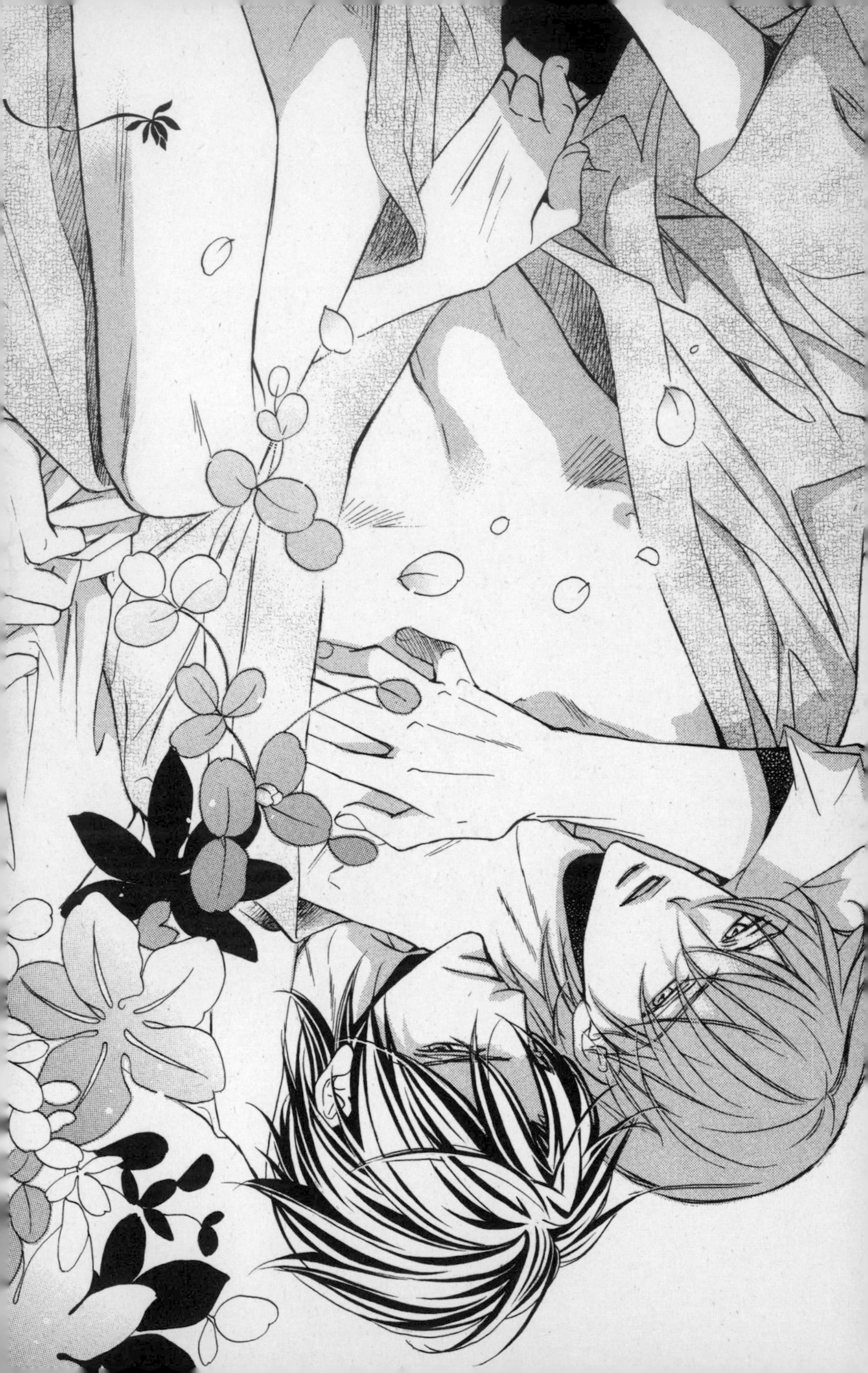

YOU WILL DROWN IN LOVE
Art and Story by Hinako Takanaga

KIMI GA KOI NI OBORERU © Hinako TAKANAGA 2009
First published in Japan in 2009 by KADOKAWA SHOTEN PUBLISHING CO., LTD., Tokyo.
English translation rights arranged with KADOKAWA SHOTEN PUBLISHING CO., LTD.,
Tokyo through TUTTLE-MORI AGENCY, INC., Tokyo.
English text copyright © 2010 BLU

ISBN: 978-1-4278-1804-1

First Printing: May 2010
10 9 8 7 6 5 4 3 2 1
Printed in the USA

This "Pure Romance" is anything but...

Passing his college entrance exams isn't the only thing Misaki has to worry about! Being romanced by a suave and older tutor is the concern, especially when the tutor in question is his brother's best friend and a famous porn novelist! Suddenly Misaki's "normal" life transforms into an educational journey filled with unfamiliar feelings and nonstop insanity.

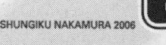

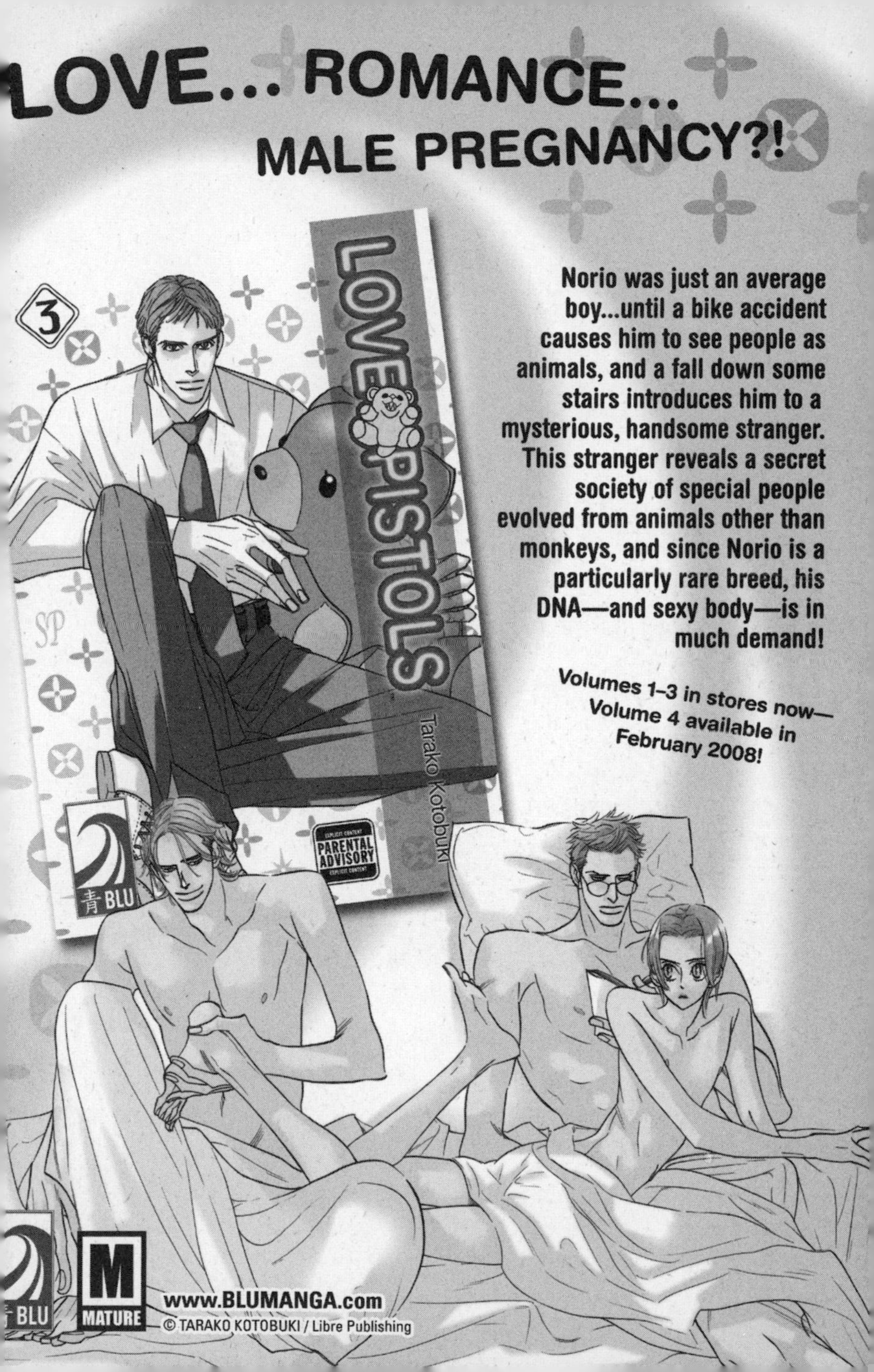
LOVE... ROMANCE...
MALE PREGNANCY?!
Norio was just an average boy...until a bike accident causes him to see people as animals, and a fall down some stairs introduces him to a mysterious, handsome stranger. This stranger reveals a secret society of special people evolved from animals other than monkeys, and since Norio is a particularly rare breed, his DNA—and sexy body—is in much demand!
Volumes 1–3 in stores now—
Volume 4 available in
February 2008!
LOVE PISTOLS
3
Tarako Kotobuki
PARENTAL ADVISORY
EXPLICIT CONTENT
青 BLU
M
MATURE
www.BLUMANGA.com
© TARAKO KOTOBUKI / Libre Publishing

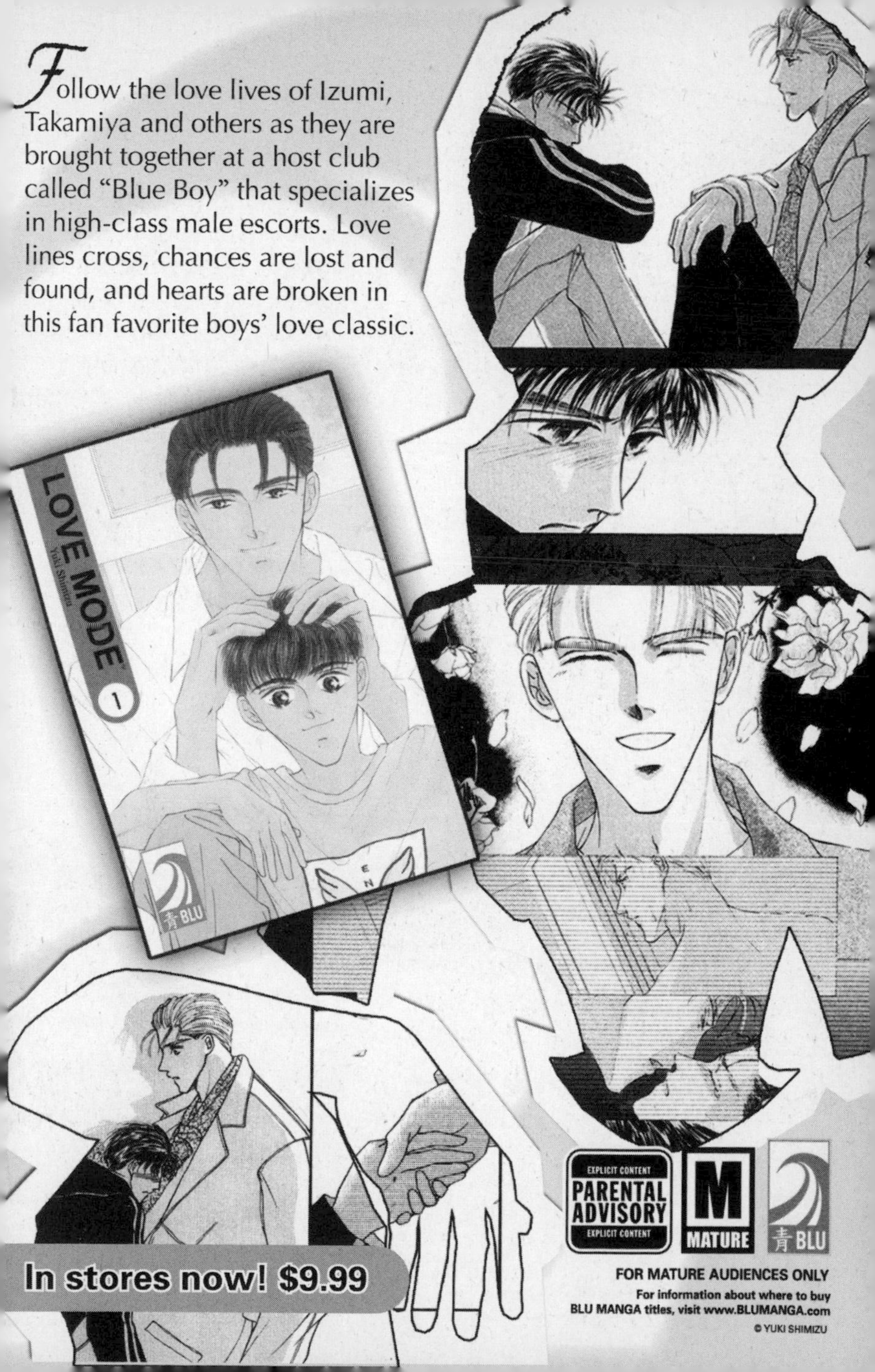
Follow the love lives of Izumi, Takamiya and others as they are brought together at a host club called "Blue Boy" that specializes in high-class male escorts. Love lines cross, chances are lost and found, and hearts are broken in this fan favorite boys' love classic.
LOVE MODE
Yuki Shimizu
1
青 BLU
EXPLICIT CONTENT
PARENTAL ADVISORY
EXPLICIT CONTENT
M
MATURE
青 BLU
In stores now! $9.99
FOR MATURE AUDIENCES ONLY
For information about where to buy BLU MANGA titles, visit www.BLUMANGA.com
© YUKI SHIMIZU

SHOUT OUT LOUD!
SAKENDE YARUZEI
1
SATOSUMI TAKAGUCHI
青 BLU

Hisae Shino is an unemployed anime voice actor who also has to support his son Nakaya, a sophomore in high school. The sweet and naive Shino will take any job he can get—even if it means boys' love radio dramas! When he gets paired up with the super-cool Tenryuu, the two bond...to a degree that Shino never intended!

YES, SIR.
THE WHOLE LINE SHOULD TAKE ABOUT TEN SECONDS.
I HAVE A QUESTION.
UGH.
THAT BLOND BASTARD!
COULD YOU NOT LOOK AT ME LIKE THAT, PLEASE?
NO HARM IN A LITTLE FUN.
MM...
SHINO.
YOU'LL CATCH A COLD THERE.
IS THIS REALLY THE FACE...
...OF A FATHER?
PLEASE... STOP...

High school is difficult enough, especially when you live in the shadow of your stunningly attractive older brother...

Kotori is often teased for being superficial, and with a gorgeous brother like Kujaku, you can't really blame him for thinking that looks are everything. However, once Akaiwa steps into the picture, Kotori's life is heading for a lesson in deep trust, self-confidence, and abiding love.

Suzuki Tanaka

MENKUI!

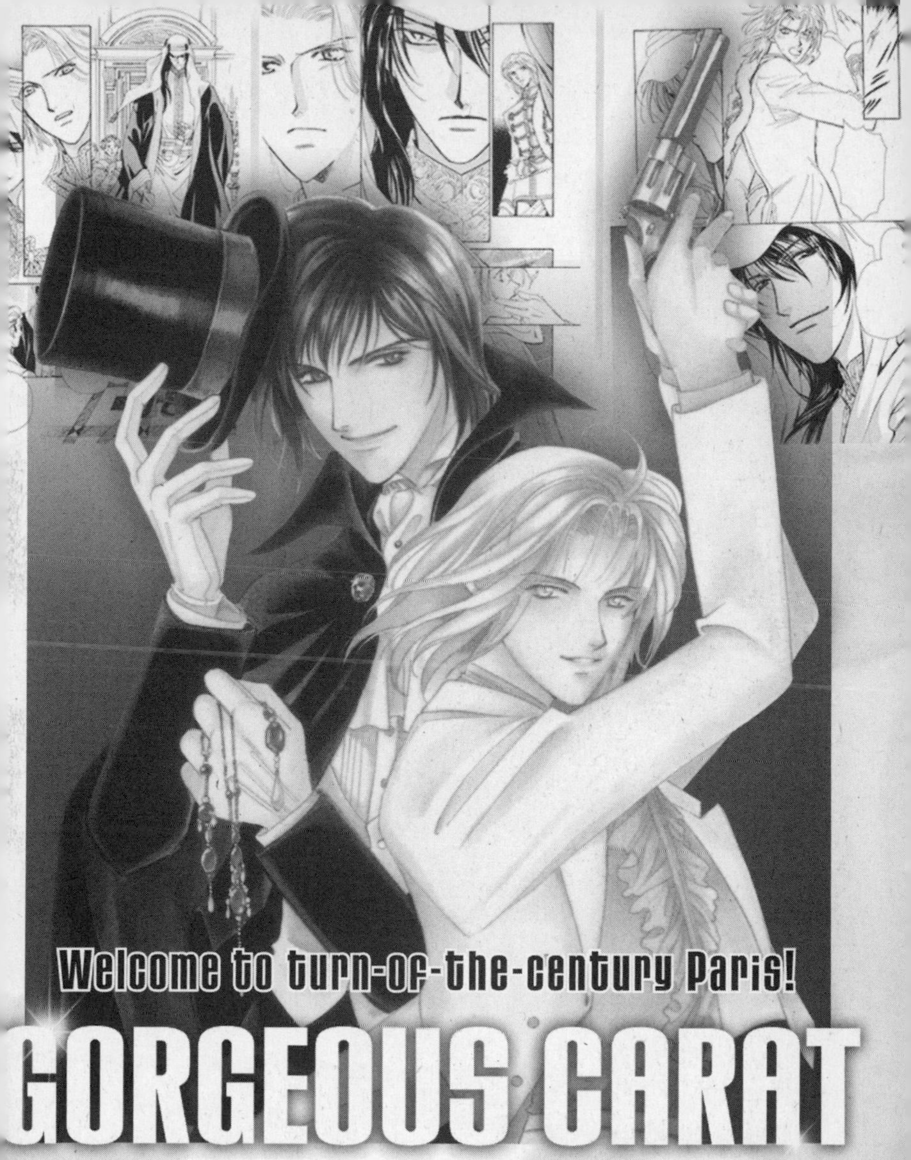

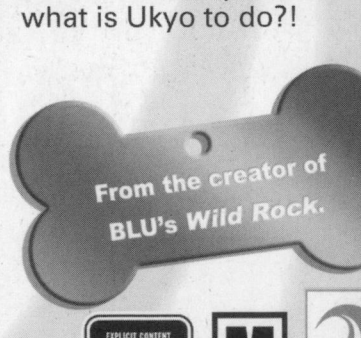

Liberté! Egalité! Fraternité!...and Love.

Become enraptured by a thrilling and erotic tale of an unlikely pair of lovers during the tumultuous times of the French Revolution. Freed from a high-class brothel, noble-born Jacques becomes a servant in Gerard's house. First seduced by his new master's library, Jacques begins to find himself falling for the man as well...but can their love last in the face of the chaos around them?

Where schoolwork is the last thing you need to worry about...

When Keita is admitted to the prestigous all-boys school Bell Liberty Academy, his life gets turned upside down!

Filled with the hottest cast of male students ever put together, this highly anticipated boys' love series drawn by You Higuri (*Gorgeous Carat*) is finally here!

GAKUEN HEAVEN

青 BLU

YOU HIGURI ✿ SPRAY

stop

blu manga are
published in the
original Japanese
format

go to the other
side and begin
reading